Congress and the Making of the Indian Nation

Volume — I

ACADEMIC FOUNDATION

Congress and the Making of the Indian Nation

Volume – I

INDIAN NATIONAL CONGRESS

CHIEF EDITOR

Pranab Mukherjee

EDITORIAL BOARD

Convenor

Anand Sharma

Aditya Mukherjee, Mridula Mukherjee,
Sucheta Mahajan, Rizwan Qaiser,
Bhashyam Kasturi

ACADEMIC FOUNDATION

NEW DELHI

First published in 2011
by

ACADEMIC FOUNDATION
4772-73 / 23 Bharat Ram Road, (23 Ansari Road),
Darya Ganj, New Delhi - 110 002 (India).
Phones : +91-11-23245001 / 02 / 03 / 04.
Fax : +91-11-23245005.
E-mail : books@academicfoundation.com
www. academicfoundation.com

Cataloging in Publication Data--DK
Courtesy: D.K. Agencies (P) Ltd. <docinfo@dkagencies.com>

Congress and the making of the Indian nation : Indian National Congress / chief editor, Pranab Mukherjee ; convenor, Anand Sharma ; editorial board, Aditya Mukherjee ... [et al.].
2 v. cm.
ISBN 13: 9788171888580
ISBN 10: 8171888585

1. Indian National Congress. 2. India--Politics and government--20th century. 3. India--Politics and government--21st century. 4. India—History—20th century. I. Mukherjee, Pranab, 1935- II. Mukherjee, Aditya.

DDC 324.25408309 22

Typeset by Italics India, New Delhi.
Printed and bound in India.

10 9 8 7 6 5 4 3 2 1

Contents: Volume I

(THE PRESENT VOLUME)

Contents: Volume II

(THE COMPANION VOLUME)

Foreword

PRANAB MUKHERJEE

This book is not only a short history of the Indian National Congress but to a considerable extent the history of the Indian people over the last 125 years. The Congress, since its inception in 1885, was not just a political party but a platform on which all shades of nationalist opinion were reflected. During the freedom struggle the Moderates, Extremists, Socialists, Communists, Liberals and Capitalists were all attracted to the Congress which led the anti-imperialist national movement in India. This was so because in the struggle against British colonialism the Congress represented the interests of the Indian people as a whole and not that of any particular class, caste, linguistic group or religious community. While the colonial rulers tried to divide the country into myriad fragments, the Congress spearheaded what one of the early nationalists, Surendranath Banerjea, termed the process of the Indian *'nation in the making'*.

Even after Independence, although the common fight of the entire Indian people against colonial rule had ended, the Congress still retained this inclusive all India national character. People from diverse economic and social backgrounds, belonging to different castes, regions and linguistic groups rallied behind the Congress not only at points of crisis such as an external threat or a war but over a sustained period of time. This was critical especially in the early years after independence in keeping the country together and fighting fissiparous tendencies which had been created and nurtured by the colonial rulers. This was particularly so because the casteist and communal parties which were promoted by colonial administrators and had emerged as the chief prop of British rule in later years did not die out after the colonialism was overthrown but continued to pose a threat to the unity and integrity of the country.

The all-inclusive, open-ended character of the Congress was also critical in successfully taking on the challenge of building democracy and creating and nurturing democratic institutions in a poor, backward and extremely diverse country. As Jawaharlal Nehru often pointed out, this was an unique experiment in history. And the Congress rose gloriously to this challenge. A democracy could be built only by an inclusive and open party and not by a party which represented narrow interests and suppressed any other political forces which contended for power. The Congress in fact provided space within itself for representatives of diverse interests to function.

This open-endedness of the Congress party also meant that it was a dynamic party, always open to change. In fact, the Congress continuously evolved over time, reflecting the changes in the internal situation, as the deepening of democracy gave voice to more and more sections of Indian society. It also remained fleet-footed in responding to the rapidly changing global economic and political situation and evolved suitable strategies and tactics to deal with it. For example, while the Congress created and led the economic strategy of the 1950s and 60s, referred to as the Nehruvian consensus. It was again the leader in creating a consensus for Economic Reforms in the 1980s and 90s. It must be remembered, however, that while being always open to change, the Congress never abandoned the four basic values bequeathed to it by the freedom struggle, i.e., maintaining India's political and economic sovereignty, democracy, secularism and a pro-poor orientation.

In the history of the evolution of the modern Indian nation, apart from the Congress, no other party has so far been successful in representing and indeed celebrating the rich diversity of this country while simultaneously weaving together this diversity into the unity of the Indian nation. Most other parties have tried to grow by trying to mobilise a particular caste, class or religious community, often leading to intolerable violence against other sections. This poses a serious threat to the unity and integrity of the country and its survival as an inclusive, multicultural democracy. The Congress is the only party capable of continuing to take on the task of keeping the country together and democratically taking its people forward, particularly the poor and the disadvantaged.

This book gives us a glimpse of how the Congress, over the past 125 years, traversed the path of Indian nation-building through extremely difficult challenges, both external and internal. This glorious history should serve as a guide and an anchor in helping the country negotiate future challenges.

1 The Emergence of the Indian National Congress

The Indian national movement or the liberation struggle against the British colonial rule was a multi-class popular movement of the Indian people. This more-than-a-century-long struggle led to a 'national revolution' overthrowing the mightiest colonial empire, and setting an example to the rest of the world. The movement was essentially 'national' in the sense that it cut across class, caste, religion, gender, and age. Seldom has a revolution in any country attracted the finest of its people from such diverse spheres. Social and religious reformers, poets, writers, musicians, philosophers, traders, industrialists, political thinkers, statesmen, all joined hands with the common people, gave direction to and learnt from their initiative to bring about one of the biggest mass movements in human history.

This movement was spearheaded by the Indian National Congress which operated as the platform representing all shades of nationalist opinion. The Congress since its establishment in December 1885 in Bombay, has retained this all-inclusive, open-ended character. In fact, its very formation marked the coming together of numerous strands of anti-colonial protest which had been evident since the early 19th century.

Impact of Colonial Rule

Various factors were responsible for the advent of modern nationalism in India. The most important in this regard was the colonial economic exploitation of India and its people. Foreign domination and the policies followed by the British government affected almost all sections of the Indian society. Suffering at the hands of the colonial government united different sections like peasants, artisans, intelligentsia and capitalists against the imperialist rule. Besides, British rule introduced changes like administrative and economic unification of the country and the railway network. This allowed people from different parts of the country to communicate with each other.

Modern education introduced Indians to ideas of liberty and equality. They came to realise that the colonial government was teaching Indians only the English language without providing access to the benefits of modern and scientific education. Further, the advent of vernacular press served as a vehicle for putting forward and popularizing new ideas. People from different parts of the country were able to discuss various national issues—a process through which a vigorous nationalist literature soon emerged.

Another factor contributing to the development of a nationalist consciousness was the British officials' denigration of all Indian things. The Christian missionaries also criticized Indian society as being primitive with its caste rigidity and superstitions. According to them, India was in need of enlightenment and governance by England, the most advanced nation of Europe during the early 19th century. This argument was rejected by many nationalist leaders who then sought to counter it by turning to India's glorious past in order to arouse self-pride amongst Indian people. They propagated India's history highlighting its glorious achievements.

The racial arrogance of the colonial rulers led to discriminatory practices. For instance, in a dispute between an Englishman and an Indian, the testimony of the Englishman was considered to be more authentic than that of the 'native'. Apart from this, Indians were kept out of European clubs and confined to separate railway compartments.

Social and Religious Awakening

This period also witnessed intellectual and cultural stirrings amongst the Indian people. There was a growing awareness that the conquest of India by just a handful of foreigners had been possible because of the internal degeneration of Indian society. It was also realised that certain elements of modern thought like reason and humanism could help in removing these weaknesses. Reform was needed in both social and religious aspects of Indian life.

Some social and religious reformers strove for a synthesis of the best in Eastern and Western thought in order to promote reason and humanism and address the evils in the Indian society. Raja Rammohan Roy was one of the pioneers of this line of thought. He established a socio-religious reform organisation called Brahmo Samaj. He was a champion of women's rights and addressed various issues related to them like the practice of *Sati*, child marriage and restrictions on widow remarriage. He strongly advocated modern education for Indian women. In the religious sphere, he condemned the rigidities of the caste system and opposed the practice of untouchability. He opposed Brahmanical ritualism in religious practice and also condemned idolatry. Other reformers like Ishwar Chandra Vidyasagar, Keshub Chandra Sen, M.G. Ranade, Jyotiba Phule and Swami Vivekananda also addressed these issues.

Some social reformers sought to return to the purity of Hindu scriptures, primarily the Vedas. According to them, the salvation of Indian society lay in conforming to Vedic ideas and rituals as much as possible. Sati, child marriage, caste system, idolatry, and ritualized Brahmanism were criticised as deviations from the simple Vedic religion and spirituality. Swami Dayanand Saraswati, who established the Arya Samaj in 1875, advocated a simplified, non-ritualized Hinduism. He also favoured the study of Western sciences and endorsed education as a vehicle of social change. Gurukuls and English schools were established by the Arya Samaj which also supported women's education.

Some of the strongest criticisms on the caste system came from the reform movements among the lower castes. Jyotibha Phule and Narayan Guru were two strident opponents of the caste-based Hindu society. Narayan Guru argued that even though the outward appearance of the leaves varied, the content and the juice of all the leaves of one tree was always the same. Narayan Guru called for 'one religion, one caste and one God for mankind'.

Syed Ahmad Khan was another prominent reformer who addressed the issue of advancement of Muslims in colonial India. He advocated adoption of English education as means of ensuring the progress of Muslims in India. He established the Anglo-Oriental College in Aligarh where students were taught a mix of Western and Indian subjects. Mohammad Iqbal was another reformer who opposed religious ritualism. There were social reform organisations among the Parsees in this period too. For the Sikhs, social reform started at the end of the 19th century with the establishment of Khalsa College in Amritsar.

The cumulative impact of this rethinking about Indian society created self-awareness about the need to reassess India and the road to its future. This was by way of a cultural ideological struggle which paved the way for the national movement.

Pre-Congress Associations

By the 1870s, a strong nationalist sentiment had developed in India which eventually led to the establishment of the Indian National Congress in 1885. However, there were many organisations which attempted to serve Indian interests before this.

As education expanded in India, the dissatisfaction with colonial rule also increased, especially in the second half of the 19th century. In 1866, the East India Association was set up by Dadabhai Naoroji in London to educate the British public about the situation in India. Surendranath Banerjea set up the Indian Association in Calcutta in July 1876. In Pune, M.G. Ranade set up the Poona Sarvajanik Sabha; Madras Mahajan Sabha was established in 1884 and Bombay Presidency Association in 1885. Now an all India association was on the cards.

The first session of the Indian National Congress was held in December 1885 with 72 delegates under the presidentship of W.C. Bonnerjee.

There was one Scotsman, namely A.O. Hume, a retired civil servant, amongst these 72. Unlike most civil servants in India, Hume deeply loved India and its people. He played a major role in organizing the Indian National Congress and acted as its General Secretary in the initial years of its formation. He wished to channelise the new ideas and aspirations of the Indian people in the late 19th and early 20th century towards 'constitutional agitation'. The Congress aimed at formulating public opinion and popular demands and presenting them before the Government of India, promotion of national unity and communication between national workers from across the country. The Congress met every year in different parts of the country. The delegates consisted of lawyers, journalists, teachers, traders and industrialists and landlords. In 1890, Kadambini Ganguly, the first woman graduate of Calcutta University, addressed the Congress session.

Early Nationalists

The early nationalist leaders had a deep understanding of British rule and its objectives in conquering India. Dadabhai Naoroji wrote a book called *Poverty and Un-British Rule in India* in 1901 which discussed the drain of wealth from India to Britain apart from other ill-effects of colonialism. The Indian economy had been turned into a colonial economy to meet the needs of England rather than those of the Indian people. India was exploited through foreign trade and Indian agriculture was impoverished because of high revenue demands and harsh revenue settlements. This forced peasants to sell their land to merchants and turn into landless labourers working in return for wages. Further, high revenue demands forced peasants to plant cash crops rather than food grains without regard to their own survival. In Bengal, peasants were forced to cultivate indigo so that cheap dyes could be procured for British textile industry. This forced commercialization led to food shortages and famines. The recurrent famines from 1896-1900 left 90 lakh people dead.

The benefits of the Industrial Revolution of the 18th and 19th century in Europe were not allowed to touch India. Indigeneous industry was destroyed since it could not compete with the cheap machine-made goods imported from England. Raw materials grown in India fed the British textile mills in Manchester. The self-sufficient rural village was disrupted—urban handicrafts collapsed, as did the rural artisan industries.

Early nationalist leaders believed that British Parliament was unaware of the real administrative malpractices being carried out in India. They believed that it was essential to educate public opinion in Britain about the situation of the Indian people along with creating national unity on political issues in India as well. To this end, a journal called *India* was published by the British Committee of the Indian National Congress in London set up in 1889. They hoped to win self-government for India by placing their demand for constitutional reforms before the British government.

One of their most significant demands was the expansion and reform of the Legislative Councils in India. In response to this came the Indian Councils Act of 1892 by which the number of members in the Legislative Councils was increased. Of these members, only a few were elected, that too by an extremely narrow electorate. By the start of the twentieth century, the Congress had raised the demand for self-government. Other demands which the Congress made included administrative reforms leading to Indianization of higher services and change in the attitude of administrators towards Indians. British foreign policy was opposed and annexation of Burma, attack on Afghanistan and suppression of tribals in India were condemned. They also asked for reforms aimed at expansion of primary education among the Indian masses. The defence of civil liberties was deemed important especially as the government began to come down heavily on Indian nationalists. In 1897, the government of Bombay arrested Bal Gangadhar Tilak and other journalists, sentencing them to long terms of imprisonment.

The methods adopted for political work by the early nationalists were constitutional agitations within legal limits leading to slow, orderly, political progress. The attitude of the British government was largely dismissive towards the Congress. Lord Curzon, Viceroy of India from 1898 to 1905, claimed that Congress was tottering to its fall. Others dismissed it as an inconsequential body representing a microscopic minority which was a breeding ground for sedition. In a letter of 1891 to Gopal Krishna Gokhale, who was disappointed with the government's two-line reply to a memorial meticulously drafted by the Poona Sarvajanik Sabha, Ranade explained:

> You don't realise our place in the history of our country. These memorials are nominally addressed to government. In reality they are addressed to the people, so that they may learn how to

think in these matters. This work must be done for many years, without expecting any other results, because politics of this kind is altogether new in this land.

This phase in Congress history dominated by the so-called early nationalists is sometimes seen as having been largely ineffective. Their methods are looked down upon as mere prayers and petitioning. This is not so. The early nationalists played a crucial role in undermining the British imperial ideological hegemony or domination of the colonial perception over Indian people, where they were being led to believe that British rule was benevolent, and was beneficial to India. Over nearly half a century of intense intellectual activity, through books, pamphlets, newspapers and speeches, they were able to make a convincing argument that Indian progress would occur not via British rule but by overthrowing it. The nationalist economic argument against colonialism remained the underlying principle for Indian nationalists not only throughout the national movement but even after independence.

2 The Militant Nationalists

By the turn of the century, there was a shift in the tone of the Congress. Political leaders and activists now wanted to go beyond the political methods of the early nationalists. There were many factors that contributed to this shift.

The Indian Councils Act of 1892, mentioned earlier, had failed to satisfy anyone. In 1898, a law was passed making it an offence to excite feelings of disaffection towards the foreign government; in 1904, the Indian Official Secrets Act restricted freedom of the press. Bal Gangadhar Tilak was imprisoned in 1897 and the appointment of Curzon as Viceroy only fuelled anti-Congress attitudes. The British government sought to restrict higher education for Indians and control universities through the Indian Universities Act of 1904. This led to disaffection amongst educated Indians who were now attracted to the new radical political ideas.

International events also influenced Indian politics. The rise of modern Japan and its victory in the Russo-Japanese war of 1905 demonstrated that a small Asian country could defeat a mighty European power. Nationalist movements in Turkey, Egypt, Ireland and Russia further encouraged Indian nationalists. The earlier method of demanding reforms was now seen as redundant and self-government came to be seen as the objective of the movement.

A radical trend had already emerged in Bengal and Maharashtra. Leaders like Bal Gangadhar Tilak in Maharashtra and Rajnarain Bose in Bengal had endorsed no-tax campaigns. Tilak had turned Ganpati and Shivaji festivals into national symbols in Maharashtra. Now this militant nationalist trend within the Congress came to be represented by leaders like Tilak, Bipin Chandra Pal, Lala Lajpat Rai and Aurobindo Ghosh.

Bengal Partitioned

It was, however, a political step by the British government which provided the platform for a full flowering of radical methods. On 20 July 1905, Lord Curzon issued an order dividing Bengal into two parts. East Bengal and Assam with a Muslim majority were separated from West Bengal, a predominantly Hindu-majority area. The official explanation for this step was that the province was too big to be well administered. However, Indian public opinion saw it as an attempt at containing the widespread nationalist sentiment in Bengal. H.H. Risley, Home Secretary to Government of India, commented in December 1904, "Bengal united is a power. Bengal divided will pull in several different ways."

This move was opposed by the leaders of the Congress and Bengal. In addition, a popular movement against partition emerged in which various sections of society like zamindars, merchants, lawyers, students, the urban poor and women participated. The partition was seen as a challenge to Indian nationalism and an attempt at the division of Bengalis on communal lines. On 7 August 1905 a huge rally was held in Calcutta. 16 October 1905, the day the partition was promulgated, was observed as a day of national mourning. People fasted, walked barefoot and bathed in the Ganga. Rabindranath Tagore wrote the famous song, 'Amar Sonar Bangla' and huge crowds went around singing it. *Bande Mataram* became the theme song of the movement. Hindus and Muslims tied *rakhis* on each others' wrists to symbolize unity. Foreign cloth was burnt in huge bonfires and shops selling foreign cloth were picketed. Swadeshi and boycott became special features of this movement.

Apart from this, national educational institutions were set up by nationalists so that students could get an alternative to colonial education. In the anti-partition agitation, students and upper-middle class women were most active. From then on, women took an active part in the national movement. The swadeshi movement spread to other areas of India and become a nation-wide movement.

The government took repressive measures to suppress the movement. The press was gagged, students beaten up, meetings and singing of Bande Mataram in public was banned. In Punjab, Lala Lajpat Rai and Ajit Singh were deported; Chidambaram Pillai in Madras and Hari Sarvottam Rao in Andhra were arrested. Tilak was arrested and sentenced to six years of imprisonment. By 1908, the government had succeeded in stifling the movement, but nationalist sentiments were far from dead.

Growth of Revolutionary Nationalism

When the anti-partition movement was suppressed by the government, many of the youth in Bengal took to the cult of the bomb. They were influenced by Irish terrorists and Russian Nihilists. In 1906, a newspaper called *Yugantar* was set up which argued that force must be countered by force. These revolutionary nationalists adopted violent methods like assassination of influential British officials and dacoities to procure funds and arms.

The two most important secret societies established to carry out these activities were Anushilan Samiti and Jugantar. In April 1908, Prafulla Chaki and Khudiram Bose threw a bomb at a carriage in Muzaffarpur, which they mistakenly thought carried a British judge Kingsford. An attack was carried out on the Viceroy, Lord Hardinge, by Sachindranath Sanyal and Rash Behari Bose in December 1912. Most of these nationalists were arrested, tried and hanged. Between 1908 and 1918, about 186 nationalists were convicted or killed.

Congress after the Partition of Bengal

By 1907, the early nationalists had exhausted their historical role. The government believed that the Congress led by this group could be easily subdued since it had no mass base. It was in this context that Lord Curzon had declared that the Congress was tottering to its fall. He refused to meet the Congress president or its delegation. Once the militant nationalist trend grew strong, the British wanted to weaken the national movement by a complex policy of repression–conciliation–suppression. They sought to repress the militant nationalists, conciliate the early nationalists through political reforms and then, once the early nationalists were on their side, they could go ahead and annihilate the militant nationalists. But this policy did not quite work.

Surat Split

Lord Minto, the Viceroy of India from 1905 to 1910, came up with a scheme for reform of Legislative Councils in which he wanted the co-operation of the early nationalists. This led to a split in the Congress since at this time, the popular swadeshi movement was going on. The early nationalists agreed to cooperate but the militant nationalists were opposed to it. At the Surat session of the Congress held in 1907, the split became official. In the years from 1905 to 1907, there were many disagreements between the two groups on various issues. The militant nationalists had wanted to extend the Swadeshi movement to the rest of India but the early nationalists opposed it; militant nationalists wanted to extend the boycott of foreign goods to boycott of the government as a whole, but again the early nationalists disagreed. Aurobindo Ghosh was active on the militant side and wanted a split so that they could go their own way. Pherozeshah Mehta, who led the early nationalists, also favoured a split as he felt that the militant approach would destroy Congress as an organization. Tilak among the militant nationalists and Gokhale among early nationalists were opposed to a split but their views did not prevail. The split at Surat was quite acrimonious. The government now launched a massive attack on militant nationalists: their newspapers were suppressed and Tilak was deported to Burma for six years. Aurobindo Ghosh was also arrested, Bipin Chandra Pal and Lala Lajpat Rai retired from politics temporarily. With the militant nationalists repressed and the early nationalists lacking any support in the country, political activity slowed down.

Formation of Muslim League

A little before this, in 1906, the All India Muslim League had been established at Dhaka under British encouragement by a few Muslim leaders led by the Nawab of Dhaka who argued for a separate political path for India's Muslims. Their argument was for cooperating with the British government in order to make social and educational advancement possible for the Muslims. They also wanted separate electoral safeguards for the Muslims in India based on the argument that they formed a numerical minority in the country and needed to be protected from domination by the majority Hindus.

Indian Councils Act, 1909

Soon after these developments, in 1909, the Indian Councils Act was passed based on Morley-Minto scheme of reforms. According to these reforms, the number of elected members in imperial and provincial Legislative Councils was to be increased. One Indian member would be included in the Governor-General's Executive Council. However, these councils lacked any real power and were merely advisory bodies. Morley, the Secretary of State for India, said, "If it could be said that this chapter of reforms led directly or necessarily up to the establishment of a Parliamentary system in India, I, for one, would have nothing at all to do with it." Under this Act, the system of separate electorates was introduced for Muslims. This led to the growth of Muslim communalism based on separate electoral reservations.

National Movement during the First World War: Home Rule Leagues

The outbreak of the First World War and the involvement of India as a British colony in the war had some severe consequences for India. It meant heavy taxation, high prices for ordinary goods, shortage of basic commodities—all of which generated a lot of misery among the common people. As such, resentment against colonial rule was on the rise and the people were ready to join a movement.

In 1914, Tilak was released after six years of imprisonment in Burma. He came back to a quiet country almost devoid of any political activity. His first act was to try to get back into the Congress. It was at this time that Annie Besant was also persuading early nationalist leaders to allow Tilak and other militant nationalist leaders to return to the Congress. However, at the 1914 Congress session, this did not materialize and Besant and Tilak went ahead with the formation of their own Home Rule Leagues.

In 1915, Annie Besant demanded self-government for India and Tilak stepped up political activity. Militant nationalists were allowed to rejoin the Congress in 1916. Tilak formed his Home Rule League in April 1916 and in September of the same year, Besant set up her own Home Rule. Tilak's League worked in Maharashtra, Karnataka, Central Provinces and Berar and Besant's in the rest of the country. By March 1917, Besant had 7,000 members in her Home Rule League which included Jawaharlal Nehru in Allahabad. By April 1917, 14,000 members had enlisted in Tilak's Home Rule League.

The Home Rule Leagues popularized the demand for home rule through public meetings and writings in the press and distribution of League literature. For example, three lakh copies of pamphlets arguing for self-government were sold in 1916 itself. Tilak made his famous declaration, "Swaraj is my birthright and I shall have it."

Lucknow Pact

In December 1916, the annual session of the Congress was held in Lucknow where the presence of the Home Rule League members was appreciable. Militant nationalists were welcomed back to the Congress. The demand for more constitutional reforms as a step towards self-government was made and for the first time, a joint meeting of the two Leagues was held at the Congress session. The government came down harshly on this combined force. Besant was arrested and in protest, Sir S. Subramania Aiyar gave up his knighthood. In solidarity, Mohammed Ali Jinnah, Madan Mohan Malaviya, Surendranath Banerjea joined the Home Rule League. Tilak gave a call for passive resistance. A petition for home rule was circulated with the target of getting a million signatures of peasants and workers. The Montagu announcement of 20 August 1917 was the government's response to this movement. Besant was released in September 1917 and became the president of the Congress in December 1917. However, during 1918, the Home Rule movement declined since the early nationalist leadership once again wanted to cooperate over the 1919 reforms and did not support passive resistance which Tilak had called for.

This session is also known for the Congress-League pact. Behind this pact was a sincere desire to allay minority fears about majority domination. Tilak and Jinnah were the forces behind this since both of them emphasized the importance of Hindu-Muslim unity. The two organizations passed the same resolutions at their sessions and put forward a joint scheme of political reforms based on separate electorates and self-government. There was a tremendous enthusiasm over this unity. The government was encouraged to follow a policy of constitutional concessions which took the form of Montagu-Chelmsford reforms of 1918.

Mohammed Ali Jinnah, who at a later stage in his political career, advocated the two-nation theory, strove hard to promote Hindu-Muslim unity during these initial years. When the Muslim League was formed in 1906 in Dhaka, Jinnah did not join it. A great admirer of Congress stalwarts like Dadabhai Naoroji, Gokhale, Bal Gangadhar Tilak and Annie Besant, he attended a Congress session for the first time in 1904. He functioned as Secretary to Dadabhai Naoroji who presided over the 1906 session in Calcutta. Initially he rejected the separate electorate formula on grounds of national integration. However, he was later elected to the Central Legislative Council as the Muslim member from Bombay. He used to attend the annual sessions of both the Congress and the Muslim League. He initiated the move for setting up of a League-Congress joint committee for Hindu-Muslim unity that eventually led to the Congress-League Pact of 1916. After the death of Gokhale and Pherozeshah Mehta, Jinnah seemed to have felt lonely in the Congress. Meanwhile, the Muslim League elected him as its President in 1916 and that marked his formal exit from the Congress.

The major impact of the Home Rule Movement was the popularization of the demand for self-government. Through this movement, organizational linkages were developed between town and country which proved significant in later years. This generation of nationalist leaders formed the main support base of Gandhiji's non-violent movement for India's independence.

3 And Then Gandhiji Came

Mohandas Karamchand Gandhi was born on 2 October 1869 at Porbandar in Gujarat. He became a barrister after receiving legal education in England. In 1893, he went to South Africa to join a law firm and there he got involved in the fight against racial injustice. He took up the cause of the Indians, who were predominantly indentured labourers, and the problems of the merchants who had to pay a poll tax. The Indians did not have the right to vote and were confined to certain parts of the cities. From 1893 to 1914, he spearheaded this struggle and it was during this phase that the whole idea of satyagraha evolved. Satyagraha stands for *satya* and *agrah*, i.e., struggle for truth. The emphasis was on resisting evil, not the evil-doer. The stress on non-violence by Gandhiji was not a weapon of the weak but something which could only be practised by the brave. He put many of his ideas into practice by starting a settlement or an ashram at Phoenix in South Africa where he gathered like-minded people who practised the concept of 'bread-labour'. This meant that everyone worked in a commune like farm, sharing the work and the food. He set up a newspaper called *Indian Opinion* in which he expressed the grievances of the Indians and framed petitions to the government. He also set up another ashram called Tolstoy Farm which was similar to the settlement in Phoenix.

This satyagraha in South Africa was important in the evolution of Gandhiji's political approach. Here, he worked with the masses and poor people belonging to different religions. This experience helped him in organizing Indians later during the freedom struggle. He was warmly welcomed on his return to India in 1915. For one year after his return, he travelled around the country to familiarize himself with the main problems. Soon after this, he was engaged in three formative struggles in Champaran (1917) in Bihar, Kheda and Ahmedabad (1918) in Gujarat. All three struggles were based on local issues and dealt with the economic demands of the peasants and workers. The tenants of Champaran found indigo cultivation unprofitable but were forced to take it up. Their protests were suppressed with a heavy hand by the planters, who were mostly Europeans and the government sided with the planters. When Gandhiji reached Motihari, the headquarters of the district, for investigations, he was served with an order to leave the place. But, he disobeyed and pleaded guilty. The prosecution was withdrawn and he was allowed to continue with his investigations. This led to the appointment of a commission by the government to enquire into the issue. The commission recommended abolition of indigo cultivation and gave redress to the tenants. The success in Champaran of the new method of satyagraha triggered its adoption elsewhere in the country. The weapon of satyagraha was also used to secure a waiver of land revenue in Kheda in Gujarat in years of famine or crop failure.

The Kheda Satyagraha saw the entry of Sardar Vallabhbhai Patel into public life, giving up a lucrative legal practice. It also brought Gandhiji and Sardar Patel together. They educated the peasants about their right to question the government's authority to tax them. The peasants were told to defy coercion with civility. The peasants courted arrest after removing crops from land wrongfully attached. The government was forced to suspend revenue assessment in the case of poor peasants. The Kheda campaign laid the foundation of an awakening among the peasants of Gujarat.

Gandhiji then organized the textile workers in Ahmedabad. Before he entered the scene, Anusuyaben Sarabhai, the sister of Ambalal Sarabhai, one of the leading millowners of Ahmedabad, had been carrying on educational work in the labour areas. She sought Gandhiji's advice when a dispute arose between the weavers and the mill-owners in 1918. Gandhiji, instead of trying to force the hands of the mill-owners, persuaded them to accept the principle of arbitration. He and Sardar Patel became arbitrators on behalf of the labourers. The workers went on strike. Gandhiji advised the workers not to resume work until their demands were secured. After a few days, the workers' morale went down with the loss of wages and signs of starvation at home. Gandhiji declared he would have no food and would use no conveyance until the workers succeeded. It was literally a fast unto death. He arranged for some alternate work for the workers so that they could earn some living. The fast had its effect and soon a solution was found with Sarladevi, the wife of Ambalal Sarabhai, playing a key role in persuading the mill-owners to find a solution. This episode laid the foundation of a strong union between Congress leaders and the workmen and of a permanent organization called the Textile Labour Association.

India after the First World War

The international situation after the war gave a fillip to the growth of nationalism. The Imperial powers had promised self-determination to their colonies so as to get support from them for the war. However, these promises were conveniently forgotten when the war ended. In reaction, nationalism took an aggressive turn when the colonial people realized that there was no prospect of self-government. The war had also helped the colonial subjects to overcome their feeling of racial inferiority *vis-à-vis* their rulers. The Russian revolution of 1917 inspired the people of the colonies to rise up against their masters.

In India, two major legislative changes were introduced during the immediate post-war years: the Montford Reforms and the Rowlatt Act. The former was a constitutional reform scheme and the latter intensified the repressive powers of the government. The Montagu–Chelmsford reforms scheme led to the enactment of the Government of India Act, 1919. Under this act, the provincial Legislative Councils were to be expanded and most of its members were to be elected. The provincial governments were given greater powers under the system of Dyarchy. Some subjects called reserved subjects like finance and law and order remained under the authority of the provincial Governor and others called transferred subjects like education, public health and local self-government were to be controlled by ministers responsible to legislatures. But the government retained total control over finances and it could overrule the ministers on any grounds. At the Centre, two houses of legislature were established, the lower house called the Legislative Assembly and the upper house called the Council of State. However, this legislature had no control over the Governor-General and his executive council just as the Provincial legislatures had little control over the Provincial Governor. Provincial governments were controlled totally by the Centre.

Indian nationalists remained dissatisfied with these reforms. The Congress met in a special session at Bombay in August 1918 and rejected these reforms demanding effective self-government. It repudiated the assumption in the Montagu-Chelmsford report that Indians were not fit yet for responsible government.

The second major legislation was the Rowlatt Act promulgated in March 1919. It was passed despite every Indian member of the Central Legislative Council opposing it. At the end of the war, the government decided to strengthen its capacity to repress political activity through legislation which was clearly outside the limits of the rule of law. The proposed act empowered the government to imprison any person without prior trial and conviction by a law court on grounds of suspicion alone. There was a widespread resentment towards this act among the people who saw it as an insult since it came after the war when they were expecting progressive constitutional changes. Gandhiji called for satyagraha and formed a Satyagraha Sabha which was joined by the members of the Home Rule Leagues. A call for hartal accompanied by fasting, prayer and defiance of specific laws was given. On 6 April 1919, the start of the Satyagraha was announced. In most places, hartals were accompanied by violence and disorder.

In Punjab, two Congress leaders, Dr. Saifuddin Kitchlew and Dr. Satyapal were arrested on April 10 provoking an assault on the town hall and the post office in Amritsar. Europeans including women were attacked. This brought on martial law under which public meetings were banned. April 13 saw a massive gathering of people in Jallianwala Bagh in Amritsar protesting against the martial law and the arrest of Congress leaders. Without any warning, General Dyer opened fire on the unsuspecting and unarmed people. According to government estimates, 379 people were killed. Following upon this incident, martial law was intensified in Punjab. The infamous order under which people had to crawl before Europeans was passed. Gandhiji withdrew the Rowlatt Satyagraha on 18 April 1919, dismayed by the violence.

The entire country was horrified at the violence and atrocities in Punjab. It was as if the mask of enlightenment and civilization that covered the brutality of imperialism had been shed in one day. People understood the true nature of colonial rule and the extent to which it could use force in order to maintain its foothold in India.

4 Khilafat and Non-Cooperation

This untold repression by the British government served to brought Hindus and Muslims close even more than before. With the Lucknow Pact, Hindus and Muslims were brought together for political work and the post-war repression united them against the British rule. Symbolizing this unity, Swami Shraddhanand, an Arya Samaj leader, was asked to preach in the Jama Masjid at Delhi, and Dr. Kitchlew was given the keys to the Golden Temple in Amritsar.

Further, after the war, Muslims in India had been concerned about the fate of the Khalifa, the religious head of Muslims in Turkey. Turkey had been dismembered in contravention of earlier promises by England and the predominantly Turkish area of Thrace was taken away from it. Muslims felt that the religious power of the Turkish Caliphate should not be undermined in this manner. In November 1919, the All-India Khilafat Conference was held in Delhi where it was decided that a non-cooperation movement against the government would be started unless the demands of the Muslims are met. The Muslim League under nationalist leadership supported this cause, as did the Congress. Tilak and Gandhiji saw this as the best opportunity to strengthen Hindu-Muslim relations and unite them against colonial rule. Gandhiji declared that he would start a non-cooperation movement if the Khilafat demands were ignored by the government. Dr. M.A. Ansari headed a deputation to the Viceroy in

January 1920, which proved futile. This was followed by a Khilafat Conference at Bombay, as a result of which a deputation was sent to England in March 1920. The British Prime Minister Lloyd George's response to the representation made by the deputation struck at the very root of the Khilafat sentiment in India, as he turned down the demand for restoring to Turkey the lands taken away from it. Following this, 19 March 1920 was observed as a day of national mourning, marked by hartal, fasting and prayers.

In April 1920, Gandhiji took over the presidentship of the All India Home Rule League and, in a manifesto issued on the occasion, took the view that constitutional reforms should be given secondary place in any scheme of national reorganization. If national energy was devoted to activities like Swadeshi movement, Hindu-Muslim unity, acceptance of Hindustani as the *lingua franca* and the linguistic reorganisation of the provinces, it would bring about reforms and accelerate the achievement of self-government.

The publication of the Hunter Committee Report on the Punjab incidents in May 1920 increased the unrest in the country. The Report was viewed with disappointment and disgust by the Congress. General Dyer and other officers responsible for these actions were let off with mere censure.

Dissatisfaction with the Montagu–Chelmsford reforms, the government's refusal to repeal Rowlatt Act and the Khilafat issue cumulatively increased the widespread national discontent. Thus, in June 1920, an all-parties meeting was held in Allahabad and a programme for non-cooperation was drawn up which included boycott of British courts, schools and colleges.

On 1 August 1920 Gandhiji formally launched the non-cooperation movement. Khilafat Committee also organized All India Hartal the same day. The Congress met in September at Calcutta in a special session presided over by Lala Lajpat Rai and accepted Gandhiji's plan for non-cooperating with the government till the Punjab grievances were redressed, Khilafat demands fulfilled and Swaraj achieved.

The programme of non-cooperation adopted by the Congress called upon people to surrender their titles and honorary offices, resign from nominated seats in local bodies and refuse to attend government functions. It also asked them to boycott all foreign goods, withdraw their children from government schools and colleges, boycott British courts and establish private arbitration courts for settlement of private disputes. The people were also asked to refuse to offer themselves as recruits for service in Mesopotamia, withdraw their candidature for election to the reformed Councils and refuse to vote for any candidate who may, despite the Congress advice, offer himself or herself for election. People were encouraged to spin and weave khadi. Later, the programme included mass civil disobedience and refusal to pay taxes.

This peaceful defiance was endorsed by the Congress session at Nagpur held in December 1920. This session was also important for the organizational changes introduced in the Congress. Provincial Congress Committees were now restructured according to linguistic areas which expanded the reach of the Congress into villages and small towns. Membership fee was reduced to a nominal 4 annas so that the poor masses could become members of the party.

These changes led to a shift in the nature of the Congress—it now became a mass party in which people from different backgrounds were united in their opposition to colonial rule and for the pursuit of Swaraj. Hindus and Muslims were acting as one in this struggle against British rule. However, not everyone was happy with this mass phase of the Congress. Many leaders, like Mohammed Ali Jinnah, Annie Besant, Bipin Chandra Pal and G.S. Khaparde, still believed in constitutional methods of agitation against colonial rule and it was during this time that they left the Congress.

During 1921 and 1922, India witnessed a great mass upsurge led and directed by the Congress. An unprecedented number of people participated in this mass movement—students left schools and colleges in thousands and joined nationalist educational institutions like Kashi Vidyapith, Bihar Vidyapith and Jamia Millia Islamia. Eminent lawyers like Sardar Patel, Rajendra Prasad, Chittaranjan Das, Motilal Nehru, Asaf Ali, C. Rajagopalachari gave up their legal practice and joined Gandhiji in this movement. Funds for the movement were collected through voluntary donations given by people. Foreign cloth was burnt in huge bonfires and simple acts like spinning or weaving khadi became symbols of protest against the British rule. In July 1921, the All India Khilafat Committee gave a call to Muslims asking them not to serve in the British-Indian army. The government soon arrested the Ali brothers in September 1921 and charged them with sedition. The Congress decided to take the movement to the next level by launching civil disobedience of laws in provinces which included non-payment of taxes.

The government responded with repression. Congress and Khilafat grassroot workers had been working successfully to unite Hindus and Muslims and now their activities were declared illegal. The press was gagged. By the end of 1921, most leaders were in prison as were some 3,000 non-cooperators. The Prince of Wales' visit to India in 1921 was met with large-scale demonstrations in India and in Bombay, 53 people were killed and 400 wounded when the police tried to repress demonstrators. The December 1921 session of the Congress at Ahmedabad stated that the Congress was determined to continue this movement. All followers were asked to offer themselves for arrest, refrain from violence and promote Hindu-Muslim unity.

On 1 February 1922, Gandhiji declared that if the government did not release political prisoners and lift press controls within seven days, he would call for mass civil disobedience with non-payment of taxes. However, this did not come about because on 5 February, in Chauri

Chaura village of United Provinces, a procession of 3,000 peasants was fired upon by the police. In retaliation, the peasants set the police station on fire which led to the death of 22 policemen. Gandhiji realized that the country was not ready to practice non-violence yet and that such incidents could spread to other areas as well. Thus, in a Congress resolution passed at Bardoli on 12 February, he suspended the non-cooperation movement and asked all Congressmen to dedicate themselves to constructive work like popularization of khadi and spinning, national schools, removal of untouchability and promotion of Hindu-Muslim unity.

The Bardoli resolution shocked the nation. Some leaders believed that this retreat was also a part of Gandhian struggle while others, especially the younger members of Congress like Subhas Bose and Jawaharlal Nehru, were at that time resentful about this suspension. The government arrested Gandhiji on 10 March 1922 and sentenced him to six years' imprisonment for spreading disaffection against the government. Gandhiji made a historic statement during his trial. He pleaded guilty to the charges and said that the court should give him the highest punishment for "what in law is a deliberate crime, and what appears to me to be the highest duty of a citizen." Soon after this, the Khilafat question became irrelevant. In 1922, Turkey underwent a national revolution led by Mustafa Kamal Pasha which overthrew the rule of the Sultan. Kamal Pasha stepped up the modernization of Turkey and as part of that, he abolished the institution of the Khalifa and separated the state from religion. He nationalized education and law on European lines and also modernized agriculture and industry. All this made the Khilafat agitation eventually redundant.

Impact of Khilafat and Non-Cooperation Movements

The Khilafat agitation brought urban Muslims into the nationalist movement and contributed to a sense of national unity.

Even though apparently the Khilafat and Non-cooperation movements ended without achieving their immediate objectives, they furthered the long-term objective of building the national consciousness in India. Various sections of society had been mobilized for mass action—peasants, students, women, urban and rural poor, and artisans. This aspect of politicization of masses on an unprecedented scale made the Indian national movement revolutionary. Through pamphlets, speeches, dramas, *prabhat pheries*, songs and newspapers, the adverse effect of colonial rule on India was popularized among people. The superiority and invincibility associated with the British was successfully challenged by the Indian masses, who now gained confidence and lost their fear of the colonial masters in this process.

5 India in the 1920s

The sudden withdrawal of the non-cooperation movement encouraged an alternative political approach within the Congress. C.R. Das and Motilal Nehru advocated that the Congress must give up its boycott of Legislative Councils. Once elected to these Councils, Congressmen should obstruct their working from within and bring out their shortcomings. This would turn the Councils into political battlegrounds and arouse the public against them. However, other leaders like Sardar Patel, Rajendra Prasad and Dr. Ansari disagreed with this approach. They argued that entry into Councils would weaken both the mass base of the party as well as the nationalist sentiment among the people. They believed that it was more important to follow the Congress's constructive programme of spinning khadi, promoting Hindu-Muslim unity and temperance, and removal of untouchability.

Swaraj Party

This difference eventually led to the formation of the Swaraj Party in December 1922 by C.R. Das and Motilal Nehru. It was to work from within the Congress and follow the Congress programme except on the issue of entry into Councils. They were known as Swarajists or 'pro-changers' and those who opposed this change within Congress were termed as 'no-changers'. In order to prevent a split like in 1907,

Gandhiji advised both groups to stay and work from within the Congress.

In the 1923 elections, the Swarajists performed well, winning 42 seats out of 101 elected seats in the Central Legislative Assembly. They successfully defeated the government within the Council on numerous occasions and elected Vithalbhai Patel as the speaker of the Central Legislative Assembly in 1925, first ever to do so. The contribution of the Swarajists to the national movement was that they exposed the shortfalls of the Act of 1919 and gave visibility to the movement when the mass movement was in a passive phase and Congress was rebuilding its strength amongst the masses. But they could not bring about a change in the imperial policy and walked out of the Councils in 1926 and later in 1930 as well.

Constructive Work

The constructive work of the Congress continued in the meantime and numerous ashrams came up all over the country. Many young men and women promoted charkha and khadi as symbols of the national struggle against the colonial rule. They also worked among the tribals and lower castes for their upliftment. Nationalist educational institutions came up which provided anti-colonial education to the youth. These workers later became the organizers of the civil disobedience movement.

Emergence of New Forces

The end of non-cooperation was also the time when the spectre of communalism started to raise its ugly head. Between 1922 and 1927, 112 major communal riots took place in the country. The Muslim League, with its support for separate electorates, and the Hindu Mahasabha, formed in 1915, became active.

The 1920s in India were also remarkable for other new forces emerging on the Indian political scene. The influence of Marxist and socialist ideas among students was on the rise during this period. These were manifested in the form of a new left wing within the Congress led by Jawaharlal Nehru and Subhas Chandra Bose. They argued that the national movement, while continuing its struggle against colonialism, must also address the question of economic disparity and oppression of peasants and workers in India.

This period also saw the widespread mobilization of the youth. Youth leagues were established across the country with the first All Bengal Conference of Students being held in September 1928 under the presidentship of Jawaharlal Nehru. This increased the influence of socialism among the youth and led to the advocacy of radical solutions for the economic and social problems in India. They also demanded that complete independence, rather than a dominion status be made the goal of the freedom struggle.

Growth of Socialist Ideas

This period also saw the rise of communist and socialist groups in India. The Russian revolution inspired them and their dissatisfaction with Gandhian methods of struggle drew them further towards socialism. M.N. Roy was the first Indian to be elected to the Eastern leadership of the Communist International. The government was very wary of this increasing Communist influence in the country and in 1924, arrested Muzaffar Ahmad and S.A. Dange in the Kanpur Conspiracy case and tried them for spreading communist ideas in the country. However, this did not seem to have stemmed the growth of socialist following in India. In 1925, the Communist Party of India was formed and many workers' and peasants' parties came up across the country. These parties operated from within the national movement but advocated the socialist route to India's freedom.

In UP, peasants agitated for reform of tenancy laws. They demanded decrease in rents, debts and safeguards against eviction. In 1928, Sardar Patel led the peasants of Bardoli in a no-tax campaign which ended successfully. Trade unionism grew during these years and workers agitated for better wages, living and working conditions. The year 1928 saw many strikes—South Indian Railway workers struck work, as did railway workshop workers in Kharagpur and the workers of Tata Iron and Steel works in Jamshedpur. The most important strike was the Communist-led strike in Bombay textile mills which saw the participation of 1,50,000 workers for more than five months.

Revolutionary Nationalism

Another trend which gravitated towards socialism in this period was revolutionary nationalism. The Hindustan Republican Association (HRA) was founded in 1924 to overthrow British rule through an armed revolution. Many of its young members were arrested and tried in the Kakori Conspiracy Case of 1925 after their attempt to rob government money aboard a train near Kakori in Lucknow district of UP. Four were hanged, 4 deported for life and 17 sentenced to various terms of imprisonment. Among those hanged were Ram Prasad Bismil and Ashfaqullah Khan. Recognizing the influence of socialism, the name of the organization was changed in 1928 to the Hindustan Socialist Republican Association (HSRA) under the leadership of Chandra Shekhar Azad and Bhagat Singh. In the earlier phase, revolutionary nationalism had stood for individual acts of revenge against British officials. But now the HSRA was operating with an ideology that the change in India's political situation could only be brought about through a violent revolution by the masses. Another event which convinced them about the need for an armed rebellion was the appointment of the Simon Commission and the nation-wide protests that followed.

Simon Commission

In 1927, the British Government appointed the Indian Statutory Commission under the chairmanship of Sir John Simon to enquire into the question of further constitutional reforms for India. The Commission did not include any Indian member. The Congress met in Madras in 1927 and decided to boycott the Commission. Both the Muslim League and the Hindu Mahasabha supported it. Anti-Simon protests thus united the different political strands in the country once again.

An all-India hartal was held when the Commission arrived in Bombay in February 1928. Wherever the Commission went it was greeted with black-flag demonstrations 'Simon Go Back'. The demonstrators were suppressed through police attacks and lathi-charges. It was in one of these clashes that Lala Lajpat Rai received lathi-blows on his head and succumbed to his injuries later. As an answer to the Simon Commission, an All-Party Conference was held in order to evolve a common scheme of constitutional reforms. This resulted in the Nehru Report drafted by Motilal Nehru and finalized in August 1928. But this report was not accepted by the All-Parties Convention held in Calcutta in December 1928, due to the opposition of communal parties like the Muslim League, Hindu Mahasabha and the Akalis. Jinnah rejected the Nehru Report and put forward his Fourteen Points which were made up of the demands of different communal organisations.

However, in the meantime, the death of Lala Lajpat Rai had angered the HSRA members and on 17 December 1928, Bhagat Singh, Chandrashekhar Azad and Rajguru assassinated Saunders, a police officer. A few months later on 8 April 1929, in order to make their ideas known to the people, Bhagat Singh and B.K. Dutt threw a bomb in the Central Legislative Assembly. The bomb was harmless and they stayed in the hall and threw pamphlets saying that the bomb was meant to 'make the deaf hear'. They were arrested and during their trial, they made their famous speeches propagating their ideas. In Bengal, revolutionary activities were on the rise. In 1930, an armoury in Chittagong was raided and attacked by Surya Sen and his followers.

The government swung into action and arrested many of these leaders. They were tried and sentenced to various terms of imprisonment, deportation as well as death. Their defence was organised by Congress leaders. Within the prison, they carried out a hunger strike in order to protest against the inhuman conditions of political prisoners. During this strike, Jatin Das died after fasting for 63 days. Meanwhile, alarmed by the popular following which Bhagat Singh and his followers were gathering, the British officials hastened their hanging. On 23 March 1931 Bhagat Singh, Rajguru and Sukhdev were hanged despite large-scale popular protests against their death punishment.

Unrelenting repression by the government soon led to the weakening of the revolutionary movement as most of its leaders were arrested, imprisoned or killed. In February 1931, Chandrashekhar Azad was killed in a police encounter; Surya Sen was arrested in 1933 and hanged. Hundreds of others were arrested and imprisoned, some were sent to the Cellular Jail in the Andamans. The government also suppressed the growing trade union and peasant movements. In March 1929, 31 trade union leaders and communists were arrested and after a four-year long trial called the Meerut Conspiracy Case, were sentenced to various terms of imprisonment.

Thus by the end of the 1920s, there was a rising nationalist feeling expressed through anti-Simon demonstrations. There was also a radical wave, especially among the youth. Jawaharlal Nehru, who had emerged as the voice of the new generation, was elected President of the Congress at the Lahore session of the Congress in 1929 where a resolution calling for Purna Swaraj was passed. Complete independence was to be the new Congress goal and on 31 December, the tricolour was adopted as the national flag and 26 January 1930 was celebrated as Independence Day. This became an annual ritual when people would reiterate their commitment to ending colonial rule in India. It was also decided that a civil disobedience movement would be launched under the leadership of Gandhiji.

6 Civil Disobedience and After

Gandhiji started the civil disobedience movement on 12 March 1930 with the Dandi March. Along with 78 followers, he walked from Sabarmati Ashram in Ahmedabad to Dandi, a village near the sea coast in Gujarat, a distance of 375 kilometres. Hundreds of government officials resigned in the villages through which he passed. Reaching Dandi, on 6 April, he picked up a handful of salt—a symbolic act of defying the government monopoly on salt and therefore, an act of protest against British authority. He declared, "I regard this rule as a curse. I am out to destroy this system of Government. ...Sedition has become my religion. Ours is a non-violent battle. We are not to kill anybody but it is our dharma to see that the curse of this Government is blotted out."

Spreading swiftly, the movement saw people defying the salt laws all across the country. Forest laws were defied in Maharashtra, Karnataka, and the Central Provinces, and people refused to pay the *chaukidari* tax in eastern India. Hartals and demonstrations were organized and people boycotted foreign goods. People refused to pay taxes, rent or land revenue and offered satyagraha. A notable feature of this movement was that a large number of women participated in it. They offered satyagraha, picketed shops selling foreign goods or liquor and actively participated in demonstrations and processions. In the North-West Frontier Province, Khan Abdul Ghaffar Khan organized the Pathans into Khudai Khidmatgars, popularly called Red Shirts, a non-violent body for fighting colonial rule. In Peshawar, two platoons of soldiers disobeyed orders by refusing to open fire on the non-violent demonstrators. This proved that nationalism had spread into the Indian army which was one of the main pillars of the colonial rule in India. In Nagaland, Rani Gaidilieu led an anti-colonial rebellion. She was captured in 1932 and sentenced to imprisonment for life. She was released only in 1947 when India achieved independence.

The government responded with its usual repressive measures—lathi charges, firing on unarmed demonstrators, arrests of leaders and satyagrahis. The Congress was declared illegal and strict controls imposed on the press. Official estimates gave 110 persons as killed and over 300 wounded in police firings. South India witnessed a wave of repression where men were beaten up by the police just for wearing Gandhi caps.

Gandhi-Irwin Pact

Meanwhile, in 1930, the first Round Table Conference was organized in London to discuss the report of the Simon Commission but the Congress boycotted it. This brought the government to negotiations with the Congress in order to persuade it to attend it. In March 1931, Gandhiji, negotiated on behalf of the Congress, and Lord Irwin, the Viceroy, came to a settlement known as the Gandhi-Irwin Pact by which the government agreed to release non-violent political prisoners, allowed the people to make salt for domestic usage and to peacefully picket the shops selling foreign cloth and liquor. With this, the Congress suspended the civil disobedience movement and participated in the Second Round Table Conference.

The Congress met soon thereafter at Karachi. The left-leaning younger leaders of the Congress were not too happy with the Gandhi-Irwin pact as it meant suspension of the movement. There was also a grave disappointment that the death sentence for Bhagat Singh had been carried out despite Gandhiji's appeal to the Viceroy for its commutation to life imprisonment. A resolution was passed at the Karachi session of the Congress in March 1931 stating that, "while dissociating itself from and disapproving of political violence in any shape or form" it admired "the bravery and sacrifice" of the three martyrs. Gandhiji's concept of satyagraha involved giving opportunities to the opponent for honest change of heart. He also believed that a mass movement demanded sacrifices from the people and that it could not continue endlessly. Thus, it was imperative that a phase of mass struggle be followed by a phase of negotiations. The Congress approved this pact under Gandhiji's persuasion.

The Viceroy having to negotiate with Gandhiji as an equal was seen as a major advance for the Congress whereby the colonial government was forced to accept the Congress as a legitimate representative of the Indian people.

As agreed in the pact Gandhiji went to England in September 1931 to attend the Second Round Table Conference but he could not persuade the government to grant freedom on the basis of immediate Dominion Status to India.

Civil Disobedience Movement: The Second Phase

In the meantime, the Great Depression of the 1930s had hit Indian agriculture also severely. Peasants found that the revenue and rent demands were becoming tougher to cope with because of the falling agricultural prices. When Gandhiji returned from England, he gave a call for resuming the civil disobedience movement. In UP, the Congress agitated for rent reduction and preventing eviction of peasants from their lands. In December 1931, Congress started a no-rent, no-tax campaign and Jawaharlal Nehru was soon arrested. In NWFP, Khudai Khidmatgars led the peasants against the high land revenue demands leading to the arrest of Khan Abdul Ghaffar Khan.

Peasant movements were initiated in other states like Bihar, Andhra, Bengal and Punjab.

The government, working under the new Viceroy, Lord Willingdon, now unleashed a wave of repression in order to completely crush the Congress. On 4 January 1932, Gandhiji was arrested along with other leaders of the Congress. Ordinances were issued to govern the country and normal administration suspended. Police atrocities reached a new high: over a lakh of satyagrahis were arrested, lands and properties of many other were confiscated, nationalist literature was banned and the nationalist press was again gagged.

Elections and Formation of Ministries under the Government of India Act, 1935

While the movement had been going on, the Third Round Table Conference met in England in 1932 in the absence of Congress leaders. However, the Muslim League participated in this as it had done in the earlier Conferences. The political developments of the preceding years led to the introduction of the Government of India Act of 1935. This act established a new federation in India based on the union of British Indian provinces and the Princely States. Provinces were to be governed through provincial autonomy. A federal legislature was to be set up in which the States had representation through nomination by the rulers. Merely 14 per cent of the people of India were given the right to vote. Moreover, the legislature did not have any power over defence and foreign affairs and the Governor-General had special authority over other subjects. In the provinces, popularly elected ministers would control all departments of governance but the Governor had special powers over them as well as the police and civil services. The nationalist leaders were dissatisfied with these limited reforms since the power would still be concentrated in the hands of British governors.

The provincial part of the Act was put into practice and elections were announced. The Congress, after a lot of debate, decided to contest these elections with the stated objective of showing the inadequacy of the Act. The Congress election campaign was successful in most of the provinces. Out of a total of 11 provinces, Congress ministries were formed in 7 and the Congress formed coalition ministries in 2 more provinces later. Only Bengal and Punjab had non-Congress ministries: the Muslim League formed a coalition with the Krishak Praja Party in Bengal and the Unionist Party governed in Punjab.

The Congress ministries in provinces worked hard for the betterment of the people. They passed many laws in their provinces which benefited the masses. Civil liberties of the people were safeguarded, restrictions on the press were revoked and the other radical organisations of peasants, workers and students. Many political prisoners were released and the powers of the police restrained. For peasants, they reduced rent, prevented eviction by law and gave protection to peasants in debt. Trade unions functioned freely and were able to secure better conditions for workers. They promoted public health, education, khadi and village industries and the people gained a new confidence in the Congress.

Muslim Mass Contact Programme

The Congress decided to initiate a Muslim mass contact programme in the CWC meeting held in February 1937. It was initiated by Nehru in order to reach out to the Muslim masses as the election results of 1937 had shown that the influence of the Congress on them had become weak. Many Mass Contact Committees were formed and their main work was to enrol Muslims as members of the Congress. Prominent Muslim Congressmen like Maulana Madani, K.M. Ashraf and Sajjad Zaheer addressed meetings in Muslim-majority areas. Congress pamphlets were brought out in Urdu. In western UP, the programme was successful in increasing Muslim membership of the

Congress. The Muslim League felt threatened by this programme and started a counter-campaign accusing the Congress of oppressing the Muslims.

Socialism and Congress

The period from the late 1920s to the mid-1930s saw the resurgence of socialism in India. The economic slump had exposed the weaknesses of the capitalist world. However, during these years, the socialist Soviet Union continued its industrial growth. As such, many young leaders, peasants and workers in India were attracted more and more towards socialism. Jawaharlal Nehru popularized the vision of a socialist India where, along with political freedom, economic and social emancipation would bring about equality in all the spheres of life. The Congress demonstrated its faith in his vision by electing him president in 1929, 1936 and 1937, and Subhas Bose in 1938 and 1939. At the Lucknow Congress in 1936, Nehru asked the Congress to accept socialism as its goal and through its agenda of economic emancipation, win over the Muslim masses from the communal leadership of the Muslim League.

At the Karachi session of the Congress in 1931, a resolution ensuring the economic upliftment of the masses from exploitation along with fundamental right of freedom and other civic rights had already been passed. The resolution guaranteed equality before the law, elections based on universal adult franchize, free and compulsory primary education, rent reduction and relief from debts for peasants. For the workers, it ensured minimum wages, limited hours of work, protection of women workers, right to organize unions and state ownership of main industries. The Faizpur session of the Congress in 1936 passed some more radical resolutions. The Election Manifesto of 1936 also ensured similar measures to reduce rent and revenue demands. In 1938, the Congress set up a Planning Committee under the chairmanship of Jawaharlal Nehru. Other leaders including

Gandhiji also argued for the intervention of public sector in running certain industries. In 1945, the Congress Working Committee adopted a resolution for the abolition of landlordism and the granting of land to the tiller.

This was also the time for the consolidation of the Indian capitalist class within the national movement. They became more active to counter the growing leftist orientation of the Congress, but they did not go over to the side of imperialism. Nor did they attempt to form a political party of their own. Some individual members of this group like Jamnalal Bajaj, Lala Shankar Lal, Vadilal Mehta *et al.,* were members of the Congress. Others gave financial help to the Congress movement like Ambalal Sarabhai, G.D. Birla and Walchand Hirachand.

The Communist Party also grew under the leadership of P.C. Joshi after 1935. This was the period when the policy of Communists was changed to that of the United Front with socialists, anti-fascists and 'bourgeois' led nationalist movements. Thus, Communist Party members now joined the Congress and accepted it as the main nationalist party. They occupied official positions within the Congress with 20 of them being in the All-India Congress Committee. In 1934, the Congress Socialist Party was founded by Narendra Deva and Jayaprakash Narayan.

The Peasants and workers had been mobilized by the non-cooperation and civil disobedience movements. The economic depression had worsened their conditions because of a fall in agricultural prices and wages. As such, peasants and workers all over the country were demanding reduction in rents, revenues and relief from indebtedness. Workers demanded better living conditions and higher wages and recognition of their trade unions. Many trade unions and Kisan Sabhas came up in different parts of the country like UP, Tamil Nadu, Bihar, Kerala, Punjab, and Andhra Pradesh.

The All-India Kisan Sabha was founded in 1936 with Sahajanand Saraswati as its president.

In 1939, at the Tripuri session of the Congress, Subhas Bose was elected president despite Gandhiji supporting the candidature of P. Sitaramayya. Bose wanted the Congress to move towards a mass struggle whereas Gandhiji and others were not convinced that the time was ripe. Eventually, he resigned from this office and founded a new party within the Congress called Forward Bloc along with other left-wing followers in April 1939. During the 1930s, the influence of left-wing politics increased amongst students and the All India Students' Federation and the All India Progressive Writers' Association were also founded. By 1939, leftist influence was substantial within the Congress as well.

International Affairs

Another significant development of the 1930s was Congress's interest in international questions. Based on its opposition to the deployment of Indian troops in the extension of imperial control abroad, Congress foreign policy by now was firmly founded upon anti-imperialism. In February 1927, a Congress of Oppressed Nationalities was held in Brussels where political exiles and revolutionaries from colonies of Asia, Africa and Latin America met. The Congress was asked to plan their common struggle against imperialism. Nehru attended the Congress and was elected to the Executive Council of the League Against Imperialism that was founded at this Congress. The Madras session of the Congress in 1927 had warned the British government that Indian people would not support any of its imperialist wars. During 1930s, the Congress opposed imperialism in all parts of the world. It also declared its opposition to fascism and nazism in Germany, Italy and Japan. The Congress declared that its sympathy lay with the countries such as Spain, Ethiopia and China which were victimized by the fascist nations.

Communal Award

While Gandhiji was imprisoned in 1932, the British government announced the Communal Award which extended separate electorates to Depressed Classes who were also seen as a minority. Gandhiji reacted very strongly to this treatment of Depressed Classes as separate from Hindus. He said that grant of separate electorates would perpetuate untouchability. He was in favour of joint electorates and universal franchize. To protest against this divisive move, he undertook a fast unto death in prison. This garnered political support all over the country and led to the Poona Pact. According to this agreement, Dr. B.R. Ambedkar agreed to abandon separate electorates for Depressed Classes. However, the number of reserved seats for them in the provinces increased from 71 to 147 and to 18 per cent of the total at the Centre.

Dr. Ambedkar was a lawyer belonging to the Mahar caste of Maharashtra. He was educated in the US on a scholarship from the Maharaja of Baroda. By the late 1920s, he had emerged as a leader of the Depressed Classes. After the Poona Pact of 1932, he formed the Independent Labour Party in 1936 which sought to mobilize peasants and workers and contested the 1937 elections in Bombay and won a few seats. In 1942, he set up the All-India Scheduled Castes Federation. He was appointed to the Viceroy's Executive Council in the 1940s.

Other organisations working for the promotion of the interests of the Depressed Classes also emerged in Punjab, Bengal, UP and Bihar. In Punjab, the Ad-Dharmis allied with the pro-British Unionist Party; in Bengal, Namasudras too allied with the pro-British Krishak Praja Party. In UP, an organisation for Adi-Hindus was set up and in Bihar, Jagjivan Ram emerged as the most prominent Harijan leader associated with the Congress. He set up the Khetmazdoor Sabha and the Depressed Classes League. The main demands of these organizations were abolition of *begar* or forced labour, grant of rights to forest land, removal of legal provisions disallowing Depressed Classes from owning land.

Gandhiji launched an anti-untouchability campaign after the Poona Pact which lasted for the next two years. Working from Satyagraha Ashram at Wardha, he devoted all his energies to opposing untouchability in all forms and practices. His famous Harijan Tour in the nine months from November 1933 to July 1934 covered 20,000 kilometres during which he collected money for the Harijan Sevak Sangh and campaigned against untouchability. During this campaign, he made speeches criticizing the malpractices in Hindu society. He argued that high-caste Hindus needed to do penance for the untold oppression of Harijans.

Communal Politics

However, despite the Poona Pact, separate electorates for Muslims, which meant that Muslims voted separately for Muslim candidates, instituted by the Morley-Minto reforms in 1909, continued to be in force. The elections held in 1937 had been based on separate electorates for Muslims. This had fuelled tendencies towards political separatism. As far as election results were concerned, the Congress did not do very well in the seats reserved for minorities—Congress candidates won in 26 out of 482 Muslim seats and out of these 26 too, 15 were won in NWFP. The Muslim League and the Hindu Mahasabha also did not fare well. However, since the programme of the Congress had been radicalized in favour of peasants and workers, many of the landlords shifted allegiance to communal parties in order to promote their own interests and thus strengthened them. It was now that the Muslim League began to propagate the two-nation theory according to which Hindus and Muslims were seen to be two distinct nations within India who could never live together. They argued that the Muslims would constantly be dominated by the numerical majority of Hindus and any democratic electoral representative structure would be inherently biased against them.

The presence of the right-wing Hindu communal parties like the Hindu Mahasabha who saw India as a Hindu country and denigrated Muslims as well as their past history in India also fuelled communal tendencies. They declared that Hindus were a separate nation and India was their country—an acceptance of the two-nation theory. Sangathan and Shuddhi movements came up among Hindus countered by Tanzim and Tabhligh movements among Muslims. The Hindu communal movements worked to prevent conversion to Islam whereas the Muslim movements tried to facilitate this. This led to the strengthening of minority fears about political and cultural domination by the majority. Since these sentiments were stronger in provinces where Muslims were in a minority like UP and Bihar, the Muslim League was also strong there. In Muslim-majority provinces like Punjab, Bengal and NWFP, Muslims felt more secure about themselves and here, ironically, the League remained weak. Also, these groups tended to support the British government politically and did not participate in the mass movements of the freedom struggle.

The nationalists opposed communal parties but were unable to contain their spread, eventually leading upto the partition of the country in 1947. Negotiations with Jinnah failed during the late 1940s since he demanded Congress acceptance of its being a Hindu party. This was impossible since Congress nationalists were committed to secularism and the notion that the Congress represented the entire people of India, irrespective of their religion, caste or language. Many Muslim leaders like Khan Abdul Ghaffar Khan and Abul Kalam Azad had been unwavering in their secularism and support to nationalist demands. After 1947, India was able to establish a secular polity but communalism in various forms continued to be a major concern for the country.

7 Princely India in the Freedom Struggle

By the middle of the 19th century, the British government had established treaty relations with most of the Princely States in India. Under British paramountcy, the internal administration of the States was left to the Princes. British residencies were established as channels for communication with the British government. In theory, the rulers had absolute power but in practice, they were subject to the dictates of the British Resident and dependent on the British government for internal and external protection. Succession policies in the States were also laid down by the Resident.

Most of the States were autocratically ruled. The economic burden on the people was heavy with high taxation, education and social services were backward and civil rights were restricted. State revenues were expended on the luxurious life-styles of the rulers and since the British provided immunity from domestic and external aggression, they felt free to ignore the interests of their people. The British government expected the States to support them in their imperialist policies, thereby acting against the development of nationalist sentiments. Thus, most of the Princes were hostile and suspicious towards the nationalist forces. The exceptions to this were States like Baroda and Mysore which sympathized with the nationalists and promoted internal political reform.

The onset of the nationalist movement in British India also had an impact on the people of the Princely States. Many revolutionary nationalists fleeing British authority came to the Princely States in the first and second decades of the 20th century and initiated political activities there.

The launching of the non-cooperation and Khilafat movements stirred the entire Indian population cutting across the borders of British India. A large number of people's organizations in the Princely States were established in Mysore, Hyderabad, Baroda, Kathiawad, Jamnagar, Indore, Nawanagar, etc. Praja Mandals or States' People's Conferences were established. In December 1927, an All India States' People's Conference was held and attended by about 700 delegates from different States. Balwantrai Mehta, Maniklal Kothari and G.R. Abhayankar assumed the leadership of the movement.

The Congress, for the first time at its Nagpur Session in 1920, enunciated its policy towards the peoples' movement in the Princely States. It called upon the Princes to grant full responsible government in their States. However, it was pointed out that though the people belonging to the States could enroll themselves as members of the Congress, they could not initiate political activity in the State in the name of the Congress. They could carry on political activity in their individual capacity as members of the local Praja Mandals. This position continued till 1935 though the cooperation between the leaders of the States' People's Conferences and the Congress leaders gradually increased. Finally, it was decided that Congress Committees could be formed in the Indian States but they were not to engage in any unparliamentary activity or direct action. This compromise formula helped to bring about harmony between the Congress and the freedom movement in the States.

From the mid-20s, the Congress started taking keen interest in the states' people's movements. In 1929, Pandit Jawaharlal Nehru in his presidential address observed, "The Indian States cannot live apart from the rest of India.... The only people who have a right to determine the future of the States must be the people of those States."

Two developments in the mid-30s brought a radical change in the relations between the Princely States and British India. The Government of India Act of 1935 projected a scheme of federation in which the States were brought into a direct constitutional relationship with British India. The States were to send representatives to the upper house of the Central Legislature called the Council of States. However, all these representatives were to be nominated by the rulers of the States rather than elected by their peoples. It would deprive the people of their rights and also create a band of hand-picked persons to stand by the British Government in the Federal legislature at any crucial time. The decision to leave the choice to the rulers to join or not to join the federation was another feature of the Act which undermined the people's legislative representation. The second major impact on the States was created by the acceptance of office by the Congress in majority of the British Indian provinces in 1937. The installation of the Congress ministries in the neighbouring British Indian provinces encouraged the Praja Mandal leaders to step up their political activities for demanding responsible government in the Princely States.

In Rajkot, the Satyagraha movement drew personalities like Gandhiji and Sardar Patel. Though Gandhiji ultimately withdrew the Satyagraha accepting his failure to change the heart of the ruler, its impact was far reaching. In Hyderabad also, a very powerful people's movement built up. In Kashmir, under Sheikh Abdullah the people organized themselves. The Congress also started showing more interest in various political activities in the States, though adhering to its old stand that the movement in the Princely States should not be conducted in the name of the Congress but in the name of the local organizations.

In a resolution passed at the Lucknow session of Congress in 1936, it was observed that, "Congress... desires to make it clear that, in its opinion, the people of the States should have the same rights of self-determination as those of the rest of India, and that the Congress stands for the same political, civil and democratic liberties for every part of India. The Congress, however, desires to point out that the struggle for liberty within the States has, in the very nature of things, to be carried on by the people of the State themselves."

After this, the Haripura session of Congress in 1938 dealt with the problems of the States in detail. It considered the states to be integral parts of India and desired the same political, social and economic freedom in the States as in the rest of India. The demand for 'Purna Swaraj' put forward by the Congress was for the whole of India inclusive of the States.

Jawaharlal Nehru was elected president of the All India States' People's Conference in 1939 at its session held in Ludhiana. He exhorted the Praja Mandals to step up the agitations in the States to uphold the rights and dignities of the people. Important leaders like Ramanand Tirtha and Ravi Narayan Reddy of Hyderabad, U.N. Debar and Balwantrai Mehta in Saurashtra and Kathiawad region and Sheikh Abdullah in Kashmir spearheaded the movement in these States.

During the Quit India movement, Congress formally extended the call for launching a struggle to the people of the States as well. The constitutional changes, likely to take place in the near future also underlined the necessity of having an organic relationship between the Princely States and the Government of India. In the post-World War II period, when the withdrawal of the British from India became increasingly clear, the future of the Princely States occupied the attention of national leaders both in the Congress and in the Muslim League.

The Cabinet Mission of 1946 had proposed a federal scheme for free India. In the memorandum of 12 May 1946, while explaining the consequences of the withdrawal of British power and the emergence of independent India, it had observed, "Thus, as a logical consequence and in view of the desires expressed to them on behalf of the Indian States, His Majesty's Government will cease to exercise the powers of paramountcy. This means that the rights of the States which flow from the relationship to the Crown will no longer exist and that all the rights surrendered by the States to the paramount power will return to the States."

Though the Congress never agreed to this interpretation of paramountcy, some of the Princely States decided to declare independence. They hoped that the British Government would come to their aid and they found support in Jinnah. He emphasized that the Indian States were sovereign states, except in so far as they had entered into treaties with the Crown. British India could do nothing to them. To say that the Governor General or the British Parliament could lay down that every Indian State was bound to enter one Constituent Assembly or the other was not constitutional. If the States liked to come in, they could do so by agreement, but there was no way of forcing them in.

Nehru reacted to this strongly and pointed out that by no test of sovereignty could an Indian State be defined as sovereign. Congress pressure forced the British government to act and the Political Department was taken away from British control and was placed under two new State Departments of the two future Dominions. Sardar Patel headed the States Department of India. Both Nehru and Patel acted firmly on this issue. They were fortified by the support of the States' people. So, when the Nizam of Hyderabad and Travancore-Cochin expressed their desire to declare independence, Sardar Patel acted swiftly.

The Mountbatten Plan of June 1947 envisaged a division of India into two dominions with the Princely States choosing their course of action. The definition, scope and relevance of paramountcy came into question. Since paramountcy was going to lapse, technically, the States would have the choice to join either dominion or even be independent. However, Mountbatten and the British government ruled out the possibility of independence for the States by giving their support to the integration of States in the Dominions. In the few instances where rulers expressed a tendency towards independence, for instance in Hyderabad, Travancore and Junagadh, popular movements for responsible governance came into play against independence.

The AICC, in its resolution of 15 June 1947, made the position of the States quite clear by stating, "The arrangements made under paramountcy in the past dealt, inter alia, with the security of India as a whole. In the interests of that security, various arrangements were agreed to limit the power of the States' authorities and at the same time grant them protection. The question of the security of India, as well as other matters, are as important today as at any time previously and cannot be ignored in deciding the future of the States. The AICC cannot admit the right of any State of India to declare its independence and to live in isolation from the rest of India. That would be a denial of the course of Indian history and of the objectives of Indian people today. The AICC trusts that the rulers of the States will appreciate fully the situation, as it exists today, and will, in full cooperation with their people, enter as democratic units in the Indian Union, thereby serving the cause of their own people as well as India as a whole."

During the next few weeks, the ground was prepared to bring in all the 565 States into the Indian Union. Through the people's organizations in various States the Congress secured public support from the States in favour of the Indian Union. Most of the rulers saw the writing on the wall and gave up the hope of separate States. Most of the States took their decisions before 15 August 1947, except Jammu & Kashmir and Hyderabad. Hyderabad came into the Indian Union after police action and the Maharaja of Kashmir eventually joined the Indian Union in the wake of invasion from Pakistan.

In the transitory provisions of the Constitution which came to exist from the 26 January 1950, some of the bigger States like Hyderabad, Mysore, Travancore-Cochin, were given the status of "B" Category States. A number of small States were clubbed together to form States' unions like Saurashtra and Patiala and East Punjab States Union (PEPSU). After the reorganization of the States on linguistic basis in the mid-50s, the integration of Princely States with India was complete. The Congress under the leadership of Nehru and Patel had successfully integrated the Princely States with the rest of India and thereby contributed enormously to the unity of the Indian nation.

8 National Movement During the Second World War

The Second World War broke out on 1 September 1939 when Germany attacked Poland. England entered the War on 3 September and without consulting the Indian leaders, declared India as a partner in its war effort. To begin with, the Congress leaders were eager to support the anti-fascist forces because of their earlier stand of opposition to fascism. In fact, Gandhiji expressed his distress at Westminster Abbey and the House of Parliament in London being bombed and offered unstinted cooperation to Britain. However, the dilemma before the Congress was how to come to the assistance of Britain while they were under its subjugation. At a Congress Working Committee meeting in Wardha in mid-September 1939, different strands of opinion emerged within the party on the issue of support to the war. Subhas Bose and the Socialists saw the war as an imperialist one. They wanted Congress to go in for a mass struggle immediately, taking advantage of Britain's predicament. Jawaharlal Nehru neither wanted India to join the war till she was free nor was in favour of a struggle as advocated by the Socialists. Finally, Nehru's stand prevailed with Gandhiji's support. The resolution censured fascist aggression but explained that India could not come out on the side of the Allies while being unfree. The Congress called for Britain to make true its claims that the war was for freedom by giving India its independence. If this was done, Indians would join the Allies in the war against fascism.

The reaction of the Viceroy to this resolution was predictably hostile. In a statement issued on 17 October 1939, he repeated the line that there was disunity among the Indians and pitted the Muslim League and the Princes against the Congress. All that was offered was a consultative committee without any real powers and talks at the end of the war between all parties to amend the 1935 Act. Gandhiji was dismayed by this response, especially as he had been unconditional in his offer of support to Britain from the beginning of the war. He charged the government with continuing the old policy of "divide and rule". He summed up the response thus: "The Congress asked for bread and it has got a stone." The CWC at its meeting on 23 October endorsed Gandhiji's reaction by calling upon the Congress ministries to resign, which they immediately did.

Subhas Bose, Congress Socialist party leaders, Communists and Royists termed the war as an imperialist one and mobilized opinion for a movement against the British. Subhas Bose was willing to leave the Congress if need be and set up a parallel organization which would direct the movement. In his view, the mass of Congressmen and the mass of people would come behind his group. However, the Communists and the Congress Socialists disagreed with this assessment and felt Gandhiji's leadership was essential for a successful movement. Nehru, could see the merits on both sides but eventually went along with Gandhiji.

The year 1940 saw the Muslim League making the demand for Pakistan at its all-India session held in Lahore in March. The League demanded a reconsideration of the 1935 Act on the basis of sovereign states in the Muslim majority areas in the north-west and east of India. This demand was based on the two-nation theory advocated by Jinnah since the 1930s. This theory argued that Hindus and Muslims were not two communities within India but two different nations which must constitute different territorial units. The League advocated that Congress would institute Hindu raj in independent India and Muslims would be persecuted under it. As such, political and cultural survival of Muslims depended on this demand for an autonomous area. They now launched a campaign of vilification against Congress calling it a Hindu party, and emphasizing the impossibility of co-existence between Hindus and Muslims. This generated anxieties amongst the Muslim masses regarding their future in a free India. The Muslim League received the support of the British in this demand and once this resolution was adopted, the British were able to constantly refer to differences amongst Indian leaders as the reason why Britain could not give India its independence.

Individual Satyagraha

By the end of 1940, Gandhiji was asked to lead the Congress and his decision was to start individual satyagraha. This was to be a protest by chosen individuals against participation in the war. The pledge of the satyagrahi was: "It is wrong to help the British war effort with men or money." Vinobha Bhave was the first satyagrahi and Nehru the second. Gandhiji explained to the Viceroy that it was necessary to clarify that the Indian people were not participating in the war effort contrary to British claims. The motive behind offering individual satyagraha was to gear Congress organization for another mass movement. By 15 May 1941, more than 25,000 satyagrahis had been arrested. After their release from prison, Indian leaders were concerned about the security of India. The CWC passed a resolution in December 1941 offering to cooperate in the war effort if Britain promised complete independence after the war.

In March 1942, Stafford Cripps came to India to obtain the cooperation of Indians for the war. This was partly a response to the pressure of the US and Chinese leaders. The Cripps offer promised

India Dominion Status and a Constituent Assembly after the war. It conceded the essentials of Pakistan by allowing provinces to have separate agreements with Britain. Defence of the country continued to be under the control of the British, indicating the lack of any desire to part with authority in the present. Even Nehru who considered Cripps to be a friend was dismayed by the proposals. The offer of Dominion Status rather than full independence was not acceptable to the Congress. Dominion Status would have entailed membership of the British Commonwealth of Nations and allegiance to the British Queen. The Congress also objected to the fact that the representatives of the states would be nominated by the rulers and not elected by the people. Last of all, they opposed the right of the provinces to secede from the Centre because they saw it as an attempt to divide the country.

Quit India Movement

The failure of the Cripps Mission convinced Gandhiji and Nehru that there was no point in looking towards Britain for any substantive political settlement during and after the war. The reluctance to start a mass movement at a time when Hitler was knocking at Britain's door was at an end. Gandhiji proposed a resolution for the CWC in July 1942 which called for the British to 'Quit India' and for the Indian people to fight the Japanese invasion non-violently.

On 8 August 1942, 'Quit India' resolution was passed at the AICC meeting at Gowalia Tank in Bombay. Gandhiji made it clear that the Congress demand was not for anything specific like ministries or abolition of the salt tax but for nothing less than freedom. He exhorted them to 'do or die' in the struggle for independence. He said, "We shall either free India or die in the attempt; we shall not live to see the perpetuation of our slavery." Gandhiji laid down specific tasks for different groups: soldiers were told to refuse to fire on their own people, officials to declare allegiance to the Congress,

Princes to accept sovereignty of their own people, peasants, "who have the courage and are prepared to risk their all", not to pay land revenue.

The next day on 9 August Congress leaders including Gandhiji, Nehru, Patel and Maulana Azad were arrested. In reaction, lakhs of people reached the scene of the 8 August meeting at Gowalia Tank in Bombay, and clashed with the authorities. The next few days saw hartals, public demonstrations, processions and defiance of the law. The major storm-centres were UP and Bihar. A mass upsurge took place all over the country. Forms of protest were many: police stations, courts, post offices, railway stations and other symbols of authority were attacked by huge crowds. Satyagrahis offered arrest in large numbers. Crowds numbering a few thousand removed railway tracks while smaller groups disrupted communications. Strikes in schools and colleges were rampant. Hundreds of news sheets or patrikas mushroomed all over the country. Workers went on strike in Ahmedabad, Bombay, Jamshedpur, Ahmednagar and Poona. Bihar and East UP witnessed a virtual rebellion. The initial message was taken to the villages by students of Banaras Hindu University who hijacked trains and took them inside villages, raised slogans and mobilized people. Tirhut division in Bihar was cut off from the rest of the country for two weeks. It is estimated that in 10 districts of north and central Bihar, 80 per cent of police stations were captured or temporarily evacuated.

Government repression took the form of imposing collective fines, whipping of suspects, burning of entire villages and even firing and machine-gunning from low-flying aircrafts. Over 10,000 people were killed in police and military firing. Sixty thousand were arrested by the end of 1942. Such brutal and large scale repression was not seen since the revolt of 1857. An underground movement also emerged during this period. The important leaders of this movement were Achyut Patwardhan, Aruna Asaf Ali, Ram Manohar Lohia, Sucheta

Kripalani, Jayaprakash Narayan and others. They were active in different parts of Bombay Presidency, Kerala, Andhra, UP, Bihar and Delhi.

An unusual feature of the movement was the parallel governments which came up in some parts of the country. The most famous was in Ballia in east UP where Chittu Pandey asked the Collector to hand over power to him. However, it lasted only for a week. Another parallel government came up in Tamluk in Midnapore district of Bengal. Known as the Jatiya Sarkar, this lasted almost two years from December 1942 to September 1944. Satara in Maharashtra saw a parallel government known as the Prati Sarkar with Nana Patil as its leader. Here, peoples' courts were set up, prohibition was enforced, and village libraries set up. The Prati Sarkar continued till 1945.

Gandhi-Jinnah Talks

Gandhiji was released in May 1944 on medical grounds. On the part of the Congress, at Rajaji's initiative, Gandhiji entered into talks with Jinnah. Gandhiji gave his support to Rajaji's proposals, which envisaged setting up of a Union with India and Pakistan forming two regions in it and pursuing a common policy on Defence, Commerce, Communications and other essential purposes. It also envisaged Muslim League endorsing the demand for independence and cooperating with the Congress in the formation of a provisional government. Further, a Commission would be appointed after the war to demarcate Muslim majority areas in north-west and eastern India. A plebiscite would be held in these areas to determine the issue of separation from India. Gandhiji and Jinnah met in September but this scheme did not commend itself to Jinnah, who insisted on Gandhiji agreeing to the two-nation theory and partition without plebiscite. Gandhiji now busied himself with constructive work which was to help the reorganization of the Congress party through activities like membership drives, training programmes and fund collection.

9 Towards Freedom

Wavell Plan

In the last year of the War, the Viceroy formulated a new political plan known as the Wavell Plan. It was only when the war ended in Europe in May 1945 that he was allowed to put forward this proposal to the Indian leaders.

The Congress leaders were now released to participate in the Simla Conference held in June 1945 to discuss the Wavell plan. The scheme was to constitute a politically representative Executive Council which would include all major political interests. However, very soon, Jinnah declared that all Muslim representatives to the Conference would be League nominees. He also demanded that only a two-third majority in the Council could take decisions on matters objected to by Muslims. While the Viceroy found Jinnah's demand unacceptable, he did not wish to put the whole onus of failure on the League. The Viceroy's objection to Jinnah's claim to be the sole spokesman of all Muslims did not imply an acceptance of the Congress position but was motivated by an unwillingness to alienate the Unionist Party members who had supported the British during the War. The Congress rejected Jinnah's claim and asserted its right to nominate a Muslim member to the Council. Due to persistent disagreement, the Simla Conference failed to reach any political compromise.

By then, the Labour Party had gained power in England defeating the Conservatives at the polls. This was, indeed, a good augury. The King, in his speech to the new Parliament, promised to do the utmost to promote, in conjunction with the leaders of Indian opinion, early realization of full self-government in India. This reflected the priority accorded to the Indian problem. Soon thereafter, Lord Wavell was summoned to England for consultations and fresh elections were announced in India both to the Central and the Provincial Legislatures. On his return from England, Lord Wavell announced the Government intention to convene a Constitution making body as soon as possible and said that, immediately after the elections, he would discuss with the representatives of the Legislative Assemblies in the Provinces to ascertain whether the proposals made earlier were acceptable or any alternative scheme was preferable. He said he would have discussions with the representatives of Indian States to ascertain in what way they could participate in the Constitution making body. The British Prime Minister, Clement Attlee too explained the Government intentions in a broadcast on September 19, 1945.

These announcements, however, were received with a feeling of disappointment by all sections of Indian public and by the Congress in particular. The reason was that the proposals did not contain any declaration of independence to India. Besides this, the latest announcement contained other shortcomings. The AICC considered these at its Bombay session and declared them to be inadequate and vague. The new Secretary of State for India, Lord Pethick-Lawrence clarified the Government's intentions and followed it up with a Parliamentary delegation which was really in the nature of a goodwill mission.

Indian National Army

At the end of the War, an important issue achieved significance. This was the trial of the officers and soldiers of the Indian National Army (INA). The INA had been established by Indian officers of the British Indian army who went over to the Japanese for assistance after the latter captured Malaya and Singapore. The fall of Singapore resulted in the capture of 45,000 Indian soldiers by the Japanese. Along with the officers and soldiers, members of the Indian community in these regions also joined the INA. The INA looked to the Congress and the Indian people for direction. The INA became a part of the Japanese army when the latter decided to invade India. However, they only wanted a token force of 2,000 men whereas the INA leaders wanted to take 20,000 men along. Subhas Bose came to Singapore in July 1943 with the help of the German and the Japanese armies. In October 1943, he set up the provisional government of free India which declared war on the Allies and was recognized by the Axis powers. A hope emerged among Indian civilians: funds were collected and young men and women enrolled into INA. Subhas Bose called upon Gandhiji to bless this army in its 'holy war of India's liberation'. Only one battalion was allowed to accompany the Japanese army to India. On the way, they faced ill-treatment and discrimination from the Japanese which resulted in demoralization. They could not reach India and had to retreat to South-East Asia where, at the end of the War, they surrendered to the British army who, in turn, put them on trial for treason.

In 1945, three officers of the INA, Shahnawaz Khan, Gurdayal Singh Dhillon and Prem Sehgal were put on trial at the Red Fort. The charge was a serious one—treason and disloyalty to the Crown. The Government hoped that conducting this trial publicly in Red Fort, public opinion would turn against INA upon learning of its brutalities during the war. Nehru stated that these men were misguided patriots and called for leniency towards them, especially in the context of

British professions of extending self-government in India. Other Congress leaders also took up the issue. The AICC session in Bombay held in September 1945 passed a resolution supporting the cause of the INA and calling for lenient treatment of these officers. Legal luminaries like Bhulabhai Desai, Tej Bahadur Sapru, K.N. Katju and Asaf Ali appeared in defence of the officers. Nehru donned his lawyer's robes after many years to plead their case in court. The Congress organized an INA Relief and Enquiry Committee which gave some money and food to the men on their release and tried to secure employment for them.

The INA was the main issue highlighted during Congress election campaigns for 1945-46 elections. The press took it up in a major way and editorials were published daily praising the INA men and condemning the British government. Public meetings were held in many cities to express popular resentment against the British and in solidarity with the officers, an INA Day and an INA Week was observed. The Commander-in-Chief of the British Indian Army conceded in November 1945 that the general feeling amongst army men was in favour of leniency and given this, recommended minimal punishment.

Students demonstrated in support of the INA men. Two of the more well-known protests were in Calcutta, the first in November 1945 and the second in February 1946. In November, Communist and Forward Bloc students marching to Dalhousie Square, the seat of the government in Calcutta clashed with the police whereupon two died and 52 were injured. In February 1946, the procession was led by Muslim League students along with Congress and Communist students. Here again, there were arrests, defiance of Section 144 and a lathi-charge. Later, troops were called in and 36 civilians were killed in the firing. Due to public pressure, the sentences of the three officers were commuted to cashiering and forfeiture of pay.

Mutiny in the Royal Indian Navy

Another manifestation of popular resentment against continued British rule was the mutiny in the Royal Indian Navy. This began on 18 February 1946 when 1,100 Indian naval ratings of *HMIS Talwar* struck work at Bombay in protest against racial discrimination and poor food. One of the ratings, B.C. Dutt, was arrested for writing 'Quit India' on the walls of the ship. The next day saw ratings from other establishments join the strike. Congress, League and Communist flags were hoisted on the masts of the ships. Ratings left their ships and went around Bombay in lorries, waving Congress flags.

The common people showed sympathy with the strikers, joining them in putting up barricades, attacking Europeans, fighting pitched battles from house-tops, burning police stations and other symbols of authority. In Bombay, 30 shops, 10 post offices, 10 police posts, 64 food grain shops and 200 street lamps were destroyed. Lakhs of workers came out into the streets in response to the call for a strike. Two hundred twenty-eight civilians died while 1046 were injured. Shopkeepers showed their support by hartals and public transport services came to a halt. There was a display of solidarity all over the country and there were sympathetic strikes by naval establishments in Karachi, Madras, Vishakapatnam, Calcutta, Delhi, Cochin, Jamnagar, the Andamans, and also in Bahrain and Aden. Seventy-eight ships and 20 shore establishments involving 20,000 ratings were affected. The government sent out troops to crush the revolt in Bombay. On the advice of the leaders of the Congress and the League, the ratings eventually surrendered and were subjected to a naval enquiry.

Labour and Peasant Unrest

During the war, workers' and peasants' discontentment had not found any expression. After the war ended, the anticipation of freedom was expressed in an unprecedented mass upsurge. Labour unrest now became widespread in the country. Post and telegraph workers struck work all over India in July 1946. Railway workers went on strike in South India in August 1946. In all, 1,629 strikes occurred in 1946 involving nearly 2 million men and the loss of more than 12 million man-days. The main issue was working conditions and decrease in real wages. One of the most well-known peasant movements was the Tebhaga movement in Bengal in which the sharecroppers vowed to pay only one-third and not the prior demand of one-half of the produce to the landlords. The struggle of the Warli tribals in Maharashtra was directed against illegal exactions, exploitation and low wages by the landlord-moneylender-official nexus. The Kisan Sabha supported the demands of the tribals. Further, there were no-rent struggles by peasants in different areas of Punjab like Patiala, Una, Kangra, Ferozepur and Pathankot. In Travancore, agricultural workers were mobilized by the Communist party in support of the people's struggle against the feudal autocracy. This was known as the Punnapra-Vayalar revolt.

In the meantime, elections to the Central and provincial assemblies were announced in September 1945. This turned into a contest between the Congress with its ideal of a united free India and the League with its Pakistan demand. The election was projected as a popular vote on Pakistan by the League campaign. In Punjab, the League campaign received the support of religious leaders and involved vilification of the Unionist Party as well as the Congress. In the Central Assembly elections, the Muslim League won all the reserved Muslim seats, securing 89 per cent of the Muslim vote. Elections to the provincial legislative assemblies were held in the beginning of 1946. Ninety per cent of the general seats were won by Congress candidates. The Muslim League secured the reserved Muslim seats.

Cabinet Mission

The decision to send a mission to India to negotiate a political settlement was taken by the Cabinet in London on 22 January 1946.

The mission came with the objective of setting up a national government and putting into motion the machinery for transfer of power. The ministers, Stafford Cripps, A.V. Alexander and Pethick-Lawrence, were given powers to take decisions without referring back to England. On 15 March 1946, Prime Minister Attlee declared that a minority would not be allowed to place a veto on the progress of the majority, indicating a shift away from the pro-League stand adopted earlier by the British government.

After consulting the Indian leaders, the ministers came around to the view that Pakistan was not viable and that safeguards for minorities must be within the framework of a united India. The ministers came up with a scheme announced on 16 May 1946 for establishment of a three-tiered constitution for India. Provinces were divided into three sections: Section A comprised Madras, Bombay, United Provinces, Bihar, Central Provinces, and Orissa; Section B was made up of Punjab, Sindh and NWFP; and Section C comprised Bengal and Assam. There would be a common Centre supervising defence, foreign affairs and communications. A province could come out of a section only after the first general elections. After 10 years, a province could ask for a reconsideration of the section or union constitution.

The Congress did not want to wait till the first election for any province to leave the section. It wanted that any province should have the option not to join the section in the first place. Here, they were expressing the concerns of Assam and the NWFP who did not want to be part of their respective sections which were dominated by states with Muslim majority. The League wanted that the union constitution could be questioned at the very outset by any province rather than after a period of 10 years. The lack of clarity about whether these sections were binding upon the provinces comprising them generated a lot of controversy and intensified Congress-League disagreement. The Congress eventually decided to accept the 16 May statement while maintaining its opposition to compulsory grouping. The League accepted the plan primarily because compulsory grouping conceded the principle of Pakistan. However, the continuation of ambivalence about the nature of grouping led to the withdrawal of League acceptance at the end of July 1946.

Interim Government and Communal Violence

In early September, Nehru was sworn in as the vice-president of the Interim Government. There were debates on the sovereignty and the status of the Constituent Assembly. But the Legislatures started electing their representatives to the Constituent Assembly. The Muslim League refused to participate in this exercise and observed August 16 as "Direct Action" Day to achieve Pakistan through non-constitutional means. Direct Action Day witnessed orgies of violence in Calcutta. The Muslim League government of Bengal abetted these riots in which over 5,000 people were killed and many rendered homeless. A judicial enquiry was demanded by the Congress. Nehru compared the Bengal government to the fascist regime of Hitler. In October, riots broke out in Bihar as a reaction to the Calcutta killings. This led to widespread attacks on Hindus in Noakhali and Tipperah in East Bengal in October. Thousands were rendered homeless and looting, abduction of women, forced conversion and killings were rampant. The Bengal government did little to control the situation. Gandhiji went on a peace mission to Noakhali in early November 1946. He walked barefoot through the villages of Noakhali. The idea was to persuade the Muslims to reassure the Hindus about their safety and ask them to return to their homes. Many Muslims in Noakhali wanted him to go and see the destruction which had occurred in Bihar and the state of the Muslims there. He went to Bihar in March 1947 where he saw his task as getting the Hindus to repent for their deeds. The Congress ministry of Bihar was energized by his presence and it took up relief and rehabilitation in a big way.

The Viceroy insisted on incorporating League members in the Interim Government arguing that else, civil war would become inevitable. On 25 October 1946, League members entered the government, barely 15 days after the Noakhali riots. From the very beginning, it was clear that the League nominees in the Interim government had not forsaken direct action. Rather, they saw the Interim government as one of the fronts of the direct action campaign for Pakistan. Within the Interim government, the League members adopted a method of non-cooperation intended to render the exercise redundant. Later, they participated in civil disobedience campaigns against elected ministries in Punjab, NWFP and Assam.

Constituent Assembly

The League stayed away from the Constituent Assembly and when it was convened in December 1946, Jinnah remarked that it was a move to appease the Congress. This deadlock was sought to be resolved by talks in London in December 1946. However, these talks did not yield any results and the statement by the British government issued on 6 December 1946 adopted an interpretation of grouping favourable to the League. The Congress decided to accept this interpretation but even that failed to bring the League into the Constituent Assembly. At the end of January 1947, the League passed a resolution at its session in Karachi calling for a boycott of the Constituent Assembly and dissolution of the Cabinet Mission plan. Congress members of the Interim government pointed out that it was now clearly unacceptable for League members to continue in the government without coming into the Constituent Assembly. However, this did not affect the functioning of the Constituent Assembly and League members continued to be in the Interim government.

On 20 February 1947, the British Prime Minister Attlee issued a new statement in the Parliament regarding the future of India. The terms of this statement temporarily shifted political focus away from the issues which had so far occupied the Congress leadership and the League. It was announced for the first time that the British would leave India by June 1948 and that Mountbatten would be the new and the last Viceroy of India. This statement was positively received in Congress circles as proof of British intention to leave India. Partition of the country was implied in the proviso that if the Constituent Assembly was not found adequately representative, power would be inherited by more than one Central government. The Congress was relieved that at least the Constituent Assembly could carry on its work of framing the constitution for free India. Nehru's appeal to Liaquat Ali Khan to work out some political compromise given the forthcoming departure of the British did not receive any constructive response.

Last Viceroy

Lord Mountbatten came to India on 22 March 1947 as the new Viceroy. The few weeks before his arrival had witnessed widespread rioting in Punjab which the government was struggling to control. Muslim League had launched an anti-ministry movement in Punjab bringing down the Unionist-Akali coalition ministry at the beginning of March. Given the collapse of law and order in the province and the active involvement of League volunteers in attacks on non-Muslims, the CWC was forced to pass a resolution demanding that Punjab must be partitioned if the country was divided. This was the situation which met Mountbatten on his arrival in India. He had been instructed in London to explore the possibilities of union and division in India after which he was to advise the government in England about the form which the transfer of power to India should take.

Within two months of his arrival, he realized that the Cabinet Mission plan could not work for India. He found it impossible to convince Jinnah to accept anything other than a sovereign Pakistan. The administrative situation of the country had deteriorated further and the cooperation of the political parties was vital for the functioning of the Interim government. The Mountbatten Plan, as the 3 June plan was called, advanced the date of departure and stated that India would achieve Dominion Status in August 1947. According to this, the country would be divided but maximum unity retained. This implied the partition of Punjab and Bengal so that the Hindu majority areas of these provinces would be retained in India. Two boundary commissions, overseen by Sir Cyril Radcliffe, would be set up to demarcate the boundaries of the two Dominions in Punjab and Bengal. The NWFP was to choose either Dominion through a referendum and a plebiscite was to be held in Sylhet district of Assam for the same purpose. The Princely States were given the choice to join either of the two Dominions. India's membership of the British Commonwealth was a top priority for the government on account of future defence interests in the subcontinent.

Communal Massacres

Meanwhile, communal riots broke out in Punjab leading to widespread arson, rioting, killings and the beginning of the migration of people. Refugee camps came up in Rawalpindi, Delhi, Panipat, Kurukshetra, Wah and many other places. Congress reluctantly accepted the partition of the country despite its long-term commitment to unity of India in the hope that it would stem civil war and contain communal violence. Many leaders and people hoped that when the passions had subsided, the two countries would once again come together. Thus, while the country did achieve freedom through a phase of negotiations with the communal leadership and the British government, communalism as a mass phenomenon could not be uprooted.

The League was also not entirely happy with this Plan. Jinnah felt that it did not concede Pakistan in full and that what they had inherited was a moth-eaten version of their demands. Nonetheless, the Plan was formally accepted by both the parties as the best solution under the circumstances and on 23 June 1947, the provincial assemblies of Punjab and Bengal voted in favour of the division of the two provinces. Even Gandhiji, who had once declared that India could be partitioned only over his dead body, now expressed his helplessness in the face of the overwhelming public acceptance of partition. He advised people not to accept the demarcation of political boundaries as a division in their hearts and keep alive the hope for a union of the two countries in the future.

Congress and Partition

For Congress leaders, acceptance of partition was the last resort for avoiding civil war. It did not amount to an acceptance of the two-nation theory since India was visualized as a multi-religious and multi-cultural entity. In any case, the number of Muslims who stayed back in India exceeded those who constituted Pakistan. Any talk of India following Pakistan and declaring itself as a Hindu state was summarily dismissed by the nationalist leadership. It was a brave task indeed to frame a secular constitution and build a secular polity in the backdrop of the communal violence and the formation of Pakistan. Even Jinnah, when asked for advice by Muslims who chose to stay in India after independence, told them to be loyal citizens of India. In an address to the Pakistan Constituent Assembly on 11 August 1947, he argued for a state divorced from considerations of religion, caste or creed. However, these ideas did not guide the formulation of state policy in Pakistan. It was a nation founded upon the principle of safeguards for religious minorities, and yet, it did not provide these same safeguards to the non-Muslim minority populations now within its territory. The worst predicament was faced by the pro-Congress Pathans in NWFP who boycotted the referendum as they were not given the option of independence that they desired. Instead, the province was to choose between India and

Pakistan. Their fate was linked to a regime which continued to be hostile towards them.

The Indian Independence Act was passed by the British Parliament in July 1947. On 15 August 1947, in a midnight session of the Constituent Assembly in New Delhi, Nehru took over as the Prime Minister of India. Multitudes greeted this occasion with joy and celebration while countless others were too stricken with the wounds of communal violence to rejoice. In Calcutta, Gandhiji preferred to spend the day in silence, spinning, fasting and praying for an end to the carnage. In New Delhi, the new government with Nehru at the helm started out on the difficult and challenging task of rebuilding free India.

10 The Nehru Era

India was fortunate to have leaders who were tremendously popular and could communicate with the people and represent their aspirations. As dedicated and imaginative leaders, their power was derived from democratic values. Nehru stood at the head of a virtual galaxy of leaders—Sardar Patel, Maulana Azad, Rajendra Prasad and C. Rajagopalachari at the Centre and G.B. Pant, B.G. Kher, B.C. Roy and Morarji Desai in the states. These were all men with experience of organizing a movement and a party and being at the heads of legislatures and governments. The challenge of building an independent, democratic, secular, modern and prosperous India out of the "mud and filth" left behind by colonialism (to use a description by Rabindranath Tagore) was a huge one. Nehru and his team rose gallantly to meet this challenge.

The Making of the Constitution

The newly independent state inherited a rich legacy from the national movement. The Congress party had given priority to upholding the right of free expression throughout the years of the national struggle. It was this tradition that was reflected in Nehru's first Cabinet and the Indian Constitution adopted in 1950. Of the 14 members of Nehru's Cabinet in 1947, 5 were non-Congressmen, B.R. Ambedkar,

S.P. Mookerjee, John Mathai, C.H. Bhabha and Shanmukham Chetty, making it a national government.

In the years when the Indian Constitution was being drafted, the basic principles and the broad structure of the Constitution bore the imprint of Congress ideology. In respect to fundamental rights, directive principles of state policy and other features in the Constitution, such as the abolition of separate electorates, the policies advocated by the Congress were reflected. The Congress Working Committee and AICC would discuss and ratify each and every important resolution before it went to the Constituent Assembly. The Indian Constitution provided for universal adult franchize, a demand taken up by the Congress since the late 19th century. The Constitution laid down a democratic and parliamentary form of government for India. It took three years to put the Constitution together and, on 26 January 1950, the Indian Constitution was adopted making India a republic. Dr. Ambedkar, Chairman of the Drafting Committee of the Constitution, emphasized the point that India was not a 'Federation of States' but a 'Union of States'. Explaining the difference, he argued that a federation resulted when different states signed agreements joining or creating a federation. By this logic, they could also leave the federation at some point in time. In the case of India, the constituent states were not independent entities willingly entering into a federation or having the choice to opt out in the future. Rather, they were part of a Union which was indestructible. The Union was divided into states for reasons of administrative convenience but as a society, as a country, all states together formed a whole.

The Constitution was also the instrument for removal of social injustice and ensuring equality. Thus, political rights were extended to all adults without distinction of religion, caste or gender. Untouchability was formally abolished and later in 1955, its practice was made punishable. Seats in legislatures and educational institutions and government jobs were reserved for Scheduled Castes. These were meant initially for a period of 10 years only but have been extended till now.

The tribes were sought to be protected through safeguards given in the constitution and concerted efforts were made in this direction by the governments at the Centre and in the states. The policy of Nehru's government was to preserve the social and cultural heritage of the tribals in India. Later Tribal Welfare Departments were actively urged to take literacy, education and Panchayati Raj institutions to tribal areas in all the states.

Partition and the Communal Challenge

Soon after independence, fierce and widespread communal riots broke out in many parts of India. Nehru was aware that communalism was a major threat to India and carried out a massive campaign against it through radio broadcasts, public speeches, speeches in Parliament and private letters including letters to Chief Ministers and most of all by his personal example of fearless resistance to communal violence. This campaign was also aimed at reassuring Muslims that they would be safe in India. With the establishment of Pakistan, the Hindu communal forces became strident in their stance. They declared 15 August as a day of mourning and launched an attack on the government for what they saw as its policy of Muslim appeasement. Their ideology struck root among the disaffected refugees. Very soon, riots broke out in Delhi.

The slander of national leaders especially Gandhiji became a common feature. 'Gandhiji Murdabad' reverberated at Hindu Mahasabha meetings. When Gandhiji asserted that Pakistan government be paid Rs. 55 crore, its share of immovable assets, despite its engagement in hostilities in Kashmir, the Hindu communalists sharpened their attack on him. Gandhiji undertook an indefinite fast in January 1948 in Delhi in an effort to bring about communal peace. He broke it after he was assured by the government that communal harmony would be maintained.

A few days later, on January 30, 1948, as he came to his usual prayer meeting, Gandhiji was shot dead by Nathuram Godse, a member of the Hindu Mahasabha and the RSS, and a close associate of V.D. Savarkar. The assassination shocked the entire country, as it was clear that the Mahatma had fallen a victim to communal forces. Communal forces received a setback after the murder of Gandhiji. Nehru realized that it was not just the act of a fanatic but behind it was the ideology of the RSS which he described as a fascist organization. With Nehru's full support, Sardar Patel, the Home Minister, placed the RSS and Hindu Mahasabha under a ban. The ban on RSS was lifted only in July 1949 when it gave an undertaking that it would function under severe restrictions. The Hindu Mahasabha dissolved itself. The sacrifice of the Mahatma was not in vain. For at least a decade, communal forces were pushed on to the back foot and could not raise their head.

Another major issue which Nehru's government had to deal with was the rehabilitation of six million refugees who had been rendered homeless due to the communal carnage which accompanied Partition. The rehabilitation of Punjabi refugees was completed only by 1951. New townships for refugees had to be established. Nilokheri, near Delhi, was developed as part of this endeavour to resettle the refugees from Punjab. Similarly, in the eastern part of the country, the refugees from East Bengal were rehabilitated. The question of refugee rehabilitation involved negotiations with the government of Pakistan. In April 1950, Nehru signed a pact with Liaquat Ali Khan, the Prime Minister of Pakistan in which the two governments reassured each other that they would protect their minorities.

Integration of the Princely States

One of the many problems immediately after independence was the integration of the Princely States. Earlier in the year, Patel had used persuasion as well as pressure to integrate most of the States into the Union. Some States had joined the Constituent Assembly in April 1947 but others had stayed away, with some desiring independence. Patel used the threat of popular struggles to persuade the States to join the Union. By 15 August 1947, all but three of them—Kashmir, Hyderabad and Junagadh—had joined India.

In the case of Junagadh, the Nawab acceded to Pakistan but the people revolted. The Nawab fled to Pakistan and the Indian Government took over the administration of Junagadh. The Nizam of Hyderabad declined to accede to either India or Pakistan but, after a swift police action, Sardar Patel succeeded in bringing Hyderabad within the Indian Union. It is interesting to note that contrary to the expectations of Nizam and Pakistan, the Muslims in both Hyderabad and the rest of the Indian Union opted to stay in India.

The problem regarding Jammu and Kashmir, however, remained. It had a border with Pakistan, was ruled by a Hindu Maharaja, and the Muslims formed the majority of the population. The National Conference, affiliated to the All India States' People's Conference and headed by Sheikh Abdullah, was very close to the Congress and to Nehru. The Maharaja asked for a standstill agreement for a year to make up his mind. Pakistan had already formally accepted this and the Indian stand in any case was that the people's wishes should be ascertained via elections. Pakistan, however, was not confident that the popular verdict would go in its favor and jumped the gun. In October 1947, Pakistan invaded the valley. As the invaders marched forward to take over Srinagar, the Maharaja acceded to India. Pursuant to this, Indian troops repelled the invaders and under UN auspices, a cease-fire agreement was arrived at. Jammu and Kashmir, though under the Indian Union, continues to enjoy a special status, distinct from other provinces. The integration of the Princely States with the neighbouring provinces in the Indian Union was regarded as one of the greatest achievements of Sardar Patel, backed by eminent leaders of Praja Mandals and other bodies affiliated to the All-India States' People's Conference.

The Economic Challenge

The economic critique of colonialism developed by Congress leaders during the years of the national movement had highlighted the subordination and colonial structuring of the Indian economy to suit the needs of the British economy. On the basis of this understanding, the national leadership evolved a perspective to overcome this colonial structuring so that backwardness and underdevelopment could be fought. This became the foundation of the economic policies adopted after independence. The emphasis was on building a planned, self-reliant economy through rapid industrialization, growth in agriculture and public sector intervention in strategic industries making it a mixed economy.

In 1947, the Economic Programme Committee of the AICC with Nehru as its convener spelt out that defence, key industries and public utilities would be under the public sector. An Industrial Policy Resolution was adopted in 1948 which stated that nationalization of existing industries would be considered after a period of 10 years. A Planning Commission was set up in 1950 under the chairmanship of Nehru. At the AICC session in Bangalore held in July 1951, Nehru presented a report outlining his concept of a Welfare State and the means to achieve it. All these were incorporated in the First-Five Year Plan launched in 1951. In 1954, this resolution was reviewed and a major change in favour of socialistic pattern of society was proposed. This was adopted at the historic Avadi session of the Congress in 1955. Following this, the Industrial Policy Resolution was modified in

1956. This triggered the growth of the public sector. The Second Five-Year Plan reflected this changed policy by the entry of public sector into heavy and capital goods industry on a massive scale.

The overall economic performance during the Nehru years was remarkable. India's national income grew at 4 per cent per annum between 1950 and 1964. This was roughly four times the rate of growth achieved during the last half century of colonial rule and compared very favourably with that of other countries, like Japan, in their early stages of industrialization. Comprehensive land reform measures were introduced within the democratic framework, a rare feat in world history. During the first three five-year plans, agriculture grew at an annual rate of over 3 per cent which was more than seven times higher than what was achieved in the last half century of colonial rule. It again compared very favourably with other countries like Japan and China. Industrial growth during these years reached a figure of 7 per cent per annum. But more important, the focus on basic and heavy industries reduced India's nearly hundred per cent dependence on advanced countries. By 1960 India needed to import only 43 per cent of the capital equipment or machinery out of its total fixed investments. By 1974 the dependence on imports in this area had come down to a mere 9 per cent. This was the great Nehruvian achievement in rapidly converting our political independence achieved in 1947 into economic independence.

The development of infrastructure was, especially in the areas of education and health, another area Nehru focussed on. Basic education received a new impetus. Removal of adult illiteracy, universalization of primary education, large scale training of manpower in areas of science and technology by setting up institutions of higher learning in these areas became immediate objectives. Maulana Abul Kalam Azad was put in charge of the Education portfolio in the Congress government at the Centre. The setting up of a University Education Commission under the

Chairmanship of Dr. S. Radhakrishnan in 1948, followed by the setting up of a Secondary Education Commission under the Chairmanship of Dr. A. Lakshmanaswami Mudaliar, helped in laying a solid foundation for the development of school and higher education. Nehru played a seminal role in providing an impetus to the growth of a scientific temper and the setting up of a chain of national institutions and laboratories to promote indigeneous research and technological development. In 1948, the Atomic Energy Commission was set up laying the foundations for the advances made by India in the sphere of nuclear science and related areas. In 1958, the Congress government came out with its famous Scientific Policy Resolution, drafted by Nehru himself.

Nehru had brilliantly anticipated that 'knowledge' would become the key factor of production in the future. That India can participate in the globalization process in today's world of high technology, with any degree of competitiveness and equality, is largely due to the spadework done since the early years after independence, particularly the great emphasis laid on human resource development in the sphere of science and technology.

The Language Issue

Though the Congress had accepted language as the basis for formation of states since 1921, the experience of Partition urged it give top priority to unity. The Jaipur session of the Congress reiterated the acceptance of linguistic divisions in principle. A Committee comprising Nehru, Sardar Patel and Pattabhi Sitaramayya was set up to examine the issue. The Committee report was not in favour of further linguistic divisions. It felt that any effort at re-drawing the boundaries of the states might harm unity, by dislodging the administration, disrupting economic development and accentuating linguistic rivalries. However, the success of the struggle for a separate state in Andhra in 1953 encouraged other states to demand autonomy or re-drawing of boundaries on the basis of language. In 1953, the States Reorganization Commission was set up by Nehru. The states were eventually reorganized on grounds of language by the end of 1950s.

Another aspect of the language problem was the dispute over the official language to be adopted in the country. The Constitution declared Hindi, in the Devnagari script, as the language of administration throughout the country. The change to Hindi from English was to be effected by 1965. No link language was specified in the Constitution. In 1956, the report of the Official Language Commission recommended that Hindi should start progressively replacing English in the functioning of the Central government. This was opposed by members from Tamil Nadu and West Bengal. It was felt that this would be disadvantageous to the people in non-Hindi speaking areas in the matter of job opportunities. The reaction in Tamil Nadu was particularly violent. There was resentment over what the agitators characterized as attempts by the North to dominate over the South. The Dravidian parties gathered strength in the process. The conflict between Brahmins and non-Brahmins surfaced adding to the tension. In 1963, the Dravida Munnetra Kazhagam launched a massive movement against Hindi, paralyzing the Congress Party machinery. Nehru gave an assurance that English would continue to be the associate language for official purpose until non-Hindi states voluntarily agreed to implement the Constitutional provisions for making Hindi the *lingua franca* of the country. Following this assurance, the DMK gave up its demand for secession from India.

Foreign Policy

When India became independent in 1947, it was natural that she sought to express herself in international forums. Nehru did this by defining and adopting the policy of non-alignment. Besides keeping a neutral distance from military blocs, Nehru defined this policy as the struggle to maintain independence from imperialism. India led the other newly-independent colonies into this policy and thus offered an alternative to membership in either of the two blocs. Nehru outlined five principles of peaceful coexistence among countries, termed the Panchsheel, which envisaged mutual respect for each other's territorial integrity and sovereignty, non-aggression, non-interference in internal affairs, equality and mutual benefit, and peaceful coexistence. These principles became the basis of the Non-Aligned Movement.

The Political Dimension

After independence, the Congress underwent a change in character. From being a platform for an anti-colonial movement, it turned into a more organized political party. However, the features of ideological flexibility, openness in its approach to other political strands and democratic procedures were retained within the party. It is well known that Nehru and Patel did not see eye to eye on many important issues, yet this did not come in the way of their relying on each other in running the country till Patel's death in 1950. P.D. Tandon was elected Congress president in 1950 despite Nehru's opposition to his candidature. Nehru and many other leaders resigned from the CWC compelling Tandon to step down. From 1950 to the Avadi session of the Congress in 1955, Nehru was the president of the Congress along with leading the government.

He was the star campaigner for the party in the first general elections held in 1951-52. His campaign covered 40,000 kilometres during which he addressed 35 million people. The main issue in this campaign was communalism. The participation of the 173 million-strong electorate in the elections was remarkable. About 46.6 per cent of the eligible voters cast their votes. The Congress won nearly 75 per cent of the seats in the Lok Sabha and 68.5 per cent in the state legislatures. Elections were seen as the primary method of political participation for the rural and urban poor. Women as well as tribals voted in large numbers. It was evident that elections were fair, free and orderly.

It is a great tribute to the triumph of the secularist ideal under Nehru's leadership that even after the cataclysmic events leading to the partition of the country where communal frenzy led to hundreds of thousands being killed and millions made homeless, within three years a peaceful election could be held on the basis of a secular constitution. A secular India was the response to Pakistan (made in the name of Islam) not a Hindu India.

The 1950s and the 1960s were also marked by cleavages in the party. During the freedom movement, the Congress had attracted people with diverse political views and economic interests. They worked together for the sole aim of ousting the British rulers. After independence, the differences were heightened. In 1951, J.B. Kripalani quit the Congress with his followers because of differences with Nehru over the relative importance of the parliamentary and the organizational wings. Kripalani wanted the government to consult the Congress Working Committee on important matters like appointments for high political offices but Nehru insisted on unfettered freedom for the government to function. On the eve of the first general elections, some leaders including P.C. Ghosh left the Congress to form the Kisan Mazdoor Praja Party. C. Rajagopalachari left the Congress in 1959 to form the Swatantra Party.

During these years, Nehru tried to ensure that the Congress remained a party that welcomed diversity. When the Socialists left the Congress believing it to have become a right-wing party, Nehru made several attempts to woo them back and seek their cooperation in nation building. He was concerned that the Congress should maintain a leftist orientation. With the Communists leaving the Congress in 1945, and adopting a hostile stance since 1947, and the Socialists leaving Congress in 1948, the Left forces in the Congress were considerably weakened. When he could not bring the Left back into the party, he decided to take the initiative himself for radicalizing party policies in the spheres of social equality, equity and economic development. At the Congress session in Hyderabad in 1953, the scope of land reforms was extended and at the Avadi session in 1955, "the socialistic pattern of society" was adopted as the objective. In the Nagpur session held in 1959, he proposed a resolution for introduction of cooperatives in agriculture. In January 1964, the Congress session was held in Bhubaneshwar where the commitment to socialism was reiterated.

The transformation of the Congress from a party leading a movement to a party heading a government, inevitably brought in problems of factionalism, weakening of contact with the masses, tendencies of power-seeking and even corruption. For some years, Nehru was able to contain this but a stage came when even he could not check the stagnancy. At the session in Avadi held in 1955, a resolution was adopted directing the Working Committee to take firm steps to ensure that organizational discipline was duly observed. In 1963, the loss of three by-elections made the party sit up and take notice of the stagnancy which had set in. The party had been in power for many years and the organizational side had clearly suffered. K. Kamraj, the Chief Minister of Madras, and Nehru put together a plan to reinvigorate the party and bring about a balance between the party and its parliamentary wing. Under this plan, called Kamraj Plan, prominent leaders were asked to relinquish official positions, approach the masses and try to restore their confidence in the party. Three hundred resignations from ministerial posts including those of all members of the Union Cabinet and all Chief Ministers followed. Of these, Nehru accepted the resignations of 6 Cabinet ministers and 6 Chief Ministers.

However, this plan came too late. By this time, Nehru's health was failing and he could not follow it through. He passed away on 27 May

1964. Nevertheless, the Congress during the Nehru era achieved great success in many fields, including political stability in the country in its most formative years. It helped the nation in framing for itself a democratic constitution and in creating a strong and vibrant parliamentary structure. Its performance in the first three general elections was better than that of all other parties.

India during the years from 1951 to 1964 settled on a road to stability and prosperity. The Constitution had been adopted and the refugee problem had more or less been settled. This was the beginning of the rebuilding of the polity and the economy. The basic objectives of democracy, civil liberties, secularism, economic development and planning and socialism seemed within reach. The linguistic issues were dealt with as were the tribal problems, planning was initiated, foreign policy charted out, elections set in place and administrative structure established and the blueprint of a welfare state laid out.

This was no mean achievement. India's success in combining development with democracy became a model for other newly independent third world countries. As Nehru was keenly aware, this was a path 'uncharted in history'. Nehru, the pre-eminent builder of independent India had set India on a course which many other countries were to try and follow with varying degrees of success.

11 Indira Gandhi

On Nehru's death in May 1964, Gulzari Lal Nanda, the senior-most minister in his Cabinet, was made the interim Prime Minister. Even during Nehru's last days, some of the powerful Central and state leaders of the Party had formed themselves into an informal group evidently with a view to guiding and directing the Congress politics in the post-Nehru era. This group came to be known as the Syndicate. It initially consisted of K. Kamaraj, N. Sanjiva Reddy, S. Nijalingappa, Atulya Ghosh and S.K. Patil. Subsequently, C.B. Gupta and quite a few other leaders joined it. Barring Kamaraj, the rest were conservatives. Morarji Desai, known for his conservative ideas, also moved closer to the Syndicate at a later stage. There were many names that were discussed, but the choice was narrowed down to Morarji Desai and Lal Bahadur Shastri.

The Shastri Era

Kamaraj, who was then the Congress President, consulted the members of the Congress Working Committee, state Chief Ministers, the Deputy Leader and Chief Whip of the Congress Parliamentary Party (CPP) and eight other leaders to decide the leader of the Congress Parliamentary Party. There was a broad consensus in favour of Lal Bahadur Shastri. He became the Prime Minister on

2 June 1964. Indira Gandhi became the Minister for Information and Broadcasting.

An experienced minister in Nehru's cabinet, Lal Bahadur Shastri was the first choice of the party leadership to resolve intra-party conflicts. Though India had taken giant strides, a lot was yet to be done for socioeconomic development if the objectives of self-reliance, eradication of poverty, removal of illiteracy and promotion of health were to be achieved. A hostile China continued to be a threat at the borders. Shastri affirmed his commitment to the principles of socialism and turned his attention to the task of reinvigorating rural society. The land reforms proposed by the Congress in the 1950s had still to be fully implemented and rural economy was still underdeveloped. Shastri took forward the process of technological development of Indian agriculture—the Green Revolution—the foundations for which had been laid in the Nehru period. This was to lead India transforming herself from a food deficient country to a food surplus country in a short period under Indira Gandhi's leadership.

Even as Shastri was engaged in tackling economic problems, Pakistan launched military action to take over certain border areas in Gujarat, and followed it up with a full-scale war in the autumn of 1965. Shastri demonstrated to the world that India could defend its territory with the modest resources at her command. The aggression by Pakistan was effectively checked. The Indian troops even crossed over to Pakistani territory near Lahore. However, the hostilities ceased after a while, following pleas for amicable settlement by a number of countries. The Soviet Union brought the Prime Ministers of India and Pakistan together at a conference in Tashkent in 1966 to arrive at a mutually acceptable agreement. While the country was rejoicing over the triumph of Shastri and the leadership he provided to the Indian defence forces, news came of his death in Tashkent on 10 January 1966.

G.L. Nanda was again made interim Prime Minster to get time to choose another leader. The exercise proved to be more difficult now than in 1964. The ideological differences between the various groups in the party were sharper. The conservatives within the party looked upon Morarji Desai as the most appropriate choice. The radical elements, on the other hand, preferred Indira Gandhi. The preference was not merely because she was the daughter of Nehru. Earlier, in 1959, she had been the President of the Congress and at that time had demonstrated her political skills. In the Shastri Cabinet, she had served as the Minister of Information and Broadcasting.

The two groups openly canvassed for their respective candidates. Kamaraj, as the Congress President, preferred Indira Gandhi. As one wedded to socialistic ideas, Kamaraj did not like to have Morarji Desai, known for his conservative policies, as the head of the government. However, Kamaraj did not follow the "consensus" method now. He allowed the CPP to choose their leader by a battle of the ballot. Indira Gandhi was chosen as the leader of CPP defeating Morarji Desai, receiving 355 votes as against Desai's 169. She became the Prime Minister at the age of 48.

Challenges before Indira

The challenges she faced were many. She tackled the Punjab problem by accepting the demand for a Punjabi suba. She also accepted the Naga rebels' demand for autonomy. The economic situation demanded attention. Economic recession prevailed and drought worsened the situation further. The drought and famine situation was handled effectively but one of the measures taken to resolve the economic plight proved to be counter-effective. This was the devaluation of the rupee by 35.5 per cent. It failed to increase exports and attract foreign capital. The Green Revolution, a strategy of introducing high-yield seeds and fertilizers in order to jump-start a sharp rise in food production, was taken forward in her time.

Between 1967-68 and 1970-71, food grain production rose by 35 per cent. India was no longer seen as standing with a begging bowl before the Western countries and successive droughts were handled without foreign aid.

Foreign policy was another field which demanded application of a new approach. For example, the United States used its position as a supplier of financial aid, food and capital investment to India to twist India's arm towards taking a pro-US line on Vietnam. However, she went ahead to decry the US bombing of Vietnam. In addition, Indira Gandhi chose to develop links with the Soviet Union in order to build a counter-alliance to the US-China-Pakistan axis.

Two features of the political system were a source of great trouble for Indira Gandhi. One was the decline of Parliament as an institution. Members of Parliament took to undisciplined behaviour and she was often the target of attack. The party was another trouble spot, beset with groupism and factionalism. Her own position in the party was not secure. Though she was the Prime Minister, the important portfolios were held by leaders not chosen by her.

Indira Gandhi had hardly taken the reins of office when the country went in for General Elections. Apart from the factionalism within the Congress, this was the period of extreme "anti-Congressism" where opposition parties of completely divergent views and ideologies joined hands to form anti-Congress fronts. Lohiaites, socialists, communal Jan Sangh, communists, the right wing Swatantra Party, Akalis etc., all made opportunistic alliances against the Congress. As a result, the Congress Party suffered an unexpected defeat at the polls in Bihar, UP, Rajasthan, Punjab, West Bengal, Orissa, Madras and Kerala, besides securing a reduced majority in the Lok Sabha. The vote share of the party went down to 41 per cent while the number of seats now stood at 284 seats in a house of 520. The worst aspect was that the decline in the states had now reached the Centre. If one analyses the election results in terms of social groups, it was evident that the rich and middle peasants had deserted the Congress.

The poor electoral performance of the party again brought up the issue of leadership. The Syndicate was critical of the "dismal performance" of the Government under Indira Gandhi's leadership. Secondly, her style of functioning as the Prime Minister of India seemed to have offended Kamaraj and his colleagues. One of the factors that strengthened the position of Indira Gandhi was the near rout of the Syndicate leaders in the general elections. The only prominent Syndicate leader elected was Sanjiva Reddy. She had been the star and the only all-India campaigner and vote-catcher for the Congress. Her unchallenged leadership of the Congress parliamentary party (CPP) was now established giving her a free hand in forming a Cabinet and deciding the portfolios.

As on the past two occasions, Morarji Desai was an aspirant for the Prime Ministership. But a contest was averted and he was offered the position of Deputy Prime Minister which he accepted. However, this was merely a formal position without any real authority. This time, a pressure group in the CPP, backed by the Congress President Kamaraj, a few Chief Ministers and some members of the Congress Working Committee saw to it that Indira Gandhi was made the Prime Minister.

Mid-term polls took place in four states in February 1969 and the position of Congress deteriorated further. The rate of economic growth had slowed down considerably. Corruption was rampant, unrest in the countryside and discontent in urban areas was widespread. The election results shocked Congressmen and the differences within the party now came to a head. The leftist "Young Turks" did not keep quiet. One of them, Chandra Shekhar, launched a frontal attack on Morarji Desai for not setting up a commission of inquiry into the affairs of the Birlas. The CWC took serious note of this and warned party men against indulging in personal attacks. It asked Indira Gandhi as the leader of the Congress Parliamentary Party to curb this tendency on the part of the members of Parliament. Undeterred, the Young Turks carried on their pressure tactics by criticizing the party bosses for failure to implement the 10-point programme for socioeconomic development. This was followed by the severe indictment of the party leadership by the Congress Forum for Socialist Action (FSA). C. Subramaniam, President of Tamil Nadu Congress Committee, warned in a report that the party would not make much headway in the 1972 elections unless it adopted a radical programme of socialist action. He wanted the party's goal to be declared as democratic socialism. He referred to the feeling among the people that Congress was incapable of attacking the vested interests. Different proposals were mooted to prevent a debacle in the 1972 elections. Some favoured an understanding with "like-minded" parties in the Parliament, to form a stable coalition. Indira Gandhi preferred a radical socialist action programme as a solution.

Against this backdrop, the Congress held its session in Faridabad in 1969, which turned out to be a significant event. On the eve of the session, Indira Gandhi expressed the view that the Congress should not move to the extreme left or extreme right but stick to the middle course with democratic socialism as its objective. The coalition idea was not favoured either by her or the Party President, S. Nijalingappa.

The differences within the party were also founded on ideological grounds. After the electoral defeat, the Congress leaned left-ward. For instance, the 10-point programme in May 1967 adopted by CWC which comprised control over banks, insurance, land reforms, abolition of princely privileges, ceilings on urban property and curbs on business monopolies. The right-wing Syndicate did not appreciate this and wanted better ties with the USA and suppression of Leftist groups. At Faridabad the intra-party wrangles had set the stage for a split. Morarji Desai was the target of a severe attack from the leftists and the "Young Turks". Bhagwat Jha Azad, who was a member of

Indira Gandhi's Cabinet, accused some of his ministerial colleagues of sabotaging the implementation of the 10-point programme. Indira Gandhi came to Morarji Desai's defence at the open session but her differences with Nijalingappa over issues like linguistic reorganization of the country, mixed economy, and the role of public sector surfaced. The action taken by Nijalingappa against some of the Young Turks for attacking Desai exacerbated the situation. Nijalingappa sought to make amends in his concluding remarks by reiterating his faith in democratic socialism.

In the weeks following the Faridabad session, the warring groups prepared themselves for the next round of confrontation. The unexpected death of Dr. Zakir Hussain, President of India, and the choice of his successor became the new bone of contention between the warring groups. Indira Gandhi preferred a President of her choice with whom she would have a rapport. Her opponents in the Party wanted to have a President of their choice. Their choice was Sanjiva Reddy, who was then the Speaker of the Lok Sabha. The decision was to be taken at the Central Parliamentary Board meeting at Bangalore on the eve of the AICC session. She assumed control of the Finance ministry and declared the nationalization of 14 major banks by a presidential ordinance within days of the Bangalore meeting. This was welcomed enthusiastically by the people. This was her way of showing to the Syndicate that she was the one in control. Following this, Morarji Desai resigned from the Cabinet.

However, V.V. Giri, who was the acting President, announced his candidature for the Presidentship as an independent. The Syndicate was surprised by this move of a veteran Congress leader to oppose the official party nominee. Meanwhile, Giri appealed for a "conscience vote". This was probably the first time that such an appeal had been made. Over the years, elections had been conducted on party basis leaving no scope for the voter to exercise his franchize according to his conscience. It was considered that a conscience vote would break party discipline with dangerous consequences for the stability of the Government, if the party happened to be in power. Giri's plea created a new situation. At the end of it all, Giri got elected with the support of one-third of the party MPs and MLAs, turning the course of the history of the Congress Party.

Nijalingappa served show-cause notices on Central Ministers for violating party discipline and voting for Giri. Indira Gandhi questioned his authority to take action against party MPs over the head of the CPP. There were over 100 MPs who favoured disciplinary action against those who voted for Giri. They wanted to precipitate a showdown if the CWC failed to act. Indira Gandhi countered this with a threat to recommend dissolution of the Lok Sabha.

In the next few weeks, the events took the direction of a compromise. The CWC came out with a resolution on the need to avert a split in the party. The move for disciplinary action was given up. The supporters of Indira Gandhi in CWC relented in their attack on the Syndicate and Nijalingappa. In the process, the Syndicate lost its strength to a considerable extent. Nijalingappa, however, warned against the "personality cult" developing in the country, referring indirectly to the signature campaign started by Indira Gandhi to convene a meeting of AICC to replace Nijalingappa by a leader of her own choice.

The CWC soon met under Nijalingappa and expelled Indira Gandhi from the party and directed the CPP to elect a new leader. One group rejected this directive leading to a formal split creating two Working Committees and two CPPs. The group owing allegiance to Nijalingappa, now called Congress (O) did not have enough strength to stake its claim to run the Government. The group owing allegiance to Indira Gandhi, called Congress (R) had to rely on independents and certain opposition groups like the communists, DMK, etc., for support. Two hundred twenty of the party's Lok Sabha MPs supported Indira and only 68 went with the Syndicate. In the AICC,

446 out of 705 members joined the Congress (R). The formal split at the national level had its repercussions elsewhere in the country and the party split into two in all the states.

The Aftermath of the Split

Meanwhile, Indira Gandhi's group held its AICC meeting at which Nijalingappa was replaced by Subramaniam as Congress President, an interim arrangement till regular election took place. Now her position as leader of the party and the government was established.

In pursuance of the Congress Party resolutions, Indira Gandhi initiated steps on many fronts. She set up the Monopolies and Restrictive Trade Practices Commission in 1969 to check concentration of economic power. The existing land reform laws were to be implemented stringently. The Fourth Five-Year Plan was launched. Due to this programme, her support among the poor and middle classes increased. Another step was the abolition of privy purses and other privileges of the ex-rulers of the Princely States. The legislative measure to carry this out was adopted in the Lok Sabha but lost in the Rajya Sabha. The purpose was then achieved through a presidential order derecognizing the Princes. The Supreme Court struck this down. This provoked Indira Gandhi to seek a fresh mandate from the electorate after dissolving the Lok Sabha.

Garibi Hatao

Elections to the Lok Sabha were held in 1971, a year ahead of the schedule. This was the first time that Indira Gandhi was contesting elections on her own. She gave the pro-poor slogan of 'Garibi Hatao' highlighting the need for removal of poverty and hunger. Her opponents turned the campaign into an effort for removing her from power. When asked by the press about the major issues in the campaign, she said, "I am the issue." Her rivals called for 'Indira Hatao' to which she responded with 'Garibi Hatao'.

In this mid-term poll, the Congress (R) secured an overwhelming majority winning 352 out of 518 seats in the Lok Sabha. One of the first acts of the government now was to amend the Constitution to delete property rights from the list of fundamental rights and to abolish privy purses. In the elections to five state assemblies too, the Congress (R) performed well. As a result, the Election Commission recognized it as the real Congress, allowed it to call itself Indian National Congress without any suffix and restored the frozen Congress symbol of two bullocks to it. But, Indira Gandhi's supporters preferred the "Calf and Cow" symbol it had adopted after the 1969 split and dropped the suffix "R". The morale in the Congress Party was boosted by the way Indira Gandhi carried on the administration and projected the image of the country.

Formation of Bangladesh

Around that time, a liberation movement had begun in East Pakistan under the leadership of Sheikh Mujibur Rahman. On 25 March 1971, Pakistani armed forces cracked down upon the civilian people of East Pakistan and perpetrated genocide on an unprecedented scale. About 10 million refugees migrated from East Pakistan and took shelter in India, leading her to point out that, "an internal problem of Pakistan has become an internal problem of India also." Human rights were violated and world opinion went against Pakistan. Indira Gandhi stood by the suffering people. On 3 December 1971, Pakistan attacked India. India reacted by recognizing the provisional government of Bangladesh and joined with Mukti Bahini of Bangladesh to resist Pakistan. War with Pakistan broke out on both the eastern and north-western fronts. On 16 December, Pakistani army in East Bengal surrendered and East Pakistan was liberated. A new nation known as Bangladesh emerged. With the surrender of Pakistan in the eastern front, Indira Gandhi declared unilateral cease-fire and a battered Pakistan had no option but to accept it.

Indira Gandhi was at the height of her power in the wake of the 1971 war. She was hailed as Durga, an incarnation of Shakti. The war was seen as her personal success. After all, she had mobilized world opinion on Bangladesh, travelling to all the major capitals of the world except the US which was avowedly hostile. The political fallout of the war was evident in the electoral success of the party in the Assembly Elections of March 1972. It won everywhere, including West Bengal. Soon after this, in 1974, India successfully performed an underground nuclear detonation and became a member of the nuclear club. Despite this, she continued to favour disarmament. At a UN conference on human environment held in 1972 at Stockholm, she also stressed the importance of environmental conservation.

The growing popularity of Indira Gandhi and the Congress could not be borne by the opposition parties, particularly those who had left the Congress, and the rightist groups. They all combined in a Grand Alliance on the eve of the 1971 elections. The Grand Alliance parties however did not fare well in the elections. This was an unnatural coming together of the leftist and rightist groups, inspired solely by anti-Congress sentiments. There was no other meeting ground in terms of either agenda or ideology. In desperation to unseat the Congress, they decided to support any movement which was opposed to the government. An unfavourable atmosphere loomed in the economic crisis resulting from the impact of immigration of Bangladeshi refugees and the subsequent war with Pakistan, rising prices, food shortages and growing scarcity of jobs which caused much disaffection. Other facets of the crisis included the drain of foreign reserves and drought due to monsoon failure in 1972 and 1973. The oil shock of 1973 led to a spurt in the prices of petroleum goods, and foreign exchange reserves in many countries decreased appreciably. There were food riots in many areas and soon this disaffection led to large-scale industrial unrest. Strikes occurred in many areas during 1972 and 1973 leading to a 22-day all-India railway strike in May 1974. The strike was repressed and the government's popularity among the working class suffered another setback. In UP, in May 1973, the Armed Constabulary mutinied, leading to a violent clash with the army sent in to suppress it, killing more than 35 constables and soldiers. Demonstrations, protests and strikes continued during the years 1974 and 1975.

Factors leading to the Emergency

Two mass agitations in Bihar and Gujarat were launched turning the socioeconomic discontent into a political movement. In January 1974 in Gujarat, popular anger over high food prices created conditions of anarchy. This was expressed as a student movement and supported by opposition parties. Strikes, arson, looting and rioting became rampant. President's rule was imposed in the state followed by the dissolution of the Assembly and fresh elections to it were announced for June 1975. Soon after this, in Bihar, a students' movement against the government was launched in March 1974. It was led by Jayaprakash Narayan who gave a call for 'total revolution'. He came out of political retirement and demanded the resignation of the Congress government in Bihar, and asked people to pay no taxes and establish parallel people's governments across the state. It was supported by students, traders, middle classes and a section of the intelligentsia. This was an extra-constitutional and undemocratic movement aimed at unseating the government at any cost. The students clashed with the police on several occasions, leading to 27 deaths in one week. The movement gradually spread to other parts of the country as well. Indira Gandhi refused to succumb to this pressure and did not dissolve the assembly. The movement lost its strength by the end of 1974. The student support dwindled; the poor had never really been mobilized. Indira Gandhi challenged Jayaprakash Narayan to a real electoral battle rather than this unconstitutional approach which he had adopted.

However, the electoral battle was sidelined by the verdict of the Allahabad High Court against Indira Gandhi in the election petition filed by Raj Narain, who had opposed her in her constituency in the Lok Sabha polls and lost. Justice Sinha had dismissed the more serious charges and had convicted Indira Gandhi on the technical and trivial, even frivolous offences against the election law. The verdict charged her with violating the election law to win her seat and invalidated her election, disallowing her from contesting elections for six years. Indira Gandhi rejected this verdict and appealed to the Supreme Court which allowed her to continue in office. Soon, the results of the Gujarat assembly elections showed that Congress had secured 75 seats as against 87 of the opposing Janata Party in a house of 182.

These two events strengthened the Janata Party and soon they demanded that Indira Gandhi should resign. On 25 June 1975, in Delhi, they announced that a campaign of mass agitation and civil disobedience to force her to resign would be launched on 29 June. Jayaprakash Narayan asked the people to obstruct the functioning of the government and asked the army, police and bureaucracy to disobey this 'corrupt' government. In response, Indira Gandhi declared a state of internal emergency in the country on 26 June 1975.

The JP movement suffered from many shortcomings. Even though Jayaprakash Narayan could not be faulted on his integrity and selflessness, his ideology remained vague. During the 1950s, he criticised parliamentary democracy and advocated a partyless democracy. During this movement in Bihar, he advocated 'total revolution'. But he never really defined its political, social or economic implications. He himself was not an authoritarian leader but the ambiguity of his ideas provided scope for totalitarian elements. It led him to accept support from parties which had nothing in common with his ideas or agenda. Communal groups like

Jan Sangh and Jamaat-i-Islami, the RSS, Socialists and Naxalites—all entered his movement making it impossible to outline any coherent political ideology. The good organizational strength of the RSS and Jan Sangh soon dominated the cadre of the movement, with Jayaprakash Narayan remaining only responsible for mass mobilization. The undemocratic nature of the movement was evident in its aim of wanting to overthrow the government in Bihar and the Central government at any cost.

The methodology adopted by the movement was also unconstitutional. Demonstrations and rallies, gheraos of the legislatures and government offices were aimed at forcing the government and the legislators to resign. The army, police and civil services were encouraged to disobey the government. On 25 June 1975, they declared their intention of gheraoing the PM's residence to force her to resign. They wished to intimidate her into giving up office.

The period of the emergency saw the suspension of normal political procedures and fundamental rights, arrests of the leaders of the Grand Alliance, and enforcement of press censorship and strict discipline. Extreme communal and leftist organizations were banned. More than one lakh people were arrested over the 19 months of the Emergency. Powers of the judiciary were reduced drastically. Unlimited state and party power was concentrated in the hands of the Prime Minister.

Vast sections of the population welcomed it initially since general administration improved. But, civil rights activists took exception to the curbs on freedom of expression and personal liberties. Unfortunately, in certain spheres, over-enthusiasm led to compulsion in enforcement of certain programmes like compulsory sterilization and clearance of slums. Sanjay Gandhi had, by then, emerged as a leader of great significance. It was due to his support to family planning that the government decided to pursue it more vigorously.

He also promoted slum clearance, anti-dowry measures and promotion of literacy but in an arbitrary and authoritarian manner much to the annyonce of the popular opinion.

General Elections and the Janata Phase

On 18 January 1977, Indira Gandhi ordered elections to the Lok Sabha, releasing political prisoners and removing curbs on freedom of expression. The decision to call off the Emergency and hold the elections showed the strength of Indian democracy. The Grand Alliance fought these elections under the banner of Janata Party and secured an impressive victory, except in the southern states. It won 330 seats out of 542 in Lok Sabha. The Congress was defeated and it readily resigned from office. The world was impressed with this return to the democratic path in India.

The Janata Party took over the reins of Government and set up the Shah Commission to inquire into the alleged emergency excesses. Jagjivan Ram and some other Congressmen left the party in February 1977 and formed a new party known as Congress for Democracy. It joined forces with the Janata Party.

The impact of defeat in the general election in 1977 was severe. Congress could only win 154 seats in the Lok Sabha, Indira Gandhi herself was defeated in Rae Bareilly by Raj Narain. Sanjay Gandhi was defeated in Amethi. Congress did not get any Lok Sabha seat in UP, Bihar, Haryana and Punjab; Madhya Pradesh and Rajasthan returned only one member each to the Lok Sabha on the Congress ticket. The performance in West Bengal, Orissa and Gujarat was equally dismal. Only the South stood by the Congress solidly and Maharashtra gave a marginal majority to the Congress. Y.B. Chavan, was chosen as the leader of the Congress Party in the Parliament.

On the organizational front there was almost a knee-jerk reaction. Many people demanded the resignation of the Congress President and members of the Working Committee. Indira Gandhi accepted the verdict of the people and assumed the responsibility of the defeat. A section of the Congress leaders demanded that Congress must get rid of Indira Gandhi and her supporters. K. Brahmananda Reddy was elected Congress President defeating Siddhartha Shankar Ray and 10 members were elected to the Working Committee.

The 81-year old Morarji Desai took over as the Prime Minister in March 1977. One of the first acts of his government was the dismissal of Congress ministries in 9 states. In the ensuing elections, in June 1977, the Janata Party won in 7 states. Sanjiva Reddy was elected as President in July 1977 with the support of the Janata Party and its allies. The Janata government spent the first two weeks in euphoria and in dismantling the structures of the Emergency. Indira Gandhi was found guilty of committing a breach of privilege of the Parliament and sent to Tihar Jail from the Lok Sabha. All such actions only helped to generate sympathy in her favour among the public.

Indira Gandhi was soon engaged in regaining the lost confidence of the people. An incident in July 1977 in Bihar (Belchi) where Harijans were massacred provided an opportunity for her to visit the place and express her sympathies in the cause of the downtrodden. This helped in her campaign when she contested the bye-election to the Lok Sabha from the Chikmagalur constituency in Karnataka held in November 1978. She was returned to the Lok Sabha and took her place as the leader of the Opposition.

In the meanwhile, ministers deposing before the Shah Commission squarely placed the blame for the Emergency on Indira Gandhi's shoulders. The Janata Party and a section of the Congress leaders started a campaign against her on all fronts. She was arrested on 3 October 1977 on the charge of abusing the office of the Prime Minster by obtaining illegal benefits from industrialists by seeking some jeeps for her party candidates in the election of 1977. The whole nation was stunned at the triviality of the allegations. However, the next day the judge acquitted her by pointing out that there was no case.

The AICC was summoned to condemn the atrocious, vindictive act of the Janata Party government but instead of condemning the Janata government's action, the session criticized Indira Gandhi and her so-called coterie. Hereafter, she was ignored in major party decisions. In the selection of party candidates for the Assembly elections in June 1977 neither her services were called for nor was she consulted in major policy matters. So, her supporters started a move to have a requisition meeting of the AICC members to replace K. Brahmananda Reddy and elect Indira Gandhi as the Congress President.

The Janata Party failed to deal with many important problems. Social tensions in rural areas accelerated; their opposition to Nehruvian economic policies did not bring out any alternative framework; inflation rose to more than 20 per cent in 1979. On top of this, the constituent parties of Janata Party started clashing with each other. Soon, the party broke up in 1979 with Charan Singh forming a government that lasted only a few months.

Second Split and Indira Gandhi's Return to Power

A National Convention of Congress workers was held in Delhi on 1 and 2 January 1978. Indira Gandhi was elected President and authorized to constitute the Working Committee, Central Parliamentary Board office bearers, Provincial Congress Committees (PCCs) and other subordinate Congress Committees. Ultimately, the Party split formally.

Elections were to be held in Andhra, Karnataka, Maharashtra, Assam and Arunachal Pradesh in February 1978. The Election Commission refused to recognize Indira's group as the Congress. So the symbol of "Calf and Cow" was retained by the other faction led by Sanjiva Reddy and the suffix "I" was added to the faction led by Indira

Gandhi. A new reserved symbol "Hand" was allotted to the party. The Party headquarters and bank accounts were not given to the faction led by Indira Gandhi. So, a new party headquarters was established at 24, Akbar Road. For all legal purposes, this party was considered as a new Party and the other faction was called "Congress" till Congress (I) was recognized as "Congress" by a court verdict in 1982. However, people gave their verdict in favour of Indira Gandhi's party much earlier by putting her party in power with two-thirds majority in Andhra and Karnataka. In Maharashtra, it swept the Vidarbha region by winning almost all the seats. As no party got a clear majority in Maharashtra, a coalition government of the two factions of the Congress was formed. In Assam, the party did not do well and won only eight seats. However, the victory spree demonstrated the popular support which Indira enjoyed. The common people saw the attempts by the Janata government to imprison her as vindictive and sympathized with her.

By the end of 1979, elections were ordered to the Lok Sabha, two years ahead of schedule and Indira Gandhi's Congress was returned with a thumping majority of 353 out of 529 seats giving it a two-thirds majority. She became the Prime Minister once again in 1980. One of the first acts of the Congress government was to dissolve the governments in nine states where the Janata Party ruled. In the subsequent elections, the Congress swept the polls in all these states except in Tamil Nadu. Now, 15 out of 22 states were under Congress rule.

Soon after she assumed office, Sanjay Gandhi was killed in an air crash. After getting over this personal loss, Indira Gandhi devoted herself vigorously to the problems awaiting to be resolved. An important event of that period was the Summit Meeting of Non-Aligned Movement hosted by India in March 1983. Her contribution in shaping the NAM was regarded quite significant. Similarly, she took an active role in the meeting of Commonwealth Heads of

Government Meet (CHOGM) and many other international forums. Indira Gandhi's growing popularity attracted many youngsters to the Congress. By then Kamaraj had died and his supporters in Tamil Nadu returned to the Congress (I).

In this period, growing communal, linguistic and caste conflicts were issues of major concern. Moreover, terrorism raised its head in Punjab, Kashmir and Assam. Besides these, the problem of the people of Indian origin in Sri Lanka was becoming complex. In Assam, the problem centred on illegal Bangladeshi immigrants. In Sri Lanka, she supported the aspirations of the people of Indian origin, without affecting the national integrity and sovereignty of Sri Lanka.

In Punjab, the Akali Dal presented a series of demands, including formation of a separate Khalistan. The Government was prepared to concede anything but secession. The terrorists, backed by Pakistan, were disrupting law and order, gunning down innocent people and damaging public property. In dealing with legitimate demands, she had earlier accepted the demand for a Punjabi-speaking state in March 1966 and made Chandigarh a Union Territory which would be the capital of both Punjab and Haryana. This took away the political grounding of the Akali Dal and now, they started taking up more and more communal demands and terrorism struck root in Punjab. The terrorists were targeting Hindus and creating a reign of terror in the state. In 1984, Indira Gandhi ordered the Indian Army to liberate the Golden Temple in Amritsar from the hold of terrorists. This was portrayed as an attack on the Sikh community and their religion and calls for revenge were raised by terrorists against her. On 31 October 1984, she was shot dead by two of her own security men. She thus paid the ultimate price in the service of the nation, trying to retain its integrity and secular character.

Indira was a lion-hearted lady who successfully steered the country through some of its worst economic and political crises. She won the hearts of the poor and they responded to her assassination as if they had lost their protector. Kitchen fires were not lit for days in the huts of the poor in remote villages as the news spread that she was no more.

12 Rajiv Years

The choice of a successor to Indira Gandhi did not prove difficult. The Congress Parliamentary Board members formally presented their recommendation to the President and Rajiv Gandhi was sworn in as the Prime Minister on 31 October 1984. He had already entered politics in June 1981, after the death of Sanjay Gandhi in June 1980, by getting elected to the Lok Sabha from Amethi. In 1983 he had become one of the seven new General Secretaries of the Congress.

Challenge of Terrorism and Fissiparous Tendencies

When Rajiv Gandhi took the reins of Government, the situation was grave. In reaction to Indira Gandhi's assassination by her two Sikh guards, there were nationwide riots against the members of the Sikh community. Nearly 2,800 people were killed in Delhi alone. The first task of Rajiv Gandhi was to quell the riots and restore confidence among the Sikh community. Another crisis that had to be handled was the Bhopal Gas Leak tragedy in which 2,000 people lost their lives and thousands were affected. The next task was to secure a mandate from the electorate.

The general elections to the Lok Sabha were anyhow due in a few months in the normal course. He considered it necessary to hold the elections on schedule as that would help him get the people's mandate also. The elections demonstrated the people's sympathy and love for Indira Gandhi. The party under her son's leadership was returned with an unprecedented majority. Of the 543 seats, 415 had been secured by the Congress Party, a record not achieved ever before in its history. This was attributed not only to the 'sympathy wave' but also to the desire on the part of the electorate to ensure unity and integrity of the country.

However, more complex than these was the problem of terrorism in Punjab and Assam on the one hand, and the ethnic issue concerning people of Indian origin in Sri Lanka. Soon after assuming office, he had ordered the release of key Akali leaders in January 1985 who had been detained since the days of Operation Blue Star and lifted the ban on the All India Sikh Students Federation. He ordered an enquiry into the anti-Sikh riots in Delhi and elsewhere in November 1984, and soon talks began with Akali leaders in order to find a settlement to the Punjab problem. In August 1985, he announced a settlement with Shiromoni Akali Dal led by Sant H.S. Longowal according to which the major Akali demands were conceded and others were to be reviewed. The elections were fixed for September 1985. However, Longowal was assassinated on 20 August, the very day he announced that Akalis would take part in the elections. Not long thereafter, the Akali Dal Government led by Barnala got destabilized and had to quit. The State was back under the Central rule. Along with this, lawlessness and killings of innocent people escalated. The Punjab problem called for fresh initiatives and Rajiv came out with an action plan. This included "Operation Black Thunder", a smoothly carried out operation to clear the Golden Temple of arms and gunmen. A number of incentives were offered to the state to tackle the problem of terrorists. While all this was a setback to the terrorists the final solution to the problem was to take a few more years.

In the case of Assam too, Rajiv Gandhi succeeded initially in defusing the crisis by reaching an accord with the main warring group on 15

August 1985. Apart from the general grievance of underdevelopment, their agitation was against the influx of illegal Bengali-speaking immigrants who had reduced the Assamese to a minority in their own region. According to this accord, foreigners who had come between 1951 and 1961 were to be given full citizenship, including the right to vote, and those who came between 1961 and 1971 would not have voting rights for 10 years. Those coming after 1971 would be deported. This put an end to the agitation by the students and cleared the way for elections to the state assembly. The student agitators, under the banner of Assam Gana Parishad, formed the government.

However, a series of agitations began in different parts of the country including one in the North-East for Bodoland. The Gorkhas of West Bengal were also agitating for greater degree of independence. In Bihar, the Jharkhand agitation started. In Mizoram, there had been insurgency for a number of years under Laldenga and Rajiv Gandhi arrived at an accord to put an end to it. Meanwhile, the unrest in Jammu and Kashmir was assuming serious proportions. In July 1986, the government of G.M. Shah was dismissed and President's rule imposed. Rajiv Gandhi entered into an alliance with Farooq Abdullah for the assembly elections in 1987. However, Abdullah proved to be ineffective and after that, the secessionist movement became active in the state.

Initiatives in Foreign Policy

The Sri Lankan Tamils issue was another major concern of the Rajiv Gandhi government. In 1983, thousands of Sri Lankan Tamils took refuge in Tamil Nadu when the Tamil areas in the north-east of Sri Lanka became the site for heavy repression by the government. The government had ordered the blockade of these areas and when India sent relief supplies, these were turned back by the Sri Lankan navy. This area was the base for the Liberation Tigers of Tamil Eelam

(LTTE), an organization fighting for Tamil independence from Sri Lanka.

After discussions with the Sri Lankan government, an Indo-Sri Lanka Agreement to establish peace and normalcy was signed on 27 July 1987. According to this agreement, the Tamil areas would get substantial autonomy, the LTTE would be dissolved and the Indian army would come to the help of Sri Lanka if necessary. The accord was not popular among certain sections of the Sinhalese and the Tamils. The Sinhalese resented the intervention of a foreign army and the Tamils were unhappy with the forced disarming of the LTTE. After signing the accord, Rajiv Gandhi was even attacked with a rifle by one of the sailors at the guard of honour ceremony. The whole world condemned this heinous attack on him and admired his cool and fortitude amidst grave provocation. The Indian Army agreed to a phased withdrawal from Sri Lanka which began in 1989.

On the Western border, Pakistan was not quiet. When Rajiv Gandhi became the Prime Minister the relations between the two countries were marked by a high degree of mutual suspicion. Before he could do anything to repair the strained relations, new fissures developed. These arose from a routine military exercise carried out by the Indian army in the deserts of Rajasthan after due notice to Pakistan. Pakistan retaliated by stepping up the troop movements on her side of the border not only across Rajasthan but also Punjab. The tension was soon relieved following official level talks and the pull-back of the troops on both the sides. It was a few months later that Rajiv Gandhi undertook a visit to Islamabad at the invitation of Pakistan and signed accords with his counterpart Ms. Benazir Bhutto, which envisaged both countries abiding by the Simla Agreement. However, this did not stop Pakistani support to terrorism in Punjab and Kashmir.

He visited China in 1988, being the first PM since Nehru in 1954 to do so. The aim of the visit was to improve trade, extend consular contacts and set up mechanisms to solve long-standing problems. To build good relations with China, India did not condemn the massacre at Tiannanmen Square in June 1989. He also visited the US in 1985 where the US agreed to give India a super-computer for processing weather data. Rajiv developed a very close relationship with the Soviet leader, Gorbachev. He was very keen on foreign affairs and expended a lot of time on it. Apart from visiting foreign countries, the two main issues which he took up were nuclear disarmament and struggle against apartheid.

As far as disarmament is concerned, he followed in his mother's footsteps by getting governments in different parts of the world to put pressure on the nuclear super-powers to disarm. He shared this passion with Gorbachev. In November 1986, on Gorbachev's visit to Delhi, a plan for disarmament was spelt out known as the Delhi Declaration. The Action Plan for Nuclear Disarmament was presented by Rajiv in June 1988 at the UN General Assembly. According to this plan, all nuclear weapons were to be eliminated by 2010. Rajiv got most of the Commonwealth countries, except the UK, to support him in his struggle against apartheid. He set up the AFRICA (Action for Resisting Invasion, Colonialism and Apartheid) Fund at the Non-Aligned Summit meeting at Harare in 1986. In support of the independence of Namibia, Rajiv Gandhi gave diplomatic recognition to SWAPO, the main nationalist organization and popularized the cause at all international gatherings which he attended.

Rajiv's Vision for the 21st Century

Unconventional and dynamic in his approach, Rajiv Gandhi created quite a stir when he questioned the "vested interests" within the party and called them "power brokers". The occasion for this was the Centenary Celebrations of the Congress Party in Bombay in 1985. He was keen to democratize the party and bring in the youth. Similarly, he was frank to admit that the funds earmarked for development schemes did not reach the targeted groups but gone into the hands of middlemen. He found many shortcomings in the way the state governments implemented the centrally-funded schemes at the grassroots level.

The strengthening of Panchayati Raj Institutions was a very important objective that Rajiv Gandhi took up on a war footing in order to meet some of the above deficiencies. A National Perspective Plan for Women drafted in 1988 was meant to provide reservation of 30 per cent of seats for women in panchayati raj bodies. He decided to amend the Constitution to provide for direct funding to the local bodies by the Centre instead of having to go through the state governments. This provoked a lot of criticism and opposition from vested interests. He ultimately failed to get the necessary legislation passed, as in the Rajya Sabha all the opposition parties combined to defeat the relevant Constitutional Amendment Bill.

He also initiated the Jawahar Rozgar Yojana to provide employment to at least one member of every poor family in a village for 50-100 days in a year. This concept was to later evolve into the National Employment Guarantee Scheme. His new education policy was to focus on the rural areas and envisaged model schools in each district under the name of Navodaya Vidyalaya.

Like Indira Gandhi before him, Rajiv Gandhi was also acutely aware of the issue of environmental sustainability. A new ministry of environment was created in his time and environmental clearance was made mandatory for all big projects. He proposed that a Planet Protection Fund be created.

Rajiv Gandhi found it difficult to carry on with some of the members of the old guard. They also found his style of running the party with meticulous professionalism not in tune with their approach. Some senior leaders were removed from the party and a few were replaced by younger persons. In his anxiety to make quick changes, he shuffled and reshuffled his team both in the Party and the Government frequently. Even some of his colleagues who acted as his main advisers in the early years of his Prime Ministership deserted him, when he refused to toe their dictated line. The promises of reform in the party, which he made in his famous Bombay speech as a corollary to his attack on the "power brokers" in the party, could not be fulfilled. Party elections, long overdue, were put off again and again. But he introduced other measures to deal with the tendency of politicians to cross the floor. The Anti-Defection Act was passed in 1985. He also favoured greater freedom for government media.

Rajiv Gandhi repeatedly reminded the country of the necessity of preparing for the 21st century and took some dramatic steps in that direction. He spearheaded India's computerization programme. He reduced import duties on components and foreign competition was allowed in this sector. He wanted India to participate in the information and communication revolution. Every district was to be connected with the Central Government through a computer network. He set up six 'technology missions' which aimed at applying science and technology to six areas which were grossly underdeveloped. These were drinking water, literacy, health of pregnant women and children, milk production, edible oil production and telephonic communication.

Besides stressing the use of modern technology like computers and decentralization of decision-making at the community level, Rajiv Gandhi's government initiated moves for removing controls over industries and demystifying the budgetary process. The process of economic reform which had started with Indira Gandhi's return to power in 1980 was taken forward considerably by Rajiv Gandhi, preparing the ground for the big shift that was to occur in 1991. The report of the Economic Administration Reforms Commission, headed by L.K. Jha, came in handy for him to take steps towards liberalization in the industrial sector. During his tenure from 1984-1989, the economic growth rate was 5.5 per cent, breaking the barrier of the 3 to 3.5 per cent growth rate which the Indian economy was hovering around for quite some time.

The Political Challenge and the Resurgence of Opportunistic Anti-Congressism

Rajiv Gandhi also made efforts for strengthening the capability of Indian Defence Forces and arming them with the latest weapons. Among the many deals towards this end was the one involving the purchase of howitzer guns from the Swedish firm, Bofors. This turned out to be the root cause of one of the biggest crisis ever faced by any Government in the past. The Swedish Radio reported that millions of dollars had been paid as bribes to Indian officials by the Bofors to get the contract. This triggered nationwide agitation for enquiry and action against those found guilty. This came on top of a few other allegations over the purchase of submarines from West Germany and appointment of an American detective agency Fairfax to investigate into the dealings of some industrialists. The opposition mounted an agitation demanding Rajiv's resignation.

Added to these, Rajiv Gandhi faced innumerable problems from within the party. The electoral debacle in Haryana, Kerala and West Bengal also damaged the image of the Party. V.P. Singh, Arun Nehru and others, who were very close to him in earlier years, left the Party and joined the opposition parties.

By then, the five-year term of Rajiv Gandhi's Government was coming to an end. The first year and a half of his tenure was quite smooth sailing for him. He was projected as a leader with a clean image and as a man of vision, keen to prepare the country technologically for meeting the challenges of the 21st century. This euphoria heightened the people's expectations which could not be fulfilled. The second half of his term was not that smooth. His problems were aggravated by a severe drought in many states following the failure of the southwest monsoon. However, the worst drought situation of 1987-88 was handled most efficiently.

But, by far the most serious problem was the one created by the Bofors deal. On this issue, all the opposition parties were united. They demanded his resignation on the basis of a report of CAG, and the Opposition members of the Lok Sabha resigned *en masse* in mid-1989. It paved the way for electoral adjustment among the non-Congress parties reviving the practice of opportunistic anti-Congressism as a central mode of political mobilization rather than substantive ideological issues. It was against the backdrop of a series of unfavourable factors that Rajiv Gandhi ordered the general elections to the Lok Sabha in November 1989.

The National Front

The right-wing opposition parties that had earlier combined and broken up, started moving closer once more to give a united fight to the Congress. They combined under the banner of a National Front, keeping intact their separate identities. The National Front had electoral adjustments with the Left Front and the BJP. By then, V.P. Singh had left the Congress Party and aligned himself with the Janata Dal, a constituent of the National Front.

A disturbing feature of this period was the coming together of many otherwise diverse anti-Congress groups like the Left and the BJP, ensuring their support to V.P. Singh. This association lent political legitimacy and credibility to BJP and also blurred the mark of communalism from its image to some extent. This political collusion also led to the coming together of regional and national secular non-Congress parties with the Left parties and the BJP. By October 1988, the Janata Dal came into being with the merger of Jan Morcha, Janata Dal, Lok Dal and Congress (S).

The Bofors deal and the Nehruvian concept of secularism became the main issues at the polls. The latter had come to the fore with the Vishwa Hindu Parishad's claims over the site at which Babri Masjid had been erected and its moves to build a temple for Lord Rama there. This had led to communal clashes. The VHP went ahead with the laying of the foundation stone a few days prior to the Lok Sabha elections. The BJP secured electoral advantage from this move.

The 1989 elections were marked by unprecedented violence and the results went against the Congress Party. In fact, no party could get the majority to form the government. The Congress emerged as the single largest party with 197 seats and 39.5 per cent of the vote share and as such was invited to form the government with the help of its allies. But, Rajiv Gandhi chose to stay in the Opposition. The National Front took the reins of government with V.P. Singh as the Prime Minister. The Congress Party reposed its faith in the leadership of Rajiv Gandhi undeterred by the election reverses. In the Southern states, the party's performance was quite impressive. Both Andhra and Karnataka had been recaptured by the Congress. Soon after the Lok Sabha elections, the Assembly elections were held in eight states. In most of these, Congress suffered heavy losses. Only in Maharashtra and Arunachal Pradesh could it form the government.

However, the scenario did not remain static. The National Front government soon got into trouble, some inherent in the very composition of the Front and some others made by itself. In the latter category, fell the now famous Mandal Agitation. In his zeal to project himself and his Front as the champion of the downtrodden, V.P. Singh sought to implement the recommendations of the Mandal Commission set up during the Janata rule in 1977-1979 in respect of reservation quota for backward classes in educational institutions and employment. The recommendations reserved 27 per cent of the jobs in government and public sector undertakings for the backward classes. This increased the total reservations to 49.5 per cent since

SCs and STs already had a reservation of 22.5 per cent. Reservations in educational institutions and promotions were also to be implemented in the future.

This announcement was criticized by many: even people in support of reservation as a policy thought that the suddenness of the decision was unacceptable. Political allies of the government opposed it as a unilateral move on the part of V.P. Singh. Others pointed out that the method of identifying backward classes was faulty and that no consensus had even been attempted before the announcement. The worst impact was on society: it divided people into castes and engendered caste politics and resentment among the youth. It was also argued that this policy benefited only the elites among the backward classes without helping the really deserving, making it a subject of caste-based political mobilization.

The youth in North India reacted sharply and violently. The students realized that the reservation of nearly half of government jobs would mean a severe restriction of career opportunities and also that this would not help the really underprivileged sections. Students led the agitation and were supported by teachers, government officials and housewives. Anti-Mandal protestors attacked public property, burnt buses, organized demonstrations and meetings and discussions in the press. The agitation was widespread in urban North India and in many cities like Delhi, Kanpur, Varanasi, protestors were fired upon by the police and some students attempted self-immolation. The main theme in this anti-Mandal agitation was against caste as an organizing principle of society and as a criterion for securing jobs. Caste identities were consolidated in the process and caste consciousness rose sharply among students.

During the 1980s, a new party called the Bahujan Samaj Party emerged in North India under the leadership of Kanshi Ram and later, Mayawati. This party declared that winning elections and entering the government was its primary aim. Initially, it sought to mobilize the backward castes and the minorities. In recent years, it has, become a party of Dalits which forms alliances with any other major political party in order to gain political office.

Apart from this, the problem of terrorism in Punjab and Jammu and Kashmir continued. The V.P. Singh government withdrew the Indian Peace Keeping Force from Sri Lanka and following this, there was infiltration of LTTE into Tamil Nadu creating a serious law and order problem. The V.P. Singh government did not last long. The BJP withdrew its support from the government on the Ram Mandir issue. One of the constituent parties of the Front, headed by Chandra Shekhar, broke away and with the backing of the Congress, formed the government. This government lasted only a few months.

Rajiv Gandhi Lost Life for the Nation

Elections to the Lok Sabha were ordered in May 1991. The Congress Party went to the polls well prepared. Being in the Opposition, the party leaders devoted greater attention to the strengthening of the organization at the grassroots level.

For two decades, organizational elections had not taken place in the party. Periodically, attempts were made towards this but they did not materialize. The PCCs were set up with nominated members and the Central leaders decided PCC presidents. However, in order to promote a more effective interaction between the grassroots level party workers and the leadership, training camps, workshops, etc., were organized. This helped the Central leadership to get a first hand idea of the needs and aspirations in each constituency and take suitable steps to fulfill those. Rajiv Gandhi planned the election strategy on the basis of scientific assessment of the party's prospects in each state and chose the party nominees with great care. He himself undertook extensive tours to campaign for the party candidates. This took him to Sriperumbudur in Tamil Nadu to campaign for the Congress candidate. On the evening of 21 May 1991 he reached the venue of the election meeting. All of a sudden, there was a loud bomb explosion close to him. Within seconds, his body was found blown to pieces.

Like Mahatma Gandhi, and his mother, Rajiv sacrificed his life in the cause of the country. His mother paid the price for trying to bring peace in Punjab and he became the victim of his efforts to settle the ethnic issue in Sri Lanka. The LTTE, which had harboured a grievance against him, was suspected to have masterminded the killing of Rajiv Gandhi. He was the youngest among the three martyrs all of whom significantly died in the cause of maintaining secularism, unity and harmony between communities.

Rajiv Gandhi was no more but the electoral campaign he built up paid rich dividends. In the elections, the Congress was returned to the Lok Sabha with enough strength to form a government. But, the question of leadership remained. Sonia Gandhi made it clear that she would not like to be considered for it. Senior leaders agreed to elect P.V. Narasimha Rao as Congress President. In the first election in two decades on February 27, 1992, Rao was formally elected as President. Fifty-seven nomination papers, each signed by 10 PCC members from different states, were submitted in support of Rao's candidature. After the election results were published, again through the process of consultation and consensus, P.V. Narasimha Rao was unanimously chosen the leader of the Congress Parliamentary Party. This marked the beginning of a new phase in Congress history.

13 Narasimha Rao Government

The Phase of Economic Reforms

Narasimha Rao took over as the ninth Prime Minister of India in 1991, heading a government supported from the outside by Jharkhand Mukti Morcha and the independents. It was creditable that his government completed its full term, making him the first person outside the Nehru-Gandhi family to serve as Prime Minister for five continuous years. He was also the first Prime Minister from South India.

Economic Reforms

The major achievement of this government was the carrying forward of the process of economic reform which the Congress party had outlined in its election manifesto. The process of liberalization of the Indian economy and a gradual opening up and participation in the globalization process had started with Indira Gandhi after her return to power in 1980 and was taken forward by Rajiv Gandhi. The minority government of Narasimha Rao was able to give this process a big push in 1991. The deep economic crisis faced by India had made immediate action necessary. The balance of payments was critical and repayment of foreign debts seemed difficult. Domestic inflation had reached the alarming figure of 16 per cent in August 1991. Industrial production was disrupted and exports had declined.

Foreign exchange reserves stood at 1,000 crore in June 1991, enough for just seven days of imports.

The crisis had been anticipated by Rajiv Gandhi who started the process of reform with measures like deregulation of industry, flexibility of the exchange rate and partial lifting of import controls. An acclaimed economist, Manmohan Singh, a former governor of the Reserve Bank of India, was appointed Finance Minister to steer the economy out of this crisis. The measures contemplated were reducing the fiscal deficit which for the Central government was over 8 per cent of GDP, partial privatization of the public sector, increasing investment in infrastructure, trade reforms and changes in the regulation of foreign direct investment, relaxation of controls over industry, etc.

This move towards economic reforms was criticized by many on the ground that it meant moving away from the well-trodden path of Nehruvian Socialism. In the meeting of the Subjects Committee of AICC held in Tirupati on 15 April 1992, Pranab Mukherjee, on behalf of the Congress, argued that Nehruvian Socialism was based on the vision of a society which provided equality of opportunity and a good life to all its citizens. The Indian Nation Congress still stood by its commitment to this vision outlined by Nehru and reaffirmed that Democracy, Socialism, Planning, Secularism, Self-Reliance and Non-Alignment were the basic tenets of Congress ideology. However, self-reliance did not mean an insular economy. Self-reliance meant accepting the challenge of making Indian industry competitive and the Indian rupee convertible in the international market. It was also pointed out that Indira Gandhi and Rajiv Gandhi had creatively updated the Nehruvian model. Further, it was argued that in the years immediately after independence, Indian industry was weak because of the years of colonial exploitation and had therefore required state support. But now, it had come of age and could compete internationally. The new policy initiatives did not mean acceptance of *laissez faire*. State orientation and guidance would continue for the economy in general and industry in particular. This economic policy of the Congress was based on the concept of change with continuity.

The impact of liberalizing the economy was seen in an influx of foreign portfolio investment and in permitting Indian firms to raise capital on international markets. The share of foreign firms could now go upto 51 per cent in joint ventures. Procedures for FDI approvals were considerably simplified. Tariffs were reduced from an average of 85 per cent to 25 per cent. In 1991-92, total foreign investment in India stood at US $132 million and by 1995-96, it had increased to $5.3 billion. By 1992, inflation had been brought down to 9 per cent. Industrial licensing was decreased with only 18 industries now subject to it. Easing of government controls in service sectors like communications and insurance, and the entry of private enterprize in infrastructural sectors like aviation and telecoms led to rapid growth in output. This turn-around is one of the fastest economic recoveries in recent times. What makes it more remarkable is that it has been achieved with very little adverse social consequences like unemployment. The structural adjustment programme adopted by India as part of economic reforms was rated as one which caused least damage to vulnerable sections of society even in the short run compared to other countries going through the same process.

The major objective of these reforms was economic growth with social justice. Growth was fashioned as a tool to transform society in a direction which empowered the poor, the backward, women, Dalits and minorities. One of the most significant results of the reform measures was reduction in the number of people living below the poverty line. The political stability of the government and the available public sector base built up in earlier years allowed these far-reaching changes to be carried out.

In these years, an agenda of development through education and elimination of poverty was actively pursued. Various measures were introduced: extending ration shops in drought-prone areas, desert areas and hill and tribal areas, a national old-age pension scheme, a national family benefit scheme to help BPL families in case of death of bread-earners, a national maternity benefit scheme for below poverty line (BPL) families, a new mid-day meal programme to improve nutrition and increase school attendance of 11 crore children in classes I to IV, a new Employment Assurance Scheme to provide guaranteed employment in 120 of the poorest districts of the country, a Rashtriya Mahila Kosh to provide financial support to working women and women entrepreneurs, a Mahila Samriddhi Yojana to make women economically independent. The investment in rural development and poverty alleviation during the period 1991-1996 was Rs. 34,000 crore, thrice the amount spent in the previous five years.

Foreign Policy

In the field of foreign policy, India came out in support of the new political changes in South Africa. In the Middle East, India called for Palestine and Israel to settle their long-standing dispute peacefully. While continuing to uphold the demand of the people of Palestine for their state, India established diplomatic relations with Israel. During these years, India moved towards the non-proliferation of weapons of mass destruction with the eventual aim of eliminating nuclear weapons. This effort was supported by President Clinton of the US. However, this was done without compromising the country's sovereignty. Accordingly, the nuclear security and ballistic missiles programme was carried on and military spending was increased with a view to meeting any threat from the neighbouring countries. The role of Pakistan in sponsoring acts of terrorism against India was highlighted in international forums. This was the period when India developed close links with the ASEAN countries, described by some as the 'Look East' policy. Relations with Iran were developed which enabled India to gain the support of China and Iran in the United Nations Human Rights Commission when Pakistan proposed a resolution in 1994 condemning the human rights violations in Kashmir.

Restoration of Normalcy in Kashmir and Punjab

In 1996 and later in 2002, elections were held in Jammu and Kashmir which restored democratic procedures in the militancy-ridden state. The 2002 elections brought a Congress-PDP coalition to power in the state. In Punjab, elections were held for the first time in four years of President's rule in February 1992 which brought the Congress to power in the state. Along with state forces, political activists played an exemplary role in fighting terrorism in Punjab so that the normal democratic process could be resumed. This experience emphasized that communal tendencies have to be opposed both politically and ideologically along with a firm but sensitive use of state power.

Demolition of Babri Masjid and Resurgence of Communalism

1992 saw the demolition of the Babri Masjid, built by a governor of Babur at Ayodhya in the early 16th century. In time, this site came to be disputed by some Hindus as being Lord Rama's birthplace. Since the mid-1980s, the VHP had started a campaign to 'liberate' Ram Janambhoomi and demolish the mosque and rebuild a temple there. In 1989 when the V.P. Singh government came to power with the outside support of BJP, CPI and CPM, the BJP adopted the Ram Janambhoomi issue as its agenda and in 1990, it organized a rath yatra led by L.K. Advani which enhanced communal tensions. On 6 December 1992, the VHP organized a huge rally of volunteers in Ayodhya and demolished the Babri Mosque while top BJP leaders looked on. Kalyan Singh, the BJP Chief Minister of UP, and BJP leaders at the Centre had repeatedly assured the Supreme Court and the Parliament that the structure would be protected. In fact, the destruction took place with the collusion of the state government.

The destruction of the disputed structure, which was widely reported in the international media, unleashed large-scale communal violence, the most extensive since the Partition of India. Massive rioting occurred across the country, and almost every major city including Delhi, Mumbai, Kolkata, Ahmedabad, Hyderabad, Bhopal struggled to control the unrest. It is estimated that about 3,000 people lost their lives in the riots. The Union Cabinet sacked the Kalyan Singh ministry on the very night of December 6. A red alert was sounded in most parts of the country and the army staged flag marches in sensitive areas with curfew being clamped in several towns. The choice before the government was—firing on the crowd which would have led to a violent Hindu backlash; non-intervention which would leave communal forces unchecked. On 7 December the government announced a ban on all communal organizations.

In a resolution taken up for discussion at the AICC meeting on 10 June 1994, it was stated, "December 6, 1992 is a permanent blot on the nation's history and came about because BJP showed utter contempt for the rule of law and indulged in treachery of the worst kind....AICC calls upon every Congressman and woman to work even more devotedly to foil the designs of communal forces and to isolate from public life the brand of politics that all communal parties like BJP preach, propagate and practice."

Panchayati Raj and the 73rd and 74th Amendments

On 15 May 1989, Prime Minister Rajiv Gandhi had introduced the Panchayati Raj constitutional amendment bill in the Lok Sabha. While introducing the bill, he had explained its rationale : "We learnt that a grassroots administration without political authority was like a meal without salt. We learnt that however well-intentioned our district bureaucracy might be, without effective elected authority the gap between the people and the bureaucracy could not be closed. We learnt that the vacuum created by the absence of local level political authority had spawned the power brokers who occupy the gap between the people and their representatives to distant Vidhan Sabhas and the ever more remote Parliament. We learnt that corruption could only be ended by giving power to the panchayats and making panchayats responsible to the people. We learnt that inefficiency could only be ended by entrusting the people at the grassroots level with the responsibility for their own development. We learnt that callousness could only be ended by empowering the people to send their own representatives to institutions of local self-government."

However, the bill could not become law at that time as it was not passed by the Rajya Sabha. It was re-introduced in the parliament by the Narasimha Rao government and passed as the 73 Amendment in 1992. It gave *panchayats* constitutional status. It was brought into effect on 24 April 1993. It was meant to establish "democracy at the grassroots level as it is at the state level or national level". Along with this came the 74th Amendment which established local self-government for towns and cities as well. The *gram sabha* or village assembly as a deliberative body to decentralize governance was envisaged as the foundation of the Panchayati Raj system. A uniform three-tier structure of *panchayats* at village (*gram panchayat*), intermediate (*panchayat samiti*) and district (*zilla parishad*) levels was instituted. All the seats in a *panchayat* at every level would be filled by elections from respective territorial constituencies. Not less than one-third of the total seats for membership as well as office of chairpersons of each tier was to be reserved for women. Reservation for weaker castes and tribes (SCs and STs) was also provided at all levels in proportion to their population in the *panchayats*. By 2007-2008, the number of elected institutions had risen to 2.4 lakh and the number of elected representatives stood at 28 lakh. More than 10 lakh women have been elected to these institutions, constituting about 37 per cent of all those elected. This is the largest experiment in decentralization of governance in the history of humanity. Representative and direct democracy are combined in a way which deepens democracy. The efforts begun during Rajiv Gandhi's tenure now bore fruit.

The Mandal Commission and the Issue of Casteism

During its initial years, the government moved to implement parts of the Mandal Commission's report on the basis of a Supreme Court judgement. Twenty-seven per cent of the jobs were reserved for OBCs in the Central government and in public sector enterprizes. Institutions like the National Commission for Backward Classes and the National Backward Classes Finance and Development Corporation were established. The government established the Dr. Ambedkar Foundation and converted the Dr. Ambedkar University in Lucknow into a Central University. The government launched the Indira Awas Yojana to provide houses free of cost to scheduled castes and scheduled tribes below the poverty line. The million wells scheme was also launched to provide irrigation to farmers belonging to the scheduled castes and the scheduled tribes.

In a resolution taken up for discussion at an AICC meeting of 10 June 1994, it was stated, "AICC calls upon every Congress worker to remain vigilant against ....poisonous and pernicious casteism, just as vehemently as it is opposed to the politics of communalism. AICC congratulates the government for the peaceful manner in which it has implemented the recommendations for the Mandal Commission on the basis of the judgment of the Supreme Court. But AICC firmly rejects the politics of hate that is sought to be propagated by certain political parties and leaders."

Electoral Defeat

The Congress lost in the state assembly elections held in Gujarat, Bihar, Andhra Pradesh, Karnataka, Sikkim and Goa in 1994 while it won in Orissa, Arunachal Pradesh and Manipur. Analyzing the causes for the poor showing of the party, it was pointed out in the CWC meeting held on 5 April 1995 in New Delhi that the party had suffered reverses due to internal indiscipline, loss of touch with the grass-roots workers, inadequate publicity of the successes of the government during election campaigns as well as the failure of party leaders to reach out to minorities and SCs/STs. It was generally felt that the party should be revamped and propaganda refocussed on the pro-poor economic reforms. Opposition propaganda should be aggressively dealt with through organization of training camps and political conferences.

This Congress government was notable for many achievements: restoration of normalcy in Punjab, introduction of bold economic measures, improvement of the situation in Jammu and Kashmir and Assam, decreasing the volatility of caste and communal politics. However, despite this, in the 1996 general elections, the Congress faced electoral defeat. Narasimha Rao retained the leadership of the Congress party until late 1996 after which Sitaram Kesri took over.

14 Years in Opposition

The main concern of the party now was the growing political instability at the Centre. In May 1996, the BJP-led government lasted only 13 days in office. The Congress, being the single largest party after the 1996 elections with 140 seats, provided outside support to the two United Front governments led by H.D. Deve Gowda and I.K. Gujral respectively in order to avert fresh elections and counter BJP-led communal politics. With the ministry led by I.K. Gujral as prime minister, the Congress fell out over the report of the Jain Commission about Rajiv Gandhi's assassination. The report indicted DMK in the assassination and the Congress asked for its removal from the ministry. However, the government refused to comply and on 28 November 1998, the ministry resigned after the Congress withdrew support to it. This experiment failed on account of the fact that the United Front governments could not fulfil their own Common Minimum Programme and continued attempts to undermine the Congress politically.

Under the presidentship of Sitaram Kesri (1996-1998), the party continued to criticize the policies of the United Front governments as and when they differed from Congress policies. In June 1997, the Congress Working Committee criticized the United Front government for the continuing economic downslide. During these years, Congress influence waned considerably in the Hindi belt. In

1996 elections, in UP, a Congress-BSP alliance did not work and a short-lived BJP-BSP combine came to power. Caste-based politics represented by BSP had attracted Dalits away from the Congress who, along with Muslims, had traditionally constituted its social base in this area. Lalu Prasad Yadav in Bihar and Mulayam Singh Yadav in UP represented an alliance of lower castes and Muslims which undercut the base of the Congress. On the other hand, the BJP with its strident Hindu communal politics had weaned away the upper castes.

Towards the end of 1997, Jagannath Mishra, a Congress leader from Bihar, floated a new party called the Bihar Jan Congress and S. Bangarappa Reddy from Karnataka established the Karnataka Vikas Party. A senior Congressman, K.C. Pant, distanced himself from the Congress in January 1998 and declared his intention of supporting the BJP in the upcoming elections in the interest of stable governance. Now drastic action was necessary to revive the fortunes of the Congress.

Sonia Gandhi takes Charge

Eventually, Sonia Gandhi was persuaded to take over the party leadership in 1998. Earlier in 1991 after Rajiv Gandhi's death, she had refused the offer. In May 1995, she had again refused to lead the breakaway Congress group led by Narayan Dutt Tiwari and Arjun Singh. She campaigned for the party in 1998 polls, and the Congress was able to win 141 seats in this election, though it did not do well in the Hindi belt. On 6 April 1998, Sonia Gandhi was ratified as the Congress President at the AICC session in New Delhi.

In her opening remarks at this AICC session, she listed her priorities for the party: return of the grassroots workers; involvement of youth and intelligentsia in the party; immediate revival of the party in UP, Bihar, Tamil Nadu and West Bengal; setting-up of a task force to implement her decisions; a monitoring committee to report to her directly; restructuring of AICC, PCCs and DCCs; no lethargy between elections; revamping frontal organizations; transparency and accountability in functioning; a committee to provide intellectual inputs to MPs and MLAs and public donation to form bulk of Congress resources. She sought to take the reform momentum forward by setting the target of 8 per cent economic growth for the country. In her opening address to this AICC session, she said, "This is a vast agenda and it will constructively absorb the energy of our active workers....Sycophancy should have no place in the party. We must say what we mean and mean what we say." Within the party organization, she replaced the post of Joint Secretary with the post of Secretary, a post to which she appointed 10 party men.

The Election Manifesto of 1998 defined the Congress perspective towards coalition governments clearly. The Congress refuted the claims of the United Front government that the days of single-party rule were over and that a conglomeration of regional parties at the Centre could adequately reflect the federal character of the polity. The Congress argued that a combination of regional parties could never evolve a common national approach or programme and could not rise above local ethnic/linguistic considerations. The Congress's concept of stability was the stability of ideas, of policies and of programmes leading to human development and social harmony.

To take stock of the party position, the Congress held a conclave at Pachmarhi in September 1998. This meeting was meant for a reassessment of the party and the development of a new programme outlined by Sonia Gandhi. Various questions were discussed: growth of communal and casteist politics, empowerment of Dalits and other backward groups, and improving the party position in UP and Bihar. In a redefinition of the party's economic programme, the need for ensuring an efficient public distribution system, land reforms and the establishment of panchayati raj institutions were emphasized. The party president argued that, "Our economic policy has to be multidimensional, no one dogma, no one formula for us," and affirmed, "Abolition of poverty in the next 10 to 15 years is our main goal."

However, the conclave was significant for the political stand it took. In her concluding remarks, the Congress president said, "The fact that we are going through a coalitional phase at national level politics reflects in many ways the decline of the Congress. This is a passing phase and we will come back again with full force and on our own steam. But in the interim coalitions may well be needed." She thus asserted that in the long run the Congress would be able to govern on its own, but at same time anticipated what was to happen in 2004, and said that coalitions could be needed in the interim or in the short run.

In another step forward, the Congress party reserved 33 per cent of seats in all party committees for women and a minimum of 20 per cent for SCs, STs, OBCs and minorities. This was done at a special one-day session of the AICC held in New Delhi on 18 December 1998. At this meet, the Congress president again reiterated that the party was not entirely against forging alliances with like-minded parties.

Within nine months of taking over as party president, she seemed to have galvanized the party. The Congress won in assembly elections in Madhya Pradesh, Rajasthan and Delhi. As many as 15 state governments were headed by the Congress at one point. On 17 April 1999, the BJP government lost the no-confidence motion on the floor of the house after AIADMK withdrew its support to the government. She encouraged a rapprochement with AIADMK leader Jayalalitha through Subramanian Swamy: they were able to bring down the Vajpayee government and the country was headed for another Lok Sabha election in 1999. The Congress won 114 seats in this election. The Congress, being the second largest party, staked its claim to form the government. At the CWC meeting on 25 April 1999 in New Delhi, the Congress president explained that the party wanted to discharge its constitutional responsibility by providing an alternative government. Most of the non-BJP parties supported the Congress while other parties like BSP, SP, RSP and Forward Bloc did not. This meant that the Congress could not back up its claim to the formation of government with the requisite numbers. The BJP-led National Democratic Alliance assumed power at the Centre.

In the meantime, the BJP government had carried out another round of nuclear tests at Pokhran in May 1998. At the CWC meeting held on 14 May 1998, the President, Sonia Gandhi, made the following remarks about the Pokhran tests:

> I would like to place on record in this formal meeting of the Congress Working Committee the pride we feel in the achievement of our nuclear scientists and engineers for putting India's nuclear capability in the front rank....The nuclear question is a national matter; not a partisan one. On this, every Indian stands united.

However, she also reiterated the party's commitment to a nuclear weapon-free and non-violent world, especially India's commitment to peace in the region for fostering economic growth and poverty alleviation. The Congress accused the government of inventing a security threat to justify its nuclear test and rejected the justification of its being an exercise in self-defence. Clarifications were elicited from the government about the so-called deterioration in security environment. The Congress argued that nothing had happened recently to justify the nuclear exercise.

Sonia Gandhi's projection as PM in the 1999 election campaign led to fierce opposition from within the party on account of her 'foreign origin'. On 15 May 1999, Sharad Pawar, P.A. Sangma and Tariq Anwar in a letter to the party president demanded that the Constitution be so amended as to ensure that only "natural born" citizens become the president, vice-president and the prime minister of the republic. In response to this letter, Sonia Gandhi resigned from the post of party president. The CWC disapproved of the claims made by these three leaders and reiterated its faith in her leadership. After this experience, she sought to reverse the legacy of personal bitterness and political animosity towards her. The UPA could not have come to power without her effort in forging alliances and building relationships with those very parties which had been at the core of anti-Congressism.

During the Kargil war of May 1999, the Congress party condemned the incursion by the Pakistan army. The party organized relief work for the refugees in Kargil sector of Jammu and Kashmir. It also condemned the government for its gross negligence in allowing such a dangerous situation to develop in the country. Addressing the CWC on 20-21 July 1999, the Congress president pointed out that the infiltration sponsored by the Pakistan military had been carried out for many months and reports had been reaching the government. Soon after this, a major terrorist attack occurred in US on 11 September 2001. The CWC met in Delhi on 19 September and issued a statement condemning the attacks. CWC expressed its support and sympathy for the victims and pointing to India's fight with terrorism stated, "India has experienced a very persistent terrorist movement against its sovereignty and its people....The scars of terrorism sponsored, aided and abetted from across the border are still writ large in several cities of India,...The Congress Working Committee expects that in combating the global terrorism, the world community will fully take into account India's concerns and predicament in the face of sustained cross border terrorism."

BJP's use of State Power to further Communal Agenda

Vajpayee's government set about using education for political ends. School curricula and textbooks were altered, with history textbooks coming in for special attention. New history books were introduced in which historical facts were distorted and many prejudiced statements made. For instance, in the Class X social sciences textbook called *Contemporary India* written by Hari Om, Gandhiji's assassination was not even mentioned. It was only after nationwide protests against this deliberate omission that a small paragraph was included in the reprint of the book about the event. However, Godse's (Gandhiji's assassin) identity and his linkages with the RSS were not mentioned. In another instance of similar prejudice, a Class IX social science textbook for students of Gujarat stated that every minority community in India was 'foreign', implying that only Hindus were the 'true' inhabitants of the country. The Minister for Human Resource Development, Murli Manohar Joshi, a firm supporter of the RSS/VHP ideology of Hindu Rashtra, was the force behind this move. In order to pre-empt opposition from autonomous organizations like ICHR, UGC and ICSSR, the government set about appointing pliant and pro-RSS individuals to key posts there so that this programme could be seen through. Reacting to this gross abuse of power and communalization of education, Sonia Gandhi wrote to the Prime Minister on 21 October 1998, condemning the government's move to amend the basic structure of the Constitution dealing with minorities and educational rights. In her letter, she wondered why the curricula were sought to be "Indianised, nationalised, spiritualized? What does this mean? Is it implied that curricula hitherto have been un-Indian or anti-Indian? That curricula have been colonial or foreign, not related to the past and present realities of India? That curricula have been soulless and devoid of ethical values?" The Congress chief accused the Vajpayee government of trying to impose a concept of nationhood which was both "biased and untrue".

Ever since BJP came to power again in 1999 as the leader of the National Democratic Alliance (NDA), the VHP, Bajrang Dal and the RSS began abusing state power to achieve their goal of Hindu Rashtra. The demand for building the Ram temple in Ayodhya escalated in 2002 so much so that the government had to intervene and rein in the VHP. This had a direct impact on the communal situation in Gujarat which witnessed a communal carnage against Muslims for almost three months in 2002. The events of Gujarat brought shame to the whole country.

The rioting began at Godhra, a small town in Gujarat, where 58 people were burnt to death in a fire that engulfed a compartment of the Sabarmati Express. The victims were all Hindus, *kar sewaks* who were returning from Ayodhya. This provoked widespread riots in many cities of Gujarat. The riots left around 2,000 dead and 2,00,000 homeless. Religious places were targeted and killings, looting, burning of public property became common. Violence spread to villages leading to a large-scale exodus.

A report by the National Human Rights Commission concluded that the Modi government in Gujarat had failed to protect the rights of the people through its inaction against non-state elements. Soon, many allies of the NDA like Lok Janshakti Party, Telugu Desam Party and Trinamool Congress withdrew their support from the government and demanded the removal of the Gujarat chief minister. Apart from this, Sonia Gandhi also demanded a commission of enquiry headed by a sitting judge of the Supreme Court to be set up, action against the guilty and rehabilitation programme for the victims. This was followed by her speech in Porbandar in which she alleged that Gandhiji's Gujarat was being converted into Godse's Gujarat.

While the BJP returned to power in Gujarat in 2002, it lost the parliamentary elections to the Congress-led alliance in 2004. It was generally believed that Gujarat had been the cause of the downfall of the NDA government.

15 Congress in Coalition

A party conclave was held in Simla from 7 to 9 July 2003 to formulate a strategy for the forthcoming elections in 2004. Among the anti-BJP opposition parties, the Left groups as well as the Rashtriya Janata Dal were willing to support the Congress. The Samajwadi Party in Uttar Pradesh had also expressed its readiness to work out a seat sharing arrangement with the Congress. The party was a partner in five states and these parties could also be part of the alliance. The Simla Sankalp taken by the party at the close of the conclave on 9 July 2003 urged every individual to work for defeating religious fundamentalism of all kinds and communal forces led by BJP. The party programme for the elections was also outlined: rural development, empowerment of backward and weaker sections, economic reforms, increasing the transparency of governmental institutions and combating the criminalization of politics.

The strategy for the upcoming assembly elections was discussed at the CWC meeting held in New Delhi on 28 August 2003. It was decided that the corruption and failures of the BJP government would be highlighted in the election campaign. The Congress won these elections in Delhi but lost in MP, Rajasthan, Chhattisgarh and Mizoram. BJP went to the polls with its 'India Shining' slogan, but this did not prevent its rejection by the electorate. In the parliamentary elections of 2004, the Congress-led UPA was successful in regaining the power.

Memorable Renunciation by Sonia Gandhi

Congress contested these elections in alliance with 19 parties forming the United Progressive Alliance (UPA) and won the largest number of seats with 218 out of 540 seats and got an assurance of support from the Left Front (62 seats). Sonia Gandhi, the architect of this remarkable recovery, was unanimously elected leader of the Congress legislature party on May 15. On 16 May, UPA and its supporters unanimously elected Sonia Gandhi as the Prime Ministerial candidate. On 18 May, however, she resigned from the leadership of the Congress parliamentary party and named Manmohan Singh as her choice for the prime minister.

In her address to the Congress Parliamentary Party meeting of 18 May 2004, she said, "Throughout these past six years that I have been in politics, one thing has been clear to me. And that is, as I have often stated, that the post of Prime Minister is not my aim....Power in itself has never attracted me, nor has position been my goal. My aim has always been to defend the secular foundation of our country and the poor of our country – the creed sacred to Indiraji and Rajivji." This sacrifice was widely appreciated and served to enhance her stature among people and in the party. Not since the days of the freedom struggle was such a complete separation of the objective of personal power and the objective of achieving social ideals seen. People looked upon Sonia Gandhi's renunciation of power as reminiscent of the Mahatma.

Manmohan Singh, the fourteenth Prime Minister of India, spelt out his priorities thus: "This is a mandate for change; for strengthening the secular foundation of our republic, to carry forward the process of social and economic change which benefits the poorer sections of our community, particularly our farmers and workers. We will ensure that we have a development strategy to empower our people to realise their vast latent potential."

National Advisory Council and Social Legislation

A National Advisory Council was set up with Sonia Gandhi at the head and representatives of civil society groups as its members to assist the government in policy formulation. The Right to Information Act (RTI) was enacted by the Government of India in October 2005 largely at the initiative of the National Advisory Council and with the strong support of Sonia Gandhi. The Act applies to all States and Union Territories of India, except the State of Jammu and Kashmir—which is covered under a state-level law called the J&K Right to Information Act. Under the provisions of the RTI Act, any citizen may request information from a "public authority" which is required to reply within 30 days. The Act also requires every public authority to computerize their records for wide dissemination and to publish certain categories of information reducing the need for formal enquiries. The law was passed in 2005, relaxing outdated secrecy regulations. Refusal to comply brought on penalties. This empowered the common people like never before and also promoted transparency in administration and all other public sectors.

The legislation was regarded as one amongst the most progressive in the world. After the right to vote, RTI was the most timely and important step which led to empowering legislations, strengthening of Indian democracy and ensuring accountability. This movement sought to ensure that resources meant for the poor reach them. The popular response to the Act has been tremendous as it has been welcomed by a public tired of rampant corruption and official high-handedness. In the first year of RTI, 42,876 (not yet official) applications for information were filed with Central public authorities.

The Congress-led UPA government also enacted the path-breaking National Rural Employment Guarantee Act in 2005 which is being implemented in all districts to provide 100 days of legally guaranteed employment to each rural household in public works programmes like water conservation and harvesting, afforestation, rural connectivity, flood control and protection such as construction and repair of embankments, etc. The NREGA achieved the objectives of rural development and employment as well as growth with equity. Inclusive growth agenda had been the cornerstone of Congress policies in the first term of the UPA government. National Rural Employment Guarantee Act was hailed as a landmark legislation, which created the largest social security net in the world, making people partners in India's growth story.

A very important feature of this Act was that it addressed the poorest sections without consideration of caste or community. Another significant feature in the implementation of the Act was that it worked better in areas where the poorer sections were mobilized. By December 2008, over nine crore people had been provided employment of which women formed 48.77 per cent, SCs formed 30.95 per cent and STs accounted for 24.08 per cent. The total amount of wages disbursed by this time was Rs. 572.57 crore. Not only has livelihood security been provided to lakhs of poor rural families but durable community assets have also been created. Further, the implementation of the Act has strengthened other institutions like banks, post offices, insurance companies and panchayati raj institutions.

Apart from NREGA, the government also started and achieved considerable progress on the ambitious and comprehensive Bharat Nirman programme to transform rural India by expanding and providing irrigation, all-weather roads, houses for the poor, drinking water, electricity for all poor families and phone connectivity in all villages. It brought comfort and hope to crores of our farmers and their families by increasing the maximum sale price and procurement prices for crops. By January 2009, 54,697 villages had been electrified and 52,01,372 households provided electricity of which 43,58,742 were BPL households. Further, by December 2008, a total of 21.83 lakh habitations were covered under the Accelerated Rural Water Supply Programme and 190.23 lakh rural houses constructed under the Indira Awas Yojana. In addition to this, farmers were freed from debts with loan waivers to the tune of Rs. 65,000 crores. Credit to farmers was increased threefold, reducing interest rates on crop loans to encourage investment in agriculture and by extending irrigation facilities. In 2007-08, a record production of 230 million tonnes of food grains was achieved.

The government also launched the National Rural Health Mission in 2005 which improved the quality and accessibility of primary health care in villages through the training of Accredited Social Health professionals (ASHAs). By December 2008, 6.48 lakh ASHAs had been selected and Rogi Kalyan Samitis had been established in 565 District Hospitals, 5,267 Community Health Centres and 16,628 Primary Heath Centres. Janani Suraksha Yojana was launched all over the country to promote safe delivery of children and the number of beneficiaries stood at 51.50 lakh during 2008-09.

In accordance with the belief that justice delayed is justice denied, the Congress government passed the Gram Nyayalaya Act in 2008. Setting up of *gram nyayalayas* at the headquarters of the intermediate *panchayats* and mobile courts in the rural areas would make speedy, efficient and substantial justice possible.

The weaker sections of society were considerably empowered through various measures. In 2006, the Forest Rights Act was passed which gave scheduled tribes and traditional forest dwellers rights over land they cultivated in forest areas. Reservations for OBC students were ensured by law in all professional institutions in 2007 and scholarships for scheduled castes, scheduled tribes, minorities and

OBCs were enhanced to pursue college and university education. A new act protecting women from domestic violence was enacted in 2006 which, for the first time, also recognized a woman's legal right to reside in her marital home.

For the first time, a separate Ministry of Minority Affairs was created in May 2004 and the Rajinder Sachar Committee was set up to look into the social, economic and educational status of the Muslim community in the country. The implementation of the recommendations of the Sachar Committee is already underway and an Equal Opportunity Commission will be established by law. The Prime Minister's 15-point programme was launched in June 2006 with physical and financial targets for minorities in all welfare programmes of the Central government.

However, caste politics received a fillip with the victory of BSP in assembly elections in May 2007 in UP. Mayawati attained a clear majority. She had been the Chief Minister of UP three times before this, from June to October 1995, March to September 1997 and May to August 2003. When she was sworn in the fourth time, she said that her aim was to legally ensure social justice and provide employment and other facilities to weaker sections. How to win back the Dalits to the Congress fold remained a challenge before the party in the coming years.

In keeping with their election promises, the government introduced various social security schemes for the underprivileged sections—the Aam Admi Bima Yojana (life insurance cover) for one and a half crore landless households, the Rashtriya Swasthya Bima Yojana (medical insurance cover) for six crore unorganized sector workers living below the poverty line and the Indira Gandhi National Old Age Pension scheme for citizens over 65 years of age and living below the poverty line. For the urban poor, the Jawaharlal Nehru National Urban Renewal Mission (JNNURM) was implemented in 2005 for a period of seven years with an outlay of Rs. 1 lakh crore in 63 cities for upgrading infrastructure and for providing basic services to the urban poor. By January 2009, 293 basic services projects and 566 integrated housing projects had been approved under this scheme. Governance reforms under JNNURM have increased the availability of housing in 63 cities of 31 states. A major programme for improving power supply in 1,420 towns and cities was introduced.

The National Commission for Protection of Child Rights (NCPCR) was set up in March 2007 under an Act of Parliament. Its mandate was to ensure that all laws, policies, programmes and administrative mechanisms were in consonance with the child rights perspective as enshrined in the constitution of India and also the UN Convention on the Rights of the Child. New laws have also been passed to prohibit child labour and child marriage. New schemes to improve the nutritional status of children, especially girls, and to educate them have been launched. In continuation of its commitment to protection of child rights, the UPA government enacted the Right to Education Act in 2010 which makes education a fundamental right for children. It is now legally enforceable for every child to demand free and elementary education between the ages of 6 and 14 years.

Foreign Affairs

This government also earned India a new respect and stature internationally. The United Nations declared 2 October, the birthday of Mahatma Gandhiji, as the International Day for Non-Violence due to the sustained efforts of Sonia Gandhi in this direction. The foreign policy followed by the government yielded results in the shape of civil nuclear agreements with USA, Russia, France and Kazakhstan.

The Indian National Congress commemorated the centenary of the Satyagraha movement on 29-30 January 2007, by convening an international conference on "Peace, Non-violence and Empowerment: Gandhian Philosophy in the 21st Century". The Conference brought together representative leadership delegations from 91 countries and

122 organizations, including nobel laureates, heads of states/ governments, economists, philosophers and Gandhian thinkers. Enriching deliberations in the conference underscored the enduring relevance of Gandhian philosophy, which was summed up in the conference declaration, presented by Ahmed Kathrada, freedom fighter and prisoner of conscience. The declaration articulated the collective desire of the conference to declare October 2 as the International Day of Non-Violence.

The Chair of the Conference, Sonia Gandhi wrote to eminent world leaders including UN Secretary General, Nelson Mandela, Archbishop Desmond Tutu, Brazilian President Lula da Silva, President of Ghana and the Africa Union John Agyekum Kufuor, Spanish Prime Minister José Zapatero, British Prime Minister Tony Blair. The momentum gathered through a concerted effort of the party was supported by the Government and Prime Minister Dr. Manmohan Singh initiated the process for seeking a UN resolution. This historic initiative culminated in unanimous adoption of India's resolution co-sponsored by 142 countries, was moved by Anand Sharma, Minister of State for External Affairs in the United Nations General Assembly on 15 June 2007. A special session of UNGA was convened on 2 October 2007 with a special address by Congress President Sonia Gandhi in the UN General Assembly.

The policy towards US was characterized by a growing cordiality and recognition of mutual interest. A similar tendency is evident in India's relations with China in this period, fuelled by mutual economic needs.

A significant milestone of the Congress-led UPA government was the civil nuclear energy cooperation agreement with the global community, breaking three decades of isolation. India's impeccable credentials as a nuclear power and its principal position on nuclear non-proliferation was acknowledged in the India-specific waiver by the Nuclear Supplier group, paving the way for India's integration with the global community.

The Indo-US civilian nuclear agreement, known also as the Indo-US nuclear deal, refers to a bilateral accord on civil nuclear cooperation between the United States of America and India. The Indo-US joint statement provided the framework for this agreement. It was agreed that India would separate its civil and military nuclear facilities, placing all its civil nuclear facilities under the scrutiny of the International Atomic Energy Agency (IAEA). In return, the USA offered civil nuclear cooperation with India. The aim of this agreement was to ensure energy supply for India's rapidly growing economy.

Apart from the Congress, the agreement was supported by many political parties like the RJD and the DMK, ex-military chiefs, bureaucrats and scientists but severely criticized by other political groups on the ground that it went against India's national interests. Apart from the Left groups, anti-nuclear organizations also opposed the agreement. Initially the Samajwadi Party supported the Left Front in opposing the agreement. Subsequently, it came round to voting for the government in a vote of no-confidence. The government won the vote on the floor of the house by a majority of 275 to 256 despite the withdrawal of support by the Left Front. It is interesting to note that 10 BJP MPs cross-voted on the side of the government in this vote of confidence.

The Congress-led UPA government also nurtured the South-South Cooperation, ensuring India's leadership of the developing world. The first IBSA summit was held during this period, bringing together three vibrant democracies—India, Brazil and South Africa from three continents—Asia, South America and Africa. IBSA has since then emerged as a significant political grouping which articulates the position of the developing world in all international forums.

For dealing with internal and external security threats, the government raised new battalions and set up new hubs for anti-terrorist forces across the country. A National Investigation Agency was established. Early in 2009, Pakistan was forced to admit under diplomatic pressure from India that its agents were behind the terrorist attacks in Mumbai on 26 November 2008. The well-coordinated and brutal attacks occurred across Mumbai killing at least 173 people and wounding 308. However, the inaction of the Pakistani government in this regard despite evidence given by India against Lashkar-e-Taiba, the terrorist organization involved in these attacks, has harmed the agenda of peace being pursued by India.

Spectacular Economic Performance

The government during these years has maintained a high rate of economic growth. For the first four years of the Congress-led UPA government, about 9 per cent rate of growth was maintained, which was nearly 2 to 3 times faster than that of the advanced economies including the US, Japan and the Europe area and way above the global growth rate of about 5 per cent. The bold economic reforms initiated by the Congress government during 1991-1996 were continued by later governments leading to substantial economic growth. The full benefits of the changes are being realized only now. The fruits of liberalization reached their peak in 2006-07, with India recording its highest GDP growth rate of 9.4 per cent. With this, India became the second fastest growing major economy in the world, next only to China. With per capita income growing at over 7 per cent per annum and a series of anti-poverty measures substantial fall in the poverty ratio was witnessed in the new millennium. As of 2009, about 300 million people had escaped extreme poverty.

Another very important feature of the rapid growth in this period was that it was sustainable as it was powered primarily by savings and investment generated internally. All the debt sustainability figures showed that India's external debt situation was reaching more and more manageable levels with the capacity to service debts improving rapidly. This was reflected in her debt service ratio falling rapidly to levels much lower than other developing countries except China. A very revealing comparison with China however shows that while the Chinese growth model is driven by foreign capital, the Indian model was principally reliant on indigeneous capital. This provides food for thought for those who counterpoise China's independence to India's succumbing to the so-called 'Washington Consensus'. India in other words was promoting economic reform and achieving rapid economic growth without compromising the values of self-reliance, sovereignty and equity, values of the freedom struggle and the Nehruvian era.

Summing up the achievements of the UPA government, a Congress spokesperson said that this government had given the people of India a right to quality transparent governance, a right to new respect for India and a right to basic health and education. Through the NREGA, National Rural Health Mission and various other schemes the government had empowered people with the Right to Employment, thereby generating the world's largest rural employment programme. A right to inclusive growth and the consolidation of fiscal initiatives were also significant achievements. This government has also been responsible for path-breaking social legislation like the Domestic Violence Act and the Right to Information Act.

16 Second Innings under Sonia Gandhi's Leadership

The Lok Sabha elections of 2009 again returned the Congress-led UPA to power with the Congress securing 206 seats. The UPA gathered 262 seats in all and with the support of other allies like RJD and LJP was able to form the government. 2009 elections were the first occasion when the Congress named a prime ministerial candidate in Manmohan Singh. With the Congress securing 29 per cent of the vote share in the election, the growth of the regional parties was somewhat checked.

Manmohan Singh's leadership has provided an image of stability and sobriety of the government. This is vital for the Congress at a time when it is projecting itself as a party of responsible governance. An able leadership of government was combined with the exemplary and selfless leadership of the party by Sonia Gandhi. She was seen as the architect of one of the sharpest recoveries of the electoral fortunes of the Congress. From 114 seats in 1999 when she had barely taken over as party president the Congress now had 206 seats and the UPA 262. No wonder Sonia Gandhi has the unique distinction of presiding over the Congress party for the longest period in its 125-year history, over 10 years since 1998!

Rahul Gandhi's Initiatives

In these elections, the Congress did well in many states where it had empowered the state leadership to take charge of the campaign. This was true of Delhi, Haryana, Rajasthan, Andhra Pradesh and Maharashtra. In UP, the special interest taken by Rahul Gandhi and the support of significant sections of Muslims helped the party. In addition to this, a concerted campaign was carried out at the national level by Congress president Sonia Gandhi and Prime Minister Manmohan Singh. The selfless devotion of the former and the personal image of integrity of the latter drew large sections of voters to the party.

Rahul Gandhi also played a prominent role in the election campaign of 2009. He had entered active politics during the election campaign of 2004 and was appointed General Secretary of the party in 2007. In 2009, his focus was on democratization of the party and giving the youth a greater role in the party and the government. At a press meet, when he was asked how he could speak of democracy in the party while he himself belonged to a dynasty, he said, "I agree it's a paradox. But I have got this opportunity. I could say I don't want it. I'm saying I want to work for this country, let me try to steer it in a positive direction."

Rahul Gandhi is only continuing the emphasis on mobilization of the youth and democratization of the party structure that had first been taken up by Rajiv Gandhi. Rajiv Gandhi had championed the right to vote for 18-year olds and his government had declared Swami Vivekananda's birthday on January 12th as National Youth Day. The Congress has now started a campaign to bring youth from all sections of society into the political mainstream through the Indian Youth Congress (IYC) and the National Students Union of India (NSUI). For the very first time in any political party, there are hundreds of elected youth leaders in Punjab and Uttarakhand. This is a practical demonstration of the party's commitment to open up new political spaces for the youth of the country in a democratic manner.

Shift from Casteism and Communalism to Overall Development

During its tenure in office, the Congress has made a conscious attempt to shift the focus from caste-based politics towards developmental issues. This is both a strategy to counter caste-based politics as well as to address issues of underdevelopment. The legislation relating to NREGA, NCPCR, RTI, right to education, food security and health are manifestations of this shift. The positive political impact of these pro-people measures was proved during the 2009 elections. To take a case in point, state subsidized rural housing and medical insurance provided in Andhra Pradesh endeared Congress to the poor. In recognition of the need to reconnect with the masses, many efforts have recently been launched to consolidate the party at the grassroots.

In this context, the efforts led by Rahul Gandhi in reaching out to the poor in UP aim at rebuilding the party. During his visits to villages in UP, he was welcomed by crowds of youth, Dalits and Muslims. This reflected a growing response to the Congress as a secular party as opposed to the divisive politics of the BJP and BSP. For the youth, he is an energetic young leader with a novel approach to Indian politics. He attempts to connect the youth with the sociopolitical issues of the country through a new campaign called *'Aam Aadmi Ka Sipahi'* through which youth are involved in propagating and ensuring the effectice implementation of the government's pro-people policies. For the Muslims, the Congress is the only political party that refuses to have anything to do with BJP, especially in the post-Godhra period. This has enhanced the trust that the youth and the minorities place in the Congress as a national party. Further, the refusal by Sonia Gandhi and Rahul Gandhi to take governmental positions reflects a reorientation of the leaders towards rebuilding the party and seeing themselves as servants of the people and not their rulers. In a way, this also reflects the growing realization that the party needs to re-engage with its social base.

Both the UPA government and concerned citizens are currently engaged in discussions regarding a Communal Violence Bill. This concern has arisen from past experiences in the cases of communal disturbances in Godhra and the Babri demolition and its aftermath. In these instances, assurances about maintenance of peace from state governments had prevented the Centre from taking any active steps to prevent rioting. This Bill seeks to increase the powers of the Central government for dealing with such situations. The Bill will allow the Centre to declare an area in a state as communally disturbed and scrutinize the actions of the state government in dealing with such situations. Special courts will be set up to address registered cases dealing with communal violence in such areas.

The Women's Reservation Bill is another important legislation in the pipeline. It has recently been passed in the Rajya Sabha. It is a historic piece of legislation, representing a step forward for Indian women. It is hoped that increasing the number of women in legislatures would empower women and enhance sensitivity to women's issues.

In April 2010, Sonia Gandhi was re-appointed as the Chairperson of the National Advisory Council. This ensures that the government implemented policies in keeping with the party's focus on the common man. It would maintain the party's position amongst the electorate. The reason why the NAC was revived now may be found in the difficulties faced by the government when the Women's Reservation Bill was tabled in Parliament. Her presence as NAC chief would ensure that important legislation like the Food Security Bill do not get watered down. The party is committed to bringing about the Food Security Bill ensuring sufficient food for all people, particularly the most vulnerable sections of society. By this law, every family living below the poverty line either in rural or urban areas will be entitled to 25 kg of rice or wheat per month at Rs. 3 per kg. Subsidized community kitchens will be set up in all cities for homeless people and migrants with the support of the Central government.

In May 2010, the second UPA government completed one year in power. It has been generally accepted that the Indian economy escaped the worst impact of the global economic downturn primarily because of the economic policies of the previous decade and the strong foundations laid in the Nehru era. However, inflation, based on high prices of food grains, continues to be a challenge. Major concerns continue to relate to containment of Maoist violence and external security threats. India's traditional enemy, Pakistan, is strengthened by being an ally of the US, in its 'war against terror' in Afghanistan. China, now an economic giant, is in no mood to be conciliatory towards India on strategic or economic issues. For the party, the focus on issues related to economic development and empowerment of the underprivileged continues to counter the casteist and communal forces in the country.

The nature of India's freedom struggle had a great impact on the nature of its independent polity. Many lessons learnt during the course of the national movement became the guiding principles of free India. Even though political equality, in theory, was granted to the citizens of India soon after independence, the leaders were well aware of the social and economic inequality which persisted and which continues to plague the country till today. Many issues, not just regarding economic development but also social mindsets, continue to be points of concern. The ease with which caste and religion become effective tools of political mobilization and violence is something which India is still struggling to control. Despite India's secular polity, parochial tendencies of caste, region and religion are all too often used to determine the course of politics. The Congress is the only party which can lay claim to 125 years of political existence in India, as also to having led the nation in the freedom struggle and the most formative years thereafter. Along with countering internal and external security threats and promoting overall economic development, reduction of inequality and poverty, tackling the growth of chauvinistic tendencies and preventing divisive politics remain some of the party's biggest challenges in the future.

Congress and the Making of the Indian Nation

Volume — II

ACADEMIC FOUNDATION

Congress and the Making of the Indian Nation

Volume — II

ANNEXURES

INDIAN NATIONAL CONGRESS

CHIEF EDITOR

Pranab Mukherjee

EDITORIAL BOARD

Convenor

Anand Sharma

Aditya Mukherjee, Mridula Mukherjee,
Sucheta Mahajan, Rizwan Qaiser,
Bhashyam Kasturi

ACADEMIC FOUNDATION

NEW DELHI

First published in 2011
by

ACADEMIC FOUNDATION
4772-73 / 23 Bharat Ram Road, (23 Ansari Road),
Darya Ganj, New Delhi - 110 002 (India).
Phones : +91-11-23245001 / 02 / 03 / 04.
Fax : +91-11-23245005.
E-mail : books@academicfoundation.com
www. academicfoundation.com

Cataloging in Publication Data--DK
Courtesy: D.K. Agencies (P) Ltd. <docinfo@dkagencies.com>

Congress and the making of the Indian nation : Indian National Congress / chief editor, Pranab Mukherjee ; editorial board, Anand Sharma, convenor ; Aditya Mukherjee ... [et al.].
2 v. cm.
ISBN 13: 9788171888580
ISBN 10: 8171888585

1. Indian National Congress. 2. India--Politics and government--20th century. 3. India--Politics and government--21st century. 4. India—History—20th century. I. Mukherjee, Pranab, 1935- II. Mukherjee, Aditya.

DDC 324.25408309 22

Typeset by Italics India, New Delhi.
Printed and bound in India.

10 9 8 7 6 5 4 3 2 1

Contents: Volume II

(THE PRESENT VOLUME)

ANNEXURES

Contents: Volume I

(THE COMPANION VOLUME)

Annexure I

List of Congress Sessions

Sl. No.	*Names of Congress President*	*Session, Place & Date*	*Total No. of Delegates*
1.	Womesh Chandra Bonnerjee	1st Session/Bombay Dec. 28-30, 1885	72
2.	Dadabhai Naoroji	2nd Session/Calcutta Dec. 27-30, 1886	434
3.	Badruddin Tyabji	3rd Session/Madras Dec. 27-30, 1887	607
4.	George Yule	4th Session/Allahabad Dec, 26-29, 1888	1248
5.	William Wedderburn	5th Session/Bombay Dec. 26-28, 1889	1889
6.	Pherozeshah Mehta	6th Session/Calcutta Dec. 26-30, 1890	677
7.	P. Ananda Charlu	7th Session/Nagpur Dec. 28-30, 1891	812
8.	Womesh Chandra Bonnerjee	8th Session/Allahabad Dec. 28-30, 1892	625
9.	Dadabhai Naoroji	9th Session/ Lahore Dec. 27-30, 1893	867
10.	Alfred Webb	10th Session/ Madras Dec. 26-29, 1894	1163
11.	Surendra Nath Banerjea	11th Session/Poona Dec. 27-30, 1895	1584
12.	Rahimatulla Mohammad Sayani	12th Session/Calcutta Dec. 28-31, 1896	784
13.	C. Sankaran Nair	13th Session/Amraoti Dec. 27-29, 1897	692

14.	Ananda Mohan Bose	14th Session/Madras Dec. 29-31, 1898	614
15.	Ramesh Chunder Dutt	15th Session/Lucknow Dec. 27-30, 1899	739
16.	N.G. Chandavarkar	16th Session/Lahore Dec. 27-29, 1900	567
17.	Dinshaw Edulji Wacha	17th Session/Calcutta Dec. 26-28, 1901	896
18.	Surendra Nath Banerjea	18th Session/Ahmedabad Dec. 28-30, 1902	471
19.	Lal Mohan Ghose	19th Session/Madras Dec. 28-30, 1903	538
20.	Sir Henry Cotton	20th Session/Bombay Dec. 26-28, 1903	1010
21.	Gopal Krishna Gokhale	21st Session/Benares Dec. 27-30, 1905	757
22.	Dadabhai Naoroji	22nd Session/Calcutta Dec. 26-29, 1906	1663
23.	Rash Behari Ghose	23rd Session/Surat Dec. 26-27, 1907	1600 approx.
	Rash Behari Ghose	23rd Session (contd.)/Madras Dec. 28-30, 1908	562
24.	Madan Mohan Malaviya	24th Session/Lahore Dec. 27-29, 1909	243
25.	William Wedderburn	25th Session/Allahabad Dec. 26-29, 1910	636
26.	Bishan Narayan Dar	26th Session/Calcutta Dec. 26-28, 1911	446
27.	R.N. Mudholkar	27th Session/Bankipore Dec. 26-28, 1912	207
28.	Nawab Syed Mohammed Bahadur	28th Session/Karachi Dec. 26-28, 1913	349
29.	Bhupendranath Bose	29th Session/Madras Dec. 28-30, 1914	866

30.	Satyendra Prasanna Sinha	30th Session/Bombay Dec. 27-29, 1915	2259
31	Ambica Charan Majumdar	31st Session/Lucknow Dec. 26-30, 1916	2298
32.	Mrs. Annie Besant	32nd Session/ Calcutta Dec. 26-29, 1917	4967
33.	Syed Hasan Imam	(Special Session)/Bombay Aug. 29-Sept. 1, 1918	3845
34.	Madan Mohan Malaviya	33rd Session/Delhi Dec. 26-31, 1918	4865
35.	Motilal Nehru	34th Session/Amritsar Dec. 26-30, 1919	7031
36.	Lala Lajpat Rai	(Special Session)/Calcutta Sept. 4-8, 1920	-
37.	C. Vijayaraghvachariar	35th Session/Nagpur Dec. 26-31, 1920	14582
38.	Hakim Ajmal Khan (Acting President for C.R. Das)	36th Session/Ahmedabad Dec. 27-28, 1921	4728
39.	C.R. Das	37th Session/Gaya Dec. 26-31, 1922	3248
40.	Abul Kalam Azad	(Special Session)/Delhi	
41.	Mohammad Ali	38th Session/Cocanada Dec. 28, 1923-Jan. 1924	6188
42.	M.K. Gandhi	39th Session/Belgaum Dec. 26-27, 1924	1844
43.	Sarojini Naidu	40th Session/Kanpur Dec. 26-28, 1925	2688
44.	S. Srinivasa Iyengar	41st Session/Gauhati Dec. 26-28, 1926	3000
45.	M.A. Ansari	42nd Session/Madras Dec. 26-28, 1927	2711
46.	Motilal Nehru	43rd Session/Calcutta Dec. 29, 1928-Jan. 1, 1929	5221

47.	Jawaharlal Nehru	44th Session/Lahore Dec. 29-31, 1929	-
48.	Vallabbhai J. Patel	45th Session/Karachi Mar. 29-31, 1931	-
49.	Ranchod Lal Amrit Lal (Banned)	46th Session/Delhi Apr. 24, 1932	-
50.	J.M. Sengupta (Banned)	47th Session/Calcutta March, 1933	-
51.	Rajendra Prasad	48th Session/Bombay Oct. 24-28, 1934	-
52.	Jawaharlal Nehru	49th Session/Lucknow Apr. 12-14, 1936	-
53.	Jawaharlal Nehru	50th Session/Faizpur Dec. 27-28, 1936	-
54.	Subhash Chandra Bose	51st Session/Haripura Feb. 19-21, 1938	-
55.	Subhash Chandra Bose	52nd Session/Tripuri Mar. 10-12, 1939	2285
56.	Abul Kalam Azad	53rd Session/Ramgarh Mar. 19-20, 1940	-
57.	J.B. Kripalani	54th Session/Meerut Nov. 23-24, 1946	-
58.	B. Pattabhi Sitaramayya	55th Session/Jaipur Dec. 18, 1948	-
59.	Purushottam Das Tandon	56th Session/Nasik Sept. 21-22, 1950	-
60.	Jawaharlal Nehru	57th Session/New Delhi Oct. 18-19, 1951	1440 approx.
61.	Jawaharlal Nehru	58th Session/Hyderabad Jan. 15-18, 1953	1700 approx.
62.	Jawaharlal Nehru	59th Session/Kalyani Jan. 23-24, 1953	1400 approx.

63.	U.N. Dhebar	60th Session/Avadi (Madras) Jan. 21-23, 1955	1500 approx.
64.	U.N. Dhebar	61st Session/Amritsar Feb. 11-12, 1956	1600 approx.
65.	U.N. Dhebar	62nd Session/Indore Jan. 5-6, 1957	1100 approx.
66.	U.N. Dhebar	63rd Session/Gauhati Jan. 18-19, 1958	-
67.	U.N. Dhebar	64th Session/Nagpur Jan. 9-11, 1959	-
68.	Indira Gandhi	May, 1959	-
69.	N. Sanjiva Reddy	65th Session/Bangalore Jan. 16-17, 1960	-
70.	N. Sanjiva Reddy	66th Session/Bhavnagar Jan. 6-7, 1961	-
71.	N. Sanjiva Reddy	67th Session/Patna Jan. 5-6, 1962	-
72.	K. Kamaraj	68th Session/Bhubaneshwar Jan. 9-10, 1964	-
73.	K. Kamaraj	69th Session/Durgapur Jan. 9-10, 1965	-
74.	K. Kamaraj	70th Session/Jaipur Feb. 10, 1966	-
75.	S. Nijalingappa	71st Session/Hyderabad Jan. 10-11, 1968	-
76.	S. Nijalingappa	72nd Session/Faridabad Apr. 27-28, 1969	-
77.	Jagjivan Ram	73rd Session/Bombay Dec. 28-29, 1969	-
78.	Shankar Dayal Sharma	74th Session/Calcutta Dec. 28-29, 1972	-
79.	D.K. Barooah	75th Session/Chandigarh Dec. 31, 1975-Jan. 1, 1976	-

80.	Indira Gandhi	76th Session/New Delhi Jan. 1-2, 1978	-
81.	Indira Gandhi	77th Session/Calcutta Dec. 29-30, 1983	-
82.	Rajiv Gandhi	78th (Centenary) Session/Bombay, December 28, 1985	-
83.	P.V. Narasimha Rao	79th Session/Tirupati (A.P.) April 14-16, 1992	-
84.	P.V. Narasimha Rao	Surajkund (Haryana) March 27-28, 1993	950
85.	P.V. Narasimha Rao	Talkatora Stadium, New Delhi, June 10- 11, 1994	880
86.	Sitaram Kesri	Calcutta, August 8-10, 1997	1075
87.	Sonia Gandhi	New Delhi, April 6, 1998	1000
88.	Sonia Gandhi	Panchmarhi (M.P.) Sept. 4-6, 1998	250
89.	Sonia Gandhi	Talkatora Stadium (Special session), New Delhi, December 18, 1998	-
90.	Sonia Gandhi	Talkatora Stadium, New Delhi, May 25, 1999	-
91.	Sonia Gandhi	Shimla (H.P.) July 9, 10, 11, 2003	-
92.	Sonia Gandhi	Special session/ Talkatora Stadium, New Delhi, August 21, 2004	-
93.	Sonia Gandhi	Hyderabad, January 2006	12,000

Annexure II

Extracts from Select Resolutions/Manifestos

1. Non-Cooperation Resolution, Special Session, Calcutta, September 1920
2. Extracts from the Resolution on Complete Independence, Lahore, 1930
3. Extracts from the Resolution of the Congress Working Committee on Poorna Swaraj, Lahore, January 26, 1930
4. Extracts from the AICC Resolution, Karachi, March 1931
5. Extracts from the AICC Resolution on Quit India, Bombay, August 8, 1942
6. The Congress Election Manifesto 1946
7. Extracts from the Resolution on Socialist Pattern of Society, Avadi (Madras), January 1955
8. Extracts from the Resolution on Economic Policy, Bombay, December 1969
9. Extracts from Resolution on the Political Situation, Bombay, December 1969
10. Extracts from The Centenary Resolve, Bombay, December 28, 1985
11. Text of the Pachmarhi Declaration at the brainstorming session of the Congress Party, September 6, 1998
12. Text of the Shimla Sankalp, July 9, 2003
13. Extracts from the Congress Manifesto 2004
14. Extracts from the Congress Manifesto 2009

Non-Cooperation Resolution, Special Session, Calcutta, September 1920

Following is the resolution dealing with Non-cooperation which was moved by Gandhiji and carried by 1886 delegates against 884 at the Congress session, held at Calcutta in September 1920.

In view of the fact that on the Khilaphat question both the Indian and Imperial Governments have signally failed in their duty towards the Muslims of India and the Prime Minister has deliberately broken his pledged word given to them, and that it is the duty of every non-Muslim Indian in every legitimate manner to assist his Muslim brother in his attempt to remove the religious calamity that has overtaken him;

And in view of the fact that, in the matter of the events of the April of 1919, both the said Governments have grossly neglected or failed to protect the innocent people of the Punjab and punish officers guilty of unsolidierly and barbarous behaviour towards them, and have exonerated Sir Michael O'Dwyer who proved himself directly responsible for most of the official crimes and callous to the sufferings of the people placed under his administration, and that the debate in the House of Lords betrayed a woeful lack of sympathy with the people of India, and systematic terrorism and frightfulness adopted in the Punjab, and that the latest Viceregal pronouncements is proof of entire absence of repentance in the matter of the Khilaphat and Punjab;

This Congress is of opinion that there can be no contentment in India without redress of the two aforementioned wrongs, and that the only effectual means to vindicate national honour and to prevent a repetition of similar wrongs in future is the establishment of Swarajya.

This Congress is further of opinion that there is no course left open for the people of India but to approve of and adopt the policy of progressive non-violent Non-co-operation inaugurated by Mahatma Gandhi until the said wrongs are righted and Swarajya is established;

And inasmuch as a beginning should be made by the classes who have hitherto moulded and represented public opinions and inasmuch as Government consolidates its power through titles and honours bestowed on the people, through schools controlled by it, its Law Courts and its Legislative

Councils, and inasmuch as it is desirable in the prosecution of the movement to take the minimum risk and to call for the least sacrifice compatible with the attainment of the desired object, this Congress earnestly advise;

(a) surrender of titles and honorary offices and resignation from nominated seats in Local Bodies;

(b) refusal to attend Government levees, durbars, and other official and semi-official function held by Government officials, or in their honour;

(c) gradual withdrawal of children from schools and colleges owned, aided or controlled by Government, and, in place of such schools and colleges, the establishment of national schools and colleges in the various Provinces;

(d) gradual boycott of British Courts by lawyers and litigants, and the establishment of private arbitration courts by their aid for the settlement of private disputes;

(e) refusal on the part of the military, clerical and labouring classes to offer themselves as recruits for service in Mesopotamia;

(f) withdrawal by candidates of their candidature for election to the Reformed Councils, and refusal on the part of the voters to vote for any candidate who may, despite the Congress advice, offer himself for election;

(g) boycott of foreign goods;

And inasmuch as Non-co-operation has been conceived as a measure of discipline and self-sacrifice without which no nation can make real progress, and inasmuch as an opportunity should be given in the very first stage of Non-co-operation to every man, woman and child for such discipline and self-sacrifice, this Congress advises adopting of Swadeshi in piece-goods on a vast scale, and inasmuch as the existing mills of India with indigenous capital and control do not manufacture sufficient yarn and sufficient cloth for the requirements of the Nation, and are not likely to do so for a long time to come, this Congress advisees immediate stimulation of further manufacture on a large scale by means of reviving hand-spinning in every house and hand-weaving on the part of the millions of weavers who have abandoned their ancient and honourable calling for want of encouragement.

Extracts from the Resolution on Complete Independence, Lahore, 1930

This Congress, in pursuance of the resolution passed at its session at Calcutta last year, declares that the word "Swaraj" in Article 1 of the Congress Constitution shall mean complete independence and further declares the entire scheme of the Nehru Committee's report to have lapsed and hopes that all Congressmen will henceforth devote their exclusive attention to the attainment of complete independence for India.

Extracts from the Resolution of the Congress Working Committee on Poorna Swaraj, Lahore, January 26, 1930

We believe that it is the inalienable right of the Indian people, as of any other people, to have freedom and to enjoy the fruits of their toil and have the necessities of life, so that they may have full opportunities of growth. We believed also that if any Government deprives a people of these rights and oppresses them, the people have a further right to alter it or abolish it. The British Government of India has not only deprived the Indian people of their freedom but has based itself on the exploitation of the masses, and has ruined India economically, politically, culturally and spiritually. We believe therefore that India must sever the British connection and attain Purna Swaraj or complete independence.

Extracts from the AICC Resolution, Karachi, March 1931

Mahatma Gandhi moved the resolution on the declaration of the Fundamental Rights. The text was drafted by Jawaharlal Nehru:

This Congress is of opinion that to enable the masses to appropriate what 'swaraj', as conceived by the Congress, will mean to them, it is desirable to state the position of the Congress in a manner easily understood by them. In order to end the 'exploitation of the masses, political freedom must include real economic freedom of the starving millions. The Congress, therefore, declares that any constitution which may be agreed to on its behalf should provide, or enable the Swaraj Government to Provide, for the following:

Fundamental Rights and Duties

I. Fundamental rights of the people, including:

1) Every citizen of India has the right of free expression of opinion, the rights of free association and combination, and the right to assemble peacefully and without arms, for purposes not opposed to law or morality.

2) Every citizen shall enjoy freedom of conscience and the right freely to profess and practise his religion, subject to public order and morality.

3) The culture, language and script of the minorities and of the different linguistic areas shall be protected.

4) All citizens are equal before the law, irrespective of caste, creed or sex.

5) No disability attaches to any citizen, by reason of his or her religion, caste, creed or sex, in regard to public employment, office of power or honour, and in the exercise of any trade or calling.

6) All citizens have equal rights and duties in regard to wells, tanks, roads, schools and places of public resort, maintained out of State or local funds, or dedicated by private persons for the use of the general public.

7) Every citizen has the right to keep and bear arms, in accordance with regulations and reservations made in that behalf.

8) No person shall be deprived of his liberty nor shall his dwelling or property be entered, sequestered or confiscated, save in accordance with law.

9) The State shall observe neutrality in regard to all religions.

10) The franchise shall be on the basis of universal adult suffrage.

11) The State shall provide for free and compulsory primary education.

12) The State shall confer no titles.

13) There shall be no capital punishment.

14) Every citizen is free to move throughout India and to stay and settle in any part thereof, to acquire property and to follow any trade or

calling, and to be treated equally with regard to legal prosecution or protection in all parts of India.

Extracts from the AICC Resolution on Quit India, Bombay, August 8, 1942

....The Committee approves of and endorses that resolution and is of opinion that events subsequent to it have given it further justification and have made it clear that immediate ending of British rule in India is an urgent necessity both for the sake of India and for the success of the cause of the United Nations. The continuation of that rule is degrading and enfeebling India and making her progressively less capable of defending herself and contributing to world freedom.

The Committee has viewed with dismay the deterioration of the situation of the Russian and Chinese people and records its high appreciation of their heroism in defence of their freedom. This increasing peril makes it incumbent on all those who sympathise with the victims of aggression, to examine the foundations of the policy so far pursued by the Allied Nations, which have led to repeated and disastrous failure. It is not by adhering to such aims and policies and methods that failure can be converted into success, for past experience has shown that failure is inherent in them.

These policies have been on freedom as so much on the domination of subject and colonial countries and the continuation of the imperialist tradition and method. The possession of empire, instead of adding to the strength of the ruling power, has become a burden and a curse. India, the classic land of modern imperialism, has become the crux of the question, for by the freedom of India will Britain and the United Nations be judged and the peoples of Asia and Africa are filled with hope and enthusiasm.

The ending of the British rule in this country is thus a vital and immediate issue on which depend the future of the war and the success of freedom and democracy. A free India will assure this success by throwing all her great resources in the struggle for freedom and against the aggression of Nazism, Fascism and Imperialism. This will not only affect materially the fortunes of the war, but will bring all subject and oppressed humanity on the side of the United Nations, and give these nations, whose ally India would be, the moral and spiritual leadership of the world. India in bondage and the taint of that imperialism will continue to be the symbol of British imperialism and the taint of the imperialism will affect the United Nations.

The peril of today, therefore, necessitates the independence of India and the ending of British domination. No future promises or guarantees can affect the present situation or meet that peril. They cannot produce the needed psychological effect on the mind of the only the glow of freedom now can release that energy and enthusiasm of millions of people which will immediately transform the nature of the war.

The A.I.C.C., therefore, repeats with all emphasis the demand for the withdrawal of the British power from India. On the declaration of India's independence, a Provisional Government will be formed and free India will become an ally of the United Nations, sharing with them in the trials and tribulations of the joint enterprise of the struggle for freedom. The Provisional Government can only be formed by the co-operation of the principal parties and groups in the country. It will thus be a composite Government representative of all important sections of the people of India. Its primary functions must be to defend India and resist aggression with all the armed as well as the non-violent forces at its command, together with its Allied Powers, and to produce the well-being and progress of the workers in the fields and factors and elsewhere, to whom essentially all power and authority must belong. The Provincial Government will evolve a scheme for a Constituent Assembly which will prepare a constitution for the government of India acceptable to all sections of the people. This Constitution, according to the Congress view, should be a federal one, with the largest measure of autonomy for the federating units and with residuary powers vesting in these units .... Freedom will enable India to resist aggression effectively with the people's united will and strength behind it.

The freedom of India must be the symbol of and prelude to the freedom of all other Asiatic nations under foreign domination. Burma, Malaya, Indo-China, the Dutch Indies, Iran and Iraq must also attain their complete freedom. It must be clearly understood that must not subsequently be placed under the rule or control of any other colonial Power.

While the A.I.C.C. must primarily be concerned with the independence and defence of India in the hour of danger, the Committee is of opinion that the future peace, security and ordered progress of the world demand a world federation of free nations, and on no other basis can the problems of the modern world be solved. Such a world federation would ensure the freedom of its constituents, the prevention of aggression and exploitation by one nation over another, the protection of national minorities, the advancement of all backward areas and peoples, and the pooling of the world's resources for the common good of all. On the establishment of such a world federation, disarmament would be practicable in all countries; national armies, navies and air forces would no longer be necessary and a World Federal Defence Force would keep the world peace and prevent aggression.

An independent India would gladly join such a world federation and co-operate on equal basis with other countries in the solution of international problems.

Such a federation would be open to all nations who agree with its fundamental principles. In view of the war, however, the federation must inevitably, to begin with, be confined to the United Nations. Such a step taken now will have a most powerful effect on the war, on the peoples of the Axis countries, and on the peace to come.

The Committee regretfully realizes, however, that despite the tragic and overwhelming lesions of the war and the perils that overhang the world, the Government of few countries are yet prepared to take this inevitable step towards world federation. The reaction of the British Government and the misguided criticism of the foreign press also make it clear that even the obvious demand for India's independence is resisted, though this has been made essentially to meet the present peril and to enable India to defend herself and help China and Russia in their hour of need. The Committee is anxious not to embarrass in any way the defence of China or Russia, whose freedom is precious, and must be preserved, or to jeopardize the defence capacity of the United Nations. But the peril grows both to India and these nations, and submission to a foreign administration at this stage is not only degrading India and reducing her capacity to defend herself and resist aggression, but is no answer to that growing peril and is no service to the peoples of the United Nations. The earnest appeal of the Working Committee to Great Britain and the United Nations has so far met with no response and the criticisms made in many foreign quarters have shown an ignorance of india's and the world's need, and sometimes even hostility to India's freedom which is significant of a mentality of domination and racial superiority which cannot be tolerated by a proud people conscious of their strength and the justice of their cause.

The A.I.C.C. would yet again, at this last moment, in the interest of world freedom renew this appeal to Britain and the United Nations. But the Committee feels that it is no longer justified in holding the nation back from endeavouring to assert its will against an imperialist and authoritarian Government which dominates over it and prevents it from functioning in its own interest and in the interest of humanity. The Committee resolves, therefore, to sanction for the vindication of India's inalienable right to freedom and independence, the starting of a mass struggle on non-violent lines, on the widest possible scale, so that the country might utilise all the non-violent strength it has gathered during the last 22 years of peaceful struggle. Such a struggle must inevitably be under the leadership of Gandhi and the Committee requests him to take the lead and guide the nation in the steps to be taken.

The Committee appeals to people of India to face the dangers and hardships that will fall to their lot with courage and endurance, and to hold together under the leadership of Gandhiji and carry out his instructions as disciplined soldiers of Indian freedom. They must remember that non-violence is the basis of the movement. A time may come when it may not be possible to issue instructions or for instructions to reach our people, and when no Congress Committee can function. When this happens every man and woman who is participating in this movement must function for himself or herself within the four corners of the general instructions issued. Every Indian who desires freedom and strives for it must be his own guide, urging him on along the hard road where there is no resting place and which leads ultimately to the independence and deliverance of India.

Lastly, while the A.I.C.C. has stated its own view of the future government under free India, the A.I.C.C. wishes to make it quite clear to all concerned that by embarking on a mass struggle it has no intention of gaining power for the Congress. The power, when it comes, will belong to the whole people of India.

The Congress Election Manifesto 1946

For sixty years the National Congress has laboured for the freedom of India. During this long span of years its history has been the history of Indian People, straining at the leash that has held them in bondage, ever trying to unloose themselves from it. From small beginnings it has progressively grown and spread in this vast country, carrying the message of freedom to the masses of our people in the towns as well as the remotest villages. From these masses it has gained power and strength and developed into a mighty organization, the living and vibrant symbol of India's will to freedom and independence. From generation to generation it has dedicated itself to this sacred cause, and in its name and under its banner innumerable countrymen and countrywomen of ours have laid down their lives and undergone suffering in order to redeem the pledge they had taken. By service and sacrifice it has enshrined itself in the hearts of our people; by its refusal to submit to any dishonour to our nation it has built up a powerful movement of resistance to foreign rule.

The career of the Congress has been one of both constructive efforts for the good of the people and of unceasing struggle to gain freedom. In this struggle it has faced numerous crises and come repeatedly into direct conflict with the armed might of a great empire. Following peaceful methods, it has not only survived these conflicts but has gained new strength from them. After the recent three years of an unprecedented mass upheaval and its cruel and ruthless suppression, the Congress has risen stronger than ever and become more loved by the people by whom it has stood through storm and stress.

The Congress has stood for equal rights and opportunities for every citizen of India, man or woman. It has stood for the unity of all communities and religious groups and for tolerance and goodwill between them. It has stood for full opportunities for the people as a whole to grow and develop according to their own wishes and genius; it has also stood for the freedom of each group and territorial area within the nation to develop its own life and culture within the larger framework and its has stated that for this purpose such territorial areas or provinces should be constituted, as far as possible, on a linguistic and cultural basis. It has stood for the rights of all those who suffer from social tyranny and injustice and for the removal for them of all barriers to equality.

The Congress has envisaged a free, democratic State with the fundamental rights and liberties of all its citizens guaranteed in the constitution. This constitution, in its view, should be a federal one with autonomy for its constituent units, and its legislative organs elected under universal adult franchise. The federation of India must be a willing union of its various parts. In order to give the maximum of freedom to the constituent units there may be a minimum list of common and essential federal subjects which will apply to all units, and a further optional list of common subjects which may be accepted by such units as desire to do so.

The constitution shall provide for fundamental rights, among them the following:

1. Every citizen of India has the right of free expression of opinion, the right of free association and combination, and the right to assemble peacefully and without arms, for a purpose not opposed to law or morality.

2. Every citizen shall enjoy freedom of conscience and the right freely to profess and practice his religion, subject to public order and morality.

3. The culture, language and script of the minorities and of the different linguistic areas shall be protected.

4. All citizens are equal before the law, irrespective of religion, caste, creed or sex.

5. No disability attaches to any citizen by reason of his or her religion, caste, creed or sex, in regard to public employment, office of power of honour, and in the exercise of any trade or calling.

6. All citizens have equal rights in regard to wells, tanks, roads, schools and places of public resort, maintained out of State or local funds, or dedicated by private persons for the use of the general public.

7. Every citizen has the right to keep and bear arms, in accordance with regulations and reservations made in that behalf.

8. No person shall be deprived of his liberty, nor shall his dwelling or property be entered, sequestered, or confiscated, save in accordance with law.

9. The State shall observe neutrality in regard to all religions.
10. The franchise shall be on the basis of universal adult suffrage.
11. The State shall provide for free and compulsory basic education.
12. Every citizen is free to move throughout India and to stay and settle in any part thereof, to follow any trade or calling, and to be treated equally with regard to legal prosecution or protection in al parts of India.

The State shall further provide all necessary safeguards for the protection and the development of the backward or suppressed element in the population, so that they might make rapid progress and take a full and equal part in national life. In particular, the State will help in the development of the people of the tribal areas in a manner most suited to their genius, and in the educational and social and economic progress of the scheduled classes.

A hundred and fifty years and more of foreign rule have arrested the growth of the country and produced numerous vital problems that demand immediate solution. Intensive exploitation of the country and the people during this period has reduced the masses to the depths of misery and starvation. The country has not only been politically kept under subjection and humiliated, but has also suffered economic, social, cultural and spiritual degradation. During the years of war this process of exploitation by irresponsible authority in utter disregard of Indian interests and views, and an incompetence in administration reached a new height leading to terrible famine and widespread misery. There is no way to solving any of these urgent problems except through freedom and independence. The content of political freedom must be both economic and social.

The most vital and urgent of India's problems is how to remove the curse of poverty and raise the standard of the masses. It is to the well-being and progress of these masses that the Congress has directed its special attention and its constructive activities. It is by their well-being and advancement that it has judged every proposal and every change, and it has declared that anything that comes in the way of the good of the masses of our country must be removed. Industry and agriculture, the social services and public utilities must be encouraged, modernized and rapidly extended in order to add to the wealth of the country and give it the capacity for self-growth, without dependence on others. But all this must be done with the primary object of benefiting the masses of our people and raising their economic, cultural and spiritual level removing unemployment, and adding to the dignity of the individual. For this purpose it will be necessary to plan and coordinate social advance in all its many fields, to prevent the concentration of wealth and power in the hands of individuals and groups, to prevent vested interests inimical to society from growing and to have social control of the mineral resources, means of transport and the principal methods of production and distribution in land industry and in other departments of national activity, so that free India may develop into a co-operative commonwealth. The State must, therefore, own or control key and basic industries and services, mineral resources, railways, shipping and other means of public transport. Currency and exchange, banking and insurance, must be regulated in the national interest.

Though poverty is widespread in India, it is essentially a rural problem, caused chiefly by overpressure on land and lack of other wealth-producing occupations. India, under British rule, has been progressively ruralised, many of her avenues of work and employment closed, and a vast mass of the population thrown on the land, which has undergone continuous fragmentation, till a very large number of holdings have become uneconomic. It is essential, therefore, that the problem of the land should be dealt with in all its aspects. Agriculture has to be improved on scientific lines and industry has to be developed rapidly in its various forms-large-scale, medium and small- so as not only to produce wealth but also to absorb people from the land. In particular, cottage industries have to be encouraged, both as whole-time and part-time occupations. It is essential that in planning and the development of industry, while maximum wealth production for the community should be aimed at, it should be borne in mind that this is not done at the cost of creating fresh unemployment. Planning must lead to maximum employment, indeed to the employment of every able-bodied person. Landless labourers should have opportunities of work offered to them and be absorbed in agriculture or industry.

The reform of the land system, which is so urgently needed in India, involves the removal of intermediaries between the peasant and the State. The rights of intermediaries should therefore, be acquired on payment of equitable compensation. When individualist farming or peasant proprietorship should continue, progressive agriculture as well as the creation of new social values and incentives requires some system of co-operative farming suited to Indian conditions. Any such change can, however, be made only with the goodwill and agreement of the peasantry concerned. It is desirable, therefore, that experimental co-operative farms should be organized with State help in various parts of India. There should also be large State farms for demonstrative and experimental purposes.

In the development of land and industry there has to be a proper integration and balance between rural and urban economy. In the past, rural economy has suffered, and town and city have prospered at the cost of the village. This has to be righted and an attempt made to equalize, as far as possible, the standards of life of town dwellers and villages. Industry should not be concentrated in particular provinces, so as to give a balanced economy, to each province, and it should be decentralized, as far as this is possible, without sacrifice of efficiency.

Both the development of land industry, as well as the health and well-being of the people, requires the harnessing and proper utilization of the vast energy that is represented by the great rivers of India, which is not only running to waste but is often the cause of great injury to the land and the people who lived on it. River commissions should be continued to undertake this task in order to promote irrigation and ensure an even and continuous supply of water, to prevent disastrous floods and oil erosion, to eradicate malaria, to develop hydroelectric power and in other ways to help in raising the general standard of life, especially in the rural areas. The power resources of the country have to be developed rapidly in this and agriculture. Adequate arrangement should be made for the education of the masses with a view to raising them intellectually, economically, culturally and morally, and to fit them for the new forms of work and services which will open out before them. Public health services which are essential for the growth of the nation should be provided for on the widest scale, and in this, as in other matters, the needs of the rural areas should receive especial attention. This should include special provisions for maternity and child welfare. Conditions should thus be created in which every individual has an equal opportunity for advance in every field of national activity and there is social security for all.

Science in these innumerable fields of activity has played an ever-increasing part in influencing and moulding human life and will do so in even greater measure in the future. Industrial, agricultural and cultural advance, as well as national defence, depend upon it. Science research is, therefore, a basic and essential activity of the State, and should be organized and encouraged on the widest scale.

In regard to labour, the State shall safeguard the interests of industrial workers and shall secure for them a minimum wage and a decent standard of living, paper housing, hours of work and conditions of labour in conformity, as far as economic conditions in the country permit, with international standards, suitable machinery for the settlement of disputes between employers and workmen, and protection against the economic consequences of old age, sickness and unemployment. Workers shall have the right to form unions to protect their interests.

Rural indebtedness has in the past crushed the agricultural population, and though owing to various causes in recent years this has grown less, the burden still continues and must be removed. Cheap credit must be made available through co-operatives. Co-operatives should also be organized for other purposes both in rural and urban areas. In particular, industrial co-operatives should be encouraged as being especially suited for the development of small scale industry on democratic basis.

While the immediate and urgent problems of India can only be effectively tackled by a joint and planned attack on all fronts—political, economic, agricultural, industrial and social—certain needs are of paramount importance today. Owing to the gross incompetence and mismanagement of the Government an incredible amount of suffering has been caused to the people of India. Millions have died of starvation, and scarcity of food and clothing is still well-spread. Corruption in the services and in all matters pertaining to supply and land control of the vital necessaries of life is rampant and has become intolerable. These urgent problems require immediate attention.

In international affairs, the Congress stands for the establishment of a world federation of the nations. Till such time as such federation takes shape, India must develop friendly relations with all nations, and particularly with her neighbours. In the Far East, in South-East Asia and in Western Asia, India has had trade and cultural relations for thousands of years, and it is inevitable that with freedom she should renew and develop these relations. India which has concluded her own struggle for freedom on a non-violent basis, will always throw her weight on the side of world peace and co-operation. She will also champion the freedom of all other subject nations and peoples, for only on the basis of this freedom and the elimination of imperialism everywhere can world peace be established.

On the 8th of August, 1942, the All-India Congress Committee passed a resolution, since then famous in India's history. By its demands and challenge the Congress stands today. It is on the basis of this resolution and with its battle-cry that Congress faces the elections.

The Congress therefore appeals to the voters-all over the country to support Congress candidates in every way at the forthcoming elections, and stand by the Congress at the critical juncture, which is so pregnant with future possibilities. In these elections, petty issues do not count, nor do individuals, nor sectaries, cries—only one thing counts: the freedom and independent of our motherland, from which all other freedoms will flow to our people. Many a time the people of India have taken the pledge of independence; that pledge has yet to be redeemed , and the well beloved cause for which it stands and which has summoned us so often, still beckons to us. The time is coming when we shall redeem it in full. This election is a small test for us, a preparation for the greater things to come. Let all those who care and long for freedom and the independence of India meet this test with strength and confidence and march together to the free India of our dreams.

[The Independence Pledge has undergone slight changes since it was first taken by Congressmen on January 26, 1930. Reproduced below is the pledge taken by Congressmen on Independence Day, 1940.]

Independence Pledge for January 26, 1946

We believe that it is an inalienable right of the Indian people, as of any other people, to have freedom and enjoy the fruits of their toil and have the necessities of life, so that they may have full opportunities of growth. We believe also that if the Government deprives a people of these rights and oppresses them, the people have a further right to alter it or to abolish it. The British Government in India has not only deprived the Indian people of their freedom but has based itself on the exploitation of the masses, and ruined India economically, politically, culturally and spiritually. We believe therefore, that India must sever the British connection and attain Purna Swaraj or Complete Independence.

We recognize that the most effective way of gaining our freedom is not through violence. India has gained strength and self-reliance and marched a long way to Swaraj following peaceful and legitimate methods, and it is by adhering to these methods that our country will attain independence.

We pledge ourselves anew to the independence of India and solemnly resolve to carry out non-violently the struggle for freedom till Purna Swaraj is attained.

We believe that non-violent action in general and preparation for non-violent direct action in particular, require successful working of the constructive programme kept before the country by Gandhiji and accepted by the Congress and in particular of Khadi, communal harmony and removal of untouchability. We shall seek every opportunity of spreading goodwill among fellowmen without distinction of caste or creed. We shall endeavour to raise from ignorance and poverty those who have been neglected and to advance in every way the interests of those who are considered to be backward and suppressed. We know that though we are out to destroy the imperialistic system, we have no quarrel with Englishmen, whether officials or non-officials. We know that distinction between the caste Hindu and Harijans daily conduct. Such distinctions are a bar to non-violent conduct. Though our religious faith may be different, in our mutual relations we will act as children of mother India, bound by common nationality and common political and economy interest.

Charka and Khadi are an integral part of our constructive programme, for the resuscitation of the seven hundred thousand villages of India and for the removal of the grinding poverty of the masses. We shall, therefore, use for our personal requirements nothing but Khadi, and so far as possible, products of village handicrafts only and endeavour to make others do likewise. We shall also try to work to the best of our ability some item or items of the constructive programme.

We pay our grateful homage to thousands of our comrades who faced grave hardships, suffered humiliations and sacrificed their life and property in the last struggle. Their sacrifice will always remind us of the duty never to rest until we have attained our goal.

We reaffirm the resolution passed by the All-Indian Congress Committee on 8th August, 1942. It demands the immediate withdrawal of the British power from India in the interest as much of India as of World Peace and Freedom for all.

This day we pledge ourselves again to a disciplined observance of Congress principle and policies and to keep in readiness to respond to the call of the Congress for carrying on the struggle for the Independence of India.

Extracts from the Resolution on Socialist Pattern of Society, Avadi (Madras), January 1955

In order to realize the object of the Congress, as laid down in Article I of the Congress Constitution, and to further the objectives stated in the Preamble and Directive Principles of State Policy of the Constitution of India, planning should take place with a view to the establishment of a socialist pattern of society, where the principal means of production are under social ownership or control, production is progressively speeded up and there is equitable distribution of the national wealth.

Extracts from the Resolution on Economic Policy, Bombay, December 1969

The Indian National Congress is pledged to the establishment of a casteless and classless society based on principles of social, economic and political justice and equality of opportunity and freedom to work. This can only be realized when democracy extends form the political to the social and the economic spheres. This stand of the Congress Party has been made clear at various Congress Session *viz.*, Karachi in 1931, Avadi in 1955, Nagpur in 1959 and Bhubaneshwar in 1964. In pursuance of the objectives an immediate programme in June 1967 and the note by Smt. Indira Gandhi was approved which indicated an outline for National Economic Policies at Bangalore in July 1969.

After long foreign domination resulting in stagnation and deterioration in the standard of the life of our people, free India entered the second half of the country with new hopes and aspirations. Independent India under the dynamic leadership of Jawaharlal Nehru launched upon a programme of planned development to attain economic growth and social progress.

Within a period of two decades, in spite of many hurdles and difficulties because of aggression by two of our neighbours and drought and famine due to the uncertainty of nature we have scored significant successes in the field of economic development.

It cannot be denied, however, that despite visible changes in the independence structure of the Indian economy, certain sections of the community have amassed enormous wealth, but taken as whole tens of million still live in conditions of poverty. These glaring inequalities are reflected in flamboyant display of material possession, and even more in the exercise of economic power to the detriment of social progress. The process of development has also brought into sharper focus regional imbalances. Rapid expansion of education has outspaced opportunities of employment.

This twin problem of poverty and unemployment requires our immediate attention. This imbalance is the root cause of the deep crisis in the country. Significant changes in the social and economic structure alone will set right this imbalance.

In this context the Indian National Congress wishes to reaffirm its socialist policy as follows:

I. to attain a rapid rate of economic growth in which prior consideration is given to the income groups farthest removed from the national minimum relating to basic needs;

II. to bring about a basic change in the existing economic relationships in society with a view to eliminate the exploitation of the weaker by the dominant;

III. to reshape the economic structure in a way which will yield maximum production without allowing the emergence of private monopolies and growth of concentration of wealth and economical power;

IV. to establish and encourage such economic and social institutions so as to strengthen and consolidate our democracy and socialism in the light of our experience of these institutions during the last two decades; and

V. to increase employment significantly and in such manner as will result in fuller utilization of manpower which is one of the most important productive resources of the society.

The Ten-Point Programme was adopted to put an end to the distortions existing in the economic life of the community. This programme is under implementation. Nationalization of 14 major banks, passage of legislation against monopolies, and the canalization of the import of many items of industrial raw materials through the public sector constitute an important landmark in the implementation of the programme. The Congress while renewing its pledge to implements this programme in its letter and spirit, emphasizes early implementation of the following items:

(i) Nationalization of General Insurance.

(ii) Abolition of privy purses and privileges of the ex-rulers.

(iii) Ceiling on urban property.

(iv) In order to ensure to the producer economic and remunerative prices even in the context of greater production and to avoid the exploitation of the producer and consumer by middlemen wholesale trade procurement of major agricultural commodities should be done in the public sector and forward trading of all agricultural produce should be immediately banned.

(v) To complete expeditiously the programme of bringing the bulk of the import trade into the state sector, and to enable the public sector to play a predominant role in the export trade.

Agricultural Development and Agrarian Prosperity

Major, medium and minor irrigation schemes should continue to receive priority in Central and State Plans. However, special attention needs to be given to the encouragement of research investigations to increase agricultural production on dry lands. A major forward thrust in the technological transformation on unirrigated farming is most necessary for the fuller exploitation of land resources and to enable the so far underdeveloped areas and helpless farmers to have better income and living conditions. We spend crores of rupees in an unplanned ad hoc famine relief measures in the event of the failure of the meager rainfall in areas outside the good monsoon belts. Only the introduction of new technology can help improve the yield and income by over 100 per cent in transforming the outlook and economic position of the farming community in such areas, besides providing opportunities of employment to the unemployed and underemployed engineering graduates, because their skill would be greatly needed in helping the dry areas to march forward in production. A new deal for farmers in dry areas would not only help to erase a major source of poverty and economic instability but will also open the door to gainful and satisfying employment to our young and technically qualified persons.

The basis for extension of credit has largely been the ownership of property. The transformation from a capitalist to a socialist society can become a reality only if the basis of extension of credit is consciously changed form credit-worthiness of persons to credit-worthiness of activities. There is great need to give a new orientation to the various agricultural extension programmes. The cultivators with small holdings should receive priority in credit from the nationalized banks under a suitable system of guarantee by the State Governments. Cooperative credit society should in addition meet the financial requirements of more and modern agricultural inputs. Rural cooperatives of the small and medium cultivators should be encouraged for mutual help and avoidance of middlemen in the marketing of produce and agricultural inputs. Credit facility covered by suitable system of State guarantee should be made available from nationalized banks and cooperatives financial institutions, to landless labourers to enable them to take up subsidiary occupations such as dairy farming, animal husbandry, poultry, etc.

The Congress calls upon the Central and State Governments to:

(a) organise special programmes for dry farming;

(b) develop suitable crop varieties for dry lands;

(c) ensure adequate allocation of credit and other inputs;

(d) Strengthen all the supporting services, especially cooperatives and agro-industries.

Land Reforms

The Congress recognizes the crucial importance of Land Reform, both as a measure of social justice and as an important input of agricultural development. State Governments should adopt the following steps as a matter of urgency:

(a) All laws passed so far relating to Land Reforms should be fully implemented by 1970-71;

(b) Abolition of all remaining intermediaries by the end of 1970;

(c) Review of existing provisions relating to resumption of land with a view to make them more stringent;

(d) Conferment of security of tenure on actual tillers of the land;

(e) Settlement of surplus land with landless labourer;

(f) Recovery of lands wherever held in excess of the statutory minimum including lands held under Benami ownership and distribution thereof thereafter to the landless labour;

(g) Consolidation of holdings throughout the country;

(h) Setting up special tribunals for speedy disposal of land reforms litigation;

(i) Provision of legal aid to tenants and share-croppers in cases of tenancy disputes;

(j) Association of prospective beneficiaries with the actual implementation of land reform;

(k) A vigorous programme for assignment of Government wasteland suitable for cultivation to landless labour with special preference to Scheduled Castes and Scheduled Tribes within two years and provision of adequate financial assistance of improvement of such land.

Industrial Policy

The Congress recognizes that the major thrust of any industrial policy must be towards stimulating the growth of productive forces. With this object in view, licensing procedures and other regulatory mechanisms should be designed to prevent the evils of concentration of economic power and growth of monopolies.

It is essential to clearly define the respective areas within which the public and private sectors are to operate. In this context it is necessary to enlarge the role and scope of the public sector.

In order to promote proper growth and functioning of the public sector, it is essential to urgently implement the following measures:

(a) Public sector enterprises must be ensured greater autonomy and each must be judged only in terms of its performance;

(b) Sound personnel policies must be immediately evolved together with a comprehensive system of incentives and performance evaluation. Immediate steps should be taken designed to reduce the production costs through better inventory control maximization of production from the installed capacity etc.;

(c) Evolution of a sound pricing policy;

(d) Workers of industrial plants should participate increasingly in the management so that they can have a sense of belonging.

These necessary reforms shall be taken up for implementation forthwith.

As an essential corollary to a sound and effective industrial policy, certain reforms of public financial institutions are essential both in the realm of the policies pursued by these institutions and in respect of their management. The object of both these reforms is to make the financial institutions subserve priorities of Plan and social objectives. It should be an important objective of the new industrial licensing policy now under formulation to protect adequately the interest of small-scale industry. The present area of reservation for small-scale industry should be enlarged and the reservations properly enforced.

Organic links should be established between small-scale industry and large-scale industry. Special responsibility should be cast on large enterprises both in the public and private sectors to encourage the establishment of ancillary units for production of parts and components.

Processing Industries based on Agricultural produce should be reserved for industrial cooperatives of agriculturists and small entrepreneurs and emphasis should always be laid to encourage cooperative movement for rural development.

Licensing policies and procedures and the lending policies of financing institutions should alike be oriented towards provision of all facilities for new entrepreneurs so that there might be widest diffusion of opportunities for the blossoming of the entrepreneurial talent among India's educated youth.

Taxation

The Central Government should appoint an expert group to examine, investigate and suggest legal and administrative measure:

(i) to unearth black money and prevent its proliferation;

(ii) to reduce tax arrears and prevent evasion and avoidance of tax;

(iii) to examine various exemptions in the matter of taxation;

(iv) to deal with tax avoidance through the formation of Trusts, etc.

Urban Problems

The Congress is of the opinion that it is necessary to take a fresh look at the problems, arising out of the rapid growth of metropolitan cities and other urban areas. Effective measures should be undertaken to provide housing sanitation and to prevent air and water pollution besides providing inexpensive transport specially for students, working class, etc. The plight of the scavengers in carrying the night soil in outmoded and degrading manner needs urgent solution.

Slum Clearance

Separate Housing Corporations should be set up to replace slum dwellings by inexpensive but *pucca* structures in order to provide basic amenities to the slum dwellers.

Basic Drugs at Reasonable Prices

The Drugs Control Act should be strictly enforced. Basic drug should be made available at reasonable prices.

Children's Welfare

The nutritional requirements of three groups; pre-school children, pregnant mother and nursing will have to be given high priority. The protein needs of children of 0-5 age-group are particularly critical as unless these are satisfied physical and mental growth are impaired and irreparably damage. Therefore, first priority should be given to the provision of balanced diet to every child in the age of 0 to 5 to grow into a normal health human being. In view of the vastness of the problem and meager resources of the State a beginning may be made towards the implementation of this programme by initially covering under the scheme children belonging to harijan *bastis,* tribal pockets and slum areas. A scheme of special national cess to raise a children's fund should be worked out.

Home Sites

Among the strain and deprivations to which landless labour and others who hold small holdings are exposed is the absence of even minimum shelter. As the Congress Manifest has emphasized it is essential that home sites of suitable size are provided to all such families free of cost in deserving cases and to concessional rates to others. The State Governments should take immediate and effective step to make available to landless labour and others in similar circumstances this basic amenity of life.

Drinking Water

There has been in recent years considerable emphasis on the need to provide drinking water in all villages which are without a source of drinking water. A recent survey reveals that over a lakh of villages were without a source of drinking water and over a lakh and a half had inadequate sources. This should infuse a sense of urgency in the implementation of drinking water programme so that by the end of the Fourth Plan no village should remain without this basic requirement of human existence.

Unemployment

We must deal with the problem of widespread unemployment in the rural and urban areas on the basis of the highest national priority. In order to achieve this the following measures have already been taken within the framework of the Fourth Five-Year Plan, namely:

1. Enlargement of the size of State Plans involving large out-lays for programmes such as major irrigation, minor irrigation and rural electrification which have been facilitated through the support provided by nationalized banks to the borrowing programmes of the State Governments and the electricity boards;
2. Acceleration of a programme for large network of rural workshop for hiring and servicing of tractors, electric motors and pump-sets and agricultural implements.
3. As an earnest of determination to make significant dent on the problem of unemployment it is resolved to take following additional measures:
    i. Large-scale recruitment of skilled and unskilled labour from the ranks of unemployed and for the creation of capital assets which lend themselves to labour-intensive construction;
    ii. Rural works e.g., reclamation of land, soil conservation, afforestation, minor irrigation, feeder roads, cattle development and other programmes of area development;
    iii. Special stimulus to be given to undertaking in public and private sectors to promote ancillary industries;
    iv. Promotion of agro-based industries;
    v. Enlargement of allocation for housing, slum clearance and urban improvement programmes with support from the financial institutions.

Curbing of Wasteful Expenditure

All citizens of India and more especially those sections of our community who are fortunate to live in comfort when million are denied the satisfaction of their most elementary needs should create and sustain throughout the period of economic development an atmosphere of austerity and total abstinence from conspicuous consumption.

The Central and State Governments, statutory corporations, municipal bodies and private individuals should meticulously avoid all wasteful expenditure; vulgar display of wealth and ostentatious expenditure where possible be abolished or strictly controlled. Those who seek to serve the public including Ministers, other elected representatives of the people and Government servants, should voluntarily undertake to reduce wasteful expenditure connected with their official position, especially in matters like travel, transport, consumption of electricity, furnishing of houses, and entertainment both on private and public account.

Swadeshi

Congress deplores the craze among the affluent for things foreign especially when goods of comparable quality and utility are being increasingly manufactured in the country. In order to develop pride in India's industrial achievement, it is necessary once again to propagate the Swadeshi Movement.

The objectives and programmes outlined above are designed to create a strong self-reliant and socialist India in the near future. The imperatives of the social and political situation are such that a dedicated effort by the Government and all sections of the people should be made, with a sense of urgency, to implement these programmes.

Appeal

While pledging its whole-hearted commitment to the programme mentioned above the Indian National Congress fervently appeals to the countrymen in general and Congressmen in particular to strain every nerve and bear all burdens in the battle against poverty, unemployment and inequality.

Extracts from Resolution on the Political Situation, Bombay, December 1969

The Indian National Congress has a glorious heritage. Its role in liberating India from colonial rule and projecting a clear vision to the millions of our people of a promising future are achievements about which it can be proud. In the fight for National Liberation the Congress developed as a national front representing all sections of the Indian society to fight against a ruthless imperialist power.

The Congress conscious of the social content that inspired the freedom movement gave concrete expression to these aspirations in the Karachi Resolution of 1931. From time to time the Congress continued to spell out in detail these objectives with greater clarity and purpose. On attaining freedom the Congress set for the Nation the task of establishing a democratic society ensuring justice, economic, social and political and equality of opportunity and freedom to work.

At Bhubaneshwar in 1964 the Congress declared that "it is working for a revolution in the economic and social relationships in the Indian Society." It further expanded the vision stating that "the revolution will be brought about through radical changes in the attitude and the outlook of the people as well as the institutions through which they have to function."

In order to achieve this objective it became imperative to demolish some of the social and economic institutions which the foreign rulers had fostered to further their self-interest at the cost of the toiling masses. We had to achieve a transformation of the social and economic structure.

The establishment of a new order is always a difficult and challenging task specially when, the task is manifold, that is, demolition of the old and outmoded, and establishment of new and reform of large number of existing institutions which had come into existence as a result of a historical process. The vested interest of an old and established system cannot be expected to remain quiet when challenged with change and extinction. They are bound to give stiff resistance to attempts for change which adversely affect their self-interest. The extent of their opposition has in the history of mankind borne a relationship to the intensity and vigour of those who spearhead the change. As long as the established interests do not fear or face a real challenge to their vested interest they take the posture of magnanimity and sometimes even of acceptance and agreement but the moment they find that the forces of change are gathering positive momentum with a real threat to their privilege positions, they start operation with all their vigour, using all means, at their disposal.

We must face the hard reality that a conflict of interests is inherent in the very social goals for which we stand. This is a part of the age-old struggle between the forces of status quo and the forces of change. For the character and composition of any society never remains either constant or static and there comes in the life of every nation as of political parties when vast and reverberating changes have to be brought about to keep in tune with the changing mood and need of the times.

The Congress Party had adopted from time to time many progressive resolutions most of them unanimously. But a small section in the Party leadership lacked commitment to this process of change and they managed to occupy positions of vantage in the organisation and administration. In many places they became bosses in the Party structure and made the functioning of democracy within the party a farce. Even in matters of importance there was less than free and full discussion in the Party and decisions were often taken in an authoritarian manner.

Subtle and clever internal opposition by these bosses to the demand for nationalization of private commercial banks, abolition of the managing agency system, ban on company donations to political parties, abolition of privy purses and measures to curb the concentration of economic power and restriction on monopolies specially during the lat few years shed enough light on this conflict of interest and approaches within the Congress Party.

In the pre-Independence India the possibilities of conflict within the Party were comparatively less as the over-riding issue before the Party and the nation was to get rid of the foreign rule. The Congress on attainment of Independence was called upon to clearly identify and concretize its objectives in the field of social and economic change. Jawaharlal Nehru led the Party in this difficult task in the face of constant challenges but with a great degree of success. With his passing away these forces gathered strength and momentum. They came to symbolize in themselves the forces of conformism and status quo and became the rallying point for vested interest and reactionary forces.

The conflict came into open when the organizational chiefs and the Prime Minister took divergent stands publicly on important national issues at the Faridabad Congress session. The confrontation between the two approaches became apparent as the Congress President in his Presidential Address lashed out at progressive measures and openly condemned the public sector while eulogizing the private monopolies.

At Faridabad the attempt of a section of the Congress leadership to wean to Party away from its socialist objectives was powerfully challenged. This, naturally, alarmed them. They decided on a two way thrust. They started making secret plans to join hands with communal conservative and reactionary forces to defeat the new trends of change in the Party. In order to gain control of the Party machinery they indulged in political manoeuvres and manipulations for securing in majority in the organisation at all levels. Arbitrary and unconstitutional removal of three members of the Working Committee on the eve of its meeting on November 1, 1969, a rejection of a requisition for a session of the AICC signed by a majority of its members are some of the glaring instances of the efforts of the bosses to abridge the internal democratic functioning of the Congress and to change its course. Not content with this took the most extraordinary step in total violation of the Constitution of the Party and breach of canons of democratic behaviour, they sought to remove the Prime Minister from even the primary membership of the Congress.

It was evident that this was done solely with a view to get Mrs. Gandhi removed from the Prime Ministership and to have a person of their own choice installed in her place. Even in spite of the Congress Parliamentary Party expressing full confidence in her by an overwhelming majority, these bosses refused to accept the democratic verdict and continued to insist that she was no longer a member of the Congress organisation, in complete violation of the Constitution of the Congress party in Parliament. They went to the extent of splitting the party and causing a small group of the Congress Party in Parliament to sit in opposition to the Congress Party Government in Parliament. They did not even hesitate to join hands with communal and reactionary forces to dislodge the duly constituted Congress Government. They are still continuing their vendetta. In this process they have chosen to break away from the Congress and constituted themselves into a separate party styling themselves Congress (O).

This Plenary Session of the Congress holds this group, which has come to be known as Syndicate responsible for violating party discipline, splitting the Central Parliamentary Party and the organisation, subverting the internal party democracy and for having spurned the efforts of the Prime Minister, Chief Ministers and other senior members of the Working Committee towards unity and cooperation based on policies and programmes.

It is however heartening to note that the rank and file of the Party exposed this nefarious game of the vested interests and the champions of status quo and successfully defeated it. It is however certain that even some of those who have joined these bosses in the so-called Congress (O) should at any time attempt on any course of socialist action they will find themselves disillusioned for it its apparent that in spite of their professions the Congress (O) is nothing but an ally of the forces of right reaction and communalism. They are openly talking of even an electoral alliance with Jana Sangh and the Swatantra Party. The situation in the country demands that we have to contain the right reaction in the form of communalism and conservatism and also prevent violent and chaotic action by left extremists, because if either of these two forces should succeed it would destroy the unity and integrity and the democratic structure of our country and the progress towards our socialist goal.

In this context the Congress views with deep concern the large scale outbreak of communal riots in the country more so in the Gandhi Centenary Year and is convinced that these disturbances are being used for advancement of political interests on the national and international plane. It identifies the politics of communalism practiced and preached by communal parties as the main factor responsible for these disturbances. The Congress categorically rejects the reactionary theory of Indianisation of Indian Muslims and considers the call to them to prove their loyalty to India as an affront to crores of Indian citizens and a challenge to the very basis of our secular Constitution.

Tendencies of discrimination and pleadings for inequality of human beings on the basis of birth, religion, caste, colour or creed should be ruthlessly dealt with.

The task before us therefore is to remove the sense of insecurity in the minds of Indian Muslims and to generate in them and other minorities a sense of involvement in the political and administrative framework of India. The Congress has also to work and conduct its affairs in a way so as to create a sense of belonging and participation among the weaker section of the community by paying urgent attention to the social, economic and cultural needs of Harijans, the backward classes, the tribal people, Muslims and other religious minorities.

Towards this end the Congress will have to continue to keep a vigilant eye on the forces of communal hatred and darkness both at the political and administrative level.

The revitalized Congress has to assist in the tasks of social construction and economic development in a variety of ways and address itself, to the solution of many a long term as well as short-term problem of the Indian society. Congress seeks to establish democratic socialism in the country, with equal stress on democracy and socialism. The spirit of violence is wholly incompatible with democratic values and process. Organised effort has to be made to counteract the forces which are bent on fomenting violence and spreading lawlessness. Congressmen should therefore engage themselves in the programmes aimed at promoting social peace, communal harmony and national integration.

Neither socialism nor democracy can have any meaning or substance if social life and the conduct of affairs are divorced form moral values and integrity. Congressmen have to help and stimulate the efforts of the Government and the people to arrest the decline of moral standards and the growth of corrupt practices, which are coming in the way of progress and are undermining the faith of the people.

The Party has to become mass-based including the peasants and workers and attracting to its fold the youth and the intelligentsia. The Congress calls upon all the progressive forces having faith in democracy and socialism to join the Congress to help in the process of building up of new social orders.

The Indian National Congress now sets out on an arduous journey for the speedy attainment of its social and economic goals, unencumbered by the dead weight of bossism and reaction of secure in the faith that it reflects and voices fully the needs and aspirations of the people of India.

Extracts from the Centenary Resolve, Bombay, December 28, 1985

1. It is a proud moment for the Indian National Congress. Out of the millennia of history, the Congress came forth, mighty as the Himalayas, pure as the Ganga and indestructible as the spirit of India. It raised India from the depth of slavery to the sublime heights of freedom. Then it went forward to

complete the unfinished revolution: today, it celebrates the first century of its struggles and achievements and prepares itself for the high endeavours of the next.

2. It is a time to rejoice, to remember, to reflect and to look ahead. It is a time for rededication.

3. To the people of India, the Centenary represents the crowning of a great historical effort. The Indian National Congress embodies the political genius of India, which synthesizes divergent viewpoints into a unity of heart and minds towards a common purpose. It reflects the astonishing vitality of our ancient civilization which has evolved a unique pattern of belief and action out of the rich mosaic of different races, cultures, religions and life styles. Therefore, when the Indian National Congress celebrates its first hundred years, it celebrates equally the great moral and spiritual values which have sustained our ancient people in their odyssey.

4. We, the members of the Indian National Congress, spread in our millions throughout the length and breadth of the country feel proud that our great organisation has had the privilege of being the chosen instrument of the people of India for their national liberation and regeneration. The Indian National Congress led this epic battle for freedom with the weapons of truth and non-violence. The world marveled at the sight of unarmed men and women challenging the might of British imperialism, without hatred and without fear, millions and millions of ordinary men and women of India marched under the flag of the Indian National Congress with courage, with determination and with dignity. In the very act of struggling for freedom, the Indian nation was born anew, with the Indian National Congress as the harbinger and catalyst of this great re-awakening.

5. The Indian National Congress fore-shadowed the great changes of the 20th century. It came into being at a time when major historical forces had set in motion revolutionary transformations in the world. The industrial revolution had dynamised the economy of the Western world. Capitalism had pioneered unprecedented growth, but had also inevitably spawned vast imperialisms swallowing Asia, Africa and Latin America. The colonial world began to stir from its slumber. At the same time tensions and conflicts appeared within the heart of the capitalist society leading to the articulation of a new vision of social existence. A new ideological scenario was to emerge, heralding a new

era in human thought and action. Nationalism in the colonies and Socialism in the West were the potential forces that would produce mighty upheavals and change the world permanently. All this was not evident when the first Congress session was held in Bombay in 1885. However, as our organisation grew and reached out to the despairing and crushed millions of subject India, it gathered within itself the tremendous energy of the world historical forces, shaping a movement of unparalleled grandeur mirroring the India ethos.

6. In the hands of the Indian National Congress, nationalism did not become a narrow, dogmatic, exclusive and aggressive creed. It imbibed the catholicity, the tolerance and the compassion of our heritage. Even at the height of our conflict with British imperialism in 1942, the AICC, at its historic Bombay session where it adopted the 'Quit India Resolution', did not only look inward. It saw the freedom of India as a necessary prelude to the freedom of the oppressed peoples in Asia and Africa and the birth of a world federation and cooperation on an equal basis with other free nations. Even at that time the AICC pledged itself to a struggle for world freedom and against the aggression of Nazism, Fascism and Imperialism.

7. From the very beginning, the Indian National Congress represented all sections and communities. In his address to the Lahore Congress in 1893, Dadabhai Naoroji declared, "Whether I am a Hindu, a Muhammadan, a Parsi, a Christian or of any other creed, I am above all an Indian. Our country is India; our nationality is India." This sprit has always animated the Indian National Congress. The secular ideal has throughout been an article of faith with our Party.

8. The Indian National Congress forged the deeper link between political freedom and social emancipation. It symbolised the hopes and aspirations of the destitute masses of India for a life free form want. Under the inspiration of Mahatma Gandhi, whose service to the scheduled castes and tribes has gone down in our history as an unprecedented mission, it undertook a decisive battle against untouchability, oppression of women and other social evils. On the economic side, it completed the abolition of zamindari, initiated a massive land reforms programme and made determined efforts for economic decentralization. Under Jawaharlal Nehru, socialism with its promise of radical socio-economic changes, became part of the mental universe of thousands of activists. And yet, for the Indian National Congress,

socialism was not to be an imitative creed. Its path and vision had to be Indian, permeated with a deep ethical and moral content. Violence and blood-shed had to be eschewed. The dignity and freedom of the individual had to be upheld. Democracy and socialism had to be inter-twined. This monumental task of defining the Indian road to socialism fell to the lot of the Indian National Congress, because it alone was the authentic voice of the people. Our success in social transformation is a testimony to the creative application of the socialist vision to our own conditions.

9. The Indian National Congress was always conscious of the revolutionary role of science and technology in ending poverty, hunger, disease and ignorance. It was equally conscious of the fact that in the West science had been used for aggression, for domination, for exploitation and from preserving the status quo. The liberating role of knowledge had been suppressed, while its destructive role, as shown in Hiroshima and Nagasaki, had come to the fore. True to the insights of our heritage, the Indian National Congress determined for science and technology a role for the service of the masses in India and for peace and cooperation in the world at large. Man was to be enhanced, and not diminished and mutilated by science.

10. The Indian National Congress has gone from strength to strength because it has had the capacity and the vision to integrate the world historical forces with the perennial traditions and universal values of our heritage. In the perspective of our history and the history of the world, the achievement of the Indian National Congress has shed new light on the path trodden ceaselessly by mankind in quest of freedom, peace and Indian National Congress had offered solutions that are rooted in India's timeless quest for peace.

11. While playing this wider role, the Indian National Congress attended to almost every urgent problem facing the country soon after independence. The political unification of the country was accomplished in record time, by the integration of the princely States whose people had been struggling for their own emancipation side by side with the Indian National Congress in British India. This process was later completed by the integration of the French and Portuguese colonies in India, as well as Sikkim.

12. We rejoice that we have come thus far nourished by the wisdom and unremitting toil of thosc who founded our great organisation and those who guided it during the tumultuous first century of its existence.

13. On this historical occasion this Plenary Session of the Indian National Congress reverently salutes the memory of countless men and women who gave their lives to free our motherland from foreign bondage. Fortunately, a number of our respected freedom fighters are still with us. They are a source of inspiration for millions of Congress workers. Succeeding generations will wonder at the heroism and the sacrifice of the common people of India. It was Mahatma Gandhi's magic touch which possessed the alchemy to transform ordinary men and women into fearless soldiers of freedom; they defied death with 'Vande Mataram' on their lips. For those unnamed heroes of our freedom struggle, the Indian National Congress dips its banner in silent tribute and pledges itself to work relentlessly to realize their dreams.

14. The Indian National Congress was built by a galaxy of great men and women. These titans of thought and actions blazed a new trial in history. We remember the devoted scholarship of Dadabhai Naoroji which exposed the hollowness of the claim of the imperialists that they had brought progress and prosperity to India. We remember the luminous intellect and saintly conduct of Gopal Krishna Gokhale who set the tradition for intellectual debate within the Congress. We remember the irrepressible and matchless courage of Lokmanya Tilak, Bipin Chandra Pal and Lajpat Rai who fired the imagination of the youth with the unconquerable urge for freedom. Mahatma Gandhi, Motilal Nehru, Madan Mohan Malaviya, Deshbandu Chittaranjan Das, Jawaharlal Nehru, Hakim Ajmal Khan, Annie Besant, Gopalbandhu Das, Satyamurti, Sri Aurobindo, Amiya Kumar Das, Mohd. Ali, Shaukat Ali, Rabindranath Tagore, Sarojini Naidu, Vallabbhai Patel, Rajendra Prasad, Rajagaoplachari, Pattabhi Sitaramiah, Maulana Azad, Govind Ballabh Pant, Subhas Chandra Bose, Tanguturi Prakasam, Acharya Narendra Dev, Asaf Ali, Sheikh Mohd. Abdullah, G.M. Sadiq, Jayaprakash Narayan, K. Kamaraj, Lal Bahadur Shastri, Gopinath Bordoloi, Saifuddin Kitchlew, Acharya Kripalani, Swami Ramanand Tirth and many others from the Princely States, etc., adorn a gallery of portrait which echoes the heartbeats of a nation in the throes of self-discovery and transformation. The list is long and distinguished. It can never be made exhaustive, so numerous have been the great men and women who gave their all to the freedom struggle. Last but not the least, thousands of unnamed volunteers and workers at the village level swelled the ranks of the freedom fighters. The Indian National Congress places on record its debt of gratitude to all of them.

15. We have the privilege to have in our midst a stalwart and a captain of our freedom struggle, Khan Abdul Ghaffar Khan, whom we welcome with unbounded joy. For India, he is and will always be a Tribune of freedom and unity. The saga of his sacrifices both before and after freedom inspires and elevates those who work for the cause of liberty and justice.

16. An amazing blossoming of leadership took place under Mahatma Gandhi. He moulded an entire historical epoch. He gave voice to the dumb millions whose backs had been bent under the crushing burden of imperialism. His simple message of freedom touched one and all, the peasant at his plough, the worker at his spindle, the businessman at his trade, the scientist, the lawyer, the student. He brought the masses, the 'Daridra Narayan; into the freedom movement. He created a new ferment in the mind and spirit of India, out of which grew the majestic sweep of creative endeavour in every field of human activity. At his behest millions-women no less than men-marched to goal and suffering and millions prayed. A profound revolution burst upon this ancient land, characterized by the gentleness of non-violence, strengthened by Satyagraha and steeled by civil disobedience. It was a revolution which, for the imperialist power, was difficult to tackle and impossible to suppress. As a strategy it had no match. It disarmed brute force, tended to humanize tyranny and to compel respect and conciliation in the most implacable of opponents. Under the Mahatma's tutelage, mass leaders sprang up in every part of India and welded together different groups and communities in a massive and all inclusive struggle against foreign domination. Mahatma Gandhi's message lives, his truth lives; each generation will interpret in its own fashion to further the cause of India and the cause of human-kind.

17. The priceless legacy of Mahatma Gandhi was enriched by the peerless Jawaharlal Nehru whom Gandhiji had declared his political heir. Jawaharlal Nehru infused the freedom struggle with his unrivalled passion for social justice. The masses adored him, trusted him and followed him with unbounded enthusiasm. He evoked the powerful vision of an egalitarian society based on science and industry. He trained generations of India's youth to think of India's future on scientific, secular and socialist lines. Young India thrilled to his words uttered on the banks of Ravi in 1929, claiming himself to be a republican and a socialist. He lined India's battle for freedom to a worldwide struggle against imperialism and fascism and placed

India firmly on the side of progressive forces. His uncompromising allegiance to socialism and broad internationalism constituted the ideas and values from which modern India drew sustenance.

18. Out of the ashes of the colonial past, he painstakingly built the structure of modern India. This session of the Indian National Congress recalls with pride and gratitude that Jawaharlal Nehru, its President both before and after independence, fashioned the democratic institutions of the Republic, established the Planning process, gave wing to science and technology, charted the path of an independent non-aligned foreign policy in a world beset with a suicidal conflict of the military blocs, and crusaded tirelessly for the unity of India, transcending caste, creed, region and religion.

19. Under his leadership, Indian advanced progressively on the path of an independent national economy. The basic infrastructure of development came into existence. India grew in self-assurance as she gathered the means to solve the problem of poverty. We faced many a challenge to our unity and integrity but overcame them all on the strength of his leadership. The Indian National Congress and or young Republic was fortunate to have at the helm of affairs in the formative years of India's independence.

20. His noble work, and the vast treasure-house of ideas he has left behind, shall remain a perennial source of inspiration and guidance to India.

21. On the solid foundations built by Jawaharlal Nehru, the Indian National Congress continued to take the country forward under the dynamic leadership of Indira Gandhi. She was a child of the Indian revolution, combining in herself the wisdom and the inner spiritual urge of our race and the revolutionary impulses of the modern era. She recast the idiom of Indian politics and society. She sharpened the struggle for social justice. A series of radical measures, spearheaded by the historic bank nationalization, galvanized the masses. To Indira Gandhi goes the credit of demonstrating the dynamism and the vitality of India's democratic institutions, as they absorbed and channeled this vast mass upsurge for radical change. Without this skilful adaptation of our representative bodies to the dynamics of mass aspiration, democracy may well have floundered in India, as it did in some other countries.

22. Indira Gandhi also brought about the social, economic and technological changes for production of greater wealth without which the yearning for

social justice could not have found fulfillment. She inspired the agricultural revolution which has made India self-sufficient in food grains. She lifted forever the dreadful spectre of starvation and the accompanying humiliation of dependence on others for food.

23. Under her leadership science and technology matured, bringing self-reliance even in strategic areas as Atomic Energy and Space. Industry advanced rapidly, producing a vast range of sophisticated products and bringing India to the threshold of industrial greatness.

24. She struggled not for India alone, but for the oppressed and the deprived everywhere. She spoke for them as leader of the non-aligned. The voice of India seeking peace, friendship and justice found articulation in her voice. The world listened to her because she was truly the voice of resurgent India and of the emerging world order.

25. Martyrdom crowned her life. Her passion for India and for its unity and integrity will remain engraved on the minds and hearts of hundreds of millions of Indians. She gave to India and the people all she had, and in return our vast masses showered on her their unbounded love.

26. Under her, the Indian National Congress fired the people's imagination and jumped a generation. New blood coursed through its veins. New impulses of change came into it. Crises have since tested its mettle, from each of which it has emerged with greater strength. The party of freedom has become the party of social transformation, it has found a new historical destiny for itself. The party of Mahatma Gandhi, Jawaharlal Nehru and Indira Gandhi looks to a future worthy of its past.

27. The Indian National Congress has served as a bridge to join succeeding generations by inspiring, and mobilizing the idealistic enthusiasm of the youth of each generation. It has always succeeded in tempering zeal with sagacity and stimulating wisdom with restless dynamism. In the result, India did not witness a serious generation gap. The youth of India always rallied round the Congress policies and programmes. This centenary session of the Indian National Congress expresses its deep appreciation of the identification of the youth with all that it stood for during its one hundred years of eventful history and its continued faith in their equally prominent role in the year to come.

28. When Indira Gandhi was slain over a year ago, the nation faced an unprecedented crisis. In that moment of agony and ordeal the Indian National Congress, drawing from its reserves of strength born out of decades of struggle for freedom and for the reconstruction of India, provided new leadership to the country. Shri Rajiv Gandhi became the President of our party. A tormented India rose again to resume its journey.

29. The poise, the inner calm, and the steadfast vision of our leader steered the nation through a perilous time. True to the democratic tradition of the Congress, Shri Rajiv Gandhi called the General Elections and in a country-wide campaign, reminiscent of Jawaharlal Nehru and Indira Gandhi, struck an instant rapport with the vast masses. The historic and unprecedented victory of the Indian National Congress re-affirmed the abiding faith of the people of India in our organisation. Within the first year of Shri Rajiv Gandhi's assumption of office as Prime Minister, there has been world-wide acclaim for this forward-looking approach and vision for the nation's glorious entry into the twenty-first century.

30. The Indian National Congress has met the challenges to the unity and integrity of the country through democratic and peaceful methods. The Punjab and Assam Accords illustrated the strength and resilience of the Indian democracy. These have fortified national cohesion. There are few instances in contemporary history where suspicion, mistrust, hatred and violence have yielded so swiftly to political dialogue informed by the spirit and vision of unity.

31. This historic session of the Indian National Congress reminds the country that while our achievements over the past one hundred years have been brilliant by any standard, we have still to cross many hurdles in our future journey to fulfillment. The threats to unity continue. Destabilisation lurks in the shadows all the time. Fissiparous tendencies rage under careful fostering by adversary forces operating under various covers. In particular, communalism remains an ever present danger. Communal politics are the politics of reaction, and reflect a backward looking outlook. Social change in India has brought into the political mainstream hitherto suppressed and submerged groups. The Congress has written the agenda of political action giving priority to the all round betterment of these groups. This is one of the greatest contributions of the Indian National Congress to the political process

in India. However, this mass mobilization for radical socio-economic ends is anathema to forces wedded to the philosophy of status quo and to social and economic privilege. Hence, the recurrence of communalism. Hence the appeal to medieval modes of thought and feeling and resort to violence and intimidation. Hence the resources to every means to obstruct the swelling tide of change.

32. The Indian National Congress warns the people that in addition to its internal motivation, communalism has definite external ramifications. It is linked with external forces which continue to smart under their chagrin at the consolidation of India's post-independence unity. In a complex world situation, the internal forces of disunity and division are sustained and reinforced by all manner of external reaction which can ultimately be traced to neo-colonialism. This plenary session reiterates that complete separation between religion and politics is a *sine quo non* for India's secular principle. The country has lost two of its greatest leaders, Mahatma Gandhi and Indira Gandhi, who fell victim to communal frenzy. There shall be no compromise on our continued fight against communalism.

33. The fight against communalism is thus many-faceted involving the root and branch eradication of a world view based on obscurantism and fed by world reaction. Our ideological counter-offensive needs to be more systematic, in view of the persistent onslaughts by this pernicious vestige of colonialism. The fight against it should be carried on everywhere, in the schools, in the media, in the political and social institutions and in the work places.

34. Yet another disturbing feature is an orchestrated attempt to weaken the Centre. This is indeed unfortunate, considering the fact that under the inspiration of the Indian National Congress the country's life has assumed a truly national character. All our leaders, wherever they haled from, were seen and adored by the people as national leaders. The nation's problems and challenge have always engage the attention of orientation built up assiduously and nurtured through decades of magnificent vision and universal appeal, are sought to be destroyed through the instrumentality of unthinking sentiments of various kinds.

35. There is no anti-thesis between a strong Centre and strong States. In fact, in actual practice the two mutually support and reinforce each other. The

psychology and the language of confrontation, specially developed for transient political ends, will do immense harm to our social and political fabric. For the Indian National Congress, political pluralism, which has been successfully worked under the aegis of the Constitution, embodies the vision of the founders of our Republic. It signifies a Centre capable of protecting and strengthening the unity of the nation and catalyzing the all round blossoming of all part of the country in a pattern of harmonised excellence.

36. Terrorism and violence had scarred the face of our motherland in the recent past. They are totally alien to our genius. Our leaders consciously chose the path of non-violence to achieve independence and to promote development and social harmony. In our vast and diverse country the only effective and enduring method of bringing about change and of resolving conflict is that of dialogue and consent. Terrorism and violence represent a frontal attack on our ethos. They must and will be resisted with all the means at our command. They have no place in free India. This plenary session of the Indian National Congress appeals to the people to rise with al the strength to root out this menace.

37. The Indian National Congress has always symbolized national consensus on vital policy issues. Even when it was leading the freedom struggle, there were small groups of brave and courageous patriots who wanted to go their own way. There were others who saw in compromise with British imperialism the best hope for India. But the broad national current always flowed into and found expression through the National Congress. Similarly today, in spite of the existence of many parties of widely differing ideological persuasions, the Congress represents the basic national thrust for unity and socio-economic transformation. The pillars of the Congress ideology viz., democracy, secularism, socialism and non-alignment support the basic structure of national striving. This plenary session calls upon all Congress workers to strengthen the Nation's consensus around these key elements of the Congress ideology.

38. On the Indian National Congress rest the burden of building further on the achievement of Jawaharlal Nehru and Indira Gandhi. The national economy today is strong and vibrant. We have accepted the building of a independent and self-reliant economy as a major national objective. We have achieved spectacular progress in this direction by attaining food self-sufficiency and by building a sound industrial base. We have avoided the debt

trap. Our economy has successfully dealt with a deep and long-lasting international economic crisis characterized by recession, protectionism, inflation, volatility of exchange, high interest rates and shrinking concessional flows. However, the next phase in our long journey will demand hard choices, disciplined endeavour and a spirit of sacrifice.

39. The plenary session of the Indian National Congress reiterates its unshakeable commitment to our objective of growth with social justice. The vision that beckons to us is the same that inspired Jawaharlal Nehru when he spoke at the Lucknow Congress in 1936. It is the vision of a socialist society, leading to the elimination of social and economic inequalities; material well-being brought about by application of science and technology; intellectual, cultural, moral and spiritual fulfilment of the vast masses, and the creation of a new civilization in which continued development of science and technology blends with the inner repose of the human spirit. This is a task of epic proportions, in which our generation would have to struggle against all odds, reminding itself that each success is but a short step in a long and arduous climb.

40. This centenary session of the Indian National Congress declares unequivocally that anti-poverty programmes constitute the king-pin of our strategy for development. The planning process has already brought about a significant reduction in poverty. It should now be our endeavour to accelerate our drive against this curse and to eliminate it by the close of the century. The Seventh Five Year Plan will be an important bridgehead for the final victory. An essential component of this strategy is the extension of modern agriculture to all regions, all agro-climate zones and all strata of the population. The 20-Point Programme will be implemented with improved efficiency and utmost dedication. The Programme is a challenge to the administrator and the political worker alike. Above all, it is the hope of the millions.

41. This plenary session of the Indian National Congress firmly believes that eradication of poverty will require the rapid and large-scale industrialization of the country. We have already completed the first phase of our industrial revolution. We need to consolidate and to build on it further and faster. To this end, all our efforts need to be made to ensure fuller participation of labour and various factors leading to their well-being and contentment, resulting in the all-round enhancement of the national product.

42. The public sector has played a pioneering role in India's industrialization. It must continue to lead the way. It has to meet the challenge of modernisation, of absorption and development of modern technology, and of efficiency. Further progress on the path of industrialization will depend on the extent to which India's Public Sector masters the problems posed by a variety of vicissitudes, both internal and external.

43. The Indian National Congress expresses its admiration for the remarkable capacity of the Indian farmer for innovation and absorption of modern technology in agriculture. Latest techniques such as bio-technology will further improve the productivity in agriculture. We shall constantly keep pace with modern technology both in agriculture and industry; not to do so would amount to a return to poverty. As in all progressive and vibrant economic, technological upgradation will be our continued endeavour.

44. This plenary session cautions the country to remain vigilant and to be prepared for a continuing all-out effort to strengthen economic independence. This would involve a determined drive to mobilize internal resources for development and what is more important, to use such resources in a disciplined and efficient manner. All waste, extravagance, inefficiency, unethical social behaviour, and inappropriate life styles of vulgar consumption have to be put down with a heavy hand. The road to economic independence is not for the ease loving and the faint-hearted.

45. In the ultimate analysis, as the Prime Minister has said, development is about people. We need to pay much greater attention welcomes the emphasis laid by the 7th Five Year Plan on human resource development. Our policies and programmes pertaining to education, health and family planning, development of women and children, welfare of scheduled castes, scheduled tribes, backward classes and other weaker sections, development of the youth and promotion of physical culture etc. have to be integrated into our succeeding plans as comprehensive strategy to raise the material, intellectual and moral standard of the national community. Programmes of mass literacy, drinking water and housing for the poor have to be intensified. Full employment has to be provided to the population. This is a gigantic task which cannot be accomplished by Government alone. It needs to be made and sustained as a nation-wide movement in which individuals, voluntary organisations and Government have to come together for a meaningful and

systemic effort. This and this alone will promote social cohesion and liberate the Nation's vast energy for social transformation.

46. We live and function in an inter-dependent world. What happens outside our borders inevitably affects us and conditions our choices. The Indian National Congress is fortunate that its leadership was always farsighted enough to grasp the significance of international forces and their essential and underlying relationships. Our policy of non-alignment, fashioned by Jawaharlal Nehru and further creatively development by Indira Gandhi, has served us well. It has kept India out of the vortex of confrontation between the rival blocs. It has helped the cause of disarmament and peace. And it has enabled us to cooperate with all countries, irrespective of their social and political systems, on the basis of mutuality of interest and sovereign equality. This plenary session of the Indian National Congress reiterates its faith in the policy of non-alignment, as the only sane policy for a world troubled by strife, suspicion and replete with the ever-increasing spectre of mankind's total annihilation.

47. This plenary session recalls with pride how consistently India has, both before and after independence, endeavoured for the cause of peace and international cooperation and harmony. Jawaharlal Nehru, Indira Gandhi and now Shri Rajiv Gandhi has articulated the deepest yearning of humanity to remove forever the danger of nuclear war. This session links the voice of hundreds of millions of our people to the voices of peoples all over the world in demanding total nuclear disarmament. It notes that while the Geneva Summit was a positive step, purposeful and determined action has still to begin in this direction. There could be no rest for India until peace is won completely and permanently.

48. The Indian National Congress strongly condemns apartheid which is a continuing outrage on the world's conscience. We lend our full support to the brave people of South Africa who are struggling for freedom and human rights. We applaud the efforts made by the Prime Minister in finding a solution to the problem. The Commonwealth Accord reflects the disenchantment of awakened world opinion with the intransigence of a brutal and insensitive regime. The days of apartheid are numbered. The bell tolls for it. The blood of every innocent victim of this loathsome tyranny hastens its doom. This plenary session hopes that even at this late hour wisdom will prevail and the untold sufferings and hardships of the vast

majority in South Africa will be avoided. We have, however, to be prepared for the decisive blow to racism.

49. Apartheid colludes with colonialism in Namibia. The United Nations resolutions on Namibia have remained a piece of paper. This session extended its hand of solidarity to the people of Namibia in their courageous fight against oppression under SWAPO.

50. The Indian National Congress has always championed the cause of the Palestinian people for their own homeland. Mahatma Gandhi was the first to speak out for them and we have espoused their cause consistently. The Palestine Liberation Organisation is assured of our fullest support in its heroic struggle, as the authentic of Statehood.

51. The Indian National Congress expresses concern at the situation in regard to the ethnic question in Sri Lanka. While India's good office would continue to be available in finding a political solution, the Congress hopes that such a solution will be found before long, that conditions of amity will prevail in this neighbouring country and that the Tamils of Sri Lanka who have become refugees outside Sri Lanka would return to their homes to a life of a society and dignity.

52. The Indian National Congress has always stood against external interference and intervention in the affairs of independent nations. This tendency has enlarged the areas of tension of conflict and has come in the way of mutual cooperation between the developing countries. The non-aligned countries must develop a strong unit of purpose to prevent external influence from weakening their common resolve to build a just and equitable international order.

53. The world economic crisis has brought home to all, except perhaps the privileged few, the inadequacy of existing institutional arrangements. India, along with other non-aligned and developing countries, has campaigned for a dialogue on the changes needed to enable the emergence of a more equitable international economic order. The developing crisis can be resolved only through cooperation between all. To this end we must continue our efforts, even though in the short run the receptivity to new ideas may be limited.

54. India is committed to peace, friendship and amity with its neighbours. This session of the Indian National Congress wholeheartedly endorses efforts

made by the Prime Minister in this direction. The recently concluded SAARC summit in Dhaka has given a new dimension to the prospective of regional cooperation in South Asia.

55. This plenary session of the Indian National Congress is honoured by the presence of delegates of politics parties across the globe. We desire peace, friendship and cooperation with all countries. We express our appreciation and gratitude to all the political parties represented here. We hope that our mutual relations will grow and will help promote better understanding and friendship among our peoples.

56. New challenges confront us as the Congress centers its second century of dedicated service to the people of India. New tasks await us. They call for undiminished commitment to our objectives and policies. They call for determination, faith and courage in implementation. Above all they call for the closest and most intimate liaison of the Congress with the teeming millions of India who are indeed both participants and beneficiaries of the Congress programme. What is needed is not mere cooperation but operation by them since the programme is theirs. This new approach needs to be cultivated. After all, we are not just a conventional political party. We are the proud heirs to a mass movement of unparalleled historical dimensions. We have remained a mass movement for the building of a new India. And we shall continue this basic character of the Indian National Congress.

57. It is our firm belief that the challenge of building a modern society is basically a challenge to the creative energies of our people. We call upon our peasants, workers, scientists, artists, writers, poets to come together once again in a mighty movement to re-fashion our society. We should consciously evolve a new ethic of responsibility. Joint and sincere endeavour, discipline and the spirit of Swadeshi will immeasurably increase the momentum of advance. The Indian National Congress summons, from out of the historical legacy of its monumental work, the cooperation, the unflagging zeal and the unremitting labour of every citizen of this great country in this splendid adventure. While so doing, it also pledges to act indefatigable as the catalyst and the watch-dog of this entire process of transformation on behalf of the people.

58. At this moment of resolve when we set foot in the second century of the Party's existence, let there be no mistake nor doubt as to where we are

heading. Socialism remains our goal, secularism our creed, democracy our faith and non-alignment our credo in human relations across the globe. We dare to translate into reality the dreams of Mahatma Gandhi, Jawaharlal Nehru and Indira Gandhi-combined as the action-oriented dream of Rajiv Gandhi. We will continue the tested policies of the Congress *viz.*, economic self-reliance; primary to the Public Sector; deployment of advanced science and technology in the uplift of the poorest of the poor in the land; frontal attack on poverty until it is eliminated; relentless effort to raise the quality of life of the toiling farmers and workers; social equality; full safeguarding of the rights of the minorities; crash programmes for the development of the scheduled castes, scheduled tribes, women and the vast multitude known as backward classes who, in point of fact, represent or sustain the bulk of productive forces in our society. These are the vast section of our population whose progress, in the ultimate analysis, reflects the nation's.

And we shall endeavour to develop the human resources of India so as to bring about the blossoming forth of the all round personality of each one who is born in this land. Our vision will be riveted on a resplendent future and rooted in our ageless heritage. We shall press a head abreast of the most advanced nations of the world, retaining our age-old position as one of the wisest. We shall weld our nation and the world in general so as to echo the vedic hymn which says:

> सं गच्छध्वं संवदध्वं संवो मनांसि जानताम्।
> देवा भाग़ं यथा पूर्वे संजानाना उपासते।।
> समानो मन्त्रः समितिः समानी समानं व्रतं सह चित्तमेषाम्।
> समानेन वो हविषा जुहोमि समान चेतो अभिसंविशध्वम्।।
> समानी व आकृतिः समाना हृदयानि वः।
> समानमस्तु वो मनो यथा वः सुसहासति।।

> "Move together, speak together, let your minds understand in like manner;
> As the gods known and take their (exact) share;
> Let their prayers be alike, their assemblies alike,
> Common be their purposes, their minds alike;
> I shall make you partake of the same oblation;
> Attain, you all, common intention;
> (o men,) let you resolve be one, let your hearts be one;
> Let your thoughts be one so that there is thorough union amongst you."

59. We shall not falter. We shall not compromise. We shall march to our destiny.

Text of Pachmarhi Declaration: Adopted at brainstorming session of Congress Party on September 6, 1998

THANKING the Madhya Pradesh Congress Committee, its workers and leaders, and the Chief Minister of Madhya Pradesh for the excellent arrangements made for the Vichar Manthan Shivir (Brainstorming Session) at Pachmarhi.

RECALLING the noble heritage of the Party as bequeathed to it by leaders of the stature of Mahatma Gandhi, Pandit Jawaharlal Nehru, Sardar Patel, Maulana Azad, Subhas Chandra Bose, Rajaji, Acharya Kripalani, Perunthalaivar Kamaraj, Shri Lal Bahadur Shastri, Shrimati Indira Gandhi and Shri Rajiv Gandhi, among others too numerous to name individually.

RE-DEDICATING itself to the ideological sentinels of the Party:

- *Democracy,* including the strengthening of the Parliamentary system and the promotion of the third tier of governance through the Panchayats and Nagarpalikas, as enshrined in the Constitution;
- *Secularism,* that is the bedrock of our nationhood, draws its essence from catholicity, humanism and respect for every faith and religious denomination in the world, is consecrated in our Constitution, is the immutable commitment on which our democratic polity rests, and is enshrined in the Congress concept of secularism as defined in the past, the present and will continue into the future;
- *Socialism,* directed to the task of promoting equity and social justice, based on sustained, balanced and high economic growth, through an mixed economy allied to democratic institutions of governance; and
- *Non-alignment,* as relevant as even in the post-Cold War era to the conservation of our sovereignty, and our relentless struggle to end what Shri Rajiv Gandhi called the "quest for dominance" which regrettably continues to characterise international relations;

HAVING SECURED the approval of the Congress Working Committee;

PROCLAIMS the following Plan of Action and calls upon its workers everywhere in the country and abroad to work tirelessly towards the realisation of these goals and objectives:

A. Political

1. Scheduled Castes / Scheduled Tribes / Other Backward Classes / Weaker sections of society / Minorities

Notes with dismay the erosion of the affirmative action taken in favour of these sections of society in accordance with the letter and spirit of the Constitution, and

Pledges itself to vigilance and determined steps to:

(a) forestall and oppose any move to dilute reservations, the filling of vacancies, promotions and preference in government employment for these sections, as established by law.

(b) prevent any discrimination against them, ensure their safety and security and insist on stern action in regard to atrocities inflicted on them, especially their womenfolk;

(c) remove distortions and discrepancies that have crept into the implementation of policies in respect of education, subsidies and assistance in economic and poverty alleviation programmes;

(d) ensure full representation for these sections at all echelons of the Party;

(e) vigoriously pursue the 15 point programme for the Minorities as enunciated by Shrimati Indira Gandhi and reformulated by Shri Rajiv Gandhi;

(f) resolve the Babri Masjid issue expeditiously according to the law and ensure the rigorous observance of the Places of Worship Act which guarantees the status of all places of worship as they stood on Independence Day 1947;

(g) unflinchingly meet the challenge of the communal forces as represented by the BJP and its associates in the Sangh Parivar, such as the RSS, the VHP, and the Bajrang Dal, and those outside, such as the Shiv Sena, with no compromise or dilution of the well-established principles and practice of secularism, defined and evolved by the party as crucial to our nationhood.

2. Women

Regrets the failure of the Government to introduce the Constitution (84th Amendment) Bill, as prepared by Parliament's Joint Select Committee, and seeks its passage at the next session of Parliament on the basis on a broad based consensus among all political parties;

Commits itself to the substantial enhanced representation of women at all echelons of the Party organisation and in the distribution of tickets for elections to the State Assemblies and Parliament.

3. Youth

Notes that 60 per cent of the electorate is below the age of 30.

Recognises the crucial importance of the empowerment of youth as we move into the next millennium:

Underlines the necessity of

- being sensitive to their concerns and relevant to their aspirations,
- involving them in the work of the Party,
- ensuring adequate representation for them in the Party organisation and effective positions.
- and thus rejuvenating itself at the spring of youth, as it has repeatedly done over the last 113 years.

4. Population Control

Notes with concern the inadequacy of attention to the question of voluntary population control;

Decides to make this a key element of the Party programme;

Decides accordingly that any party member who becomes the parent of more than two children after the 1st Jan., 2000 would be ineligible for selection or election to any Party office or for selection as a Party candidate for any election.

5. Proposed Review to the Constitution

Notes the proposal to establish a Commission to review the Constitution;

Expresses it apprehensions regarding the ulterior motives of those piloting this wholly unnecessary proposal at present;

Stresses that the basic structure of the Constitution, including its essential secularism and the Parliamentary system, cannot be altered; and

Calls upon the Government to hold prior consultations with all political parties before taking any decisions on this issue.

6. Electoral Reforms

Decides to appoint a committee to examine electoral reforms with special reference to curbing the use of money and muscle power in elections.

7. Coalitions

Affirms that the Party considers the present difficulties in forming one-party governments a transient phase in the evolution of our polity;

Pledges to restore the Party to its primacy in national affairs;

Decides that coalitions will be considered only when absolutely necessary and that too on the basis of agreed programmes which will not weaken the Party or compromise its basic ideology.

8. National Water Policy

Considers continuing and unresolved disputes over the sharing of river waters a matter of serious concern which impinges upon the progress of the country and even its unity;

Recalls the contribution of Shri Rajiv Gandhi to the elaboration of a National Water Policy;

Decides to accord high priority to the evolution of a policy which will treat river waters as a national asset to be used and developed as a national grid for the welfare of all its people.

9. North-East

Notes with anguish the growing alienation of a section of the people of the North-East from the national mainstream owing to inadequate development;

Resolves to restore priority to the North-East in Party matters and the governance of the nation as it was when the Congress was in office at the centre.

10. Jammu & Kashmir

Views with deep concern the developing situation in the State of Jammu & Kashmir;

Expresses its deep sympathy with the innocent families who have been the tragic victims of militant activities and cross-border terrorism; and

Resolves to ensure that there is no erosion in the secular traditions of the State as secularism has always been the binding and motivating force in the State to which the Congress has consistently contributed since Independence.

11. Uttar Pradesh, Bihar and Tamil Nadu

Notes with concern the weakening of the Party in the States of Uttar Pradesh, Bihar and Tamil Nadu; and

Decides to accord the highest priority to the revival and renewal of the Party in these States.

12. Jain Commission of Inquiry—Follow Up

Expresses its profound concern at the failure of the agencies concerned to investigate the remaining leads identified by the Jain Commission, which have been pointedly brought to the attention of the Government by the Party and which the Government have committed themselves to fully investigating through the proposed Multi Disciplinary Monitoring Agency (MDMA).

Resolves not to rest till the truth, the whole truth and nothing but the truth about the dastardly assassination of its beloved leader, Shri Rajiv Gandhi, and the conspiracy, if any, behind it, is fully and completely revealed, and the guilty parties, whoever they are, punished under the law of the land.

B. Foreign Policy

Decides, to establish, as recommended, two Working Groups within the AICC's Department of Foreign Affairs to deal respectively with:

a. monitoring and preparing policy options on matters related to our neighbourhood, especially with a view to maintaining a sustained dialogue with our neighbours and servicing the party-to-party relations which the Party intends to promote with political parties in neighbouring countries;

b. updating and rendering into treaty language the Action Plan for a Nuclear-Weapons-free and Non-violent World Order presented by Prime Minister Rajiv Gandhi to the Third Special Session of the UN General Assembly on disarmament in 1988, to serve as a basis for discussions between the Party and its interlocutors on global nuclear Issues;

Directs the chairman of the Foreign Affairs Department to take steps towards sending high-powered Party delegations to China and South Africa, as recommended by the Group;

Cautions the Government against taking any precipitate decisions and accending to the CTBT, keeping in mind that no final decisions are called for over the next 12 months and that, in any case, the decision will have to be taken in consultation with all political parties;

Calls for the restoration of the national consensus on foreign policy, disrupted by the BJP-led Government.

C. Economic Affairs

Reassert its commitment to socialism and the socialistic pattern of society as spelled out at Avadi in 1955 and in subsequent resolutions of the Party;

Appreciates the remarkable recovery and impressive economic achievements secured through the reforms of the period 1991-96;

Deplores the squandering of that legacy by successive governments since the Congress demitted office in May 1996;

Reaffirms that the removal of poverty and the empowerment of the poor as effective partners in the growth process is the essence of the Party's economic policy;

Stresses the importance of redefining the role of Government at all levels to make it a more effective instrument of economic change and social transformation.

Commits itself to programmes aimed at the realisation of growth rates of 7 per cent-8 per cent per annum on average through the mixed economy model, adjusted pragmatically to meet the ends of growth with social justice;

Underlines the inescapable importance of conserving the environment to ensure sustainable development;

Demands the control of inflation and the dampening of inflationary expectations;

Urges the revival of investment and employment opportunities through policies that promote savings, productive investment, physical and social infrastructure, productivity and competitiveness, protection to industry against unfair external competition through an effective anti-dumping regime, and effective social security safety nets;

Commits itself to the direct transfer of funds to the Panchayats and Nagarpalikas for anti-poverty programmes in rural and urban areas;

Commits itself also to the reform of the educational system, in particular vocational education, to deal with the priority problem of educated unemployment among youth;

Assures the better targeting of subsidies for the poor, the needy and the disadvantaged, which will be continued and strengthened;

Agrees with the need to persist with a significant role for the public sector but equally with the need to make these viable and genuinely autonomous;

Draws attention to the challenges posed by growing urbanization and calls for special programmes to improve the quality of life in town and cities; and

Emphasises the importance of financial sector reforms, strengthening the small scale sector, energy supplies in all forms, and the centrality of agriculture and rural development in economic policy.

D. Agriculture, Rural Development and Panchayati Raj

Adopts the 35-point Programmes of Action for Agriculture, supplemented by six additional points, as recommended by the Group, dealing, *inter alia*, with larger outlays for agriculture and agriculture-related activities by the public, private and cooperative sectors; ant status of industry to agriculture; water management, including watershed management and a National Water Policy and National Grid for river waters; prevention of fragmentation and sub-division of land holdings combined with the vigorous implementation of land reforms and the maintenance of records of rights of proprietors, tenants and sharecroppers; assured supply of fertilizer, appropriate pesticides and quality seeds; cooperative credit and reasonable rates of interest within the capacity of farmers to pay; bank pass books and credit cards for access to credit; the targeting of agricultural subsidies to farmers not industrial suppliers; comprehensive crop insurance; horticulture and aquaculture; dryland and arid areas technology missions, including urgent attention to nascent problems in the cultivation of oil-seeds; agribusiness; exports of agricultural produce; the urgent passage of the Sui Generis Bill; the end of all harassment to farmers; and the elaboration and adoption of a National Agriculture Policy, etc.

Further adopts the 14 point Programmes of Action for Panchayat Raj, supplemented by one additional point, as recommended by the Group, dealing, *inter alia*, with the finances of the Panchayats in the light of recommendations by the State Finance Commissions and the terms of reference of the Eleventh Finance Commission with regard to the sound finances of the panchayats; the imperative need to elect and establish District Planning Committees, as provided for in the 74th Amendment, to serve as the foundation for the elaboration of the Ninth Five-Year Plan; the effective devolution of the functions delegated to the panchayats in pursuance of the Eleventh Schedule to the Constitution and subsequent State Legislation, including the need to establish a nexus between the functions devolved upon elected local authorities and the funds, as well as administrative and technical personnel, made available to them to carry out these functions; effective and active Gram Sabhas to ensure that Power to the Panchayats becomes Power to the People, as attempted by the Congress Government of Madhya Pradesh through its Panchayat Raj System and its Rajiv Gandhi Missions; free and fair elections, etc.

Pledges the Congress to taking all necessary action to ensure strict adherence to the letter and spirit of Part IX of the Constitution, conceived by Shri Rajiv Gandhi and brought to realisation by the Congress.

E. Organisational Matters

Approves the proposal to establish a Congress Election Authority, composed of eminent, impartial and highly respected senior Congress leaders to ensure free and fair elections at all levels of the Party;

Approves also the short-term and long-term Programmes of Action proposed by the Group for immediate implementation by the Party at all levels within the prescribed time-frames; and

Transmits to the Congress Constitution Review Committee the suggestions made by the Group for strengthening the Party organisation and its frontal organisations, including relations with INTUC.

F. Conclusion

Under the leadership of Shrimati Sonia Gandhi,

Commits itself to becoming again the Party of the brightest and the best, a Party of principles and ideology, a Party of ethics in polities; and thereby

Entitled to primacy in the country's polity as the Party which mirrors the hopes and aspirations of the millions of downtrodden and dispossessed of this country.

Text of the Shimla Sankalp, Shimla, July 9, 2003

Taking stock and reviewing the current political, social and economic situation in the country,

Being concerned with the state of the nation brought about by the massive and glaring failures of the BJP-led NDA government and its divisive policies,

Responding to the public sentiment against the sharp fall in the rate of economic growth, mounting unemployment, stagnant investment, dire distress of kisans and khet mazdoors, increasing neglect of rural India and youth, grievous damage to social harmony and amity, growing jeopardy to defence preparedness and national security, rampant corruption and scams and the erosion of the independence of the country's foreign policy,

Conscious of the uniqueness of the Indian National Congress arising from several basic features of its history, its character, its ideology and the legacy of its leadership,

Continuing to be inspired by the life and the message of Mahatma Gandhi and recalling at this critical moment the yeoman contribution to nation building and social reform of a galaxy of remarkable Congressmen and women like Jawaharlal Nehru, Sardar Patel, Rajendra Prasad, Maulana Azad, Subash Chandra Bose, Rajaji, Acharya Kripalani, Kamaraj, Lal Bahadur Shastri, Indiraji, Rajivji and many other stalwarts,

Appreciating the successful stewardship of the country under successive Congress governments at the centre and in states that have resulted in economic growth and social transformation,

Acknowledging the support, goodwill and affection of all sections of our society, particularly the weaker sections like dalits, adivasis, OBCs, minorities and women,

Taking inspiration from Smt. Sonia Gandhi's inaugural speech at this Vichar Manthan Shivir in which she has spelt out a comprehensive vision, strategy and action programme for our party, from her relentless efforts to give voice, respect and position to the karyakartas across the country, proclaims the following Shimla Sankalp:

Political Challenges

1. The Indian National Congress announces that it stands fully prepared and ready to face the national elections at any time. No sacrifice should be too great for each and every Congressman and woman to ensure defeat of the BJP and its allies in the forthcoming elections. Throughout its annals, the dedication and sacrifices of lakhs of its workers across the length and breadth of this vast country that has sustained the Congress, in and out of power. It will be the dynamism of this committed cadre along with the support of the people that will ensure the victory of the Congress under the leadership of Smt. Sonia Gandhi.

2. The Indian National Congress will launch and sustain a Jan Jagran Abhiyan across the country to expose the BJP-led NDA government's comprehensive and glaring failures on security, defence, communal harmony, economic growth, social welfare, good governance, foreign policy and probity and transparency in public life.

3. The Indian National Congress re-emphasizes its unwavering commitment to fight religious fundamentalism of all kinds. It also reiterates its resolve to combat in as determined a manner as possible the evil and cynical attempts being made by the BJP, the RSS, the VHP and the Bajrang Dal to distort and destroy the liberal and tolerant essence of the Hinduism. It will also ensure that the essence of all great religions and faiths that have flourished for millennia on the soil of our country are protected and respected.

4. The Indian National Congress rededicates itself to strengthening the forces of nationalism that celebrate India?s multiple diversities and nurture its many unities. The Indian National Congress expresses its commitment to the people that the communalization of education will not go unchallenged and that the values of our Freedom Movement, of our Constitution and of our culture will resonate in schools and educational institutions through the Bapu Sadbhavna and Shiksha Trust. It calls upon all like-minded, progressive people to participate in this historic endeavour.

5. The Indian National Congress applauds the courage of the people of Jammu and Kashmir who have reinforced their commitment to secular democracy. It was the sagacity and concern for the welfare of the people of Jammu and Kashmir and the concern for the national interest that led Smt. Sonia Gandhi to agree to the formation of a PDP-led coalition government in J&K. The Indian National Congress accords the highest priority to the success of this coalition and to the formulation and execution of an effective strategy to deal with cross-border terrorism by the Centre. At the same time, the Indian National Congress will forcefully resist all attempts at using the issue of cross-border terrorism to polarise our society on religious and communal lines.

6. The Indian National Congress is committed to the rapid and equitable development of all regions of our vast country. The special challenges and concerns of the people of the northeast will receive our undivided attention. The dangerous and nefarious political game being played by the BJP-led NDA government in collaboration with various insurgent groups will be exposed and resisted determinedly in the larger interests of our country.

7. The Indian National Congress promises the people of the country an accelerated, time-bound programme for the modernisation of defence and a programme for providing full educational and housing facilities to the

families of our armed forces and for the welfare of ex-servicemen and their families as well.

8. The Indian National Congress is firm in its commitment to Jawaharlal Nehru's vision of foreign policy. That framework has in-built flexibility to respond to the dynamics of a changing world keeping our national interests paramount. For the Congress, non-alignment has essentially meant independence in foreign policy. Recalling Rajiv Gandhi's historic efforts for the establishment of the nuclear weapons-free world, the Indian National Congress reiterates its commitment to universal nuclear disarmament. As part of this process, the Congress Party believes in the need for initiating a dialogue with our nuclear neighbours for confidence-building measures and for managing the consequences of nuclearisation.

People-Oriented Governance, Rural Transformation and Social Empowerment

9. The Indian National Congress identifies the following as the core priorities in its agenda of governance in keeping with its beacon Congress Ka Haath, Garib Ke Saath:

- The assurance of reliable power, cheaper credit, better seeds, assured irrigation and remunerative prices to kisans across the country.
- The devolution of funds, functions and functionaries so as to fully empower panchayats and nagarpalikas and make them vibrant institutions of local self-government.
- The enactment of a national rural employment guarantee by law and making employment growth for educated youth the overriding objective of all economic policies.
- The establishment of food and nutrition security for all at more affordable prices and more particularly for the destitute and vulnerable sections of our society and for those living in the poorer and backward regions of the country.
- The introduction of social insurance and other schemes for the protection and welfare of all workers but particularly for those in the unorganized sector who constitute over 93 per cent of our labour force.

- The acceleration of the implementation of land reforms and the initiation of reforms in land laws and record of rights to enable the conversion from the present system of presumptive titles to conclusive titles guaranteed by the state.
- The launching of major programmes for the economic advancement, social empowerment, political representation and legal equality of dalits, adivasis, OBCs and minorities.
- The time-bound implementation of the Mahila Sashaktikaran Sankalp adopted by the AICC on October 1, 2002.
- The start of a purposeful dialogue with private industry on how best India's social diversity could be reflected in the private sector in different ways like reservations and fiscal incentives, how privatization where inevitable can protect the welfare of the weaker sections of society and how government procurement can promote entrepreneurship among dalits and adivasis.
- The introduction of liberal loan and scholarship schemes to ensure that no boy or girl belonging to the weaker sections of society is denied the benefit of school and college education.
- The deepening of fiscal and other economic reforms to make Indian agriculture, industry and services productive and competitive and to increase public investment particularly in irrigation, power, education and health.
- The functioning of government in a completely transparent, responsive and accountable manner with special focus on major administrative, police and judicial reforms.

10. The Indian National Congress recalls with pride that it was Rajiv Gandhi who brought India into the IT, computer and telecom age. The Indian National Congress also recalls with pride that it was a Congress government that launched economic reforms in the early 1990s to consolidate and expand on the gains made in earlier decades. Social mobility and the expansion of the middle class in India is a direct consequence of the Congress's economic policies followed after Independence. The dynamic entrepreneurial base in India is a direct result of the Congress's vision and policies. The Indian National Congress is the only party that integrates pro-poor policies, programmes and perspectives

with the concerns and aspirations of the middle classses and entrepreneurial communities.

11. The Indian National Congress fully recognises that the youth are our country's most precious and productive assets. They will get the Congress's maximum political, social and economic support to realise their aspirations in education, employment and entrepreneurship.

Organisational Reforms

12. The Indian National Congress rededicates itself to a renaissance of the country's political culture along the lines identified in the Congress President's opening speech at this Vichar Manthan Shivir. It renews its commitment to major electoral reforms, among other things, to make party funding more transparent and to combat criminalization of politics.

13. The Indian National Congress decides to establish a national training institute. Every Congressman and woman will go through an annual orientation course on contemporary political, economic and social issues and constructive work.

14. In keeping with the sentiments expressed by the Congress President in her opening speech at Shimla, the Indian National Congress reiterates its firm commitment to giving grassroots workers across the country a respected place in the party organisation.

Conclusion

The Indian National Congress fought for Independence and secured it for our people. We must now fight to preserve it and its time-tested values in their truest form. Our unshakeable commitment is to the politics of principles, to democracy, secularism, economic growth and social empowerment. We now seek the support of the people to bring India back on the path of Progress with Congress under the leadership of Smt. Sonia Gandhi. We invite all progressive-thinking men and women, institutions and political movements who share our understanding of India's past, our concerns with India's present and our vision of India's future to join us in this historic endeavour.

Extracts from the Congress Manifesto 2004

Why Congress?

Managing a nation is about both leadership and values. The strength of the Congress party, and its ability to create a new future for Indians both rich and poor, young and old, urban and rural, and for its men and women, lies in the extraordinary qualities of both its leaders and the values that it espouses.

Our leaders have had the ability to see the future. Whether it was Jawaharlal Nehru, who had a vision of an Independent India or the young Rajiv Gandhi who had a dream of a 21st century India, this is a party that has always had leaders with ability too see the future. Their greatness lay in the fact that, beyond merely crafting a vision, each of these leaders had the ability to manage the process of driving the country so that it was able to translate their vision in to a shared reality.

Today every Indian can say with pride that the India he\she is living in today is the result of the dreams and implementation capabilities of a host of great Congress leaders, who created modern India over the last 50 years of independence. The vision of a 21st century where a powerful and prosperous, peaceful and progressive united India, will be among the great global powers, is what drives the Congress party even today. We have the blueprint that works. It is one that has already had several elements put in to practice. Yes, a few years may have been lost in the interim, but today we stand once again poised to translate the next elements in that vision into glorious future for a powerful and resurgent India.

Values, that are an integral part of the Indian civilization and ethos, must always be part and parcel of leadership that can bind a country together. The divisive forces that we have been witness to in the last few years have the potential of tearing asunder the fabric of our nation. Parties that merely attempt to focus on growth and do not worry or even share concerns about the social consequences of change, tend to damage the values that have built this nation into one coherent whole. The ideology for tomorrow that the Congress party espouses, includes both values that bind and growth patterns that work. This is the tomorrow from the party of tomorrow. Join us now in this endeavour.

Lok Sabha Elections 2004 Manifesto of The Indian National Congress—The Congress Party's Priorities, Plans and Programmes

Change with Continuity

Congress policies have always been anchored in a vision of an economically prosperous, socially just, politically united and culturally harmonious India. These policies have never been reduced by rote to a mindless doctrine or empty dogma or simplistic mantra. The Congress has always created space for change. It has always been pragmatic. It has always been ready to respond to new challenges. In consequence, steadfastness to basic principles has never impeded responsiveness to new requirements.

The **1950s** needed land reforms, community development, the public sector and the building of agricultural, industrial, irrigation, educational, scientific and other infrastructure. The Congress ensured that this happened.

The **1960s and 1970s** needed a direct attack on poverty, a whole new approach to agricultural growth and rural employment, the exploration and exploitation of domestic sources of oil, and the nationalization of banks to meet the requirements of not just big business houses but also give priority to farmers, weavers, cottage industries and small industries and traders, as also to fulfill social needs and aspirations. The Congress ensured that all this happened.

The **1980s** needed renewed emphasis on science and technology to solve the problems of the people, and the modernization of industry to ready India to meet the new challenges of the 21st century. It also required India to be ushered into the electronics, computers and telecommunications age in a significant way. The Congress ensured that this happened.

The **1990s** needed bolder economic retorms and liberalization and a much larger role for the private sector to accelerate growth and promote India's integration into a rapidly-changing world economic system. A redefinition of the role of government in economic development, including Constitutionally-sanctioned Panchayati Raj Institutions and municipalities to function as units of local self-government was also needed. The Congress ensured that this happened.

The Congress makes a solemn commitment to the people of India: to restore peace among all of its peoples, to strengthen the secular order through emphasis on social harmony, cultural pluralism and respect for the rule of law, and to ensure a bright and secure economic future for every family in our country.

THE LAW OF THE LAND WILL BE ENFORCED WITHOUT FEAR OR FAVOUR TO ENSURE THAT SOCIAL HARMONY AND COHESION IS MAINTAINED THROUGHOUT THE COUNTRY. THERE WILL BE NO COMPROMISE ON THIS.

Six Basics

The Congress's six basics for governance:

- *Samajik Sadhbavna* to ensure social cohesion and harmony by taking the strictest possible action against those who promote bigotry and hatred;
- *Yuva Rozgar* to accelerate growth of productive and secure employment opportunities by around one crore a year so that each family has a viable livelihood;
- *Grameen Vikas* to improve the income and welfare of kisans and khet mazdoors across the country;
- *Arthik Navotthan* to unleash the creative energies of our professionals and entrepreneurs, the cutting edge of our middle class;
- *Mahila Sashaktikaran* to provide for the political empowerment and full educational, economic and legal equality for women;
- *Saman Avsar* to provide for equality of opportunity in every way for dalits, adivasis, OBCs and religious and linguistic minorities.

These six priorities constitute the foundation of all policies of the Congress.

The Congress has consistently maintained that liberalisation and globalisation can be meaningful only if they are aimed at local-level economic and social transformation that directly benefits the poor in rural and urban India, bringing prosperity to the 6 lakh-odd villages of India and improving the living conditions of the urban poor.

The Congress will broaden and deepen economic reforms. The over-riding objective will be to attain and sustain year after year a 8-10 per cent rate of economic growth and to spread this growth over all sectors, particularly agriculture and industry. An annual growth rate of less than 4-4.5 per cent in agriculture and 10 per cent in industry is simply unacceptable.

Rozgar

The priority requirement for accelerated employment generation is to revive economic growth and sustain it across the country at between 8-10 per cent per year for well over a decade. This will be the Congress's overall objective. Faster and broad-based economic growth is an essential pre-requisite for accelerating employment generation. The Congress will also adopt policies to expand employment in the organized sector, which has fallen precipitously in the last five years. Fiscal incentives to promote employment-intensive growth will be introduced.

Continued growth in agriculture will create new employment opportunities. This is particularly so in the central, eastern and northeastern regions of the country which have still to realize their full agricultural potential. New jobs will also be created in other areas of rural development like horticulture, aquaculture, afforestation, dairying and agro-processing. These need and will be provided new investment, credit, marketing and technology inputs. A stable long-term export policy for agricultural products and commodities will be announced.

The Congress will revamp the functioning of the Khadi and Village Industries Commission (KVIC) so as to make it a modern, research-based, technology-driven, customer-focussed organization. New programmes for the modernization of the coir industry, handlooms, power-looms, handicrafts, food processing, sericulture, wool development, leather, pottery, etc., will be launched.

A national Employment Guarantee Act will be enacted immediately. This will provide a legal guarantee for at least 100 days of employment on asset-creating public works programmes every year at minimum wage, for every rural household.

A greater thrust on labour-intensive exports of textiles, handicrafts, gems and jewelry, leather, software, engineering and consumer goods will also significantly boost employment. The textile industry will receive special focus in view of the increased competition in world markets from January 2005 as mandated by the WTO.

The concerns of small-scale industry like shortage of working capital, lack of technology and marketing, delayed payments, harassment by inspectors will be addressed expeditiously. A cluster approach to the development of small-scale industry will be adopted.

Along with vastly expanded credit facilities for self-employment, the services industry will be given all support to fulfill its true employment potential. This includes not just software and IT-enabled services, not just trade, distribution and transport, not just financial and telecommunications services but also tourism. Special infrastructural facilities for substantially expanding international and domestic tourism will be created. Reforms of laws and regulations that stand in the way of growth of the services industry will be undertaken.

The Congress will also establish a National Commission to monitor the functioning of enterprises in the informal sector, the problems they face in access to technology, credit and markets and recommend corrective measures on an on-going basis.

To enhance the employability of our youth, systematic efforts will be made to vocationalise secondary education and to establish at least one industrial training institute in each development block of the country through creative public-private partnerships. The employment exchange machinery will be revamped to provide a closer linkage between demand and supply for labour.

As an indicator of how seriously the Congress takes its commitment to employment growth, an annual Rozgar Report to the Nation will be prepared and released on May 1.

Women and Children

The Congress pledges to press for the Constitutional Amendment to reserve one-third of seats in the Lok Sabha and in Vidhan Sabhas for women.

It will launch a movement for the effective implementation of social legislation such as for minimum age at marriage, anti-dowry, curbing atrocities on women, anti-sati, widow welfare, etc., as well as for minimum wages for enhancing women's welfare. Stern measures will be taken to ensure the elimination of female foeticide and infanticide. Marriage registration will be made mandatory.

Thirty per cent of all funds flowing into panchayats and nagarpalikas will be earmarked for programmes relating to the development of women and children and focus on the special needs of female agricultural labour and women cultivators. Village women and their associations will be empowered to assume responsibility for all development schemes relating to drinking water supply, sanitation, primary education and health, nutrition, biogas, maintenance of water pumps and borewells and farm forestry.

Complete legal equality for women in all spheres will be made a practical reality, especially by removing discriminatory legislation, by giving them equal share in matrimonial property, by protecting their rights to matrimonial homes and *streedhan*, by giving them equal rights of ownership of assets like houses-and land, etc. All states will be encouraged to set up family courts at the earliest.

There will be a major expansion in schemes for micro-finance based on self-help groups, especially for tribal women, women belonging to scheduled castes, women below the poverty line, rural women and women in distress, and particularly in the backward and ecologically sensitive regions and actively encourage the functioning of producer and marketing cooperatives

Some states of India, particularly in the South, have already reached replacement levels of fertility while other states will do so over this decade. But on present reckoning, four-five states of India will be unable to reach this crucial milestone for decades. The Congress will take the lead in replicating the success of other states in those states where population growth continues unabated. Population planning is not just a government programme but must become a movement of civil society as well. A sharply targeted mobilization effort will be mounted in the 150-odd districts that still have unacceptably high levels of fertility.

Panchayati Raj

Panchayat bodies that got Constitutional sanction a decade ago because of the vision and relentless zeal of Rajiv Gandhi, now need full devolution of funds, functions and functionaries. Globalisation and economic reforms must be based on strong, effective and empowered institutions of local self-government.

The Congress will ensure that all funds for poverty alleviation and rural development programmes will be credited directly to panchayat bodies. The Gram Sabha will be empowered to emerge as the foundation of the panchayati raj system. Appropriate audit systems would be established to ensure sound financial administration at the local level.

Extracts from the Congress Manifesto 2009

Why Congress?

These are national elections.

While there will be regional, state-level and local issues that are important, these are elections for a government at the Centre, one that will govern all of India, in its many diversities and fulfill its multitude of hopes and aspirations.

It is only the Indian National Congress that is anchored in the larger vision of India as a nation, while at the same time being sensitive to regional and local sentiments.

It is only the Indian National Congress that has demonstrated its commitment to a strong Centre, to strong States, and to strong panchayats and nagarpalikas. India's political system must have space for institutions at each of these three levels. Each has a vital and specific role to play.

The Indian National Congress is fighting these elections in alliance with like-minded parties in some States. These parties share the progressive vision and values of the Congress. Over the past five years, the Indian National Congress has managed a coalition government at the Centre, accommodating the views of its partners but without compromising on any of the essential principles of nation-building.

Even so, what India needs most today—what every Indian needs most today–at the national level is a party with an All-India perspective and with an All-India presence. The Indian National Congress is the only such party.

The Indian National Congress is the party that, under the leadership of Mahatma Gandhi, led our people into freedom from colonial rule. It is the party whose leadership, by the admission of Dr. Ambedkar himself, made our Constitution possible.

The Indian National Congress is the party that, under the leadership of Jawaharlal Nehru, established the foundations of the modern Indian nation-state with its abiding commitment to parliamentary democracy, secularism, economic development, and science and technology.

Learning from experience at every step, the Indian National Congress is the party that has responded creatively to the challenges of the times through the establishment of a vast public sector manufacturing base in the fifties; through bank nationalization and the Green and White Revolutions spearheaded by Indira Gandhi in the late-sixties and seventies; through prudent liberalization and the IT Revolution created by Rajiv Gandhi in the eighties; bolder economic reforms in the nineties; and unprecedented economic growth over the past five years. It is the only party that is forward-looking, the only party that believes a better future is the right of every Indian.

The achievements of India since 1947 are the achievements of its people – of its farmers and farm labour, its organized sector and unorganized sector workers, its managers, its scientists and engineers, its teachers, doctors and other professionals, its entrepreneurs and businesspersons. It has been the privilege of the Indian National Congress to have provided the political leadership that heralded these accomplishments under the Prime Ministerships of Jawaharlal Nehru, Lal Bahadur Shastri, Indira Gandhi, Rajiv Gandhi, Narasimha Rao and Dr. Manmohan Singh.

The Way Forward

The Indian National Congress says what it means and means what it says. The Indian National Congress promises what it can do and will do what it promises. The Indian National Congress is irrevocably committed to ensuring that government functions in the interest of the people for whom it exists and for whom it works.

The Indian National Congress has always believed that the correct approach to governance is to address the daily concerns of the people and solve their problems. It is to be responsive and accountable to the needs of the people. It is that governance is a partnership between the electors and the elected and that the perceived gap between the people and those in power must be significantly narrowed.

Dr. Manmohan Singh as Prime Minister has led the country with dignity and firm resolve. His integrity, maturity and wisdom, together with his unique expertise and experience, makes him best qualified to lead the nation and handle the many challenges that India faces, both at home and abroad.

Towards Faster and more Inclusive Growth

The Indian National Congress is fully aware that the world economy faces the worst crisis in 50 years. This crisis has been caused by a failure of financial markets in the USA and in other developed countries. However, the Indian economy has shown considerable resilience under the most adverse international circumstances. This is the outcome of the policies of successive Congress governments. This is the direct result of a vibrant public sector that is the legacy of Jawaharlal Nehru, government ownership of banks that is the legacy of Indira Gandhi, and a strong private sector that matured and flowered during the tenure of Rajiv Gandhi and thereafter.

The average rate of economic growth during the self-declared India Shining period of the BJP was just 5.8 per cent per year, as compared to 8.5 per cent during the five year tenure of the Congress-led UPA government. 2008-09 has proved to be a difficult year for growth, yet the Indian economy will grow at about 7 per cent. That is why our immediate priority is to revive the economy and restore the high growth witnessed in the first four years of the Congress-led UPA Government.

The Indian National Congress will put in place measures to ensure that the momentum of growth is maintained. Three stimulus packages have already been announced. Interest rates have been reduced. Credit flows to industry have been encouraged and assured. The impact of these policies will be felt in the coming weeks and months.

The focus of the new measures will be to stimulate demand in the domestic economy and to ensure that there is more purchasing power in the hands of the people and more liquidity in the hands of companies. Public investment in agriculture and infrastructure, which has increased appreciably over the past five years, will be stepped up further. Within 45 days of forming the new Government, the Indian National Congress will present the regular Budget for the year 2009-10 with the basic objective of returning to the path of faster and more inclusive growth, which is so essential for fulfilling all our social and economic objectives.

In keeping with the promises made in our 2004 Manifesto, the Congress-led UPA government had set up a number of very important commissions including the Administrative Reforms Commission, the National Commission on Enterprises in the Unorganised Sector, the National Farmers Commission, the National Knowledge Commission and the National Manufacturing Competitiveness Council. Their valuable recommendations will be taken up for implementation in a systematic manner and without any delay.

The Work Programme: 2009-2014

In addition to consolidating and taking forward the numerous missions, programmes and schemes launched during 2004-2009, the Indian National Congress makes the following solemn promises to the people of our country.

- *We will guarantee the maximum possible security to each and every citizen.*

Our policy is zero-tolerance towards terrorism from whatever source it originates. We have already initiated the process of equipping our police and other specialist security forces with the latest weapons and technology to meet terrorist threats. This process will be taken forward vigourously. More specialist battalions will be raised and positioned in key locations across the country.

Citizenship is a right and a matter of pride. With the huge IT expertise available in our country, it is possible to provide every Indian with a unique identity card after the publication of the national population register in the year 2011.

- *We will ensure the highest level of defence preparedness and also take further steps for the welfare of the defence forces and their families.*

During the BJP-led NDA government, over Rs. 24,000 crores of funds meant for defence modernisation were simply not spent. In the last five years, modernisation of our defence forces has resumed substantially. This will continue at a rapid pace. The Indian National Congress also pledges to make India's defence forces technology-enabled and equipped with modern weapons, aircraft, ships and delivery systems to repel any threat from land, sea or air.

Recognizing their special concerns, a new and separate department of ex-servicemen's welfare was established in 2004 by the Congress-led UPA Government. Ex-servicemen constitute a large cadre of dedicated and trained persons. We will utilize them extensively in crucial nation-building tasks.

- *We will accelerate the process of police reforms.*

The Indian National Congress recognizes the imperative of police reforms. A clear distinction between the political executive and police administration will be made. The police force will be better provisioned especially in the matter of housing and education facilities; the police force will be made more representative of the diversity our population; and police recruitment will be made more effective and training professionalized to confront new and emerging threats. Accountability of the police force will be institutionalized.

- *We will build on the success of the NREGA and take the scheme forward.*

The National Rural Employment Guarantee Act, first promised by the Indian National Congress in its 2004 Lok Sabha elections manifesto, has been an outstanding success.

While drawing on the lessons of various social audits, the Indian National Congress now pledges at least 100 days of work at a real wage of Rs. 100 a day for everyone as an entitlement under the NREGA.

- *Along the lines of NREGA, we will enact a National Food Security Act.*

The Indian National Congress pledges to enact a Right to Food law that guarantees access to sufficient food for all people, particularly the most vulnerable sections of society. The Indian National Congress pledges that every family living below the poverty line either in rural or urban areas will be entitled, by law, to 25 kgs of rice or wheat per month at Rs. 3 per kg. Subsidised community kitchens will be set up in all cities for homeless people and migrants with the support of the Central government.

- *We will guarantee health security for all.*

The National Rural Health Mission has already begun to make a noticeable impact and will be implemented with an even greater sense of urgency. The Rashtriya Swasthya Bima Yojana (RSBY) introduced by the Congress-led UPA Government offers health insurance for poor families. Expenditure on health is a major cause of indebtedness, particularly in rural areas. The Indian National Congress pledges that every family living below the poverty line will be covered by the RSBY over the next three years. Every district headquarters hospital will be upgraded to provide quality heath facilities to all.

- *We will ensure comprehensive social security to those at special risk.*

The Indian National Congress will ensure a comprehensive cover of social security to all persons who are at special risk including: (i) single-woman headed households; (ii) disabled and the elderly; (iii) urban homeless; (iv) released bonded workers; (v) members of primitive tribal groups; and (vi) members of designated "most backward" dalit communities.

- *We will be make quality education affordable to everyone.*

India today has one of the largest educational loan programmes in the world. Over the past five years, over 15 lakh students have received loans totaling more than Rs. 26,000 crores and are pursuing various professional courses.

The Indian National Congress now pledges that all students admitted to any recognized course in any recognized college/university will be provided, on a need basis, either a scholarship or an educational loan without collateral repayable over a very long period.

In order to ensure quality school education for all children, we have already made a beginning by approving the setting up of one model school in every block of the country. Every year, over the next five years, we will add one more model school in every block.

The Indian National Congress pledges to focus more sharply on outcomes and achievement levels in education and not just on enrolment. It also pledges a major programme for training of teachers and improving the physical environment in schools.

A massive expansion in higher education has been undertaken in the past two years—8 new IITs, 7 new IIMs, 5 new Indian Institutes of Science Education and Research, 30 new Central Universities, 20 new Indian Institutes of Information Technology and 374 new colleges in educationally-deprived districts. The Indian National Congress pledges to ensure that these expansion plans are implemented fully with their twin focus on excellence and affirmative action.

- *We will implement a nation-wide skill development programme.*

India is a young country with 70 per cent of the population below the age of 35. To reap the "demographic dividend", the Indian National Congress believes that there is an urgent need to put in place an extensive skill development programme so that the employability of youth is enhanced. The Congress-led UPA government has already put in place a National Skills Development Mission. Rs. 30,000 crore will be invested in this mission which is of crucial importance for the future of our youth. Funds will be provided to ensure its widest possible coverage. A wider and more comprehensive spectrum of skills will be imparted.

- *We will expand schemes for improving well-being of farmers and their families.*

In addition to continuing the programmes that were launched over the past five years, the Indian National Congress pledges that every small and marginal farmer in the country will have access to bank credit at lower rates of interest. While the massive loan waiver scheme has already been implemented and 3.68 crore farmer-families have benefited from it, the Indian National Congress now pledges to extend interest relief to all farmers who repay bank loans on schedule.

The Indian National Congress is determined to ensure that farming becomes a profitable occupation. All measures in support of this objective will be taken. Programmes for agricultural diversification, agri-processing and rural industrialization will be pursued systematically. Dairying, aquaculture, fisheries, horticulture and sericulture will receive an additional boost. The special needs of crops like tea, coffee, rubber, spices, cashew and coconut will be met. A renewed emphasis will be placed on wasteland development and afforestation.

The Indian National Congress will implement comprehensive crop insurance schemes and will also examine the feasibility of direct income support to farmers in the ecologically vulnerable regions of the country. Minimum Support Price (MSP) and procurement will be ensured at the doorsteps of farmers.

All controls on the free movement of farm commodities and processing of agricultural products and all regulations that depress incomes of farmers will be systematically eliminated.

The Indian National Congress is firmly committed to ensuring that farmers get, at a very minimum, market rates for the land that is acquired for industrial projects. The Indian National Congress also believes that farmers should be given an option to become stakeholders in such industrial ventures. As a matter of priority, the National Rehabilitation and Resettlement Bill, 2007, that could not be passed because of the obstructionist tactics of the BJP, will be taken up for passage in the 15th Lok Sabha. The Land Acquisition Act, 1894 will also be amended to ensure that the interests of land-owners are more than adequately protected.

- *We will democratize and professionalize the functioning of cooperatives.*

The Indian cooperative movement comprising about 5 lakh cooperatives with more than 22 crore members is the largest such movement in the world. It plays a crucial role in our development. The Indian National Congress has always stood for its democratic, autonomous and professional functioning and this will be ensured by enacting appropriate laws, including making a Constitutional provision.

- *We will give even greater impetus to the empowerment of weaker sections of society.*

The empowerment of the weaker sections of society—scheduled castes, scheduled tribes, OBCs, minorities and women—has been an article of faith with the Indian National Congress. This will be carried forward with emphasis on education, particularly skill-based and professional education.

Education at all stages—primary, secondary and university—will be free in all respects for boys and girls belonging to dalit and adivasi communities.

Coaching fees for all entrance exams for at least one lakh scheduled caste/ scheduled tribe students every year will be paid by the Central Government. National scholarships for boys and girls belonging to scheduled castes and scheduled tribes will be further increased.

The Indian National Congress will take steps to ensure that allocations under the Special Component Plan for scheduled castes and the Tribal Sub-Plan for scheduled tribes (first introduced by Indira Gandhi over three decades ago) are made in accordance with their proportions in the population.

An unprecedented special drive was launched by the Prime Minister and over 53,000 vacancies in government have been filled through direct recruitment or promotion of members belonging to scheduled castes and scheduled tribes. This drive will continue.

The Indian National Congress is deeply committed to pursuing affirmative action for scheduled castes and scheduled tribes in the private sector. It has already initiated a national debate on this issue. It also pledges to carve out a reservation for the economically weaker sections of all communities without prejudice to existing reservations for scheduled castes, scheduled tribes and OBCs.

For the first time, a separate Ministry of Minority Affairs was created in May 2004 and the Rajinder Sachar Committee was set up to look into the social, economic and educational status of the Muslim community in the country. The implementation of the recommendations of the Sachar Committee is already under way and an Equal Opportunity Commission will be established by law. Nearly four lakh scholarships have been awarded over the past two years alone for pre-matric, post-matric and professional courses, with more than 50 per cent of these being awarded to girl students. The Prime Minister's 15-point programme was launched in June 2006 with physical and financial targets for minorities in all welfare programmes of the Central Government. A special development package for the 90 minority-concentration districts in different states has been introduced.

The Indian National Congress is irrevocably committed to ensuring that the Constitutional rights of all minorities are protected fully, that the representation of minorities in public administration increases substantially, and that minorities recognize that the government is working for their welfare at all times. The Indian National Congress has pioneered reservations for minorities in Kerala, Karnataka and Andhra Pradesh in government employment and education on the basis of their social and economic backwardness. We are committed to adopt this policy at the national level. A Wakf Development Corporation will be established to develop wakf properties. A National Unani University will be set up. The corpus of the Maulana Azad Educational Foundation will be doubled.

The Indian National Congress introduced reservation for women in panchayats and nagarpalikas. Today, about 40 per cent of the elected representatives in panchayats are women, compared to a reservation of 33 per cent mandated for them. This is nothing short of a quiet revolution. The Indian National Congress will ensure that the Bill for reserving 33 per cent of the seats in the Lok Sabha and the State legislatures is passed in the 15th Lok Sabha and that the elections to the 16th Lok Sabha are held on the basis of one-third reservation for women.

Over the next five years, the Indian National Congress will endeavour to ensure that at least half of the country's rural women population will be enrolled as members of self-help groups linked with banks and that they will get loans from banks at moderate interest rates. The Indian National Congress also proposes to reserve one-third of all central government jobs for women.

The Indian National Congress believes that, in addition to education, business development programmes are needed on a larger-scale for scheduled castes, scheduled tribes and women. Preferential policies will be adopted in government contracts to stimulate entrepreneurial activities amongst these groups.

Social security schemes for occupations like weavers, fishermen and fisherwomen, toddy tappers, leather workers, plantation labour, construction labour, mine workers and beedi workers will be expanded.

The Indian National Congress is deeply committed to ensuring equality of opportunity and full participation of persons with disabilities, including the blind, in all sectors of life. To begin with, a comprehensive review of laws and programmes will be undertaken and the shortcomings noticed in their implementation will be removed.

- *We will combat communalism of all kinds and caste atrocities with determination.*

The Indian National Congress reiterates its unflinching resolve to combat communalism of all kinds and to deal ruthlessly with those perpetrating atrocities on weaker sections like dalits and women. The Indian National Congress believes in ensuring the right to compensation and rehabilitation for all victims of communal, ethnic and caste violence on standards and levels that are binding on every government. The Indian National Congress will propose a law that empowers the National Human Rights Commission to monitor investigation and trial in all cases of communal and caste violence.

The Indian National Congress will bring school curricula of various communal and sectarian organizations—regardless of their affiliation—under the regulatory purview of an empowered national body.

- *We will bring a sharp focus on the special needs of children, especially the girl child.*

For the first time, a National Commission for Protection of Child Rights was established in 2006. The Commission's mandate is to ensure that the welfare of children as guaranteed by various laws is protected and promoted. New laws have also been passed to prohibit child labour and child marriage. New schemes to improve the nutritional status of children, especially girls, and to educate them have been launched in the past five years. Over 18 lakh anganwadi workers and helpers have benefited from an increase in their remuneration last year.

The Indian National Congress commits itself to the universalisation of the ICDS by March 2012 and to provide an *anganwadi* in every habitation and full coverage of children up to the age of six for food, nutrition and pre-school education. The special requirements of children of migrant workers in towns and cities will be met through new programmes in association with civil society organizations. A number of programmes have already been launched to combat the still widely-prevalent phenomenon of child malnutrition and these will be infused with an even greater sense of urgency.

The Indian National Congress will introduce special incentives for the girl child to correct the adverse sex ratio and to ensure education of girl children. Girl children in districts that have an adverse sex ratio and/or low enrolment of girls, monetary incentives will be given to the girl child to be credited to the girl child's account on her completing primary school, middle school, secondary school and higher secondary school.

- *We will make elected panchayat institutions financially strong.*

Thanks entirely to the tireless efforts of Rajiv Gandhi, there are some 2,50,000 elected panchayat bodies all over the country with almost 32 lakh elected representatives. It is through such institutions that we will ensure inclusive governance which is essential for inclusive economic growth. The Indian National Congress is unwavering in its commitment to full Constitutionally-mandated devolution of funds, functions and functionaries to the panchayats. The annual allocations to gram panchayats that can be used for purposes designated as priority by the gram sabha will be substantially stepped up.

The Indian National Congress will also upgrade the technical capabilities of panchayat institutions and ensure that information technology is used extensively to enhance their effectiveness.

- *We will connect all villages to a broadband network in three years time.*

While connectivity across the country has increased manifold in recent years, the Indian National Congress pledges to bring the fruits of the IT revolution to more cities and towns. It also pledges to connect every village to a broadband network within three years. This will help locate new, non-agricultural jobs in villages and open vast new opportunities for our rural youth. Thus the vision of Rajiv Gandhi—the use of IT for rural transformation—will be realized in even greater measure. Already, IT is being used in areas like computerization of land records but we now promise a bolder, time-bound initiative.

- *We will give special focus to the small entrepreneur and to small and medium enterprises.*

Small and medium enterprises and the self-employed are the backbone of our industrial and service economy. They are the major generators of productive employment for our youth. The Indian National Congress pledges a "new deal" for SMEs and for first-generation entrepreneurs by assuring them greater access to collateral-free credit, liberating them from the multiplicity of laws and forms, and freeing them from the clutches of inspectors.

The Indian National Congress pledges a targeted cluster-based approach to the growth of SMEs. There are a very large number of such clusters already in different areas like textiles, food processing, handlooms and handicrafts, consumer goods, khadi, coir and other traditional industries, and engineering. These clusters, mostly in small and medium towns, will be given access to finance, technology and marketing and will be provided vastly improved infrastructure.

- *We will maintain the path of high growth with fiscal prudence and low inflation.*

As the experience of 2004-2009 demonstrates so vividly, rapid economic growth creates opportunities for increased government expenditure in vital areas like education, health, agriculture, social security and infrastructure. Average growth in the first four years of the Congress-led UPA government was 9 per cent per year for the first time in our history. We will strive to maintain this momentum with a relentless emphasis on growth that accelerates the generation of productive jobs for our youth. The Indian National Congress is also firmly committed to maintaining high growth with low inflation, particularly in relation to prices of essential agricultural and industrial commodities.

The Indian National Congress reiterates its commitment to the path of fiscal responsibility so that the ability of the Centre to invest in essential social and physical infrastructure is continuously enhanced. This will require that all subsidies reach only the truly needy and poor sections of our society. The Indian National Congress will continue its efforts to create and implement a national consensus on this issue.

Both the public sector and private sector are essential for India's continued high growth success story. The Indian National Congress rejects the policy of blind privatization followed by the BJP-led NDA government, but believes that the Indian people have every right to own part of the shares of public sector companies while the government retains majority shareholding. Public sector enterprises in the manufacturing sector (like energy, transport and telecom) and in the financial sector (like banks and insurance companies) will remain in the public sector and will be given all support to grow and become competitive.

The manufacturing industry in India has seen a revival in recent years and this will be sustained and deepened, particularly labour-intensive manufacturing. The emphasis in all foreign investment policies will be maximization of local value-addition and export potential. The Indian National Congress will ensure that the policies it has put in place for attracting private investment for oil exploration will also be followed for other mineral resources, including coal and iron-ore.

The Indian National Congress remains committed to ensuring the highest standards of corporate governance in private companies, especially to protect the interests of small shareholders and small investors. Regulations will be made to ensure good corporate governance, ethical business practices and accountability to all stakeholders.

- *We will introduce the goods and services tax from April 1, 2010.*

The Congress-led UPA government successfully implemented VAT throughout the country. This has brought abundant revenues to all States. The Indian National Congress now pledges to take the next decisive step and introduce a moderate goods and services tax (GST). Once GST is implemented, all other central and state-level indirect taxes such as VAT, excise duty, service tax, entertainment tax, luxury tax, etc. will stand abolished and bring substantial relief to the *aam admi*. GST will create a seamless national common market for our farmers, artisans and entrepreneurs and will boost employment. State finances, and more importantly the finances of panchayats and nagarpalikas, will be put on a sound foundation.

- *We will give a completely new look to urban governance.*

While the bulk of our population still lives and works in villages, India is rapidly urbanizing. But the provision of basic infrastructure in towns and cities has not kept pace with its requirements. A massive programme of low-cost social housing and sanitation is needed to make our urban areas more livable. Recognizing that our towns and cities are engines of creativity and innovation, the Indian National Congress pledges to create a new model of urban administration with financially-viable self-government institutions as the pivot.

- *We will offer a new deal to our youth to participate in governance.*

The Indian National Congress has always been the party that has reposed its confidence in youth. It was Rajiv Gandhi who gave all 18 year-olds the right to vote and it was he who declared Swami Vivekananda's birthday on January 12th as National Youth Day. The IT revolution that has spread in our country has opened up whole new avenues for our youth.

The Indian National Congress will design and launch a voluntary national youth corps which would enable young men and women in the age group of 18-23 to serve up to two years in constructive nation-building activities for which they will be suitably compensated.

The Indian National Congress will also make a beginning to induct youth into organs of government. As a beginning, it will reserve a proportion of seats in panchayats and nagarpalikas for men and women below the age of 35 years without detriment to the existing reservations for scheduled castes, scheduled tribes, OBCs and women.

The Indian National Congress has periodically renewed itself by inducting young men and women into the Party and entrusting them with responsibilities. Under the leadership of Rahul Gandhi, the Indian National Congress has launched a unique exercise to bring youth from all sections of society and all walks of life into the political mainstream through the Indian Youth Congress (IYC) and the National Students Union of India (NSUI). For the very first time in any political party, there are hundreds of elected youth leaders in Punjab and Uttarakhand. This exercise is now being conducted in Gujarat and Tamil Nadu and will soon encompass other parts of the country. This is a practical demonstration of the deep commitment of the Indian National Congress to open new political space and opportunities to our youth.

- *We will protect India's natural environment and take steps to rejuvenate it.*

The Indian National Congress has declared the sacred Ganga as a "national river". The Ganga River Basin Authority has been established with the Prime Minister at its head for ensuring that development needs are met in an ecologically sustainable manner. This Authority will be accorded the highest priority. Water security is of paramount concern to the Indian National Congress and steps will be taken to enhance it measurably for local communities.

India has an enormously rich biodiversity that is under threat on account of various reasons. The Indian National Congress commits itself to strengthening people's movements whose objective will be to protect and preserve our bio-resources and ensure their sustainable use.

Climate change has now emerged as a serious challenge for the world community. India too has begun to feel its impact in different ways. The Congress-led UPA government has already unveiled a National Action Plan for Climate Change. It is an acknowledgment of our responsibility to take credible actions within the overall framework of meeting the development aspirations of our people for higher economic growth and a higher standard of living. This action plan will be implemented in letter and spirit.

- *We will carry out a massive renewal of our extensive science and technology infrastructure.*

One of the most outstanding legacies of Jawaharlal Nehru is the vast infrastructure for science and technology that India possesses and which has made so many far-reaching contributions to the country's progress—in agriculture, nuclear energy, defence, space, industry, energy, telecom and IT. The Indian National Congress is firmly commited to extend full support to the modernization and expansion of our science and technology institutions and will ensure that they attract and retain the best talent from India and abroad.

- *We will pursue judicial reforms to cut delays in courts.*

Although delays in the Supreme Court have come down appreciably in recent years, delays in High Courts and district courts are still unacceptably high. The Indian National Congress has always been of the view that justice delayed is justice denied and will therefore pursue judicial reforms to ensure timely completion of the hearing and disposal of cases. As a reflection of this priority, the Gram Nyayalaya Act, a key promise of our 2004 Manifesto, was passed by Parliament last year. Setting up of Gram Nyayalayas at the headquarters of the intermediate panchayats and mobile courts in the rural areas will bring to the *aam admi* speedy, affordable and substantial justice.

- *We will continue to be sensitive to regional aspirations.*

The Indian National Congress is aware that in some large states the persistence of intra-regional imbalances in development has given rise to the demand for separate states. While it has introduced several programmes to redress these disparities, recognising the legitimacy of these concerns and acknowledging that the solution may vary from one state to another, the Indian National Congress will find pragmatic solutions to deal with these demands.

- *We will ensure energy security for our country.*

The last two years have seen a very sharp turnaround in the addition to power generating capacity. This momentum will be maintained and it will be ensured that the country adds at least 12,000-15,000 mw of capacity every year through a mix of sources—coal, hydel, nuclear and renewables. Rural electrification and reduction in distribution losses will be given the highest priority. The Indian National Congress promises a very significant increase in the share of nuclear power, both through domestic and imported technology which has now been made possible by the civil nuclear agreements. The pace of oil and gas exploration will be intensified. India's oil diplomacy will be pursued aggressively. The Indian National Congress will implement a scheme to supply energy to poor families at affordable prices.

- *We will take further steps to preserve and promote our heritage.*

India has an extraordinarily rich heritage going back centuries. The Indian National Congress will take further steps to protect, preserve and promote this heritage and ensure that its value is fully appreciated, especially by the younger generation particularly. A statutory National Heritage Sites Commission will be made fully operational. This will be an important instrument to strengthen the foundations of our pluralistic culture and inheritances.

- *We will continue to pursue an independent, pro-India foreign policy.*

The Indian National Congress has always upheld India's supreme national interests and has often braved criticism and opposition both at home and abroad in defending the country's interests. At the same time, the Indian National Congress has always believed that it is India's historic destiny to be engaged and connected with the rest of the world and, in particular, with the countries of Asia.

The foreign policy followed in the past five years has yielded handsome results: the foremost example is the agreements on civil nuclear cooperation signed with the USA, Russia, France and Kazakhstan.

India's well-thought out foreign policy and its patient but forceful diplomacy has obliged Pakistan to admit that its citizens were responsible for carrying out the dastardly attacks in Mumbai in November 2008. The Indian National Congress has striven for an enduring peace and for close economic relations with Pakistan. The Indian National Congress has also encouraged extensive people-to-people contacts between the two countries, particularly amongst the younger generation. But the Mumbai attacks have cast a long shadow on the on-going dialogue and engagement process. It is now entirely upto Pakistan to break the impasse by taking credible action against those responsible for the carnage in Mumbai. If it does so and dismantles the terrorist networks that operate from its soil, a Congress-led government will not be found wanting in its response.

The long-held policy of the Indian National Congress is that the Government of Sri Lanka should find an honourable solution to the strife in that country and ensure that all communities, especially the Tamil-speaking people, are guaranteed and enjoy equal rights within the framework of a united Sri Lanka. The Indian National Congress offers to help the parties reach an agreement as envisaged in the India-Sri Lanka Peace Accord of 1987 which remains the only basis for a politically negotiated settlement.

The Indian National Congress welcomes the return of multi-party democracy to Bangladesh and Nepal. It will work with both countries to deepen bilateral ties across a wide spectrum of areas for demonstrable mutual benefit. The Indian National Congress also believes that the two countries must take note of India's security concerns in a more meaningful manner.

The Indian National Congress has always championed the legitimate and peaceful aspirations of the long-suffering Palestinian people and urges that a viable Palestinian state be established at the earliest.

India's relationships with countries like the USA, Russia, China and Japan and with countries of Europe have been transformed by sustained diplomatic efforts since 2004. These relationships will be further deepened. India has begun a whole new process of engagement with the countries of Africa where there is great appreciation of what India has to offer to them. This engagement will be expanded.

- *The Indian National Congress will intensify the involvement of overseas Indians in development.*

The Indian National Congress takes great pride, as does the entire country, in the outstanding accomplishments of overseas Indians in different fields. The Indian National Congress also acknowledges the vital role remittances by overseas Indians play in bolstering the country's finances. The Ministry of Overseas Indian Affairs was created in May 2004 to reflect the priority that the Indian National Congress places on maximizing the contributions of the overseas Indian community to our country's economic, scientific and technological progress. A number of measures have been taken to protect the interests of lakhs of Indian workers in the Middle East. This will continue to be a matter of priority. New opportunities will be created for overseas Indians to play their rightful role in the renewal of institutions of higher learning and in starting new ventures and businesses. Four new universities will be established with 50 per cent of the seats reserved for PIO/NRI students.

Annexure IIIa

Extracts from Addresses of Congress Presidents

1. W.C. Bonnerjee
2. S.N. Banerjea
3. G.K. Gokhale
4. Dadabhai Naoroji
5. Annie Besant
6. C.R. Das
7. Maulana Mohamed Ali
8. M.K. Gandhi
9. Sarojini Naidu
10. Motilal Nehru
11. Jawaharlal Nehru (1929)
12. Vallabhbhai Patel
13. Jawaharlal Nehru (1936)
14. Subhas Chandra Bose
15. Abul Kalam Azad
16. K. Kamaraj
17. Jagjivan Ram
18. Rajiv Gandhi
19. Sonia Gandhi (2004; 2006)

A. Extracts from Addresses of Congress Presidents

W.C. Bonnerjee (Bombay-1885)

Aims and Objects of the Congress

And not it seemed a fitting occasion for answering a question that had continually been asked in the world outside during the past few weeks *viz.* what the objects and aims of this great National Congress really were. He would not pretend to reply to this question exhaustively. The ensuing proceedings would, he believed, do this more effectively than any single speaker could hope to do but he might say briefly that the objects of the Congress could for the most part be classed under the following heads:

(a) The promotion of personal intimacy and friendship amongst all the more earnest workers in our country's cause in the different parts of the Empire.

(b) The eradication, by direct friendly personal intercourse, of all possible race, creed, or provincial prejudices amongst all lovers of our country, and the fuller development and consolidation of those sentiments of national unity that had their origin in their beloved Lord Ripon's ever memorable reign.

(c) The authoritative records, after this had been carefully elicited, by the fullest discussion of the matured opinion of the educated classes in India on some of the more important and pressing of the social questions of the day.

(d) The determination of the lines upon, and methods by which, during the next twelve months, it is desirable for native politicians to labour in the public interest.

Surely there was nothing in these objects to which any sensible and unprejudiced man could possibly take exception, and yet on more that one occasion remarks had been made by gentlemen, who should have been wiser, condemning the proposed Congress as if it were a nest of conspirators and disloyalists. Let him say once for all, and in this he knew well after the long informal discussion that they had all amongst themselves on the previous day, the he was only expressing the sentiments of every gentleman present, that there were no more thoroughly loyal and consistent well-wishers of the British Government than were himself and the friends around him. In meeting to discuss in an orderly and peaceable manner questions of vital importance affecting their well-being, they were following the only course by which the Constitution of England enabled them to represent their views to the ruining authority. Much had been done by Great Britain for the benefit of India, and the whole country was truly grateful to her for it. She had given them order, she had given railways, and above all, she had given them the inestimable blessing of Western education. But a great deal still remained to be done.

The more progress the people made in education and material prosperity, the greater would be the insight into political matters and the keener their desire for political advancement. He thought that their desire to be governed according to the ideas of Government prevalent in Europe was in no way incompatible with their thorough loyalty to the British Government. All that they desired was, that the basis of the Government should be widened and that the people should have their proper and legitimate share in it. The discussion that would take place in this Congress would, he believed, be as advantageous to the ruling authorities as, he was sure, it would be to the people at large.

Surendranath Banerjea (Ahmedabad—1902)

The Drain

One of the chief causes which have contributed to the impoverishment of the people is the annual drain which, says a writer on Indian economics, "has tapped India's very heart-blood." Lord Salisbury has himself observed that "much of the revenue of India exported without a direct equivalent." The drain of the last thirty years of the 19th century has been estimated at £900,000,000 without interest, at the rate of £30,000,000 a year. This drain represents a distinct loss of national wealth and resources. As Sir George Wingate has observed:

The taxes spent in the country from which they are raised are totally different in their effect from taxes raised in one country and spent in another... In this case, they constitute no mere transfer on one portion of the national income from one set of citizens to another, but are an absolute loss and extinction of the whole amount drawn from the taxed country.

What is to be the remedy? It is simple enough, if the Government will only adopt it. The revival of old and the introduction of new industries, the wider employment of the people in the higher offices of State, a more equitable adjustment of charges between England and India in matters in which both countries are interested, would go a long way to check the drain and the material exhaustion consequent thereon. British Rule represents the Government of India by one of the most civilized nations of the world. It is a proud and glorious record. In point of culture and enlightenment and in its ideals of government, it is far removed from most Government which preceded it. But the conquerors of old soon made the conquered country their own, and returned to the people the money which they had wrung from the people. This thus stimulated the springs of domestic industry and contributed to the material prosperity of the people. Might we not ask the English Rulers of India, whose proud mission it is to govern India for the benefit of India, to return to the people the people's wealth and thus lay broad and deep the foundations of our material prosperity?

The Remedy

What are to be the means for enforcing the remedial measure for checking the growing impoverishment of the country? How is a economy to be enforced—how are the taxes to be imposed without hampering the springs of industry—how are the sources of national wealth to be deepened and widened—how is agriculture to be improved and the arts and manufactures stimulated? The sovereign remedy is to be found in the practice of the British constitution. Give the people a potential voice over the control of the public expenditure and economy will follow as surely as the night follows the day.

The Wider Employment of Our People

I have referred to the question of the economic drains and from year to year we have appealed to the Government from this platform to stop it, or if, in the present relations between England and India, this cannot be done, to curtail its volume. From a return ordered by the House of Commons, it appears that the salaries, allowances and pension to Europeans in India drawing £100 a year or more were £10,274,246 in 1889-90. It must be much more now, as exchange compensation allowance has since been added. The bulk of this vast sum of money is necessarily spent out of India. The employment of a costly foreign agency for Government of a country is, in the best of circumstances, a heavy financial burden and often a financial loss; on the case of India, it is among the primary cause of her growing impoverishment. The wider employment of the people in the public service of their own country is one of the chief remedial measures which will naturally suggest itself. Racial disqualifications have long been abolished. Merit is the sole test of qualifications for public employment. This principle has again and again been affirmed; but there is as yet wide divergence between principle and practice.

As regards the open competitive examination for the Indian Civil Service, the prospects of Indian candidates have sensibly diminished; and well they may. The marks in Sanskrit and Arabic are 500; in Greek and Latin they are 750. Roman and Greek History, each of which 500 marks are attached, are subjects which Indian students may take up; but they are handicapped by the nature of the questions set. In all these subjects, extracts from the Latin and Greek authors are placed before the students, and to be able to answer them they must know these classical languages. Is a knowledge of the classical languages necessary for the thorough mastery of Political Science which is altogether a modern branch of knowledge or even of Roman or Greek History? So many Latin and Greek passages and questions are introduced in the question papers on these subjects that I think it would be no exaggeration to say that no candidate, not knowing Latin and Greek, could hope to gain even half the maximum marks in these subjects. What is most inexcusable is the free quotation from Greek authors in the paper on Political Science. It is, therefore practically impossible for an Indian student to take up these subjects.

The Military Service

As a part of the question of the wider employment of our people in the Public Service, it is impossible not to refer to the exclusion of our countrymen from the commissioned ranks in the Army. The bravest native soldier, a born warrior, possessed, it may be, of military instincts which he has inherited from a long line of ancestors, cannot in these days rise beyond the rank of a

Subedar-Major or a Ressaldar-Major in the British Army. The youngest British subaltern, who was not born when the veteran won his spurs, in his superior military salute.

The Separation of Judicial and Executive Functions

Among the reforms which have occupied a prominent place in our programme is the question of the separation of Judicial and Executive Functions in the administration of criminal justice. We claim to have brought it within the range of practical political, and the question is now pending for final decision by the Government of India. A Memorial was presented by Lord Hobhouse and several other distinguished men, praying for the speedy introduction of this reform. The Memorial has been forwarded to the Government of India; but no orders have yet been passed. It is with some little disappointment we notice that this question has not been included among the twelve administrative problems which Lord Curzon has selected for solutions; but if it is true that justice is the bulwark of Thrones and States, then there can be no more urgent or pressing consideration than a proposal which seeks to improve the administration of justice in India, and to relieve it of the scandals which are inseparable from the present system.

The responsibilities of the present, the hopes of the future, the glories of the past ought all to inspire us with the noblest enthusiasm to serve our country. Is there a land more worthy of service and sacrifice? Where is a land more interesting, more venerated in antiquity, more rich in historic traditions, in the wealth of religious, ethical and spiritual conception which have left an enduring impress on the civilization of mankind? India is the cradle of true religions. It is the holy land of the East. Here knowledge first lit the torch. Here, in the morning of the work, the Vedic Rishis sang those hymns which represent the first yearning of infant humanity towards the divine ideal. Here was developed a literature and a language which still excites the admiration of mankind—a philosophy which pondered deep over the problems of life and evolved solution which satisfied the highest yearning of the loftiest minds. Here man first essayed to solve the mystery of life, and the solution wrapped in the rich colours of the poetic imagination and clothed with the deeper significance of a higher spiritual idea, bids fair, thanks to the genius of the greatest Hindu scientist of the age to be accepted by the world of science. From our shores went forth those missionaries who fired with apostolic fervour traversed the wilds of Asia and established the ascendancy of that faith which is the law and the religion of the nations of the Far East. Japan is our spiritual pupil. China and Siberia and the islands of the Eastern Archipelago turn with reverend eyes to the land where was born the Prophet of their faith. Our pupils have outdistanced us; and where are we hesitating, doubting, calculating, casting up moral results to satisfy ourselves that our gains have a Royal road to political enfranchisement. The triumphs of liberty have not thus been won. Japan is an object-lesson which thrusts itself upon the view. Read her history; note her wonderful self-sacrifice, her marvelous power of adaptation, her patience, her fortitude, her indomitable energy and persistency, and let the most ancient of Eastern nations derive inspiration and guidance from the youngest which has solved the riddle of Asiatic life and has harmonized the conservatism of the East with the progressive forces of the West.

G.K. Gokhale (Benaras-1905)

Partition of Bengal

Gentlemen, the question that is uppermost in the minds of us all at this moment is the Partition of Bengal. A cruel wrong has been inflicted in our Bengalee brethren, and the whole country has been stirred to its deepest depths in sorrow and resentment, as had never been the case before. The scheme of partition, concocted in the dark and carried out in the face of the fiercest opposition that any Government measure has encountered during the last half-a-century, will always stand as a complete illustration of the worst features of the represent system of bureaucratic rule—its utter contempt for public opinion, its arrogant pretensions to superior wisdom, its reckless disregard of the most cherished feelings of the people, the mockery of an appeal to its sense of justice, its cool preference of Service interests to those of the governed. Lord Curzon and his advisers—if he ever had any adviser—could never allege that they had no means of judging of the depth of public feeling in the matter.

But, Gentlemen, as has been well said, even in things evil there is a soul of goodness, and the dark times, through which Bengal has passed and is passing, have not been without a message of bright hope for the future. The tremendous upheaval of popular feeling, which has taken place in Bengal in consequence of the partition, will constitute a landmark in the history of our national progress. For the first time since British rule began, all sections of the Indian community, without distinction of caste or creed, have been moved by a common impulse and without the stimulus of external pressure to act together in offering resistance to a common wrong. A wave of true national consciousness has swept over the Province, and at its touch old barriers have for the time, at any rate, been thrown down, personal jealousies have vanished, other controversies have been hushed. Bengal's heroic stand against the oppression of a harsh and uncontrolled bureaucracy has astonished and gratified all India, and her sufferings have not been endured in vain, when they have helped to draw closer all parts of the country in sympathy and in aspiration.

The Swadeshi Movement

Gentlemen, I will now say a few words on a movement which has spread so rapidly and has been hailed with so much enthusiasm all over the country during the last few months–The Swadeshi Movement. It is necessary at the outset to distinguish it from another movement, started in Bengal, which has really given it such immense impetus–the Boycott of British goods. We all know that when our Bengali brethren found that nothing would turn the late Viceroy from his purpose of partitioning Bengal, that all their protest in the Press and on the Platform, all their memorials to him, to the Secretary of State and the Parliament were unavailing, that the Government exercised its despotic strength to trample on their most cherished feelings and injure their dearest interest and that no protection against this on any kind was forthcoming from any quarter, they in their extremity resolved to have recourse to this boycott movement. This they did with a twofold object–first as a demonstration of their deep resentment at the treatment they were receiving, and, secondly, to attract the attention of the people in England to their grievances, so that those who were in a position to call the Government of India to account might understand what was taking place in India. It was thus as a political weapon, used for a definite political purpose, that they had recourse to the boycott, and in the circumstances of their position every justification for the step they took. And I can tell you from personal experience that their action has proved immensely effective in drawing the attention of English people to the state of things in our country. But a weapon like this must be reserved only for extreme occasions.

Gentlemen, the true Swadeshi movement is both a patriotic and an economic movement. The idea of Swadeshi or "one's own country" is one of the noblest conceptions that have ever stirred the heart of humanity. As the poet asks:

Breathes there the man with soul so dead,
Who never to himself hath said,
This is my own, my native land.

The devotion to Motherland, which is enshrined in the highest Swadeshi, is an influence so profound and so passionate that its very thought thrills and its actual touch lifts one out of oneself. India needs to-day above everything else that the gospel of this devotion should be preached to high and low, to prince and to peasant, in town and in hamlet, till the service of Motherland becomes with us as overmastering a passion as it is in Japan. The Swadeshi movement, as it is ordinarily understood, presents one part of this gospel to the mass of our people in the form, which brings it within their comprehension. It turns their thoughts to their country, accustoms them to the idea of voluntarily making some sacrifice for her sake, enables them to take an intelligent interest in her economic development and teaches them the important lesson of co-operating with one another for a national end. All this is most valuable work, and those who undertake it are entitled to feel that they are engaged in a highly patriotic mission. But the movement on its material side is an economic one; and though self-denying ordinances, extensively entered into, must serve a valuable economic purpose, namely, to ensure a ready consumption of such articles as are produced by keeping the demand for indigenous things largely in excess of the supply, the difficulties that surround the question economically are so great that they require the co-operation of every available agency to surmount them.

The goal of the Congress is that India should be governed in the interests of the Indian themselves, and that in course of time, a form of government should be attained in this country similar to what exists in the self-governing Colonies of the British Empire. For better, for worse, our destinies are now linked with those of England and the Congress freely recognizes that whatever advance we seek must be within the Empire itself. That advance, moreover can only be gradual, as at each stage of the progress it may be necessary for us to pass through a brief course of apprenticeship before we are enable to the next one; for it is a reasonable proposition that the sense of responsibility, required for the proper exercise of the political practical training and experiment only. To admit this is not to express any agreement with those who usually oppose all attempts of reform on the plea that the people are not ready for it.

In my humble opinion our immediate demands should be:

(1) A reform of our Legislative Council, raising the proportion of elected members to one-half, requiring the Budgets to be formally passed by the Councils and empowering the members to bring forward amendments with safeguards for bringing the debates to a close in a reasonable time. The Presidents of the Councils should have the power of veto. The Viceroy's Legislative Council consists at present of 25 members of whom only 5 are elected, one by the Chamber of Commerce of Calcutta—a body of Europeans—and the other four by four provinces. We must ask for the proportion of elected members to be now raised to 12. Of this number, two seats may be given, one to commerce and one to certain industries, and the remaining ten should be assigned to different provinces, two to each of the three older provinces, and one each to the remaining. And, to begin with, the right of members to move amendments may be confined to one amendment each. The two members for Commerce and Industries will generally be Europeans, and they will ordinarily vote with Government. Thus even if all the ten provincial members voted together, they would be only 10 out of 25. Ordinarily they will not be able to carry a motion against the Government, but on exceptional occasions they may obtain the support of two or three men from the other side and then the moral effect of the situation will be considerable. In the Provincial Legislative Councils, we must have an increase in the number, each district of a province being empowered to send a member, the objection that these bodies will in that case be somewhat unwieldy is not entitled to much weight.

(2) The appointment of at least three Indians to the Secretary of State's Council to be returned one each by the three older provinces.

(3) The creation of Advisory Boards in all Districts throughout India, whom the heads of districts should be bound to consult in

important matters of administration concerning the public before taking action. For the present their functions should be only advisory, the Collection or District Magistrate being at liberty to set aside their advice at their discretion. Half the members of the Board should consist of the principal District Officers and such non-official gentlemen as the head of the district may appoint. The Boards must not be confounded with what are known as District Local Boards. There is at present too much of what may be called Secretariat rule, with an excessive multiplication of central departments. Districts administration must be largely freed from this and reasonable opportunities afforded to the people concerned to influence its course before final decisions are arrived at. If such Boards are created, we may in course of time expect them to be entrusted with some real measure of control over the District administration. The late Mr. Ranade used to urge the importance of such Boards very strongly. If ever we are to have real Local Government in matters of general administration, the creation of these Boards will pave the way for it. One great of the present system of administration is its secrecy. This will be materially reduced, so far as District administration is concerned, by the step proposed.

(4) The recruitment of the Judicial Branch of the Indian Civil Service from the legal profession in India.

(5) The separation of Judicial and Executive functions.

(6) A reduction of Military expenditure.

(7) A large extension of primary education.

(8) Facilities for industrial and technical education.

(9) An experimental measure to deal with the indebtedness of the peasantry over a selected area.

Dadabhai Naoroji (Calcutta-1906)

"Swadeshi" is not a thing of to-day. It has existed in Bombay as far as I know for many years past. I am a free-trader, I am a Member, and in the Executive Committee of the Cobden Club for 20 years, and yet I say that "Swadeshi" is a forced necessity for India in its unnatural economic muddle. As long as the economic condition remains unnatural and impoverishing, by the necessity of supplying every year some Rs. 200,000,000 for the salary, pension, &c. of the children of a foreign country at the expense and impoverishment of the children of India, to talk of applying economic laws to the condition of India is adding insult to injury. I have said so much about this over and over again that I would not say more about it here—I refer to my book. I ask an Englishmen whether Englishmen would submit to this unnatural economic muddle of India for a single day in England, leave alone 150 years? No, never. No, Ladies and Gentlemen, England will never submit to it.

Among the duties which I have said are incumbent upon the Indian, there is one which, though I mention last, is not the least. I mean a thorough political union among the Indian people of all creeds and classes. I make an appeal to all-call in mendicant, if you like—I am not ashamed of being a mendicant in any good cause and under necessity for any good cause. I appeal to the Indian people for this, because it is in their own hands only, just as I appeal to the British people for things that are entirely in their hands. In this appeal for a thorough union for political purposes among all the people, I make a particular one to my friends the Mahomedans. They are a manly people. They have been rulers both in and out of India. They are rulers this day both in and out of India. They have the highest Indian Prince ruling over the largest of Native State, viz., H.H. the Nizam. Among other Mahomedan Princes they have Junagad, Badhanpur, Bhopal and others.

Notwithstanding their backward education they have the pride of having had in all India the first Indian Barrister in Mr. Badrudin Tyabji and first Solicitor in Mr. Kamrudin Tyabji, two Mahomedan brothers. What a large share of Bombay commerce is in the hands of Mahomedans is well-known. Their chief purpose and effort at present must be to spread education among themselves. In this matter, among their best friends have been Sir Syed Ahmed and Justice Tyabji, in doing their utmost to promote education among them. Once they bring themselves in education in a line with the Hindus, they have nothing to far. They have in them the capacity, energy and intellect, to hold their own and to set their due share in all the walks of life—of which the State services are but a small part. State services are not everything.

Whatever voice I can have, I wish Government would give every possible help to promote education among the Mahomedans. Once self-government is attained, then will there be prosperity enough for all, but not till then. The thorough union, therefore, of all the people for their emancipation is an absolute necessity.

All the people in their political position are in one boat. They must sink or swim together. Without this union all efforts will be vain. There is the common saying—but also the best commonsense—"United we stand—divided we fall"

Mahomedans and Hindus were, he said, the two eyes of India. Injure the one and you injure the other. "We should try to become one in heart and should act in unison; if united, we can support each other; if not the effect of one against the other will tend to the destruction and downfall of both."

Lastly, the question of social reforms and industrial progress—each of them needs its own earnest body of workers. Each requires for it separate devoted attention. All the three great, purposes—Political, Social and Industrial—must be set working side by side. The progress in each will have its influence on the others. But as Mr. Morley truly and with deep insight says: "Political principles are, after all, the root of our national greatness, strength and hope," and his other important utterance which I repeat with this one sums up the whole position of the Indian problem. He says: "the meddling wrongly with economic things that is going to the very life, to the very heart, to the very core of our national existence."

Annie Besant (Calcutta-1917)

The Awakening of the Women

The position of women in the ancient Aryan civilization was a very noble one. The great majority married, becoming, as Manu said, the Light of the Home; some took up the ascetic life, remained unmarried, and sought the knowledge of Brahman. The story of the Rani Damayanti, to whom her husband's ministers came, when they were troubled by the Raja's gambling; that of Gandhari, in the Council of Kings and warrior chiefs, remonstrating with her headstrong son; in later days, those of Padmini of Chittor, of Mirabai of Marwar—the sweet poetess, of Tarabai of Thoda the warrior, of Chand Bibi the defender of Ahmednagar, of Ahalya Bai of Indore the Great Ruler—all these and countless others are well-known.

Only in the last five or six generations has the Indian woman slipped away from her place at her husband's side, and left him unhelped in his public life. Even now, they wield great influence over husband and son, but lack thorough knowledge to aid. Culture has never forsaken them. But the English education of their husbands and son, with the neglect of Sanskrit and the Vernacular, and that of the wife, have shut the woman out from her old sympathy with the larger life of men. While the interest of the husband have widened, those of the wife have narrowed. The materializing of the husband has tended also, by reaction, to render the wife's religion less broad and wise, and by throwing her on the family priest for guidance in religion, instead as of old, on her husband, has made the religion entirely one of devotion; and lacking the strong stimulus of knowledge, it more easily slides down into superstition, into dependence on forms not understood.

Why India Demands Home Rule

India demands Home Rule for two reasons: one essential and vital, the other less important but weighty. First, because Freedom is the birthright of every Nation; secondly, because her most important interest are not made subservient to the interest of the British Empire without her consent, and her resources are not utilized for her greatest needs. It is enough only to mention the money spent on the Army, not for local defence but for Imperial purposes, as compared with the money spent on primary education.

Enough of myself. Let us think of the Mother.

To see India free, to see her hold up her head among the Nations, to see her sons and daughters respected everywhere, to see her worthy of her mighty Past, engaged in building a yet mightier Future–is not this worth working for, worth suffering for, worth living and worth dying for? Is there any other land which evokes such homage for her spirituality, such admiration for her literature, such homage for her valour, as this glorious Mother of Nations, from whose womb went forth the races that now, in Europe and America, are leading the world? And has any land suffered as our Indians suffered, since her sword was broken on Kurukshetra, and the people of Europe and of Asia swept across her borders, laid waste her cities, and discrowned her Kings. They came to conquer, but they remained to be absorbed. At last, out of those mingled peoples, the Divine Artificer has welded a Nation, compact not only of her own virtues, but also of those her foes had brought to her, and gradually eliminating the vices which they had also brought.

Chittaranjan Das (Gaya-1922)

Nationalism: The Ideal

"What is the ideal which we must set before us? The first and foremost is the ideal of nationalism. Now what in nationalism? It is, I conceive, a process through which a nation expresses itself and finds itself, not in isolation from other nations, not in opposition to other nations, but as part of a great scheme by which, in seeking its own expression and therefore its own identity, it materially assists the self-expression and self-realisation of other nations as well: Diversity is as real as unity. And in order that unity of the world may be established it is essential that each nationality should proceed on its own line and find fulfilment in self-expression and self-realisation. The nationality of which I am speaking must not be composed with the conception of nationality as it exists in Europe today. Nationalism in Europe is an aggressive nationalism, a selfish nationalism, a commercial nationalism, of gain and loss.

I contend that each nationality constitutes a particular stream of the great unity, but no nation can fulfil itself unless and until it becomes itself and at the same time realize its identity with humanity. The whole problem of nationalism is therefore to find that stream and to face that destiny. If you find the current and establish a continuity with the past, then the process of self-expression has begun, and nothing can stop the growth of nationality.

We have, therefore, to foster the sprit of Nationality. True development of the Indian nation must necessarily lie in the path of Swaraj. A question has often been asked as to what is Swaraj. Swaraj is indefinable and is not to be confused with any particular system of Government. There is all the difference in the world between Swaraj and Swarajya. Swaraj is the natural expression of the national mind. The full outward expression of that mind covers, and must necessarily cover, the whole the true development of a nation begins, because as I have said, Swaraj is the expression of the national mind. The question of nationalism, therefore, looked at from another point of view, is the same question as that of Swaraj. The question of all questions in India today is the attainment of Swaraj.

Scheme of Government

It is hardly within the province of this address to deal with any detailed scheme of any Government. I cannot, however, allow this opportunity to pass without giving you an expression of my opinion as to the character of that system of Government. No system of Government which is not for the people and by the people can ever be regarded as the true foundation of Swaraj. I am firmly convinced that a Parliamentary Government is not a Government by the people. Many of us believe that the Middle Class must win Swaraj for the masses. I do not believe in the possibility of any class movement being ever converted into a movement for Swaraj. If today the British Parliament grants provincial autonomy in the provinces with responsibility in the Central Government, I, for once, will protest against, it because that will inevitably lead to the concentration of power in the hands of the Middle Class. I do not believe that the Middle Class will then part with their power. How will it profit India, if in place of the White Bureaucracy that now rules over her, there is substituted an Indian Bureaucracy of the middle-classes. Bureaucracy is bureaucracy, and I believe that the very idea of Swaraj is inconsistent with the existence of a bureaucracy. My ideal of Swaraj will never be satisfied unless the people co-operate with us in its attainment. Any other attempt will inevitably lead to what European Socialist calls the "Bourgeois" Government. In France and in England and in other European countries it is the middle class who fought the battle of freedom, and the result is that power is still in the hands of this class. Having usurped the power they are unwilling to part with it. If today the whole of Europe is engaged in a battle of real freedom, it is because the nations of Europe are gathering their strength to wrest this power from the hands of the middle classes. I desire to avoid the repetition of that chapter of European history. It is for India to show the light to the world Swaraj by non-violence and Swaraj by the people.

To me the organisation of village life and the practical autonomy of small local centres are more important than either provincial autonomy or central responsibility; and if the choice lay between the two, I would unhesitatingly accept the autonomy of the local centres. I must not be understood implying that the village centres will be disconnected units. They must be held together by a system of co-operation and integration. For the present, there must be power in the hands of the provincial and the Indian Government; but the ideal should be accepted once for all, that the proper functioning of the central authority, whether in the Provincial or in the Indian Government is to advise, having a residuary power of control only in case of need, and to be exercised under proper safeguards. I maintain that real Swaraj can only be attained by vesting the power of Government in these local centres, and I suggest that the Congress should appoint a Committee to draw up a scheme of Government which would be acceptable to the nation.

Maulana Mohamed Ali (Cocanada-1923)

United Faiths of India

I had long been convinced that here in this country of hundreds of millions of human beings, intensely attached to religion, and yet infinitely split up into communities, sects and denominations, providence had created for us the mission of solving a unique problem and working out a new synthesis, which was nothing less than a Federation of Faiths! As early as in 1904, when I had been only two years in India after my return from Oxford, I had given to this idea a clear, if still somewhat hesitating expression in an address delivered at Ahmedabad on the "Proposed Mahomedan University", "Unless some new force"—this is what I had said on that occasion—"unless some new force other than the misleading unity of opposition, unites this vast continent of India, it will either remain a geographical misnomer, or what I think it will ultimately do, become a Federation of Religions." I had noted the strength of the bunches of telegrams that came from Bengal, still more from Mr. Das, and still more from the Punjab. I still feel that there are a strong centrifugal forces in India. And yet hope and faith and the deep yearning for freedom had even then made me realize the latent centripetal force of Indian unity. The lines of cleavage were too deeply marked to permit a unity other than federal; and yet, as I had observed in the address from which I have already quoted, the cleavage was not territorial or racial in character, but religious. For more than twenty years I have dreamed the dream of a federation, grander, nobler and infinitely more spiritual than the United States of America, and today when many of political Cassandra prophesies a return to the bad old days of Hindu-Muslim dissensions I still dream that old dream of "United Faiths of India."

Muslim Realization of Larger Indian Interests

But it was not only a case of safeguarding Muslim communal interests without leaning for support eternally on foreign Government and harbouring suspicions against sister communities. Mussalmans would have been more than human, or less than that (means, less than human) if they had been indifferent to the continued injustice done to India and Indians collectively. Having been taught by their political preceptors in the past that Government could never for long leave a wrong unredressed, they had followed the policy of "wait and see." They had waited long, and yet all that they saw was a series of wrongs done to India—wrongs which remained unrepented and unredressed. Their patience was at last giving way and they were beginning to enlist as Congress members in annually increasing numbers. This was a hopeful indication of their realizing—I hope they realize it even today—that they had to protect not only their comparatively petty communal interest but also the larger Indian national interests, which were surely theirs to protect as those of sister communities. They now realized more than ever that by being Muslims they could not cease to be Indians. The Congress sessions of Calcutta, Bombay and Delhi had progressively justified the National appellation of the Congress. But it was reserved for General Dyer to break down entirely the barrier that Sir Syed Ahmed Khan had for temporary purposes erected more than thirty years previously and to summon the Mussalmans of India to the Congress held at Amritsar in 1919 as the unsuspecting Herald of India's Nationhood. The bullets of his soldiery made no distinction between Hindu and Muslim and clearly Providence had so designed things that a community even more loyal than the Mussalmans, namely our brave Sikh brothers (hear, hear) should also die on the sacred soil of their religious capital at Amritsar with their own blood along with that of Hindu and Muslim Martyrs. There is the Hand of God!

The Blow Recalled After the Fight

Friends, I have said all that I could say on the Hindu-Muslim question and if after all this, lengthy dissertation, I leave any Hindu or Mussalman still unconvinced, of the necessity, of co-operation among ourselves and non-cooperation with our foreign master, I can say no more and must acknowledge myself beaten. One thing is certain, and it is this, that neither can the Hindus exterminate the Mussalmans today nor can the Mussalmans get rid of the Hindus. If the Hindus entertain any such designs they must know that they lost their opportunity when Mohammed bin Qasim landed on the soil of Sindh twelve hundred years ago. Then the Mussalmans were few, and today the number more than seventy millions, and if the Mussalmans entertain similar notions, they too have lost their opportunity. They should have wiped out the whole breed of Hindus when they ruled from Kashmir to Cape Comorin and from Karachi to Chittagong. And as the Persian proverb says: "the blow that is recalled after the fight must be struck on one's own jaw." If they cannot get rid of one another, and while the Mussalmans must remove all doubts from the Hindu mind about their desire for Swaraj for its own sake and their readiness to resist all foreign aggression, the Hindus must similarly remove from the Muslim mind all apprehensions that the Hindu majority is synonymous with Muslim servitude. As for myself, I am willing to exchange my present servitude for another in which my Hindu fellow-countryman would be the slave-driver instead of the foreign master of my destiny; for by this exchange I would at least prevent the enslavement of 250 million of my co-religionists whose slaver is only another name for the continued existence of European Imperialism. When at Lucknow in 1916 some Hindus complained to my late chief, Bal Gangadhar Tilak Maharaj, that they were giving too much to the Mussalmans, he answered back like a true and far seeing statesman: "You can never give the Mussalmans too much."

Today when I hear complaints that we are showing great weakness in harping on Hindu-Muslim unity when the Hindus show no desire to unite, I say: "You can never show too great weakness in your dealings with Hindus." Remembers, it is only the weak who fear to appear too weak to others. With this observation I take my last leave of this question without a proper and a lasting settlement of which we can effect nothing.

M.K. Gandhi (Belgaum-1924)

Objections Considered

But, say the critics, the spinning wheel has not taken, it is not exciting enough, it is an occupation only for women, it means a return to the middle ages, it is a vain effort against the majestic march of scientific knowledge for which machinery stands. In my humble opinion, India's need is not excitement but solid work. For the millions, solid work itself is excitement and tonic at the same time. The fact is that we have not given the spinning wheel enough trial. I am sorry to have to say that many of us have not given it serious thought. Even the members of the All-India Congress Committee have failed to carry out the series of resolutions on hand-spinning which they themselves have passed from time to time. The majority of us have simply not believed in it. In the circumstances, it is hardly just to say that spinning has failed for want of excitement about it. To say that it is merely an old woman's occupation is to ignore facts. Spinning mills are a multiplication of spinning wheels. They are managed by men. It is time that we got out of this superstition that some occupations are beneath the dignity of men. Under normal conditions, no doubt spinning will be the occupation of the gentler sex. But the State of the future will always have to keep some men at the spinning wheel so as to make improvements in it within the limitations which as a cottage industry it must have. I must inform you that the progress the mechanism of the wheel has made would have been impossible, if some of us men had not worked at it and had not thought about it day and night.

Machinery

I wish, too, you would dismiss from your minds the views attributed to me about machinery. In the first instance, I am no more trying to present for national acceptance of all my views on machinery than I am presenting the whole of my belief in non-violence. The spinning wheel is itself an exquisite piece of machinery. My head daily bows in reverence to its unknown inventor. What I do resent is the wanton and wicket destruction of the one cottage industry of India that kept the wolf from the doors of thousands of homes scattered over a surface 1900 miles long and 1500 miles broad.

Spinning Franchise

You will not now wonder at my passion for the spinning wheel nor will you wonder why I have ventured to present it for introduction in the franchise, and why Pandit Motilal Nehru and Deshbandhu Das have accepted it on behalf of the Swaraj Party. If I had my way, there would be no one on the Congress register who is unwilling to spin or who would not wear khaddar on all occasions. I am however thankful for what the Swaraj Party has accepted. The modification is a concession to weakness or want of faith. But it must serve as a spur to greater effort on the part of those who have full faith in the wheel and khaddar.

Hindu-Muslim Unity

Hindu-Muslim unity is not less important than the spinning wheel. It is the breath of our life. I do not need to occupy much of your time on this question, because the necessity of it for Swaraj is almost universally accepted. I say 'almost' because I have known some Hindus and some Mussalmans who prefer the present condition of dependence on Great Britain if they cannot have either wholly Hindu or wholly Mussalmans India. Happily their number is small.

I share Maulana Shaukat Ali's robust optimism that present tension is a mere temporary distemper. The Khilafat agitation, in which Hindus made common cause with their Mussalman brethren and the non-co-operation that followed it, caused an awakening among the hitherto slumbering masses. It has given a new consciousness to the classes as well as to the masses. Interested persons, who were disappointed during the palmy day of non-cooperation, now that it has lost the charm of novelty, have found their opportunity and are trading upon the religious bigotry or the selfishness of both the communities. The result is written in the history of the feuds of the past two years. Religion has been travestied. Trifles have been dignified by the name of religious tenets which, the fanatics claim, must be observed at any cost. Economic and political causes have been brought into play for the sake of fomenting trouble. The culminating point was reached in Kohat. The tragedy was aggravated by the callous indifference of the local authority. I must not tarry to examine the cause or to distribute the blame. I have not the material for the task even if I was minded for it. Suffice it to say that the Hindu refugees fled for fear of their lives. There is in Kohat an overwhelming Mussalman majority. They have, in so far as is possible under a foreign domination, effective political control. It is up to them, therefore, to show that the Hindus are as safe in the midst of their majority as they would be if the whole population of Kohat was Hindu. The Mussalmans of Kohat may not rest satisfied till they have brought back to Kohat every one of the refugees. I hope that Hindus would not fall in the trap laid for them by the Government and would resolutely refuse to go back till the Mussalmans of Kohat have given them full assurances as to their lives and property.

The Hindus can live in the midst of an overwhelming Mussalman majority only if the latter are willing to receive and treat them as friends and equals, just as Mussalmans, if in a minority, must depend for honourable existence in the midst of a Hindu majority on the latter's friendliness. A Government can give protection against thieves and robbers, but not even a Swaraj Government will be able to protect people against a wholesale boycott by one community of another, Governments can deal with abnormal situations. When quarrels become a normal thing of life, it is called civil war, and parities must fight it out themselves. The present Government being foreign, in reality a veiled military rule, has resources at its command for its protection against any combination we can make, and has, therefore, the power, if it has the will, to deal with our class feuds. But no Swaraj Government with any pretension to being a popular Government can possibly be organised and maintained on a war footing. A Swaraj Government is established by the free joint will of Hindus, Mussalmans and others. Hindus and Mussalmans, if they desire Swaraj, have perforce to settle their difference amicably.

Untouchability is another hindrance to Swaraj. Its removal is just as essential for Swaraj as the attainment of Hindu-Muslim unity. This is an essential Hindu question and Hindus cannot claim or take Swaraj till they have restored the liberty of the suppressed classes. They have sunk with the latter's suppression. Historians tell us that the Aryan invaders treated the original inhabitants of Hindustan precisely as the English invaders treat us, if not much worse. If so, our history is a just retribution for our having created an untouchable class. The sooner we remove the blot the better it is for us Hindus. But the priests tell us that untouchability is a divine appointment. I claim to know something of Hinduism. I am certain that the priests are wrong. It is blasphemy to say that God set apart any portion of humanity as untouchable. And Hindus who are Congressmen have to see to it that they break down the barrier at the earliest possible moment. The Vaikom Satyagrahis are showing us the way. They are carrying on their battle with gentleness and firmness. They have patience, courage and faith. Any movement in which these qualities are exhibited become irresistible.

I would, however, warn the Hindu brethren against the tendency which one sees how-a-days of exploiting the suppressed classes for a political end. To remove untouchability is a penance that caste Hindus owe to Hinduism and to themselves. The purification required is not of untouchables but of the so-called superior castes. There is not vice that is special to the untouchables not even dirt and insanitation. It is our arrogance which blinds us 'superior' Hindus to our own blemishes and which magnifies those of our down-trodden brethren whom we have suppressed and whom we keep under suppression. Religions like nations are being weighted in the balance. God's grace and revelation are the monopoly of no race or nation. They descend equally upon all who wait upon God. That religion and that nation will be blotted out of the face of the earth which pins its faith to injustice, untruth or violence. God is light, not darkness. God is love, not hate. God is truth, not untruth. God alone is great. We his creatures are but dust. Let us be humble and recognize the place of the lowliest of his creatures. Krishna honoured Sudama in his rags as he honoured no one else. Love is the root of religions or sacrifice, and this perishable body is the root of self or irreligion, says Tulsidas. Whether we win Swaraj or not, the Hindus have to purify themselves before they can hope to revive the Vedic philosophy and make it a living reality.

May I suggest for its consideration the following points?

1. The qualification for the franchise should be neither property nor position but manual work, such, for example, as suggested for the Congress franchise. Literary or property test has proved to be elusive. Manual work gives an opportunity to all who wish to take part in the government and the well-being of the State.
2. The ruinous military expenditure should be curtailed to the proportion necessary for protection of life and property in normal times.
3. Administration of justice should be cheapened and with that end in view the final court of appeal should be not in London but in Delhi. Parties to civil suits must be compelled in the majority of cases to refer their disputes to arbitration, the decisions of the Panchayats to be final except in cases of corruption or obvious misapplication of law. Multiplicity of intermediate courts should be avoided. Case law should be abolished and general procedure should be simplified. We havc slavishly followed the cumbrous and worn-out English procedure. The tendency in the Colonies is to simplify the

procedure so as to make it easy for litigants to plead their own cases.

4. Revenues from intoxication liquors and drugs should be abolished.
5. Salaries of the Civil and Military Service should be brought down to a level compatible with the general condition of the country.
6. There should be re-distribution of provinces on a linguistic basis with as complete autonomy as possible for every province for its internal administration and growth.
7. Appointment of a commission to examine all the monopolies given to foreigners and, subject to the findings of the commission, full guarantees to be given for all vested rights justly acquired.
8. Full guarantee of their status to the Indian Chiefs without any hindrance from the Central Government, subject to the right of asylum to subjects of these States who, not being offender against the Penal Code, may seek it in Self-governing India.
9. Repeal of all arbitrary powers.
10. The highest post to be open to all who may be otherwise fit. Examinations for the Civil and Military Services to be in India.
11. Recognition of complete religious freedom to various denominations subject to mutual forbearance.
12. The official language for provincial governments, legislatures and courts, within a definite period, to be the vernacular of the province; of the Privy Council, the final court of appeal, to be Hindustani, the script to be either Devanagari or Persian. The language of the Central Government and of the Central Legislature to be also Hindustani. The language of international diplomacy to be English.

These are the requirements of Swaraj as I would have it. We may not have the power to-day to take or receive or do the things I have mentioned. Have we the will? Let us at least cultivate the desire. Before I have this highly attractive, because speculative theme let me assure the Committee in charge of the drafting of a Swaraj scheme that I claim for my suggestion no more attention than it would given to any single individuals. I have incorporated them in my address only to gain greater currency for them than they would perhaps otherwise receive.

My Faith

Let me state my faith. As a Congressman wishing to keep the Congress intact, I advise suspension of non-co-operation, for I see that the nation is not ready for it. But as an individual, I cannot, will not do so, as long as the Government remains what it is. It is not merely a policy with me; it is an article of faith. Non-co-operation and Civil Disobedience are but different branches of the same tree called Satyagraha. It is my *Kalpadrum*—my *Jam-in-Jam*—the Universal Provider. Satyagraha is search for Truth: and God is Truth. *Ahimsa* or Non-violence is the light that reveals that Truth to me. Swaraj for me is part of that Truth. This Satyagraha did not fail me in South Africa, Kheda or Champaran and in a host of other cases I could mention. It excludes all violence or hate. Therefore, I cannot and will not hate Englishmen. Nor will I bear their yoke. I must fight unto death the unholy attempt to impose British methods and British institutions on India. But I combat the attempt with non-violence. I believe in the capacity of India to offer non-violence battle to the English rulers. The experiment has not failed. It has succeeded, but not to the extent we had hoped and desired. I do not despair.

Sarojini Naidu (Kanpur-1925)

Village Reconstruction

To give concrete expression to our decision in regard to these ancillary activities, the Indian National Congress should created definite departments to be governed by groups of men and women specially qualified by their capacity or enthusiasm to administer to the vital and divergent wants of the people. The main divisions might be few but should include within their sphere of responsibility all cognate matters. To my mind it is of paramount importance to formulate a practical scheme of village reconstruction on the lines of Deshbandhu Das's dream. For this purpose we must try to enlist a large band of missionary patriots of burning zeal who, set free from material wants by the pious charity of the householders of the country as in ancient times, should carry through the length and breadth of the land the beneficent evangel of self-reliance and self-respect, taking the immemorial twin symbols of the plough and the spinning wheel as the central text of the teaching that shall liberate our unhappy peasantry from the crushing misery and terror of hunger, ignorance and disease. Closely allied to the task of village reorganisation is the task of organizing the industrial workers in the crowded cities, who are so often compelled to live under conditions that degrade and brutalize them; and who dislocated from the steadying influences of the familiar traditions and associations of the rural homes they leave in search for bread, are so hopelessly exposed to the temptations of immorality and vice. It should be our endeavour to assist in securing for them improved housing, equitable and harmonious co-operation between capital and labour as a valuable joint asset of national progress.

The Education Problem

I am appalled at the criminal apathy of our general attitude towards the urgent problem of Indian education. The surpassing evil of foreign domination has been to enslave our imagination and intellect and alienate us from the glorious tradition of our national learning. We are to-day no more than the futile purpose of an artificial and imitative system of education which, entirely unsuited to the special trend of our racial genius, has robbed us of our proper mental values and perspectives, and deprived us of all true initiative and originality in seeking authentic modes of self-expression. It is pre-eminently our duty towards the young generation to so recreate our educational ideals to combine in felicitous and fruitful alliance, all the lovely regenerating wisdom of our Eastern culture with all the highest knowledge of art and science, philosophy and civic organisation evolved by the younger peoples of the West.

National Militia

In addition, I would insist with all the force at my command on including a compete course of military training as an integral part of national education. It is not the saddest of all shameful ironies that our children whose favourite lullabies are the battle songs of Kurukshetra and whose, little feet march gaily to the stirring music of Rajput ballads, should be condemned to depend for the safety of their homes, the protection of their sanctuaries, the security of their mountain and ocean frontiers, on the fidelity and strength of foreign arms. The savage Massai, the primitive Zulu, the Arab and the Afridi, the Greek and the Bulgar may all carry their tribal weapons and claim their inalienable right to defend the honour of their race, but we, whose boast it is that we kindled the flame of the world's civilization, are alone defrauded of our privilege and have become cowards by compulsion, unfit to answer the world's challenge to our manhood, unable to maintain the sanctity of our homes and shrines.

Hindu-Moslem Question

And now I approach with the utmost hesitation and regret the most baffling and most tragic of all the problems before us. I, who have dedicated my life to the dream of Hindu-Muslim unity, cannot contemplate without tears of blood the dissentions and divisions between us that rend the very fabric of my hope. I have tried to arrive at a just appreciation of the many unfortunate cases that have brought about so deep a gulf-between the two communities, and tended to quicken such a sharp and importunate sense of aloofness on the part of my Muslim brothers, which to the profound alarm and resentment of the Hindu community, manifests itself in a growing and insistent demand for separate and preferential rights and privileges in academic, official, civic and political circles of life. Though I am convinced that the principle of communal representation, whether through a joint or a separate electorate frustrate the conception of national solidarity, I am compelled to recognize that situated as we are to-day in an atmosphere so tense and dark and bitter with unreasoning communal jealousy, suspicion, fear, distrust and hatred, it is not possible to reach any satisfactory or abiding readjustment without the most earnest and patient collaboration between Hindu and Muslim statesmen of undeniable patriotism to whom we should entrust the delicate and difficult task of seeing some sovereign remedy for so devastating a disease.

I beseech my Hindu brothers to rise to the height of their traditional tolerance which is the basic glory of our Vedic faith and try to comprehend how intense and far-reaching a reality is the brotherhood of Islam, which constrains seventy millions of Indian Mussalmans to share with breathless misery the misfortunes that are so swiftly overtaking the Islamic countries and crushing them under the heel of the military despotism of foreign power.

In their turn I would implore my Muslim comrades not to permit their pre-occupation with the sorrows of Syria, Egypt, Iraq and Arabia to obliterate the consciousness of their supreme duty to India, their motherland, which must always have the first claim upon their devotion and allegiance.

If Hindus and Mussalmans would both learn to practise the divine qualities of mutual forbearance and accord to one another perfect liberty of living, without the tyranny of fanatical interruptions of one another's appointed rituals and sacrifices, if they would but learn to reverence the beauty of each other's creeds and the splendour of each other's civilizations, if the women of the two communities would but join together in the intimate friendship of their common sisterhood, and nurture their children in an atmosphere of mutual sweetness and harmony, how near we should come to the fulfilment of our heart's desire!

We should grossly fail in our duty to our neighbours were we to omit to try and foster cordial ties of sympathy and trust between ourselves and the princes and the people of the great Indian States scrupulously refraining from all interference in their internal concerns but always ready to serve in their wider interests.

Nor can we afford to ignore the claims of the Frontier Provinces, which owing to their peculiar geographical and strategic position on the map, are governed by a form of perpetual martial law. We should render them all the assistance in our power, in their efforts to obtain the normal civic and social amenities which are so abundantly enjoyed by their sister provinces.

Motilal Nehru (Calcutta-1928)

Our Social Evils

It will be clear from what I have said above that the process of forging new chains to keep us in perpetual bondage has gone on simultaneously with a long protracted, ruthless exploitation of our material resources. While, however, the Government has to answer for a great deal it must be frankly confessed that we cannot honestly acquit ourselves of all blame for our present plight. The strength or weakness of a nation depends upon the strength or weakness of the individual which keeps its component parts together. In our case this tie has not for centuries been very strong and with the march of the new order of things has lost much of what binding force it ever had. There is no over-looking the fact that we are divided into a number of large and small communities, more or less disorganized and demoralized. The Government is undoubtedly responsible for the prevailing ignorance and poverty among the masses and in a very large measure for the growing hostility among the classes. But it certainly is not to blame for the evils of our own social system, which has relegated millions of our people as good as ourselves, to the category of untouchable and depressed classes, and has put our women under restrictions which deprive them not only of many natural rights but also of the opportunity to render national service. Nor is the Government solely accountable for all the communal differences which have contributed a dark chapter to the recent history of our own times.

Reception of Nehru Report in the Country

It will be observed that the recommendations are divisible under two main heads—general and communal. Both are so inter-related that you cannot accept the one and reject the other. We cannot overlook the Lucknow resolution, whereby all parties agreed that "every one of them will stand by it (the Report) as a whole and will refuse to accept any single part of it without giving full force and effect to all other parts." There are communal and politico-communal organisations which favour dominion status and have not only joined the communal agreements as parties, but given up what they considered substantial rights for the sake of an agreed constitution. Many hundreds of public meetings have been held throughout the country attended by people of all shades of opinion, which have approved of the recommendations as a whole. It is impossible to say how many accepted the communal solution because of the draft constitution for dominion status and how many accepted the latter because of the former. We have to keep our faith with all.

The position, as I view it, is this. Here is constitution agreed upon by the various parties, invited by the Congress to frame it. These parties know that the goal of the Congress is complete independence. They do not ask the Congress to change its goal, but present to it the result of their labours such as it is, and say that they are prepared to go thus far and no further at present. They offer their co-operation and demand that of the Congress, to enable both to reach the point up to which they are prepared to go. After the point is reached they reserve liberty to themselves and to the Congress to consider the next step. Is the Congress going to refuse them this co-operation and this liberty? Is the Congress after bringing them together going to sent them back to the wilderness in isolated groups, each to shift for itself, and leave the Congress to wrangle over the respective merits of complete independence and dominion status to the end of time? If the Congress will do that, I will abdicate its proper function to guide the nation on its forward march. The occasion calls for skilful generalship, and not academic discussions which take us nowhere. The nation is knocking at your door. You must open it wide—wide enough for every one to enter, or lose your rightful place of high command. My advice to you is to accept the offer. If you do so the way to your destination is clear.

Begin at the point at which the All-Parties have now arrived and push forward with them as far as they would go, then pause and take stock of your equipment, and finally throw the strength your whole being into one great effort to reach the goal.

That is my answer to the question: how can we reach our destination?

The first, and the most obvious step is to set our own house in order. For this purpose, rally all the parties under the banner of the Congress and prepare to march shoulder to shoulder with them to the farthest end of the common road. That will be that first part of the arduous journey. I suggest the following programme for it.

1. Popularising the communal solution, agreed in at the All-Parties Conference, in the country, by intensive propaganda in the press and on the platform and organizing village to village lectures.
2. Organising similar propaganda in regard to the Delhi Unity Conference and the Madras Congress, with such improvement as this Congress might make on communal matters, others than those dealt with by the Conferences.
3. Work among the untouchables and depressed classes.
4. Organisation of labour, agricultural and industrial.
5. Other village organisation.
6. Popularising khaddar and boycott of foreign cloth.

7. Campaign against social customs which retard social intercourse and national growth, more especially a crusade against the purdah and the other disabilities of women.
8. Intensive campaign against the drink and opium curse.
9. Publicity.

It will be observed that this is a predominantly social programme. I claim no originality for any of its items and have merely selected them out of a long list which, with the exception of the first item, has been before the Congress and the country for years past. I may, however, be pardoned, when I say that, we have no so far not done much worth speaking in carrying out the constructive work.

Commonplace as this programme may appear, it is the only true foundation on which the hopes of the high priests of complete independence, as well as those of the votaries of dominion status, can be safely built. To the former I say, that the measure of their capacity, for the tremendous sacrifice that the first real step towards their goal will demand is the measure of their success in carrying out his seemingly unpretentious programme. To the latter I say, that the only change there is of dominion status being ever offered to them lies in the complete fulfilment of this very programme.

Jawaharlal Nehru (Lahore-1929)

India means the peasantry and labour and to the extent that we raise them and satisfy their wants will we succeed in our task. And the measure of the strength of our national movement will be the measure of their adherence to it. We can only gain them to our side by espousing their cause which is really the country's cause. The Congress has often expressed its good-will towards them but beyond that it has not gone. The Congress it is said must hold the balance fairly between capital and labour and zamindar and tenant. But the balance has been and is terribly weighed on one side. The only way to right it is to do away with the domination of any one class over another. The All-India Congress Committee accepted this ideal of social and economic change in a resolution it passed some months ago in Bombay. I hope the Congress will also set its seal on it and will further draw up a programme of such changes as can be immediately put in operation.

In this programme perhaps the Congress as a whole cannot go very far to-day. But it must keep the ultimate ideal in view and work for it. The question is not merely of wages and charity doled out by an employer or landlord. Paternalism in industry or in the land is but a form of charity with all its sting and its utter capacity to root out the evil. The new theory of trusteeship, which some advocate, is equally barren. For trusteeship means that the power for good or evil remains with the self-appointed trustee and the he may exercise it as he wills. The sole trusteeship that can be fair is the trusteeship of the nation and not of one individual or a group. Many Englishmen honestly consider themselves the trustees for India, and yet to what a condition they have reduced our country.

We have to decide for whose benefit industry must be run and the land produce food. To-day the abundance that the land produces is not for the peasant or the labourer who work on it. And industry's chief function is supposed to be to produce millionaires. However golden the harvest and heavy the dividends, the mud huts and hovels and nakedness of our people testify to the glory of the British Empire and of our present social system.

Our economic programme must therefore be based on a human outlook and must not sacrifice man to money. If an industry cannot be run without starving its workers then the industry must close down. If the workers on the land have not enough to eat then the intermediaries who deprive them of their full share must go. The least that every worker in field or factory is entitled to is a minimum wage which will enable him to live in moderate comfort, and human hours of labour which do not break his strength and spirit. The All-Parities Committee accepted the principle and included it in their recommendations. I hope the Congress will also do and will in addition be prepared to accept its natural consequence. Further that it will adopt the well-known demands of labour for a better life, and will give every assistance to it to organise itself and prepare itself for the day when it can control industry on a co-operative basis.

The Cry of the Peasatry

But industrial labour is only a small part of India although it is rapidly becoming a force that cannot be ignored. It is the peasantry that cry loudly, piteously for relief and our programme must deal with their condition. Real relief can only come by a great change in the land laws and the basis of the present system of land tenure. We have among us many big landowners and we welcome them. But they must realize that the ownership of large estates by individuals, which is the outcome of a state resembling the old feudalism of Europe, is a rapidly disappearing phenomenon all over the world. Even in countries which are strongholds of capitalism the large estates are being split up and given to the peasantry who work on them. In India also we have large areas where the system of peasant proprietorship prevails and we shall have to extend that all over the country. I hope that in doing so we may have the cooperation of some at least of the big landowners.

It is not possible for this Congress at its annual session to draw up any detailed economic programme. It can only lay down some general principles and call upon the All-India Congress Committee to fill in the details in cooperation with the representatives of the Trade Union Congress and other organisations which are vitally interested in this matter. Indeed I hope that the cooperation between this Congress and the Trade Union Congress will grow and the two organisations will fight side by side in future struggles.

The Congress Organisation

The past year has been one of preparation for us and we have made every efforts to reorganize and strengthen the Congress organisation. The results have been considerable and our organisation is in a better state to-day than at any time since the reaction which followed the non-cooperation movement. But our weaknesses are many and are apparent enough. Mutual strife even within Congress Committees is unhappily too common and election squabbles drain all our strength and energy. How can we fight a great fight if we cannot get over this ancient weakness of ours and rise above our petty selves? I earnestly hope that with a strong programme of action before the country, our perspective will improve and we will not tolerate this barren and demoralizing strife.

For this struggle we want efficient machinery. Our Congress constitution and organisation have become too archaic and slow moving and are ill suited to times of crisis. The times of great demonstrations are past. We want quiet and irresistible action now and this can only be brought about by the strictest discipline in our ranks. Our resolution must be passed in order to be acted upon. The Congress will gain in strength, however small its actual membership may become, if it acts in a disciplined way. Small determined minorities have changed the fate of nations. Mobs and crowds can do little. Freedom itself involves restraint and discipline and each one of us will have to subordinate himself to the larger good.

The Congress represents no small minority in the country, and though many may be too weak to join it or to work for it, they look to it with hope longing to bring them deliverance. Ever since the Calcutta resolution the country has waited with anxious expectation for this great day when this Congress meets. None of us can say what and when we can achieve. We cannot command success. But success often comes to those who dare and act; it seldom goes to the timid who are ever afraid of the consequences. We play for high stakes; and if we seek to achieve great things it can only be through great dangers. Whether we succeed soon or late, none but ourselves can stop us from high endeavour and from writing a noble page in our country's long and splendid history.

Vallabhbhai Patel (Karachi-1934)

Hindu-Muslim Unity

But before all else comes the question of Hindu-Muslim or rather communal unity. The position of the Congress was defined at Lahore. Let me recite the resolution here: "In view of the lapse of the Nehru Report, it is unnecessary to declare the policy of the Congress regarding communal problem can only be solved on strictly national lines. But as the Sikhs in particular and the Muslims and other minorities in general had expressed dissatisfaction over the solution of the communal question proposed in the Nehru Report, this Congress assures Sikhs, Muslims and other minorities that no solution thereof in nay future constitution can be acceptable to the Congress that does not give full satisfaction to the parties concerned."

Therefore, the Congress can be no party to any constitution which does not contain a solution of the communal question that is designed to satisfy the respective parties. As a Hindu, I would adopt my predecessor's formula and present the minorities with a Swadeshi fountain pen and paper and let them write out their demands and I should endorse them. I know that is the quickest method, but it requires courage on the part of the Hindus. What we want is a heart unity not a patched up paper unity that will break under the slightest strain. That unity can only come when the majority shows the path. This would be the highest wisdom. Whether unity is reached that way or any other, it is becoming plainer day after day that it is useless to attend any conference unless that unity is achieved. A conference can give us an agreement between the British and us. It can perhaps help us to come nearer to the princess. But it can never enable us to achieve unity that must be hammered into shape by ourselves. The Congress must leave no stone unturned to realize this much desired end.

Boycott and Swadeshi

In this connection, let me say a few words regarding the boycott of British goods. This idea is almost as old as the Congress. We know that after the advent of Gandhiji on the political platform, the boycott of British goods was replaced by that of foreign, not only British cloth. He interpreted it in terms of economic and social uplift, whereas the boycott of British goods as such is a political and punitive measure. This was effectively employed during the recent hurricane campaign, Now that there is at least temporary peace and we seek to reach our goal through consultation and conference, we must withdraw the political weapon. We cannot be sitting at a friendly conference table and outside making designs to hurt British interest. Whilst, therefore, we must for the time being withdraw the British goods boycott, we must intensify Swadeshi which is the birthright of every nation. Whatever we produce in our country, we must encourage to the exclusion of foreign, whether British or other. This is a condition of national growth. Thus we must encourage and carry on intensive propaganda on behalf of indigenous insurance companies, banking, shipping, and the like. We may not belittle or neglect them on the ground of their inferiority or dearness. Only by wide use and helpful criticism may be we make them cheaper and better.

Jawaharlal Nehru (Lucknow-1936)

Only Key to Solution

I am convinced that the only key to the solution of the world's problems and of India's problem lies in socialism, and when I use this word I do so not in a vague humanitarian way but in the scientific, economic sense. Socialism is, however, something even more than an economic doctrine; it is a philosophy of life and as such also it appeals to me. I see no way of ending the poverty, the vast unemployment, the degradation and the subjugation of the Indian people except through socialism. That involves vast and revolutionary changes in our political and social structure, the ending of vested interests in land and industry, as well as the feudal and autocratic Indian States system. That means the ending of private property, except in restricted sense, and the replacement of the present profit system by a higher ideal of co-operative service. It means ultimately a change in our instincts and habits and desires. In short, it means a new civilization, radically different from the present capitalist order. Some glimpse we can have of this new civilization in the territories of the U.S.S.R. Much has happened there which has pained me greatly and with which I disagree, but I look upon that great and fascinating unfolding of a new order and a new civilization as the most promising feature of our dismal age. If the future is full of hope it is largely because of Soviet Russia and what it has done, and I am convinced that if some world catastrophe does not intervene, this new civilization will spread to other lands and put an end to the wars and conflicts which capitalism feeds.

But we cannot go to it with blank minds in the hope that something good will emerge out of it. Such an Assembly, in order to be fruitful, must have previous thought behind it and a definite scheme put forward by an organized group. The actual details as to how the Assemble is to be convened, must depend on the circumstances then existing and need not trouble us now. But it will be our function as the Congress to know exactly what we are after, to place this clearly and definitely before the Assembly, and to press for its acceptance.

Communal Question

There is one more matter concerning the Constitution Act which has given rise to much controversy. This is the communal decision. Many people have condemned it strongly and I think rightly; few have a good word for it. My own view-points is, however, somewhat different from that of others. I am not concerned so much with what it gives to this group or that but more so with the basic idea behind it. It seeks to divide India into numerous separate compartments, chiefly on a religious basis, and thus makes the development of democracy and economic policy very difficult. Indeed the communal decision and democracy can never go together. We have to admit that, under present circumstances, and so long as our politics are dominated by middle class elements, we cannot do away with communalism altogether. But to make a necessary exception if favour of our Muslim or Sikh friends is one thing, to spread this evil principle to numerous other groups and thus to divide up the electoral machinery and the legislature into many compartments, is a far more dangerous proposition. If we wish to function democratically the proposed communal arrangement will have to go and I have no doubt that it will go. But it will not go by the methods adopted by the aggressive opponents of the decision. These methods result inevitably in perpetuating the decision for they help in continuing a situation which prevent any reconsideration.

I have not been enamoured of the past Congress policy in regard to the communal question and its attempts to make pacts and compromises. Yet essentially I think it was based on a sound instinct. First of all the Congress always put independence first and other questions, including the communal one, second, and refused to allow any of those other questions to take pride of place. Secondly, it argued that the communal problem had arisen from a certain set of circumstances which enabled the third party to exploit the other two. In order to save it, one had either to get rid of the third party (and that meant independence), or get rid of that set of circumstances, which meant a friendly approach by the parties concerned and an attempt to soften the prejudice and fear that filled them. Thirdly, that the majority community must show generosity, in the matter to allay the fear and suspicion that minorities, even though unreasonably, might have.

Contact with Masses

I have referred previously to the growing divorce between our organisation and the masses. Individually many of us still have influence with the masses and our word carries weight with them, and who can measure the love and reverence of India's millions for our leader, Gandhiji? And yet organisationally we have lost that intimate touch that we had. The social reform activities of the khadi and village industries and Harijan organisation keep large numbers of our comrades in touch with the masses and those contacts bear fruit. But they are essentially non-political and so, politically, we have largely lost touch. There are many reasons for this and some are beyond our control. A present Congress constitution is, I feel, not helpful in developing these contacts or in encouraging enough the democratic spirit in its primary committees. These committees are practically rolls of voters who meet only to elect delegates or representatives, and take no part in discussion or the formation of policy.

Subhas Chandra Bose (Haripura-1938)

I am afraid there is a lack of clarity in the minds of many Congressmen as to the role of the Congress in the history of our national struggle. I know that there are friends who think that after freedom is won the Congress Party, having achieved its objective, should wither away. Such a conception is entirely erroneous. The Party that wins freedom for India should be also the party that will put into effect the entire programme of post-war reconstruction. Only those who have won power can handle it properly. If other people are pitchforked into seats of power which they were not responsible for capturing, they will lack that strength, confidence and idealism which is indispensable for revolutionary reconstruction. It is this which accounts for the difference in the record of the Congress and non-Congress Ministries even in the very narrow sphere of provincial autonomy.

I do not know how or when this new order will come to India. I imagine that every country will fashion it after its own way and fit it in with its national genius. But the essential basis of that order must remain and be a link in the world order that will emerge out of the present chaos.

Socialism is thus for me not merely an economic doctrine which I favour, it is a vital creed which I hold with all my head and heart. I work for Indian independence because the nationalist in me cannot tolerate alien domination! I work for it even more because for me it is the inevitable step to social and economic changes. I should like the Congress to become a socialist organisation and to join hands with the other forces in the world who are working for the new civilization. But I realize that the majority in the Congress, as it is constituted to-day, may not be prepared to go thus far. We are a nationalist organisation and we think and work on the nationalist plane. It is evident enough now that this is too narrow even for the limited objective of political independence, and so we talk of the masses and their economic needs. But still most of us hesitate, because of our nationalist backgrounds, to take a step which might frighten away some vested interests. Most of those interests are already ranged against us and we can expect little from them except opposition even in the political struggle.

Congress and Socialism

Much as I wish for the advancement of socialism in this country, I have no desire to force the issue in the Congress and thereby create difficulties in the way of our struggle for independence. I shall cooperate gladly and with all the strength in me with all those who work for independence even though they do not agree with the socialist solution. But I shall do so stating my position frankly and hoping in course of time to convert the Congress and the country to it, for only thus can I see it achieving independence. It should surely be possible for all of us who believe in independence to join our ranks together even though we might differ on the social issue. The Congress has been in the past a broad form representing various opinions joined together by the common bond. It must continue as such even though the difference of those opinions becomes more marked.

How does socialism fit in with the present ideology of the Congress? I do not think it does. I believe in the rapid industrialisation of the country and only thus I think will the standards of the people raise substantially and poverty be combated. Yet I have co-operated wholeheartedly in the past with the khadi programme and I hope to do so in the future because I believe that khadi and village industries have a definite place in our present economy. They have a social, a political and an economic value which is difficult to measure but which is apparent enough to those who have studied their effects. But I look upon them as temporary expedients of a transition stage, might be a long one, and in a country like India, village industries might well play an important though subsidiary role even after the development of industrialism. But though I co-operate in the village industries programme my ideological approach to it differs considerably from that of many others in the Congress who are opposed to industrialisation and socialism.

The problem of untouchability and the Harijans again can be approached in different ways. For a socialist it presents no difficulty for under socialism there can be no such differentiation or victimization. Economically speaking, the Harijans have constituted the landless proletariat and an economic solution removes the social barriers that custom and tradition have raised.

Constituent Assembly

I think that, under the circumstances, we have no choice but to contest the election to the new provincial legislatures, in the event of their taking place. We should seek election on the basis of a detailed political and economic programme, with our demand for a Constituent Assembly in the forefront. I am convinced that the only solution of our political and communal problems will come through such an Assembly, provided it is elected on an adult franchise and a mass basis. That Assembly will not come into existence till at least a semi-revolutionary situation has been created in this country and the actual relationships of power, apart from paper constitutions, are such that the people of India can make their will felt. When that will happen I cannot say, but the world is too much in grip of dynamic forces to-day to admit of static conditions in India or elsewhere for long. We may thus have to face this issue sooner than we might expect. But obviously, a Constituent Assembly will not come through the new Act or the new legislatures. Yet we must press this demand and keep it before our country and the world, so that when the time comes we may be ripe for it.

A Constituent Assembly is the only proper and democratic method for the framing of our constitution, and for its delegates then to negotiate a treaty with the representative of the British Government.

No, there can be no question of the Congress Party withering away after political freedom has been won. On the contrary, the party will have to take over power, assume responsibility for administration and put through its programme of reconstruction. Only then will it fulfil its role. If it were forcibly to liquidate itself, chaos would follow. Looking at post-war Europe we find that only in those countries has there been orderly and continuous progress where the party which seized power undertook the work of reconstruction.

I know that it will be argued that the continuance of it in such circumstances, standing behind the State, will convert that State into a totalitarian one; but I cannot admit the charge. The State will possibly become a totalitarian one if there be only one party as in countries like Russia, Germany and Italy. But there is no reason why other parties should be banned. Moreover, the party itself will have a democratic basis and, unlike, for instance, the Nazi Party will prevent the future Indian State becoming a totalitarian one. Further, the democratic basis of the party will ensure that leaders are not thrust upon the people from above, but are elected from below.

Though it may be somewhat premature to give a detailed plan of reconstruction, we might as well consider some of the principles according to which our future social reconstruction should take place. I have no doubt in my mind that our chief national problems relating to the eradication of poverty, illiteracy and disease, and to scientific production and distribution can be effectively tackled only along socialist lines. The very first thing which our future national government will have to do would be to set up a commission for drawing up a comprehensive plan of reconstruction. This plan will have two parts—an immediate programme and long period programme. In drawing up the first part, the immediate objectives which will have to be kept in view will be three-fold: firstly, to prepare the country for self-sacrifice; secondly, to unify India; and thirdly, to give scope for local and cultural autonomy. The second and third objectives may appear to be contradictory, but they are not really so. Whatever political talent or genius we may posses as a people will have to be used in reconciling these two objectives. We shall have to unify the country so that we may be able to hold India against any foreign invasion. While unifying the country through a strong Central Government, we shall have to put all the minority communities as well as the provinces at their ease, by allowing them a large measure of autonomy in cultural as well as governmental affairs. Special efforts will be needed to keep our people together when the load of foreign domination is removed, because alien rule had demoralized and disorganized us to a degree. To promote national unity we shall have to develop our lingua franca and a common script. Further, with the help of such modern scientific contrivances as aeroplanes, telephone, radio, films, television, etc., we shall have to bring the different parts of India closer to one another and through a common educational policy we shall have to foster a common spirit among the entire population.

With regard to the long period programme for a free India, the first problem to tackle is that of our increasing population. I do not desire to go into the theoretical question as to whether India is over-populated or not. I simply want to point out that where poverty, starvation and disease are stalking the land, we cannot afford to have our population mounting up by thirty millions during a single decade. If the population goes up by leaps and bounds, as it has done in the recent past, our plans are likely to fall through. It will, therefore, be desirable to restrict our population until we are able to feed, clothe and educate those who already exist. It is not necessary at this stage to prescribe the methods that should be adopted to prevent a further increase in population, but I would urge public attention be drawn to this question.

Regarding reconstruction, our principal problem will be how to eradicate poverty from our country. That will require radical reform of our land system, including the abolition of landlordism. Agricultural indebtedness will have to be liquidated and provision made for cheap credit for the rural population. An extension of the co-operative movement will be necessary for the benefit of both producers and consumers. Agriculture will have to be put on a scientific basis with a view to increasing the yield from the land.

To solve the economic problem, agricultural improvement will not be enough. A comprehensive scheme of industrial development under State ownership and State control will be indispensable. A new industrial system will have to be built up in place of the old one, which has collapsed as a result of mass production abroad and alien rule at home. The Planning Commission will have to consider carefully and decide which of the home industries could be revived despite the competition of modern factories, and in which sphere large-scale production should be encouraged. However much we may dislike modern industrialism and condemn the evils which follow in its train, we cannot go back to the pre-industrial era, even if we desire to do so. It is well, therefore, that we should reconcile ourselves to industrialization and devise means to minimize its evils and at the same time explore the possibilities of reviving cottage industries where there is a possibility of their surviving the inevitable competition of factories. In a country like India, there will be plenty of room for cottage industries, especially in the case of industries including hand-spinning and hand-weaving, allied to agriculture.

Last but not the least, the State, on the advice of the Planning Commission, will have to adopt a comprehensive scheme for gradually socializing our entire agricultural and industrial system in the spheres of both production and distribution. Extra capital will have to be procured for this, whether through internal or external loans or through inflation.

How can we strengthen and consolidate the Congress while our Ministers are in office? The first thing to do is to change the composition and character of the bureaucracy. If this is not done, the Congress Party may come to grief. In every country, the Ministers come and go but the steel frame of the permanent services remains. If this is not altered in composition and character, the governmental party and its Cabinet are likely to prove ineffective in putting their principles into practice.

Secondly, the Congress Ministers in the different provinces should, while they are in office, introduce schemes of reconstruction in the spheres of education, health, prohibition, prison reform, irrigation, industry, land reform, worker's welfare, etc. In this matter, attempts should be made to have as far as possible, a uniform policy for the whole of India. This uniformity could be brought about in either of two ways. The Congress Ministers in the different provinces could themselves come together, as the Labour Ministers did in October 1937 in Calcutta, and draw up a uniform programme

At this stage I should like to say something more about the role of the Congress Working Committee. This Committee, in my judgement, is not merely the directing brain of the national army of fighters for freedom. It is also the shadow cabinet of Independent India, and it should function accordingly. This is not an invention of my own. It is the role which has been assigned to similar bodies in other countries that have fought for their national emancipation. I am one of those who think in terms of a Free India- who visualize a National Government in this country within the brief span of our own life. It is consequently natural for us to urge that the Working Committee should feel and function as the shadow cabinet of a free India. This is what President de Valera's Republican Government did when it was fighting the British Government and was on the run. And this is what the Executive of the Wafd Party in Egypt did before it got into office. The members of the Working Committee, while carrying on their day-to-day work, should accordingly study the problems they will have to tackle in the event of their capturing political power.

This brings us to the vexed problem of the collective affiliation of workers' and peasants' organizations to the Congress. Personally I hold the view that the day will come when we shall have to grant this affiliation in order to bring all progressive and anti-imperialist organizations under the influence and control of the Congress. There will, of course, be difference of opinion as to the manner and the extent to which this affiliation should be given, and the character, and stability of such organizations will have to be examined before affiliation could be agreed to. In Russia, the united front of the Soviets of workers, peasants and soldiers played a dominant part in the October Revolution, but on the contrary in Great Britain we find that the British Trades Union Congress exerts a moderating influence on the National Executive of the Labour Party. In India we shall have to consider carefully, what sort of influence organizations like the Trade Union Congress and the Kisan Sabhas will exert on the Indian National Congress in the event of affiliation being granted. We should not forget that there is the possibility that the former may not have radical outlook if their immediate economic grievances are not involved. In any case, quite apart from the question of collective affiliation, there should be the closet co-operation between the National Congress and the other anti-imperialist organizations, and this objective would be facilitated by the later adopting the principles and methods of the former.

Abul Kalam Azad (Ramgarh-1940)

Probably in the history of the Congress, the 1936 session at Lucknow marked a new ideological phase, when the Congress passed a long resolution on the international situation and placed its viewpoint clearly and categorically before the public. After this consideration of the international situation, and a resolution thereon, became an essential and integral part of the annual declarations the Congress, Thus, this decision on this subject was arrived at and placed before the world with full deliberation. These resolutions embodied at one and the same time, two declarations to the world: Firstly, we stated, what I have described as a new ideology in Indian politics, that we could not remain in isolation from the political event of the outside world, even in our present state of helplessness. It was essential that while we forged our way ahead and fashioned our future, we must not confine ourselves merely to our own surroundings but should keep a vigilant watch on the conditions of the outside world. Innumerable changes in the world have brought countries and nations nearer to one another; so that the waves of thought and action, rising in one corner of the world, flow and produce immediate reactions in other places. It is therefore impossible to-day for India to consider her problems while confining herself within her own four walls. It is inevitable that events in the outside world should have their repercussions in India. It is equally inevitable that our decisions and the conditions prevailing in India should affect the rest of the world. It was this consciousness and belief which brought about our decisions.

But whatever the roots of our problems might be, it is obvious that India, like other countries, has her internal problems. Of these, the communal problem is an important one. We do not and cannot expect the British Government to deny its existence. The communal problem is undoubtedly with us and if we want to be ahead, we must take it into account. Every step that we take by ignoring it will be a wrong step. The problem is there; to admit its existence, however, does not mean that it should be used as a weapon against India's national freedom. British Imperialism has always exploited it to this end. If Britain desires to end her imperialistic methods in India and close that dismal chapter of history, then the first signs of the change must naturally appear in her treatment of the communal problem.

What is the Congress position in regard to this problem? It has been the claim of the Congress, from its earliest beginnings, that it considers India as a nation and takes every step in the interest of the nations as a whole. This entitles the world to examine the truth of its assertion. I wish to examine afresh this question from this point of view.

There can be only three aspects of the communal problem: its existence, its importance, and the method of its solution.

The entire history of the Congress demonstrates that it has always acknowledged the existence of the problem. It has never tried to minimize its importance. In dealing with this problem, it followed a policy which was the most suitable under the circumstances. It is difficult to conceive of a different or better course of action. If, however, a better course could be suggested, the Congress was always, and is to-day, eager to welcome it.

We should attach no greater importance to it, than to make it the first condition for the attainment of our national goal. The Congress has always held this belief; no one can challenge this fact. It has always held to two basic principles in this connection, and every step was taken deliberately with these in view.

(1) Whatever constitution is adopted for India, there must be the fullest guarantees in it for the right and interest of minorities.

(2) The minorities should judge for themselves what safeguards are necessary for the protection of their rights and interest. The majority should not decide this. Therefore, the decision in this respect must depend upon the consent of the minorities and not on a majority vote.

The question of the minorities is not a special Indian problem. It has existed in other parts of the world. I venture to address the world from this platform, and to enquire whether any juster and more equitable course of action can be adopted in this connection, than the one suggested above? If so, what is it? Is there anything lacking in this approach, which necessitates that the Congress be reminded of its duty? The Congress has always been ready to consider any failure in the discharge of its duty. It is so prepared today. I have been in the Congress for the last nineteen years. During the whole of this period there is not a single important decision of the Congress in the shaping of which I have not had the honour to participate. I assert that during these last nineteen years, not for a single day did the Congress think of solving this problem in any way other than the way I have stated above. This was not a mere assertion of the Congress, but its determined and decided course of action. Many a time during the last fifteen years, this policy was subjected to the severest test, but it stood firm as a rock.

The manner in which the Congress has dealt with this problem today in connection with the Constituent Assembly, throws a flood of light on these two principles and clarifies them. The recognized minorities have a right, if they so please, to choose their representatives by their votes. Their representatives will not have to rely upon the votes of any other community except their own. So far as the question of the rights and the interest of the minorities is concerned, the decision will not depend upon the majority of the vote in the Constituent Assembly. It will be subject to the consent of the minority. If unanimity is not achieved on any question, then an impartial tribunal, to which the minorities have also consented, will decide the matter. This last provision is merely in the nature of a provision for a possible contingency, and is most unlikely to be required. If a more practical proposal is made, there can be no objection to it.

When these principles are accepted and acted upon by the Congress, what is it that obliges British statesmen to remind us so often of the problem of the minorities, and to make the world believe that this stands in the way of Indian freedom? If its really so, why does not the British government recognise clearly India's freedom and give us an opportunity to solve this problem for ever by mutual agreement amongst ourselves?

Dissensions were sown and encouraged amongst us, and yet we are taunted because of them. We are told to put an end to our communal conflicts, but opportunity to do so is denied to us. Such is the position deliberately created to thwart us; such are the chains that bind. But no difficulties or constraints can deter us from taking the right steps with courage and fortitude. Our path is full of obstacles but we are determined to overcome them.

The Muslims of India and the Future of India

We have considered the problem of the minorities of India. But are the Muslims such a minority as to have the least doubt or fear about their future? A small minority may legitimately have fears and apprehensions, but can the Muslims allow themselves to be disturbed by them? I do not know how many of you are familiar with my writings, twenty-eight years ago, in the "Al Hilal". If there are any such there, I would request them to refresh their memories. Even then I gave expression to my conviction, and I repeat this to-day, that in the texture of Indian politics, nothing is further removed from the truth than to say that Indian Muslims occupy the position of political minority. It is equally absurd for them to be apprehensive about their rights and interest in a democratic India. This fundamental mistake has opened the door to countless misunderstandings. False arguments were built up on wrong premises. This error, on the one hand, brought confusion into the minds of Mussalmans about their own true position, and, on the other hand, it involved the world in misunderstandings, so that the picture of India could no be seen in right perspective.

If time had permitted, I would have told you in detail, how during the last sixty years, this artificial and untrue picture of India was made, and whose hands traced it. In effect, this was the result of the same policy of divide and rule which took particular shape in the mind of British officialdom in India after the Congress launched the national movement. The object of this was to prepare the Mussalmans for use against the new political awakening. In this plan, prominence was given to two points. First, that India was inhabited by two different communities, the Hindus and the Mussalmans, and for this reason no demand could be made in the name of a united nation. Second: that numerically the Mussalmans were far less then the Hindus, and because of this, the necessary consequence of the establishment of democratic institutions in India would be to establish the rule of the Hindu majority and to jeopardise the existence of the Mussalmans.

Politically speaking, the word minority does not mean just a group that is so small in number and so lacking in other qualities that give strength, that it has no confidence in its own capacity to protect itself from the much larger group that surrounds it. It is not enough that the group should be relatively smaller, but that it should be absolutely so small as to be incapable of protecting its interests. Thus this is not merely a question of numbers; other factor count also. If a country has two major groups numbering a million and two millions respectively, it does not necessarily follow that because one is half of the other, therefore it must call itself politically a minority and consider itself weak.

A Basic Question for Indian Musalmans

It is now nearly thirty years since I first attempted to examine this question as an Indian Musalman. The majority of the Muslims then were keeping completely apart from the political struggle and they were influenced by the same mentality of aloofness and antagonism, which prevailed amongst them previously in the year 1888. This depressing atmosphere did not prevent me from giving my anxious thought to this matter, and I reached quickly a final conclusion, which influenced my belief and action. I saw India, with all her many burdens marching ahead to her future destiny. We were fellow-passengers in this boat and we could not ignore its swift passage through the waters; and so it became necessary for us to come to a clear and final decision about our plàn of action. How were we to do so? Not merely be skimming the surface of the position. I did so and I realized that the solution of the whole problem depended on the answer to one question: Do we, Indian Mussalmans, view the free India of the future with suspicion and distrust or with courage and confidence? If we view it with fear and suspicion, then undoubtedly we have to follow a different path. No present declaration, no promise for the future, no constitutional safeguards, can be a remedy for our doubts and fears. We are then forced to tolerate the existence of a third power. This third power is already entrenched here and has no intention of withdrawing and, if we follow this path of fear, we must need to look forward to its continuance. But if we are convinced that for us fear and doubt has no place, and that we must view the future with courage and confidence in ourselves, then our course of action becomes absolutely clear. We find ourselves in a new world, which is free from the dark shadows of doubt, vacillation, inaction, and apathy, and where the light of faith and determination, and enthusiasm never fails. The confusions of the times, the ups and downs that come our way the difficulties that beset our thorny path, cannot change the direction of our steps. It becomes our bounden duty then to march with assured step to India's national goal.

The Muslims and a United Nation

I am a Mussalman and am proud of that fact. Islam's splendid traditions of thirteen hundred years are my inheritance. I am unwilling to lose even the smallest part of this inheritance. The teaching and history of Islam, its arts and letters and civilization are my wealth and my fortune. It is my duty to protect them.

As a Mussalman I have a special interest in Islamic religion and culture and I cannot tolerate any interference with them. But in addition to these sentiments, I have others also which the realities and conditions of my life have forced upon me. The spirit of Islam does not come in the way of these sentiments; it guides and helps me forward. I am proud of being an Indian. I am a part of the indivisible unity that is Indian nationality. I am indispensable to this noble edifice and without me this splendid structure of India is incomplete. I am an essential element which has gone to build India. I can never surrender this claim.

Full eleven centuries have passed by since then. Islam has now as great a claim on the soil of India as Hinduism. If Hinduism has been the religion of the people here for several thousands of years, Islam also has been their religion for a thousand years. Just as a Hindu can say with pride that he is an Indian and follows Hinduism, so also we can say with equal pride that we are Indians and follow Islam. I shall enlarge this orbit still further. The Indian

Christian is equally entitled to say with pride that he is an Indian and is following a religion of India, namely Christianity.

K. Kamaraj (Bhubaneshwar-1964)

Land Policy

Our land policy is one example of legislative action on these lines. We have passed measures for abolition of intermediaries in land and establishing a system of peasant proprietorship, for fixation of ceiling on land holding and fair rents and for providing security of tenure to the tenants. May be, many of the provisions of these legislative enactments are not being zealously enforced in various parts of the country. Such instances should make us watchful and redouble our efforts to ensure that the legal benefits are enjoyed in fact by those for whom they were enacted. It will be useful if each Pradesh Congress Committee would constitute a small sub-committee to study the adequacy of legislation and the degree of implementation of the various land reform laws in its respective State and report to the All India Congress Committee which in its turn would review the progress made in the States.

Economic Progress

While reviewing the economic progress of the country since independence, we can look back with pride on the great strides that our country has made. I do not want to weary you with statistics of achievements in the fields of agriculture, industrial production, education, health, hygiene and social welfare. Any one can see visible advances in every one of these fields during the last decade.

But great as the progress had undoubtedly been, the problems of India are greater still.

For one thing, this progress has not been attended without certain disquieting trends in the functioning of the economy. I may refer, firstly, to the concentration of wealth and economic power in fewer hands resulting in monopolistic control over certain industries. Evasion of taxes, black-marketing in scarce materials, adulteration of food and general deterioration in business standards and commercial practices have assumed proportions against which effective steps are needed. It is necessary to cleanse our society of these evils before they disrupt organized community life.

In my view the development of the co-operative system, in which the divided is controlled, the shareholders are widespread and the management is democratic, will go a long way to prevent the concentration of wealth. If this policy is thoughtfully pursued it will build up the industrial base of the country at a rapid pace. This will also help in curbing the growth of monopolies.

Problems of Unemployment

The rapid economic development which takes place in the country should reflect itself in increasing employment opportunities and improving the standard of life of our people. I would urge the Government to give special attention to the problem of the young educated unemployed and devise means of absorbing them in fruitful occupation. Government should consider the question of starting a number of work centres with varied types of production so as to suit different aptitudes. These centres will help young men to get work-oriented and also to acquire technical skills. They should be able to train a large number of young men not only to find employment in industries and trade, but also to equip themselves to become self-employed. Opportunities should be provided for young boys and girls to become independent self-employed artisans, craftsmen and technicians by providing them with necessary loans, technical assistance, machinery on hire-purchase and the like.

Organizational Work

I have so far dealt with the social and economic problems that face the country. I shall now turn my attention to a few matters relating to our own organisation and its working. There is no doubt that the Congress in order to function effectively as a mass organisation should have its roots firmly grounded in the villages. In my view there should be a Village Congress Committee in every village as the Village Congress Committee is the best medium of mass contact. A serious handicap for Congress Committees is the lack of trained personnel who can organize and canalize the energies of the rural population into fruitful channels. It is necessary to have at least one wholetime trained Congress worker in each block so that both the organizational and development functions of the area may be attended to properly.

In the days of the national struggle the Congress worker had only the simple task of preparing the masses for the struggle ahead; but after achievement of independence our responsibilities have change and we have to attend to the social and economic needs of our people. This cannot be done without preparing a cadre of workers and giving them adequate training in various aspects of our work. It is important that the Pradesh Congress Committees should arrange for training of a large number of workers.

Fund Collection

The Congress Committees should mobilize financial support to the organisation through small collections from the masses. I am convinced that the people will be ready to make such contributions if they are properly approached. The advantage of such collections are obvious. It would enable the Congress workers to learn at first-hand the problems and grievances of the masses and undertake programme for redress.

It will be useful if the executive of the Pradesh Congress Committees meet and exchange ideas and experiences in regard to the common tasks which the Congress organisation has undertaken throughout the country. In such a meeting it would be possibly for the respective Pradesh Congress executive to explain the steps taken for implementation of the Congress programmes, the difficulties encountered and the ways in which they have been overcome. One of the ways in which this can be done is for the Pradesh Congress executives of neighbouring States to discuss common problems. It may also be useful to have a joint meeting of the Pradesh Congress executives of more than two neighbouring States. I think the mutual exchange of experiences amongst the Pradesh Congress executives will go a long way to tone up the general organisation work.

Jagjivan Ram (Bombay-1969)

Organisation versus Parliamentary Wing

An organisation of moderates wedded to the method of constitutional representation, the Congress underwent a transformation when Gandhi emerged on the scene. It functioned since then till the advent of independence as a mass movement and a united anti-imperialist front. It developed a massive organisation conforming in structure roughly to the

British administrative apparatus. Beginning at the village level and extending up through the district and provincial levels to the Working Committee which approximated to the cabinet of independent India and a President who was a symbol of the people, it dominated the Indian political scene for decades. It was relatively easier during this phase to reconcile the varying and conflicting view of its highly differentiated following because of unanimity on the objective of political independence. After the achievement of this goal, however, in 1947, it had to adjust itself to a new situation in which the locus of power shifted from Party to Government. The adjustment did not prove easy. Two Presidents quit office and some sort of a convention appeared to have crystallized. But it proved to be illusory. There was no convention; there was only an adjustment. Therefore, when Panditji passed away, instead of the Congress Parliamentary Party electing its leader, through the established democratic procedure of a free election and the organisation accepting the decision without reservation, a reverse process was initiated which sought to circumvent the free expression of the will of the members of the parliamentary party, put it in the background, and put the organisation chief in the position of a king-maker. I want to make it clear that in saying this, I am emphasizing a principle and no reference to personalities is intended. The reference is made only to underline that abridgement of denial of internal democracy invariably produces distortions.

Road to Socialism

It is sad to reflect that even though we had leaders who could compare in stature, dedication and ability to the best that the world ever produced, even though we had an organisation more massive than any political party in the world, the country has not reached anywhere near the goal which it set for itself. Many are doubting if it is on the right path. Is this debacle due to a confusion of ideas and ideals? Is it entirely because of the mass character of the Congress with its various pulls in different directions? Does the Congress have a philosophical framework with reference to which Congressmen can come to a definite conclusion in respect of matters which confront them?

The post-independence Congress had in its election manifestoes laid down as targets, the achievement of a national minimum standards, opportunities for full employment, a ceiling on personal incomes, not exceeding 40 times the national minimum to be brought down eventually to 20 times and a very elaborate programme for industries, agriculture, village and cottage industries, industrial relations, cooperation, and recommended the appointment of a permanent Planning Commission to advise and assist Central and State Governments in the practical steps that should be taken. Even before these resolutions could be implemented and the pledges made fulfilled, we set new targets. We declared that the objective of planning should be the establishment of a socialistic pattern of society and we envisaged achieving of full employment within a period of ten years.

Within a few years, even before we were anywhere near these goals, we gave a call for a revolution to be brought about through radical changes in the attitudes, outlook and ways of thinking and living of the people through fundamental changes in the social and economic structure, and made noble declaration that caste and class had no place in the social order. Karachi, Lucknow, Nagpur, Avadi, Bhubaneshwar are all important milestones on the road to socialism which has yet to be traversed.

Democracy, Socialism and Secularism: Three Pillars of Congress Policy

The humanistic strands in Indian thought which regard man as a part of divinity, as something sacred, are part of our heritage. Gandhiji's teachings are there. Nehru's vision is there. We have been able to synthesise these great strains or our thought with the humanistic strands of Western thought into our ideology of democratic socialism. We are committed to democracy, socialism and secularism—the three pillars on which the Indian National Congress stands. We all realise that in a traditionalistic backward society, democracy without socialism implies the rule of the privileged by the privileged and for the privileged and socialism without democracy implies totalitarianism. We know that secularism is in a way an old Indian ideal and not just a Western inheritance. Equal respect for all religions is ingrained in the thought structure of his country. Unfortunately, the humanistic and liberal strands of Indian thought never got integrated into the social structure, were never practiced in daily life. The West lived up to it. The concept that man is born with certain inalienable right forms the very foundation of Western democratic society. And the West progressed. Indian society reared on built-in-cumulative inequalities and disregard of man, languished. The thoughts are not new to us. In any case modern man is the inheritor of all that is noble and good in human thought. And thus, our democratic socialism is a synthesis of all that is best in the thinking of the East and West and provides an ideology superior to other sectarian ideologies, which are 'Communalistic' or 'Communitarian'.

What is to be Done?

What is to be done? Let us begin from the root—the reorganisation of agriculture and our rural economy. It is true that the method of production determines the method of distribution. If, therefore, there has to be an equalization of economic power in the rural areas, a new method of production must be adopted. Village leadership today consists of the substantial and middle farmers, and the small farmer and the landless labourer still has no place. It is still the old *zamindars* turned substantial farmers who rule the village. It is still the old dominant castes which continue to dominate the village life. The governmental machinery reflecting the caste, and class structure in the village, plays a supporting, if not a subservient role in perpetuating the existing order. All this has to change. A new leadership has to emerge and reliable agencies at the village level have to be created. These agencies must consist of local people who have a stake in development and who are dedicated. Such an agency must consist of all those who have hungry stomachs and willing hands, meager or no land and no means of production. The agency must emerge in this manner, as it were, from the soil of the village.

Land reform shall not brook delay. Elimination of intermediary tenures, ceiling on holdings, distribution of surplus and Government land among landless agriculture labour should be expedited.

The problem of landless agriculture labour is creating an explosive situation. Available surplus land will not be adequate for distribution among all of them nor will all of them be absorbed in rural works and other agricultural operations, etc. Greater attention will have to be paid, therefore, to self-employment of these millions of the submerged section in productive effort.

The programme outlined will transform Panchayats into real organs of people's will. Today, their structure, constitution, functions, powers, differ from area to area. To think in the existing context of effectively functioning Panchayats in rural areas where the majority live below the subsistence level is a mockery of the democratic ideas of Panchayati Raj. It is true that Panchayats did function in the old days and survived where nothing else survived. But those were days when the starving and the poor were content to starve. They were content to accept the privileged or the affluent as their natural overlords. That past cannot be resurrected. All men are now equal. Men can now cooperate willingly and effectively only on a footing of equality. And, there will be no equality between a needy starving person and the privileged and the affluent. The new threads, therefore, that will bind the village to the Panchayat must be different.

Another vital item of our programme—cooperation, has not made much progress in all parts of the country. Its development has not been even. In our rural areas, loyalty is still to caste or some power-group rather than to any cooperative image. Perhaps the one form of cooperation which could have broken the barriers and contributed to optimum results from agriculture was the service cooperatives. In some areas it has made spectacular progress. But there also the small farmers have not benefit much.

Indian society is a plural society. Social contact between various religious and caste groups are few and far between. Localities and habitations of these groups are also separate. In the new India that we want to create, it should be ensured that in all housing schemes, Government or otherwise, only mixed schemes are encouraged which include persons of various religions and castes. Similarly, religious festivals of all communities should be collectively observed so that it may encourage greater social integration.

Problems of Weaker Sections

I have always maintained that the problems of the Scheduled Castes and Tribes cannot be fully appreciated much less solved except in the framework of a radical reorganisation of the socio-economic order. That will take long. But even the scope of welfare projects and the manner of their implementation leaves much to be desired. It was to be expected that when the condition of these communities improved they would aspire to live as decent human beings. It was equally to be expected that with the growth of consciousness and an understanding of their rights, they would refuse to be treated as before. But wherever this trend has manifested itself, particularly in the rural areas, oppression and harassment has been renewed. It is an indication of the fact that upper caste psychology has not undergone any real change; there has only been some kind of grudging adjustment. Even the so-called liberals share the same attitude: only its expression is different. How else would one explain the much vaunted talk of pity, the much publicized desire to do some good to the depressed and suppressed communities. I have no quarrel with them but I wish that they realised that, at root, their attitude is not different in kind from the attitude of society at large. The extension of the constitutional reservation of seats for these classes for another 10 years has been a step in the right direction. But many more steps, as I have indicated, will have to be taken. All practices which segregate the Scheduled Castes from Caste-Hindus and perpetuate the discriminatory attitude should be removed. Separate colonies for Scheduled Castes should not be established. They should be mixed ones both in urban and rural areas. For all students of Scheduled Castes and Scheduled Tribes liberal stipends should be provided, technical education encouraged and facilitated, and proper representation in public service ensured.

Rajiv Gandhi (Centenary Session, Bombay, Dec. 28, 1985)

Friends,

This is a moment consecrated by history. One hundred years have passed since the Indian National Congress first met in this great city. Between then and now, India and the world have witnessed profound historical changes—changes that have affected the very structure of human thought and action. In this epoch of radical change, the Indian National Congress brought the world to India and took India to the world. Its non-violent revolution has transformed our nation. Today, it charts the path to India's greatness.

We rejoice in this moment. We rejoice in the great achievements, the great deeds of the people of India. We rejoice in the noble expressions of the human intellect and sprit represented by Mahatma Gandhi, Jawaharlal Nehru and Indira Gandhi. We rejoice in the pledge redeemed. We rejoice that the honour is ours now to carry the torch of freedom and progress.

But our joy is mixed with sorrow. Indiraji should have been here today, speaking to you in her gentle, impassioned voice. One with Bharatmata's immortal spirit, she now shines as a lodestar not only for us but for all humanity.

As I recall the great women and men who have led the Indian National Congress-the Parliament of Indian Nationalism—I feel proud and humble. I draw strength from the glorious tradition of our party and from the overflowing affection of the people of India.

May I thank dynamic Bombay and its gracious and hospitable people, for playing host to us, as they played host to our founding fathers in 1885. I, of course, have a sentimental relationship with Bombay. I was born here. Life-giving currents from every part of India flow into Bombay. It is India in microcosm.

Many distinguished delegates have come to this session from far and near, bringing to us the friendship and greetings of their parties and peoples. We appreciate this gesture. Through these honoured guests, we send our good wishes to the people of their countries.

As I stand before you this morning, my mind travels back to those fateful years when the Congress fought for India's freedom. And I think of those giants who made the Indian National Congress. Seldom has the world seen a nobler galaxy of women and men, so selfless in their devotion to the cause of freedom, so exalted in thought, so brave in action, so pure in spirit. To remember them is to live once again in those times "when the world's great age seemed to begin anew." A.O. Hume, Womesh Chandra Bonnerjee, Dadabhai Naoroji, Pherozeshah Mehta, Mahadev Govind Ranade, Badrudin Tyabji, Lokmanya Tilak, Gopal Krishna Gokhale, Surendra Nath Banerjea, Annie Besant, Bipin Chandra Pal, Lala Lajpat Rai, Mahatma Gandhi, Motilal Nehru, Madan Mohan Malaviya, Deshbandhu Chittaranjan Das, Srinivasa Iyengar, Sarojini Naidu, M.A. Ansari, Jawaharlal Nehru, Sardar Vallabbhai Patel, Chakravarti Rajagopalachari, Mazharul Haque, Satyamurthi, Rajendra Prasad, Maulana Abul Kalam Azad, Saifuddin Kitchlew, Tristao de Braganza Cunha, Gopabandhu Das, Netaji Subhas Chandra Bose, Gopinath Bordoloi, Govind Ballabh Pant, Purushottam Das Tandon, T. Prakasam, Bidhan Chandra Roy, Acharya Kripalani, Acharya Narendra Dev, Rajkumari Amrit Kaur, Rafi Admed Kidwai, Acharya Vinoba Bhave, Jayaprakash Narayan, Indira Gandhi, K. Kamaraj, Lal Bahadur Shastri, Gurmukh Singh 'Musafir', Fakhruddin Ali Ahmed and countless others. We bow in reverence to their memory. They awakened the spirit of freedom in the Indian people crushed under the oppressive burden of imperialism. Gurudev Tagore and Sri

Aurobindo Ghosh were one with the leaders of our struggle for independence in reawakening India to its true destiny.

It is our fortune that one of our great freedom, Khan Abdul Ghaffar Khan Sahib, is with us today. His life is a saga of sacrifice and non-violence. He has asked nothing for himself and has given his all to the service of his fellow men. We greet him with respect, with love, and pray he may long be with us.

We are blessed with the presence of large number of freedom fighters. We honour them for they made freedom a living reality. Their refusal to submit to the indignity of slavery, the very act of their defiance, and their luminous vision of a united and free India touched the imagination of millions. To the nameless and unsung heroes of our freedom struggle, we offer our humble tribute. Their life-blood nourishes the body of independent India.

How did the miracle of India's rebirth in freedom come about? And what did India do with its new life? The answers are to be found in the story of the Indian National Congress.

How shall we remember Mahatma Gandhi, that eternal pilgrim of freedom? Born of the very spirit of India, steeped in the tradition, the song, the legend of our ancient land—and yet he was revolutionary. Unique among revolutionaries, he marched for freedom, clad in the robe of truth, with non-violence for his staff.

He did not counter the violence of the oppressor with the violence of the oppressed. He met it by changing the oppressed from within. He freed them from fear and hatred. He ignited the greatest peaceful mass movement known to history. At his gentle summon, millions of Indian rose to assert their human dignity and walked upright with the spark of greatness in them.

Gandhiji the revolutionary was concerned with nothing less than the total reconstruction of our society. In Champaran among the impoverished peasants, in Ahmedabad among the textile workers, and in hundreds of thousands of village of India, he had seen the soul of India seared by the ruthless exploitation of the poor. He saw how India's social system had been vitiated by iniquitous practices—the oppression of the Harijans, of the women and of the poor.

To Mahatma Gandhi, the key to India's progress was the development of its villages. In his unified vision, education, agriculture, village industry, social reform, all came together to provide the basis for a vibrant rural society, free from exploitation and linked to the urban centres as equals. Our planning incorporates this basic insight.

His crusade against untouchability stirred an ossified system. His radical premise of human dignity and equality electrified millions who lived and struggled at the very margin of social existence. Independent India was to enshrine Mahatma Gandhi's war on untouchability in its Constitution.

The freedom movement transformed the status of women. Women fought along with men as comrades. In the process, the shackles that had bound them fell away. Legal safeguards and rights were to come later but Mahatma Gandhi emancipated women from slavery and oppression. What took centuries in other countries was accomplished in a matter of decades in our freedom struggle.

The mark of true revolutionary is that he sets new standards and values. Gandhiji did. Let us recall his words:

"I will give you a talisman. Whenever you are in doubt or when the self becomes too much with you, apply the following test: Recall the face of the poorest and the weakest man whom you may have seen and ask yourself if the step you contemplate is going to be of any use to him. Will he gain anything by it? Will it restore him to a control over his own life and density? In other words, will it lead to Swaraj for the hungry and spiritually starving millions? Then you will find your doubts and yourself melting away."

We cannot, and will not, rest until we have won true Swaraj for the hungry and spiritually starving millions—until we have wiped out poverty from our land. Then and only then can we claim the privilege of being true disciples of the great Mahatma.

Mahatma Gandhi called Jawaharlal Nehru 'the jewel of India.' Panditji added new dimensions to our concept of freedom. To a reawakened India, he brought intimations of mighty historical forces at work on the world stage. As the freedom struggle grew in intensity, he went out among the masses, unfolding his vision of the future: immemorial India rejuvenated by modern science, technology, and the cleansing moral force of socialism, yet retaining her identity and the age old wealth of her spiritual wisdom.

Jawaharlal Nehru destroyed the edifice of imperialism. For he knew he had the greater task of building a new society. He was a great builder. He gave India the enduring structure of democratic parliamentary institutions buttressed by the rule of law. Fundamental rights, directive principles of State policy, and safeguards for the Scheduled Castes and Scheduled Tribes together make our Constitution one of humanity's great charters of freedom and equality. We have passed through many a crisis, but democracy has continued to flourish—to the consternation of those who believed that democracy was for the rich, not for the poor. In India, democracy with all its claimant contention, is alive and vibrant.

Jawaharlal Nehru fashioned the planning process to reach the ultimate objective of a socialist. Planning is now a part of the national consensus. It was not always so. It used to be described as the road to serfdom. Those who scoffed have stayed to praise. We have a strong economy. We are firmly set on the path of self-reliance, which means more freedom, not less. Our planning process has succeeded.

Panditji built the infrastructure of science and technology with loving care. Atomic energy and space stand out as symbols of this achievement, but no field was left untouched. Let us not forget that it was Panditji who established the great laboratories, the giant irrigation dams, the fertilizer plants and the agricultural universities. This was the foundation of our self-sufficiency.

Immersed as he was in the thick of our freedom struggle, Pandit Nehru foresaw that, in the ultimate analysis, the linkages between modern agriculture and industrialisation offered the only lasing solution to the poverty of India's masses. With independence, the time came to translate into reality the dream of a vigorous, industrialized India. Panditji created the imposing structure of our industry. Leading this might effort was the public sector, a strong and dependable lever for development. He envisioned for it the commanding heights of the economy. Under his inspiration, basic industries, infrastructure, machine building, oil exploration, metals and minerals and defence industries were established in the public sector. New technology was absorbed and nurtured. New skills came to those who had never turned a simple lathe. Centres of modern industry blossomed in backward and remote areas. With confidence, the Indian people wrote a new chapter in their long and tumultuous history. Through the instrument of the public sector, Jawaharlal Nehru made the decisive break with India's colonial deindustrialised stagnation.

Panditji was the great unifier of the Indian people. India is the home of many great religions. Her many splendoured mansion of unity rests on the bedrock of secularism. Like a great teacher, he expounded in simple language the philosophy of secularism. He repeatedly warned the nation against communalism. To him, secularism was the beacon light when waves of passion threatened to submerge us.

Panditji looked at the world with the eyes of a humanist, in love with nature and with the works of man. He perceived before many others, that the splitting of the atom had changed for all time to come the universe of discourse among nations. War in nuclear age was no longer policy by other means–it was mass suicide. He saw no meaning in military block. They did not guarantee security. They only guaranteed fear. He wanted nations to cooperate, not dominate. He evolved the philosophy of non-alignment. Non-alignment is the international expression of national resurgence. It is the extension of democracy to international relations. It means independence of thought and action. Panditji abjured entanglement with power blocs, because power blocs are based on conflict, and erode the independence of countries which join them. He put forward the positive concept of peaceful co-existence and cooperation to build a better, saner world free from anxiety, suspicion and fear. This vision of a cooperative world order even today guides the Non-aligned Movement, representing the vast majority of the family of nations. It is a powerful force for freedom, peace and justice in the world. In its centenary year, the Indian National Congress is proud that India has the honour to lead the Non-aligned Movement.

All this and more is the legacy of Jawaharlal Nehru, his imperishable bequest to us in the Indian National Congress.

The smooth succession of Lal Bahadur Shastri proved the inherent strength of our democratic system. He guided the country with steadfast devotion to the basic policies of the Congress. The Congress has always stood for patriotism, simplicity, selfless service and dedication to the cause of the underprivileged, Shastriji epitomized these values.

With the sudden demise of Shastriji, once more the question arose with even greater urgency: Would a united India survive? Would its democracy endure?

Would a food-deficit country be able to preserve its independence? Would the cry of social justice remain unheeded? India's voice for freedom, peace and justice remain as firm and resonant as in the past? Or would neo-colonialism claim yet another victim? Would India once again become a petitioner in the chancelleries of the West?

The world was torn by anxiety and conflict. In Vietnam, war continued to rage. There were no signs of any lessening of East-West tensions. In India, food shortage and inflation bred serious unrest. There were intense pressures to abandon the path of planned development. It was situation to daunt the most stout-hearted.

Never known to flee from challenge, Indira Gandhi took up cudgels on behalf of the masses of India. She placed the removal of poverty at the very centre of the planning process. One radical step followed boldly upon another, establishing beyond doubt where the sympathies of the Indian National Congress lay. The nationalization of banks, the abolition of privy-purses, the takeover of the coal mines, the promulgation of radical land reforms and the creation of constitutional safety-nets for them, the formulation of a system of guaranteed prices to farmers, the setting up of a country-wide public distribution system, the large scale extension on modern technology to agriculture, the establishment of the Monopolies and Restrictive Trade Practices Commission to curb concentration of economic power, the great impetus to the growth of the public sector, the tremendous fillip to indigenous science and technology, the Pokhran test for peaceful purposes, the Space programme and the launching of the massive 20-Point Programme and the Rural Landless Labour Employment Guarantee Programme—all these electrified the nation.

The Congress in the late sixties reminded one of Panditji's address to the 1936 Lucknow Congress, where he said:

"We have largely lost touch with the masses and, deprived of the life-giving energy that flows from them. We dry up and weaken and our organisation shrinks and loses the power it had."

The people were adrift. The policies of the Congress were in confusion. There was no programme of action. At this point of crisis, Indira Gandhi revitalized the party by restoring its organic link with the masses. The sap of action began to flow once again in the veins of the organisation. The vocabulary and the idiom of Indian politics were never to be same again after her historic call for 'garibi hatao'.

Indiraji transformed the Congress from a party in which vested interest had gradually gained ascendancy into a party which identified itself totally with the hopes and aspirations of the poor. Through her unrelenting struggle against those who opposed radical change in our social and economic structure, she placed her indelible stamp on the history of our party. With unparalleled tenacity, she persuaded millions of Congresswomen and men to pursue the path of socialism to progress. She took the people into confidence on the nature of the issues which were convulsing the Congress and mobilised them behind her policies. The masses gave her the strength to face with unequalled courage the inner turmoil of the party. They manned the barricades. In 1969, the champions of the status quo had to retreat, relinquishing their control of our great organisation. The triumph of the Congress in the 1971 elections was a big blow to the forces that had thwarted social change from within the party. They were to regroup and challenge her again.

India's unequivocal stand on major international issues had disturbed, even alarmed, forces who were exerting pressures on us to deflect us from our independent policy of non-alignment. The emergence of sovereign Bangladesh and Indira Gandhi's historic role in it were anathema to neo-imperialism. Almost immediately thereafter began the collusion between external and internal forces of destabilisation. The international economic crisis, widespread drought and inflation within the country put an intolerable strain on our system. National stability was in dire peril.

To meet an unprecedented threat to the nation's stability, an emergency was proclaimed in 1975. The process of socio-economic change gathered momentum with the promulgation of the bold and dynamic 20-Point Programme. A democrat to the core to her being, Indiraji called elections in 1977. She accepted the verdict of the people who defeated her and the Congress. She knew it was an angry reaction to some mistakes that had been committed, but that the people were still with her and with the Congress. She stood by the people in their travail as they faced the tragic consequences of the reversal of national accepted policies. But many of her colleagues did not have her courage of conviction. Their vision faltered. They parted company with her. The Congress again emerged, with youth in the vanguard, as the sword arm of the poor. They voted her back in 1980, expressing their unbounded love for her and trust in her commitment to social justice.

In radicalizing the Congress, Indira Gandhi also gave new strength and vitality to the democratic parliamentary institutions of the Republic. She realigned our political process with the urges of the toiling masses. By translating the people's aspirations into epoch making legislation, policy innovations and programmes for the uplift of the poor, she made the legislature watchful guardians of the rights and needs of the people. Elections and the parliamentary process acquired ideological programmatic clarity, giving direction to national progress. She mobilised immense numbers of people from all strata, filing them with hope and deepening their allegiance to the democratic way of life. In victory as in defeat, Indiraji was the prime mover of the people's emotions and endeavours. She ensured that India's democracy would never be the plaything of vested interests.

Indira Gandhi knew, as did Jawaharlal Nehru, that social justice depended on the production and equitable distribution of wealth. She attended to the growth potential of our economy like a loving mother. The first to claim her attention was agriculture. Not just because an overwhelming majority derived their livelihood from agriculture, but because national independence and self-respect demanded that we do not stretch our hands before anyone for food. Many here will still recall the pain and the humiliation of the 'ship-to-mouth' days. She called upon our farmers and our agricultural scientists to apply modern technology to increase food production. Their heart-warning response is a matter of history. Thus were laid the impregnable foundation of self-reliance.

As she had faced not one but two oil crises, Indira Gandhi was determined to take India towards self-sufficiency in energy resources. The prodigious effort to raise oil production, trebling it in the short space of four years, is testimony to her far-sighted vision.

Indiraji had a unique relationship with India's dedicated scientific community. She was their special friend to whom they turned for counsel and encouragement. Together they placed India in the front rank of international scientific communities. A few days ago I was in Kalpakkam to inaugurate the fast breeder test reactor. India is the seventh country in the world to have such a reactor. Indiraji's monumental work in furthering indigenous science and technology has greatly strengthened the base for self-reliance.

Generations will remember with gratitude the decisive direction Indira Gandhi gave to India's industrialization and technological advance. She set exacting tasks for the public sector which responded with enthusiasm. Through the exertions of the working class and talented managers and technologist, it became the pivot of India's industrial progress. All branches and sectors of industry grew with speed, placing India among the major industrial nations of the world. The enormous range and depth of industrial progress, centred on the public sector, has served the nation well. Today, if we are poised for faster technological growth, the credit goes to Indiraji who prepared the seed-bed of modernisation.

In the international field, Indira Gandhi was the authentic voice of non-alignment, of peace and peaceful coexistence, disarmament and development. She was bold and fearless, refusing to be cowed down by pressures howsoever strong. Where the independence or sovereignty of India were in question, she never vacillated, never hesitated, never compromised. She stood like a rock in the defence of India.

The passion that ruled her was above all the passion for the unity and integrity of India. In the perspective of history, she knew how India had been subjugated because of its inability to rectify internal weaknesses and to unitedly confront external dangers. She turned the searchlight on the internal social malaise that weakened the nation—the deprivation of the scheduled castes and the scheduled tribes, the social and economic backwardness of the minorities, communalism, casteism and narrow regional loyalties. Her effort throughout was to strengthen the national fabric. Her socio-economic programmes are her greatest contribution of national integration.

But she never forgot the threats to India, external and internal, direct and indirect, military and economic. She campaigned relentlessly to alert the nation to these dangers and toiled unremittingly to strengthen our defences. She had seen again and again how the independence and unity of nations had been suborned and subverted. She was determined not to let this happen to India. Nothing would induce her to accept the dilution of an iota of India's unity and sovereignty, even at the cost of her life.

What of the future? Where do we go from here?

There is no rest for us. As Jawaharlal Nehru had said, "We cannot rest, for rest is betrayal of those who have gone and in going handed the torch of freedom to us keep alight; it is betrayal of the cause we have espoused and the pledge we have taken; it its betrayal of the millions who never rest." We cannot rest.

The history of our party tells us that, at each critical turning point, we took stock of our weaknesses and strengths to decide the direction we must take. The present situation demands a similar unsparing examination. Without self-introspection, without soul searching, movement will not be of much avail. We must see ourselves in the mirror of truth. What have we done with the legacy of our great leaders?

To answer this question, I must delve into my own political experience, short though it is. When I started my political work, it was only with the motive of being by the side of my mother. She bore with stoic fortitude the irreparable loss of a son who had been a tower of strength. She gave me no directions, no formulae, no prescriptions. She just said, "Understand the real India, its people, its problems." So I plunged into work. Millions of faces in varying moods of joy and sorrow, of eager expectation, of triumph and defeat filled my being, till they merged into the face of mother India, proud, defiant, confident but also full of sad perplexity. Always, the unspoken question haunting her face: Whiter India?

I was exhilarated by what had been achieved in the short period since independence. I was also saddened by what might have been but was not, because of weaknesses in government and in the party. I kept my counsel to myself as I was an apprentice in the great school of politics.

After two years of incessant traveling, meeting people, reading and reflection, I felt I could go to her with my perception. Listening to me, she thought I had gained some understanding of the complexities of our society. And then she began to unburden herself. She spoke of India's enduring strength and of her hopes for India, but also of her apprehensions and anxieties. She analyzed with clinical precision how the entire system had been weakened from within, how the party had once again been infiltrated by vested interests who would not allow us to move, how patronage and graft had affected the national institutional framework, how nationalism and patriotism had ebbed, how the pettiness and selfishness of persons in political positions had ruptured social fabric. She was clear that if India had to keep her 'tryst with destiny,' so much had to change. And then, suddenly, she left us. Indiraji's thoughts and reflections on the state of the nation are an abiding influence.

We have cherished our democracy. Democracy is our strength. In 1984, the people of India gave our party its largest ever majority. Their eloquent verdict strengthened the unity and integrity of India. A nation sorrowing over its beloved leader drew from its vast reserves of strength to protect the inheritance of its glorious freedom struggle.

We applied the lessons of the 1984 elections to the complex and difficult problems in Punjab and Assam. Our basic concern was to end any sense of alienation in the larger interest of national unity. We carried forward the process to reach understanding and harmony, to dispel mistrust and suspicion, and to seek the peoples' mandate for progress through brotherhood. We had no narrow partisan considerations in view. The situation demanded that we rise above mere expediency. The Congress, with its century-old tradition of nationalism, put India first.

We have no illusions that all problems have been resolved. But the democratic way of nation-building requires patience, perseverance and a spirit of conciliation. Those who have been entrusted with responsibility have to constantly keep in view the larger perspective of unity. They have to act in the same spirit in which we have acted, the spirit of the nationalism. Enduring unity comes from the willing cooperation of all.

We proclaim and celebrate the unity of India. It is a fact of transcending significance. But is it not also a fact that most of us, in our daily lives, do not think of ourselves as Indian? We see ourselves Hindus, Muslims or Christians, or Malayalees, Maharashtra, Bengalis. Worse, we think of ourselves as Brahmins, Thakurs, Jats, Yadavs and so on and so forth. And we shed blood to hold our narrow and selfish denominations. We are imprisoned by the narrow domestic wall of religion, language, caste and region, blocking out the clear view of a resurgent nation. Political parties, State Governments and social organisations promote policies, programmes and ideologies which divide brother from brother and sister from sister. Bonds of fraternity and solidarity yield to the onslaughts of meanness of mind and spirit. Is this the India for which Mahatma Gandhi and Indira Gandhi sacrificed their lives?

Turn to the great institutions of our country and you will see that too often, behind their imposing facades, the spirit and substance lack vitality. The work they do sometimes seem strangely irrelevant to the primary concerns of the masses. Attempts are made to taint the electoral process at its very source. Issues of crucial national importance are frequently subordinated to individual sectional and regional interests. Our legislatures do not set standards for other groups to follow; they magnify manifold the conspicuous lack of a social ethic. A convenient conscience compels individuals to meander from ideology to ideology seeking power, influence and riches. Political parties twist their tenets, enticed by opportunism. "The best lack all conviction and the worst are full of passionate intensity.

We are amongst the few to have the rule of law and an independent judiciary. But thousands wait for decades while an elaborate and arcane machinery grinds ever so slowly. The poor have little hope of timely redress.

We value our free press. It made a magnificent contribution to our freedom struggle. After Independence, the national media have helped to consolidate our unity and promote social and economic change. But the question the media need to put to themselves is: Does their contribution to nation building measure up to their role in the freedom struggle?

Our economy owes much to the enterprise of our industrialists. But there are some reputed business and industrial establishments which shelter battalions of law breakers and tax evaders. We have industrialists untouched by the thrusting spirit of the great risk-takers and innovators. The trader's instinct for quick profits prevails. They flourish on sick industries. Many have not cared to learn the fundamental lesson that industrialization springs from the development of indigenous technology, not from dependence on others. Industrial empire built on the shaky foundations of excessive protection, social irresponsibility, import orientation and corruption may not last long.

The trade unions have a glorious heritage of nationalism and a socially relevant radicalism. Today, they are a mere shadow of their past. They protect the few who have, oblivious of millions who have not. They feel little concern for the creation of national wealth, only for a larger and larger share in it. Nothing is considered illegitimate if one marches under the right flag. Power without responsibility, rights without duties have come to be their prerogative. Will productivity arise from such stony soil? Let us not forget that the poor and the unemployed have to sacrifice their development programmes to subsidies inefficient industry.

In the field of education, the nation has much to be proud of. Access to education has been widened immeasurably. Indian scholars are in the front rank of creative endeavour in the best institutions across the world. But the schools, the universities and the academies of the Republic, which should fill our minds with hope for tomorrow, cause us great concern. Teachers seldom teach and students seldom learn. Strikes, mass copying, agitations are more attractive alternatives. Where there should be experiment and innovation, there is obeisance to dead ritual and custom, smothering creativity and the quest for knowledge and truth. Where there should be independence and integrity, there is the heavy hand of politics, caste and corruption. Where there should be a new integration between modern science and our heritage, there is a dull repetition of lifeless formulae. Millions are illiterate. Millions of children have never been inside a school.

And what of the iron frame of the system, the administrative and the technical services, the policies and the myriad functionaries of the State? They have done so much and can do so much more, but as the proverb says there can be no protection if the fence starts eating the crop. This is what has happened. The fence has started eating crop. We have Government servants who do not serve but oppress the poor and the helpless, police who do not uphold the law but shield the guilty, tax collectors who do not collect taxes but connive with those who cheat the State, and whole legions whose only concern is their private welfare at the cost of society. They have no work ethic, no feeling for the public cause, no involvement in the future of the nation, no comprehension of national goals, no commitment to the values of modern India. They have only a grasping, mercenary outlook devoid of competence, integrity and commitment.

How have we come to this pass?

We have looked at others. Now let us look at ourselves. What has become of our great organisation? Instead of the party that fired the imagination of the masses throughout the length and breadth of India, we have shrunk, losing touch with the toiling millions. It is not a question of victories and defeats in elections. For a democratic party, victories and defeats are part of its continuing political existence. But what does matter is whether or not we work among the masses, whether or not we are in tune with their struggles, their hopes and aspirations. We are a party of social transformation, but in our preoccupation with governance we are drifting away from the people. Thereby, we have weakened ourselves and fallen prey to the ills that the loss of invigorating mass contact brings.

Millions of ordinary Congress workers throughout the country are full of enthusiasm for the Congress policies and programmes. But they are handicapped, for on their backs ride the brokers of power and influence, who dispense patronage to convert a mass movement into a feudal oligarchy. They are self-perpetuating cliques who thrive by invoking the slogans of caste and religion and by enmeshing the living body of the Congress in their net of avarice.

For such persons, the masses do not count. Their life style, their thinking, or lack of it, their self-aggrandisement, their corrupt ways, their linkages with the vested interests in society, and their sanctimonious posturing are wholly incompatible with work among the people. They are reducing the Congress organisation to shell from which the spirit of service and sacrifice has been emptied.

As we have distanced ourselves from the masses, basic issues of national unity and integrity, social change and economic development recede into the background. Instead, phoney issues, shrouded in medieval obscurantism, occupy the centre of the stage. Our Congress workers, who faced the bullets of British imperialism, run for shelter at the slightest manifestation of caste and communal tension. Is this the path that Gandhiji, Panditji and Indiraji showed to a secular, democratic India?

We talk of the high principles and lofty ideals needed to build a strong and prosperous India. But we obey no discipline, no rule, follow no principle of public morality, display no sense of social awareness, show no concern for the public weal. Corruptions is not only tolerated but even regarded as the hallmark of leadership. Flagrant contradiction between what we say and what we do has become our way of life. At every step, our aims and actions conflict. At every stage, our private self crushes our social commitment.

As action has diverged from precept, the ideology of the Congress has acquired the status of an heirloom to be polished and brought out on special occasion. It must be a living force to animate the Congress workers in their day-to-day activity. Our ideology of nationalism, secularism, democracy and socialism is the only relevant ideology for our great country. But we are forgetting that we must take it to the masses, interpret its content in changing circumstances, and defend it against the attacks of our opponents.

Mahatma Gandhi visualized the Congress as a fighting machine. Time and again we have demonstrated our fighting qualities—in the great non-cooperation movements of the twenties and thirties, in the Quit India movement of 1942, in the fifties and sixties when we carried the message of socialism to every door, in 1969-71 when the vested interests had to be fought in Parliament, in the courts and in the streets and in 1977-79 when persecution and calumny were answered by thousands of brave *satyagrahis* throughout the country. This is our tradition. We have to revive this tradition to fight for the poor and the oppressed. Only doing so shall we gain the strength to create the India of our dreams.

The revitalization of our organisation is a historical necessity. At this critical juncture, there is no other political party capable of defending the unity and integrity of the country. There is no other party capable of taking the country forward to progress and prosperity. All other parties are shot through and through with internal contradictions. The sorry, unedifying spectacle of their total incapacity, corruption, nepotism, hypocrisy has disfigured our political landscape. They have shown a cynical disregard for sensitive issues of national security. Some have not hesitated even to collude with anti-national elements. Their ideological roots are shallow, their political outlook circumscribed by region, caste and religion. Wherever they have come to power, they have retarded social and economic progress. They have no sense of history. Those who campaign for a weak Centre, campaign against the unity and integrity of India. Their slogans of welfare are spurious because true welfare comes from growth, which they have been busy destroying. It is the responsibility of the Congress to ensure that India is not left to the mercy of such forces.

We must once more generate a mass movement based on Congress ideology to fulfil this momentous task. Only with such a movement can we cleanse the party and the nation. The inner strength of our people, their unbounded patriotism, their unshakable commitment to social justice, and their aspiration for a strong and prosperous India will destroy the ugliness and enrich the creative ground of India's greatness.

How will this mass movement of epic proportions arise? What are the essentials of the Build India Movements?

The country needs a politics of service to the poor. The country needs a politics based on ideology and programme. To bring this about, we must break the nexus between political parties and vested interests. We will change the electoral laws to ensure cleaner elections. We will wage an ideological war against those who exploit the poor in the name of caste and religion.

The Congress, the custodian of the national will and the sentinel of India's freedom and unity, will be reorganized and revitalize. It will gather in its fold patriots of all sections and all communities. It will be the shield of the oppressed and the sword of the poor.

The war on corruption will go on without let or hindrance. The country needs a clean social and political environment, and the Congress is determined to give it.

Any denial of justice to the poor and the weak is in itself a crime. Our judicial institutions and legal systems have to be streamlined and strengthened. Sooner rather than later. We shall put our best brains to work on this problem.

Our administrative machinery is cumbersome, archaic and alien to the needs and aspirations of the people. It has successfully resisted the imperative of change. It must learn to serve the people. It must become accountable for results. We need structural changes at all levels. We shall have them.

The India of the future is growing in her schools and universities. But our schools and universities do not relate to the vision of the future. They continue to function in the old grooves. A new blueprint for education is being designed. It will not come out of musty corridors of the educational establishments. It will only come from a movement involving teachers, students, parents, thinkers and philosophers. Not a movement to capture more privileges, but a movement that sees the future in relation to the present and the past, a movement that uses that vast untapped energy of millions to create a design suited to our needs.

As we look back on what we have achieved, one thought keeps coming back to mind. How much faster we would have developed had we succeeded in restricting the growth of our population. Progress would have been greater not in material terms alone, but in the quality of human life. That makes the family planning programme so crucial to our future development. We need a better strategy to achieve the national goal of a stable population, healthier and better educated.

The time has come to infuse new life into the struggle against poverty. Our anti-poverty programmes, notably the 20-Point Programme, have to come out of the grip of bureaucratic sloth and inefficiency. They have to become people's programme. All the elements—education, health and nutrition, family planning land reforms and cooperatives, communications, agriculture, animal husbandry, industrial and rural crafts-all have to come together in an integrated programme to wipe out the age-old curse of poverty. The power to shape their own lives must lie with the people, not with bureaucrats and experts. Experts must help the people. Vibrant village *panchayats* must discuss, deliberate and decide the choices to be made. This is a challenge to the Congress cadres. It is up to us, the workers of this great organisation, spread in every village and every hamlet of India, to mobilize the people, to guide them, to stand by their side when they are denied their due, to fight for them and to see that resources are properly utilized, not frittered away on unproductive projects. This will keep our organisation in touch with the masses and will help us to become the true vehicle of change in rural India.

We are building an independent, self reliant economy. We have already achieved much. But more hard work is required from everyone—from scientists and technologies, from the public sector, from the private sector, from industrial workers, from farmers, from public servants, from traders, from housewives and from each one of us. We have to work hard to accelerate our agricultural and industrial development on the basis of our own resources. We have to produce more than we are doing today to invest more in future progress, and to support anti-poverty programmes. We must remember that self-reliance and eradication of poverty demand, indeed compel, the present generation bear hardship and make sacrifice. Those who are employed have a duty to the future of India. They have to be more productive and consume less so that resources can be made available for investment and for programmes to help the poor. This is a national duty—a patriotic duty.

Our life styles must change. Vulgar, conspicuous consumption must go. Simplicity, efficiency and commitment to national goals hold the key to self-reliance. The Congress Ministers, Members of Parliament, Members of State Assemblies, party functionaries and leaders at all levels must set the example. Millions of people will follow them. Austerity and Swadeshi will galvanise the masses to grow more, to produce more and to serve more.

Above all, we need to create a mass movement for strengthening India's unity and integrity, for deepening our Indianness. The Congress which won freedom for India, the Congress which has brought India to the threshold of greatness, is pre-eminently the party of India's resurgent nationalism. Our nationalism is based on our rich diversity of cultures, languages and religions. The Congress represents the multi-faceted splendour of India.

Today, communal, casteist and regional forces, sustained by external elements, are undermining our unity.

We have to be on our guard. We have to carry the message of nationalism and unity to all. We have to overcome divisive forces. Let the saga of our freedom struggle be our inspiration. Let thousands and thousands of Congress workers fan out into every village, every urban centre to revive the traditions of our glorious struggle for freedom in which all differences were transcended. We shall persuade. We shall educate. We shall bind people together. But let the divisive forces understand quite clearly that the Congress, with the strength of the masses behind it, will crush with all its might the designs of anti-national elements.

A century of achievements ends. A century of endeavour beckons to us. Our resplendent civilization, with unbroken continuity from the third millennium B.C. looks ahead to peaks of excellence in the third millennium A.D.

It falls to us to work for India's greatness. A great country is not one which merely has a great past. Out of that past must arise a glorious future.

Let us build an India.

– Proud of her independence;

– Powerful in defence of her freedom;

- Strong, self-reliant in agriculture, industry and front-rank technology;
- United by bonds transcending barriers of caste, creed and region;
- Liberated from the bondage on poverty, and of social and economic inequality; an India
- Disciplined and efficient;
- Fortified by ethical and spiritual values;
- A fearless force for peace on earth;
- The School of the world, blending the inner repose of the spirit with material progress;
- A new civilization, with the strength of our heritage, the creativity of the spring time of youth and the unconquerable spirit of our people. Great achievements demand great sacrifices. Sacrifices not only from our generation and gone by, but also from generations to come.

Civilizations are not built by just one or two generations. Civilizations are built by the ceaseless toil of a succession of generations. With softness and sloth, civilizations succumb. Let us beware of decadence.

We must commit ourselves to the demanding task of making India a mighty power in the world with all the strength and the compassion of her great culture.

To this cause, I pledge myself. Jai Hind.

Sonia Gandhi (New Delhi, August 21, 2004)

Introduction

As I stand before you, I am flooded with memories.

Memories of a young, dynamic, forward-looking leader, a Prime Minister brimming with ideas and immersed in action. Yesterday, we observed his 60th birth anniversary.

At all times Rajivji is with us. The warmth he radiated endeared him to one and all. To them he was not simply a leader—he was a friend, a colleague, a brother. I know how much he was loved and how fondly he is remembered by all Congressmen and women.

His sincerity and his dedication inspire us even today.

Let us recall how much Rajivji accomplished in his short span in politics.

It was his drive that brought about the panchayat raj revolution and empowered lakhs of women, scheduled castes and scheduled tribes in local self-government.

It was his courage that brought about a new climate of peace in troubled areas like Punjab, Assam, Mizoram, Darjeeling and Tripura.

It was his statesmanship that opened a new chapter in our relations with the USA, Pakistan and China.

It was his foresight that ushered India into the IT, computer and telecom age and launched technology missions in vital social areas like drinking water, immunization, oilseeds, literacy and energy.

It was his abiding concern for the environment that made him launch ambitious projects for the greening of India and for cleaning the sacred Ganga.

He added strength to our defence capability at the same time campaigning tirelessly for a nuclear weapons-free world.

He gave the country a new education policy, propagating a modern, scientific education based on secular and progressive values and the best of our traditions.

He opened up new horizons for our entrepreneurs, businessmen and industrialists.

Rajiv Gandhi did so much. Yet, he left us with so much more to get done. As we assemble here today, let us not just remember his work but also rededicate ourselves to his vision. What he set out to do and what he did are an example to us. But what he wanted to get done has even more relevance today.

UPA

I came into active politics in December 1997 to do all I could to strengthen the Congress party and its commitment to our founding principles.

Together, we have fought many electoral battles. Together we have shared triumphs, together we have shared defeat.

Before and during the recent Lok Sabha elections, many prophets of doom had written us off. We remained steadfast. We prevailed.

We prevailed because the people of our country chose to entrust us with their confidence. How can we ever thank them for honouring us with that sacred trust? We can do so only by serving them with our utmost dedication, and by fulfilling each one of our promises.

We prevailed because of the unsparing efforts of lakhs of Congress workers across the length and breadth of our land. They toiled hard without any regard for personal gain or reward, never discouraged by gloomy predictions. Let us acknowledge and applaud their contributions. I am aware that many Congress workers and supporters expected me to be Prime Minister. And I am grateful that all of you understood and accepted my decision. It was a decision that came from the heart.

After many years we now have both a Prime Minister and a Congress President. It is a new experience, but I have no doubt that both the party and the government will emerge stronger.

In Dr. Manmohan Singh, India has a Prime Minister of great learning, vast administrative experience and impeccable reputation. Let us welcome him today and congratulate him once again.

For all of us, a coalition at the centre is a new experience. We have adjusted easily, proving our opponents and critics wrong. And in a remarkably short period of time we announced our Common Minimum Programme.

The CMP is based very largely on our own manifesto. It details the priorities, plans and programmes of the UPA government in several areas. It has been widely welcomed as a charter that gives a new direction to our politics, to our economy and to our society. It will undo the damage caused by the BJP/NDA and, in doing so, it will honour the verdict of 2004.

Verdict 2004

That verdict was a clear, categorical, decisive rejection of the BJP and of the NDA. Their arrogance, their lust for power and their pursuit of personal profit blinded them to reality. They believed they had attained political immortality.

Obviously, the BJP did not expect to lose. It lost.

Yet, the BJP is still behaving in a manner that subverts this mandate. It has not accepted its rejection by the people, by the "*aam admi*".

We have always acknowledged that the will of the people is supreme. For six years, we played the role of a responsible opposition. Even when our views were not sought we extended our support to get legislation passed in Parliament. We supported the government's initiatives on foreign policy, on J&K and on many other issues of national interest.

Yes, we also opposed. We also demonstrated. But we did not cross the *lakshman rekha* between legitimate protest and deliberate disruption. We were always on the offensive but we were never offensive.

The BJP is clearly worried. Its *Chintan Baithaks* are now *Chinta Baithaks*. Let us be under no illusions. The BJP has not accepted the verdict of the people. And it will continue to disregard this verdict. But in doing so, it will be shown up for what it really is —anti-democratic, illiberal and hypocritical.

There is a lesson for us all here and that is— we must never fall prey to the arrogance of power. We must never lose sight of the fact that we are here to serve the people of India.

Current Political Issues

Today, I want to talk to you about some of the pressing issues before us.

Friends, we should all be concerned at what is happening in the North-East. The BJP and some of its allies have been playing dangerous games in this most sensitive region, but there are times when partisan politics need to be set aside. Insurgency has to be combated. Dialogue must be sustained. Infrastructure must be developed rapidly. The true economic potential of all the North-Eastern states must be fully realized in a way that directly benefits the people of the region.

Two years ago, our party took a bold step in forming the coalition government in Jammu and Kashmir. As a result, development work has been revived. Because of the state government's "healing touch" policy, there is a renewed sense of hope and participation among the people of the state. Of course, we cannot afford to relax our vigil against those whose seek to prevent the return of harmony to J&K. But we do need to make sure that all those willing to participate in democratic processes find a place and a voice.

Many tribal regions in a number of states are witnessing the spread of Naxalite violence. In addition to what governments are doing to meet this challenge, our party in these states also has a role to play. We must make it a mission to be true representatives of the people, involving ourselves closely with the continuing problems faced by our tribal brothers and sisters. I plan to constitute an AICC task force to make an in-depth analysis of this complex issue and come up with appropriate recommendations for our party.

Water disputes are becoming increasingly contentious. Each state has its point of view that must be heard and debated. Each state has to take care of its own interests. But aren't the interests of the country as a whole, paramount? Doesn't the country have a legitimate right to ask for .an amicable settlement? India's precious water resources need to be harnessed for the well-being of all her people. The states owe it to themselves and to the country to work together for viable solutions.

Current Economic Issues

Let me turn to other matters that concern the daily welfare of our people.

The recent Budget has emphasized agriculture, employment, education and health. This is in keeping with our manifesto. It is a matter of satisfaction that the UPA government has allocated Rs. 10,000 crore extra this year for the implementation of the CMP. This will cover largely the *"Sarva Shiksha Abhiyan"*, the food-for-work employment guarantee programme, the cooked mid-day meal scheme and health insurance for the poor. It will also enable faster completion of on-going irrigation projects.

But as a party that is answerable to the people, we know that increased spending in itself is not enough. While we increase outlays, we must focus on outcomes. The Prime Minister himself is closely monitoring this aspect through the Planning Commission. It is vital that the delivery system at the grassroots actually delivers and delivers what is planned to those with the greatest need—the poor and the disadvantaged sections of society.

I am firmly convinced, as was Rajivji, that devolution of funds, functions and functionaries to elected Panchayat institutions as provided in the Constitution, is the single most important measure to bring about a rural transformation. There must also be complete transparency and accountability in the use of these funds. The Right to Information can be used as an instrument to ensure that people themselves know how money allocated for their welfare is being spent. Our party workers and our frontal organizations must spearhead such a campaign.

In recent weeks, some states like Assam, Bihar and Gujarat have gone through the agony of floods. The Prime Minister and I have visited some of the affected areas: Many of our colleagues have been involved in rehabilitation work. It is a matter of some relief that rains have finally come in parts of the country where there were fears of drought. But the delay in rains has caused some distress. I know that the government is in close touch with the states concerned. Perhaps the time is ripe, as some eminent scientists have advocated, for the implementation of drought, flood and good weather codes. Such codes could enhance our capacity to minimize the impact of an aberrant monsoon and maximize the impact of a good monsoon as well.

Our manifesto and the CMP also makes a number of commitments for the economic and social empowerment of the weaker sections of society, including affirmative action. We accord the highest priority to fulfilling these commitments. Earlier Congress governments established separate finance and development corporations for the welfare of scheduled castes, scheduled tribes, *safai karamcharis*, backward classes, minorities and the physically challenged. These corporations need to be given full financial and infrastructure support so that they can carry out their functions in a manner so as to fulfill Dr. Babasaheb Ambedkar's dreams and aspirations.

Organisation

Let me now turn to our organization itself. Just last week, we celebrated the anniversary of our Independence. We recalled the sacrifices and contributions of freedom fighters and our unique galaxy of leaders like Mahatma Gandhi, Jawaharlal Nehru, Sardar Patel, Maulana Azad, Lal Bahadur Shastri, Indiraji and Rajivji. We have achieved whatever we have only by following in their footsteps and I am confident that we will continue to march ahead guided by the their values and principles.

It is a matter of satisfaction that we were able to overcome great odds in the recent Lok Sabha polls, emerging as the single largest party and forming the government with our allies and other secular forces. However, there is simply no room for complacency. Our performance in some states was disappointing. In some places, intra-party rivalries and in-fighting cost us dearly. In others, we have been unable to regroup effectively and turn the tide that went us in November 2003.

But in a few states we fought well, showing ourselves and the rest of the country what the Congress is capable of when it is united and disciplined behind a single purpose. We cannot afford to sit back in states where we are in the Opposition today, hoping to benefit from the so-called anti-incumbency factor. "*Padayatras*" and mass contact programmes highlighting the concerns of farmers, workers, and other weaker sections of society—this should be our daily agenda wherever we are in Opposition today.

In the next few months, we will have Vidhan Sabha elections in Maharashtra, Arunachal Pradesh, Haryana, Bihar and Jharkhand. We are preparing for these polls. Each and every election is important to us and we must work cohesively to ensure our victory.

We will soon start the process of organizational elections. I would urge all of you to participate actively in the membership drive. We should make every effort to reach out to all sections of society, particularly scheduled castes, scheduled tribes, OBCs, minorities and women. We are the only political party which provides for reservations for the weaker sections of society in our organization. However, in spite of my own attempts, representation for women continues to be disappointingly low. Let each one of us commit to remedying this situation. We must also bring in professionals from different walks of life.

I want to share with you another special concern of mine.

Two years ago, I had circulated a code of ethics and austerity to all our chief ministers and PCCs. That code has largely remained on paper. This pains me. There is so much deprivation around us. Yet, so many of us talk of the poor, while engaging in conspicuous consumption, ostentatious displays of wealth and outright wastage. We, who derive our inspiration from Gandhiji, cannot indulge in such double standards. Ultimately, our conscience must guide us to adopt norms of public conduct that stand out for simplicity and integrity.

I do believe that the time has come for the NSUI, the Youth Congress, the Mahila Congress and the Sewa Dal to think innovatively. The politics of protest and agitation will continue to be important. But a number of other tasks are equally important. Making the people aware of their entitlements and empowering them is a political activity which can most effectively be carried out by the Party. We must all recognize that there is more to politics than elections alone.

Frontal organizations should, for instance, spearhead campaigns for the implementation of legislation relating to women's rights and child welfare. Dowry, violence on women, atrocities on weaker sections, child marriage, female foeticide, to give some examples—are issues crying out for political advocacy and action. I am counting on all of you, young people particularly to take the lead. I also want INTUC to reactivate itself and take on social security concerns of crores of workers in the unorganized, informal sector.

I feel very anguished when I see the state of public hygiene around all of us. How can we let our children grow up in such conditions? I know that there are government initiatives in this area but we must return to Gandhiji and give our personal and collective effort to improving hygiene and sanitation. Today, let us resolve to launch and sustain a *"Swachha Vatavaran Abhiyaan"* in which every one of us undertakes specific tasks in villages, towns and cities. In this connection, I find it a matter of the greatest regret that in spite of laws, scavenging continues even in places like the nation's capital and Gandhiji's birthplace. How can we accept this?

Normally when the party wins an election and forms a government, the organization takes a back seat. This must not happen. It is the people who vote a party into power. And it is the party that then forms and sustains a government in office. These crucial bonds between party and government must be retained and nurtured through constant communication and interaction.

Our governments both at the centre and in states where we are in power must be extra-sensitive to the needs of ordinary Congress worker. At the same time, being in government imposes different obligations which those of us not in government must also understand and appreciate.

But a heavy responsibility rests on the shoulders of those Congressmen and women who are in government to ensure that party workers have full access to them and never feel of being neglected or betrayed. One of the reasons why we have lost in a number of states is because the government took precedence over the party. Government programmes were not seen as party programmes. The party was unable to effectively propagate and leverage the achievements of our governments. We must not let this happen.

The Ideological Battle

I have always said that our fight with the BJP is not just electoral. Our fight with the BJP is ideological. The clash between the Congress and the BJP is not a clash just for office and power. It is, at its very core, a clash between two diametrically opposing visions of India's past, between two conflicting visions of India's future.

Congress nationalism is based on the best of Indian traditions and culture, a secular, pluralistic, liberal, all-inclusive nationalism. The BJP brand of nationalism is based on divisiveness, hate, bigotry, on a rejection of what India has always stood for and cherished.

The Congress's nationalism is based on pride, while the BJP's nationalism is based on prejudice.

This is the essential message that we have to propagate. There can be no let-up in our fight against the destructive ideology of the RSS and its outfits. While our founding fathers were fighting for the freedom of our country, the RSS was busy spreading the virus of communalism in our society. Its sole objective has been to denigrate our party and our leaders. While our leaders immersed themselves in nation-building, the RSS did its best to undermine them and their efforts and weaken the bonds of amity and harmony.

There can and will be no let-up in our fight against bigotry, communalism and religious fanaticism of any kind that seeks to destroy our social peace. This is why we set up *"Sadbhavna Ke Sipahi"* after the last AICC session here two years back. This is why we set up the *"Bapu Shiksha Sadbhavna Trust"* after the Shimla Chintan Shivir last July. It is by actively participating in such initiatives that we can best counter the forces that seek to tear our social fabric apart.

Conclusion

Friends, today we rightfully share a sense of achievement. We overcame great odds and defeated our adversaries.

But now it is time to consolidate, time to fulfill our obligations. It is time to redeem our pledges, our promises and the many expectations that we have aroused. Let us not under-estimate the obstacles ahead.

But let us march ahead with confidence and conviction. Electoral ups and downs are inevitable. What matters more is whether we are at one with the people of our country, especially with the poor, the deprived and the disadvantaged. What matters more is whether we are true to our beliefs, steadfast in our commitments and transparent in our actions.

Six years ago, I asked you to join me in a journey of renewal. Together, we have sought to recapture our inspiration, to reinforce our values and to rediscover the well-springs of our strength.

That journey continues.

Let us march ahead undeflected in moments of joy, undeterred in times of disappointment, always unshakeable in our resolve.

Jai Hind.

Sonia Gandhi (Hyderabad, January 2006)

I

We are meeting in Andhra Pradesh for the fifth time and in Hyderabad for the third time, in our long 120 year-old history.

And what a glorious history it has been.

It has been a history of remarkable men and women who, by their struggles and sacrifices, brought us our freedom. They bequeathed to us democratic and secular values that form the bedrock of our Constitution.

It has been a history of enormous progress that has seen the establishment of the modem Indian nation-state and its flowering as a major political, economic and technological power in the world.

It has been a history of profound transformations. The people of India have rediscovered the wells-springs of their creativity and enterprise, and are scaling new heights of achievement.

With all humility but with confidence we can say that the Indian National Congress has decisively shaped contemporary India.

And, in turn, the Indian National Congress has been enriched by a large number of leaders and workers from Andhra Pradesh. Andhra Pradesh has produced outstanding entrepreneurs, scientists, doctors, engineers and other professionals. This land, so much part of our traditions and heritage, has also given birth to very many eminent cultural and literary personalities. Many diverse faiths and cultures have intermingled here in harmony.

Last year, the people of Andhra Pradesh not only brought the Congress back with a massive mandate in the assembly, but they also voted overwhelmingly for us in the Lok Sabha elections. This enabled us to form the Congress-led coalition government at the Centre. We owe a deep debt to the people of Andhra Pradesh, a state in which Indira Gandhi's memory is still recalled with so much affection.

II

We met last as a Plenary in March 2001 in Bangalore.

On that occasion, we had resolved to wage every war, fight every battle, make every sacrifice, to remove the BJP-led NDA government at the centre.

That milestone was reached in the May 2004 elections.

Across the country, people came out to express their resentment on the divisive politics of the BJP that had damaged social harmony. They came out to express their opposition to the elitist economic policies of the BJP, that had neglected *kisans, khet mazdoors*, weavers, workers and other weaker sections of society.

Lakhs of Congress workers all-over the country worked tirelessly and selflessly to ensure our victory.

I want to acknowledge their contributions and say that without them, without their devotion and dedication, we would not be in power today at the centre.

The Congress has always been a party of *karyakartas*. We have workers in every village, in every *basti*, in every *mohalla* of our vast country. They give us strength. No words are sufficient to appreciate their contributions. I should add here that, time and again, whether it is the earthquakes in Gujarat and Jammu and Kashmir or the floods in different states or the tsunami in the Andamans and south India, I have been moved by the spontaneous manner in which our party workers have engaged themselves in relief and rehabilitation activities.

III

Twenty months ago, we formed a coalition government at the centre with the support of parties committed to secular values. Dr. Manmohan Singh, a Congressman of integrity and learning, a man of compassion and humility, became our Prime Minister.

Under his leadership, together with our allies, we formulated a Common Minimum Programme.

This CMP is based predominantly on the Congress's own election manifesto. So, it should be clearly understood by all of us that when we fulfill a CMP pledge, we are fulfilling a commitment of our manifesto itself.

Being in a coalition is a new experience for us. But we have adapted well and have steadfastly followed the discipline and decorum of a coalition.

True, in some states we are opposing the very same parties that are supporting us at the centre. We see no contradiction in this. National challenges demand that we cooperate. But state-level issues and concerns are very different. Let our colleagues from Kerala and West Bengal have no doubts—in these states, we are opponents and we will fight as opponents.

We are running coalition governments in some states as well. I know that our party workers feel that these coalitions diminish opportunities for them. But coalition does not mean abdication of party-building. There is no doubt in my mind that though we run coalition governments, we must at the same time strengthen our party at all levels.

What have we done since May 2004?

We have restored the secular foundations of governance. No longer are external tensions being exploited for the polarization of our society.

We have fought terrorism with determination without targeting any particular section of society.

We have replaced a prejudiced, bellicose nationalism with an all-inclusive nationalism in keeping with our pluralistic ethos.

We have transformed the agenda of public debate that was obsessed with rewriting our past to a focus on the day-to-day concerns of our people. We have called a halt to the distortion of our education syllabus.

We have changed the manner in which economic reforms were perceived, from an excessive pre-occupation with FDI and privatization, to an overriding emphasis on employment, education, agriculture and health.

We have given India a new stature in the world community.

The 2004 verdict showed that our people will reject divisiveness of any kind, social or economic.

The 2004 verdict showed that our people will reject arrogance and insensitivity on the part of those who are in power.

The 2004 verdict also showed that a party that is complacent, a party that under-estimates its opponents and exaggerates its own strengths will be humbled by the people.

In that verdict lie many lessons for us also, in both the party and the government. These lessons have to be absorbed fully. They must not be forgotten.

Our Prime Minister will be speaking later on the accomplishments of the central government. But I would like to highlight some of our major initiatives that are of great political significance.

We now have the historic National Rural Employment Guarantee Act that, as the name suggests, will, for the first time, provide a legal guarantee for employment. This is an unprecedented step for which the Congress party and none else can proudly take credit.

We now have the landmark Right to Information Act. It is a major initiative for making administration at all levels transparent and accountable and for making people fully aware of their rights.

We have a huge Rupees one lakh seventy four thousand crore Bharat Nirman programme that will transform our villages, and bring new prosperity over the next four years, by investments in irrigation, housing, drinking water, electricity, roads and telecommunications.

In future, more and more of our people will live in urban areas. That is why we have launched the Jawaharlal Nehru National Urban Renewal Mission in 63 cities across the country. Over the next seven years, through this mission government will be investing about Rupees one lakh twenty thousand crore, to expand infrastructure and basic services.

We have started a National Rural Health Mission, to ensure delivery of basic health facilities to our brothers and sisters in villages. Over the next six years, the central government alone will be investing over Rupees one lakh crore in this mission.

We have doubled the allocations for the Sarva Shiksha Abhiyan and Mid-day Meals, and significantly increased spending on ICDS and nutrition programmes for women and children.

We have succeeded in increasing bank credit to farmers. Our commitment was to double the credit supply in three years and we expect to achieve this target much earlier. We are also strengthening cooperative credit institutions.

All these programmes add up to unprecedented, massive investments. The Prime Minister has taken close personal interest in each of them and I know it has not been easy for him to balance different considerations. We have to recognize that we will achieve our goals only, if we can raise and sustain the rate of growth of the economy. We have stepped up the momentum of both public and private investment. We must understand that it is imperative to grasp opportunities for faster growth, to generate more employment and resources for social sector expenditure.

I want to draw your attention to another feature of these programmes. For the most part, they benefit backward districts, the majority of which happen to be in non-Congress states. This means that, unlike the BJP, we do not play partisan politics when it comes to the needs of our people.

More importantly this means you will have to ensure these programmes are not usurped or subverted by non-Congress state governments. You will have to make people aware of their entitlements, and organize them effectively to demand and receive these entitlements. You must network more closely with activists and civil society organizations. The new Right to Information Act is your main weapon in this endeavour.

In keeping with our manifesto pledge, we have moved decisively to enact new legislation for the welfare of women and children. The Hindu Succession Act, 1956 has been amended to give women equal rights in inheritance of property. A law to prevent domestic violence against women has been passed. Our most precious resource—our children—now have a National Commission that will ensure their rights are protected.

Just a few weeks ago, as a demonstration of our unflinching commitment to social justice, the 104th the Constitution Amendment Bill was passed to provide for reservations for scheduled castes, scheduled tribes and OBCs in all private educational institutions, other than those run by religious and linguistic minorities. This will expand opportunities in higher and professional education for students belonging to the weaker sections of our society. A Bill has been introduced to give legal guarantee for reservations in government employment, for scheduled castes, scheduled tribes and OBCs. A comprehensive Bill to protect the rights and livelihood of tribals living in forest areas has also been introduced.

We have taken a number of measures to address the concerns of minorities. POTA has been repealed. A new law on the prevention of communal violence is on the anvil, and we expect Parliament to approve it soon. A National Commission on Minority Professional Institutions has been set up. A Bill to make the National Minorities Commission a Constitutional body has been introduced.

We have invigorated the defence modernization programme. We created a new department for the welfare of ex-servicemen and their families. There is a long standing demand of ex-servicemen relating to their pension benefits. We hope that this demand would be resolved soon in keeping with the pledge in our manifesto. I want to take this opportunity, to convey our greatest appreciation to the armed forces, not just for the valour with which they defend our borders, but also for the magnificent manner in which they come to the aid of our people during natural calamities.

Now that we have a government at the centre and in a number of states, we can certainly expect the concerns of the *aam aadmi* to receive the highest priority. Prices of kerosene, for instance, have not increased even though world oil prices have sky-rocketed. I know at times, governance has its compulsions but our cadres should not feel shy of highlighting people's concerns, nor should such expressions be seen as criticism of our governments at the Centre or in states.

Annexure IIIb

Other Significant Speeches

1. 'Tryst with Destiny', Jawaharlal Nehru's famous speech on the eve of India's Independence, August 14-15, 1947

2. 'The Light has Gone Out', Jawaharlal Nehru's speech broadcast on All India Radio after Mahatma Gandhi's Assassination, January 30, 1948

3. Speech by Indira Gandhi in the Lok Sabha, December 16, 1971 on the unconditional surrender of West Pakistan forces in Bangladesh

4. Indira Gandhi's Speech in the Lok Sabha, December 13, 1978 on being expelled from the House

5. 'Uphold Secular Values', Rajiv Gandhi's inaugural speech at the national symposium on 'India's Struggle against Communalism', New Delhi, October 8, 1986

6. 'Focus on Panchayati Raj', Rajiv Gandhi's speech (in Hindi) while inaugurating the Panchayati Raj Sammelan of Northern states, New Delhi, January 27, 1989

7. 'Youth and National Development', Rajiv Gandhi's speech while presenting the National Youth Awards 1986-87, New Delhi, January 18, 1988

8. Opening remarks of Congress President, Sonia Gandhi, at the AICC meeting, New Delhi, April 6, 1998.

9. Concluding Remarks of Congress President, Sonia Gandhi, at Vichar Manthan Shivir, Pachmarhi (September 4-6, 1998) on September 6, 1998

10. Congress President Sonia Gandhi's Address at 81st Plenary Session, Bangalore, March 18, 2001

11. Congress President Sonia Gandhi's Opening Speech at Conference of Congress Chief Ministers at Guwahati, April 12, 2002

12. Excerpts from the address in Lok Sabha by Prime Minister Manmohan Singh on May 10, 2005

13. Speech of Congress President Sonia Gandhi at the Congress Parliamentary Party General Body Meeting, March 4, 2010

'Tryst with Destiny', Jawaharlal Nehru's famous speech on the eve of India's Independence, Constituent Assembly, New Delhi, August 14-15, 1947

Long years ago we made a tryst with destiny, and now the time comes when we shall redeem our pledge, not wholly or in full measure, but very substantially. At the stroke of the midnight hour, when the world sleeps, India will awake to life and freedom. A moment comes, which comes but rarely in history, when we step out from the old to the new, when an age ends, and when the soul of a nation, long suppressed, finds utterance. It is fitting that at this solemn moment we take the pledge of dedication to the service of India and her people and to the still larger cause of humanity.

At the dawn of history India started on her unending quest, and trackless centuries are filled with her striving and the grandeur of her success and her failures. Through good and ill fortune alike she has never lost sight of that quest or forgotten the ideals which gave her strength. We end today a period of ill fortune and India discovers herself again. The achievement we celebrate today is but a step, an opening of opportunity, to the greater triumphs and achievements that await us. Are we brave enough and wise enough to grasp this opportunity and accept the challenge of the future?

Freedom and power bring responsibility. The responsibility rests upon this Assembly, a sovereign body representing the sovereign people of India. Before the birth of freedom we have endured all the pains of labour and our hearts are heavy with the memory of this sorrow. Some of those pains continue even now. Nevertheless, the past is over and it is the future that beckons to us now.

That future is not one of ease or resting but of incessant striving so that we may fulfil the pledges we have so often taken and the one we shall take today. The service of India means the service of the millions who suffer. It means the ending of poverty and ignorance and disease and inequality of opportunity. The ambition of the greatest man of our generation has been to wipe every tear from every eye. That may be beyond us, but as long as there are tears and suffering, so long our work will not be over.

And so we have to labour and to work, and work hard, to give reality to our dreams. Those dreams are for India, but they are also for the world, for all the nations and peoples are too closely knit together today for any one of them to imagine that it can live apart. Peace has been said to be indivisible; so is freedom, so is prosperity now, and so also is disaster in this One World that can no longer be split into isolated fragments.

To the people of India, whose representatives we are, we make an appeal to join us with faith and confidence in this great adventure. This is no time for petty and destructive criticism, no time for ill-will or blaming others. We have to build the noble mansion of free India where all her children may dwell.

The appointed day has come—the day appointed by destiny—and India stands forth again, after long slumber and struggle, awake, vital, free and independent. The past clings on to us still in some measure and we have to do much before we redeem the pledges we have so often taken. Yet the turning-point is past, and history begins anew for us, the history which we shall live and act and others will write about.

It is a fateful moment for us in India, for all Asia and for the world. A new star rises, the star of freedom in the East, a new hope comes into being, vision long cherished materializes. May the star never set and that hope never be betrayed!

We rejoice in that freedom, even though clouds surround us, and many of our people are sorrow stricken and difficult problems encompass us. But freedom brings responsibilities and burdens and we have to face them in the spirit of free and disciplined people.

On this day our first thoughts go to the architect of this freedom, the Father of our Nation [Gandhi], who, embodying the old spirit of India, held aloft the torch of freedom and lighted up the darkness that surrounded us. We have often been unworthy followers of his and have strayed from his message, but not only we but succeeding generations will remember this message and bear the imprint in their hearts of this great son of India, magnificent in his faith and strength and courage and humility. We shall never allow that torch of freedom to be blown out, however high the wind or stormy the tempest.

Our next thoughts must be of the unknown volunteers and soldiers of freedom who, without praise or reward, have served India even unto death.

We think also of our brothers and sisters who have been cut off from us by political boundaries and who unhappily cannot share at present in the freedom that has come. They are of us and will remain of us whatever may happen, and we shall be sharers in their good and ill fortune alike.

The future beckons to us. Whither do we go and what shall be our endeavour? To bring freedom and opportunity to the common man, to the peasants and workers of India; to fight and end poverty and ignorance and disease; to build up a prosperous, democratic and progressive nation, and to create social, economic and political institutions which will ensure justice and fullness of life to every man and woman.

We have hard work ahead. There is no resting for any one of us till we redeem our pledge in full, till we make all the people of India what destiny intended them to be. We are citizens of a great country on the verge of bold advance, and we have to live up to that high standard. All of us, to whatever religion we may belong, are equally the children of India with equal rights, privileges and obligations. We cannot encourage communalism or narrow-mindedness, for no nation can be great whose people are narrow in thought or in action.

To the nations and peoples of the world we send greetings and pledge ourselves to cooperate with them in furthering peace, freedom and democracy.

And to India, our much-loved motherland, the ancient, the eternal and the ever-new, we pay our reverent homage and we bind ourselves afresh to her service.

Jai Hind!

'The Light has Gone Out', Jawaharlal Nehru's speech broadcast on AIR after Mahatma Gandhi's Assassination, January 30, 1948

Friends and Comrades, the light has gone out of our lives and there is darkness everywhere. I do not know what to tell you and how to say it. Our beloved leader, Bapu as we called him, the Father of the Nation, is no more. Perhaps I am wrong to say that. Nevertheless, we will never see him again as we have seen him for these many years. We will not run to him for advice and seek solace from him, and that is a terrible blow, not to me only, but to millions and millions in this country. And it is a little difficult to soften the blow by any other advice that I or anyone else can give you.

The light has gone out, I said, and yet I was wrong. For the light that shone in this country was no ordinary light. The light that has illumined this country for these many years will illumine this country for many more years, and a thousand years later, that light will be seen in this country and the world will see it and it will give solace to innumerable hearts. For that light represented something more than the immediate past, it represented the living, the eternal truths, reminding us of the right path, drawing us from error, taking this ancient country to freedom.

All this has happened when there was so much more for him to do. We could never think that he was unnecessary or that he had done his task. But now, particularly, when we are faced with so many difficulties, his not being with us is a blow most terrible to bear.

A madman has put an end to his life, for I can only call him mad who did it, and yet there has been enough of poison spread in this country during the past years and months, and this poison has had an effect on people's minds. We must face this poison, we must root out this poison, and we must face all the perils that encompass us, and face them not madly or badly, but rather in the way that our beloved teacher taught us to face them.

The first thing to remember now is that none of us dare misbehave because he is angry. We have to behave like strong and determined people, determined to face all the perils that surround us, determined to carry out the mandate that our great teacher and our great leader has given us, remembering always that if, as I believe, his spirit looks upon us and sees us, nothing would displease his soul so much as to see that we have indulged in any small behaviour or any violence.

So we must not do that. But that docs not mean that we should be weak, but rather that we should, in strength and in unity, face all the troubles that are in front of us. We must hold together, and all our petty troubles and difficulties and conflicts must be ended in the face of this great disaster. This great disaster is a symbol to us to remember all the big things of life and forget the small things of which we have thought too much. In his death he has reminded us of the big things of life, the living truth, and if we remember that, then it will be well with India...

It was proposed by some friends that Mahatmaji's body should be embalmed for a few days to enable millions of people to pay their last homage to him. But it was his wish, repeatedly expressed, that no such thing should happen, that this should not be done, that he was entirely opposed to any embalming of his body, and so we decided that we must follow his wishes in this matter, however much others might have wished otherwise.

And so the cremation will take place on Saturday in Delhi city by the side of the Jamuna river. On Saturday afternoon, about 11.30, the bier will be taken out at Birla House and it will follow a prescribed road and go to the Jamuna river. The cremation will take place there at about 4 P.M. The place and the route will be announced by radio and the Press.

People in Delhi who wish to pay their last homage should gather along this route. I will not advise too many of them to come to Birla House, but rather to gather on both sides of this long route from Birla House to the Jamuna river. And I trust that they will remain there in silence without any demonstrations. That is the best way and the most fitting way to pay homage to this great soul. Also, Saturday should be a day of fasting and prayer for all of us.

Those who live elsewhere, out of Delhi and in other parts of India, will no doubt take such part as they can in this last homage. For them also, let this be a day of fasting and prayer. And at the appointed time for cremation, that is 4 pm on Saturday afternoon, people should go to the river or to the sea and offer prayers there. And while we pray, the greatest prayer that we can offer is to take a pledge to dedicate ourselves to the truth, and to the cause for which this great countryman of ours lived and for which he has died. That is the best prayer that we can offer him and his memory. That is the best prayer we can offer to India and ourselves.

JAI HIND.

Indira Gandhi's Statement in the Lok Sabha, December 16, 1971, on the Unconditional Surrender of West Pakistan Forces in Bangladesh

Mr. Speakers, Sir, I have an announcement to make, which I think the House has been waiting for, for sometime. The West Pakistan forces have unconditionally surrendered in Bangladesh. The instrument of surrender was signed in Dacca at 16.31 hours I.S.T. today by Lt. Gen. A.A.K. Niazi on behalf of the Pakistan Eastern Command, Lt. Gen. Jagjit Singh Aurora, GOC-in-C of the Indian and Bangladesh forces in the Eastern Theatre accepted the surrender. Dacca is now the free capital of a free country.

This House and the entire nation rejoice in this historic event. We hail the people of Bangladesh in their hour of triumph. We hail the brave young men and boys of the Mukti Bahini for their valour and dedication. We are proud of our own Army, Navy, Air Force and the Border Security Force, who have too magnificently demonstrated their quality and capacity. Their discipline and devotion to duty are well known. India will remember with gratitude the sacrifices of those who have laid down their lives and our thoughts are with their families.

Our Armed Forces are under strict orders to treat Pakistani prisoners of war in accordance with the Geneva Convention and to deal with all sections of the population of Bangladesh in a humane manner. The Commanders of the Mukti Bahini have issued similar orders to their forces. Although the Government of Bangladesh have not yet been given an opportunity to sign the Geneva Convention, they also have declared that they will fully abide by it. It will be the responsibly of the Government of Bangladesh, the Mukti Bahini and the Indian Armed Forces to prevent any reprisals.

Our objectives were limited—to assist the gallant people of Bangladesh and their Mukti Bahini to liberate their country from a reign of terror and to resist aggression on our won land. Indian Armed Forces will not remain in Bangladesh any longer than is necessary.

The millions who were driven out of their homes across our borders have already begun trekking back. The rehabilitation of this war-torn land calls for dedicated team work by it Government and people.

We hope and trust that the Father of this new nation. Sheikh Mujibur Rahman, will take his rightful place among his own people and prosperity. The time has come when they can together look forward to a meaningful future in their Shonar Bangla. They have our good wishes.

The triumph is not theirs alone. All nations who value the human spirit, will recognize it as a significant milestone in man's quest for liberty.

SEVERAL HON. MEMBERS: Indira Gandhi zindabad.

SHRI SAMAR GUHA (Contai): The name of the Prime Minister will go down in history as the golden sword of liberation of Bangladesh.

Indira Gandhi's Speech in the Lok Sabha, December 13, 1978 on being expelled from the House

SHRIMATI INDIRA NEHRU GANDHI (Chikmagalur): Mr. Speaker, Sir, and hon. Members, I am grateful for this opportunity of participating in the debate.

The Committee of Privileges submitted their report to the House on November 21, 1978. The report was taken up for consideration on December 7, 1978. I had thought that the ultimate decision about the correctness of the findings of the Privileges Committee rested with this hon. House and that, until this hon. House had fully considered the report dispassionately—each member giving his opinion in the context of the views expressed by fellow members—no member with a sense of fair-play and justice, would finally conclude that I was guilty.

My hopes were belied when I read the report in the newspapers of the proceedings of the Janata Parliamentary Party's meeting, where the only point of debate was reported to be the quantum of punishment which should be inflicted upon me.

The Janata Party, with its absolute majority, had adjudged me guilty even before the House commenced its debate on the report. Would it be unfair to conclude that the Party in power is trying to convert this House into a medieval "Star Chamber" by raising [*Interruptions*] the question of Privilege in what is essentially a question of Party politics? This is hardly conducive to a calm, judicial and impartial consideration of the merits of the case. [*Interruptions*]

If the ensuing deliberations by the entire House were considered by the Janata Parliamentary Party as an empty formality, my plea of innocence no doubt would be futile so far as the hon. Members of the Janata Party are concerned.

But this cannot dissuade me from opposing the action which the Janata Party with its overwhelming majority in this hon. House is proposing against me.

As the former Prime Minister as well. I owe an explanation to the people and to posterity—the future generations of men and women who will follow us and ponder over the traditions of this House [*Interruptions*] when the passions of the present items will have died. May I therefore reiterate emphatically and categorically that in point of fact [*Interruptions*] I have not committed any breach of privilege of the House [*Interruptions*] and that the charges leveled against me in this regard are totally untenable.

It is alleged that I was guilty of harassment of certain officers because they were collecting information in connection with a parliamentary question. It has been alleged that I initiated the action against them by calling Shri R. K. Dhawan in the presence of Shri T. A. Pai and directing him that Shri D. Sen, the Director of the C.B.I. should be called and the houses of those officers be raided. [*Interruptions*]

Sir, I have a bad cold and it seems that even clearing my throat is a provocation to the House.

The sole testimony in this regard is that of Shri T. A. Pai. Did I play any role in the formulation of the reply to be given in the House? It is not the case of Shri Pai or any other person that I did. Shri Pai admits, "at no time when I met her and she ever discussed with me the affairs of Maruti." He also admitted, "I did not get the impression (when he met me on the 15th April) that she wanted me to withhold the information or be careful at the time of answering the question."

A very large number of questions involving the collection of information on many matters, including Maruti, were constantly being asked in the House and were answered by various officers of different ministries before and after this particular question. There was never any allegation about obstruction or harassment on this score.

Besides, even a cursory examination of the evidence will clearly reveal that not all the officers who were collecting information for the Parliamentary question were proceeded against by the CBI. Government records show that no action was initiated against those officers who were actually deputed to collect in formation form Maruti. It is clear from this that the CBI cases and nothing whatever to do with the collection of information for the Parliamentary question and that they only came in handy to the Janata Party Government to implicate me in this proceeding.

What is even worse, the sanctity of this House is being used to prejudge the criminal trial that I am facing in a Court outside this House. The Janata Party Government has be that criminal case gagged me and made it impossible for me to put forth my defence in the present case. Can this be described as a reasonable opportunity of defence? I have been cribbed and confined in my defence before the House and later I shall be facing the criminal trial with an over-bearing shadow of this House looming large over those proceedings. Here is a sample of the rule of law by which the Janata Party and its leaders profess to abide.

Sir, I shall not go into the minute details of the evidence placed before the Committee on Privileges, which my colleagues Shri C. M. Stephen and Shri Venkatasubbiah have already covered. I only urge emphatically that even on the one-sided record, there is not a shred of evidence to hold me guilty of breach of privilege. The findings of the Committee, I submit, are totally unjustified and unsustainable.

The facts leave no manner of doubt that the motive which is actuating the Janata Party and its Government is not their respect for the privileges of the House but their personal vendetta against me.

The entire procedure followed by the Privileges Committee suffered from constitutional infirmities. It also sought to compel me to become a witness against myself in total violation of my fundamental rights under the Constitution. My refusal to take the oath in these circumstances is now being alleged to be another breach of privilege. I humbly submit that this is not so. I meant no disrespect whatsoever to the hon. Members of the Privileges Committee. Had it been consistent with my defence in the Court cases, I would not have hesitated to depose before the Committee in greater detail.

I also maintain that the conclusion drawn by the Privileges Committee from the text of my statement submitted to them on June 16, 1978, is not warranted. In that statement I particularly mentioned my great respect and high regard for the hon. Members of the Privileges Committee. Thereafter I pointed out the well known fact of the Janata Party's disposition towards me, a disposition which has been demonstrated by thought, word and deed, times without number. Finally, I gave expression to a reasonable apprehension on the one had, and positive allegation of bias or prejudice on the other, has not been appreciated. Incidentally, the fact that different political parties *qua* political parties are now considering this matter and formulating their respective stands even before this hon. House has taken a decision, this act, I submit, only confirms my views. This is how political parties functioned and therefore, my observations in the said statements cannot be constructed as imputations of bias.

To the Shah Commission, I had said:

"Corruption in some areas of Governmental functioning especially involving commercial dealings with the public, has always been a matter of serious concern. As Prime Minister, I received many complaints in writing or orally alleging corrupt practices on the part of various officers of the Government. These I used to forward to the concerned authorities or departments and occasionally to my staff for appropriate action.

I received complaints from some persons, including MPs about these officers, amongst others. I told Mr. Dhawan to pass on the complaints to the authorities concerned in order to verify whether there was any truth in the allegations. There was nothing special or unique about this. When such complaints were repeated or conveyed verbally to me, I sometimes directed similar action through a member of my staff."

I repudiate the allegation that I ever ordered searches or raid against these officers.

My alleged involvement in the alleged harassment of these officers was used by the Government and the Shah Commission for public denigration and character assassination. It is being used by the Janata Party to punish me for breach of privilege of this House and it is further going to sued by the Government to prosecute me in the court of law and seek my conviction. What else is political persecution? But if the Janata Party thinks that acts of persecution and victimization can destroy the ideals for which I stand, it is cherishing false dreams.

It is my proud privilege and the privilege of the Party which I have the honour to lead, to fight for the ideals of secularism and socialism for which Gandhi, Jawaharlal Nehru and we all have been struggling for more than half a century.

Never before in the history of any democratic country has a single individual, who leads the principal political opposition been subjected to so much calumny, character assassination and political vendetta of the ruling party. [*Interruptions*]

I give below a few instances of the views expressed publicly by leaders of the Janata Party who are or have been also leaders of the Government.

(a) When I was released by the learned Magistrate in Delhi on 4-10-1977, Shri Morarji Desai publicly declared that the Magistrate had committed impropriety in releasing me.

(b) In a letter to Prime Minister, the former Home Minister stated that members of the Cabinet of the Janata Party were being looked upon as a band of impotent men for not having already put me behind bars.

(c) In the Chikmagalur constituency, one hon. Minister declared that my place was in jail. Another bemoaned that the Janata Party had lost the election because the people were angry for not having punished me.

The Parties and groups which have combined to form the Janata Party had been conducting a campaign of vilification first against my father and for more than decade against me. When I decided to espouse more strongly the cause of secularism and democratic socialism, when I nationalised the banks and took other measures to offer opportunity and help to the poor and weaker sections, there was a tremendous popular upsurge. This disturbed the privileged and vested interests and the communal and obscurantist elements, which the Janata Party today represents, and they felt it impossible to fight me and my party on an ideological plane. Therefore, they changed their strategy and turned their fury against me personally. [*Interruptions*] In the historic phase of India's development one would have expected a fierce ideological debate, but nothing of the sort happened. On the contrary, political and ideological issues were deliberately side-tracked by these elements. They accused me of having flouted political morality by causing a split in the Congress. Those who had been bitter political enemies before the split and had professed strong ideological differences with one another suddenly discovered a new mutual kinship in their common hostility towards me. [*Interruptions*]

Some people have suffered during Emergency. At no time was it my intention to harass or harm anyone. [*Interruptions*]

Sir, are you guiding the House or is it being guided from some other place?

For hardship caused, I am deeply sorry. I have already expressed my regret in many public forums and do so again. Not all actions came to my notice since it is just not possible for the Head of the Government or event others to keep in touch, as the present administration well knows. [*Interruptions*]

It was I who decided to go to the people again and hold elections in 1977. This act of my Government re-asserts my abiding faith in democracy and totally disproves the accusation of authoritarianism made by the Janata Party and its allies. They continue to chant slogans of dictatorship *versus* democracy in order to hide the sinister character of the political forces which dominate them.

I may be annihilated in the course of my struggle for the ideals of socialism and secularism, but those ideals will live on and the time is not far off when they will overcome the forces of communalism, casteism, regionalism, obscurantism and capitalism which the Janata Party and its Government have unleashed [*Interruptions*] in a period of less than two years of their misrule.

It is obvious that the motivation of the ruling Party is to divert public attention from their inability to implement [*Interruptions*] their high sounding but hollow promises of February-March, 1977. [*Interruptions*]

I charge the ruling party of failure to check divisive forces, thus endangering our unity, of inaction in the face of mounting lawlessness and disorder and of callously neglecting the interests of Harijans [*Interruptions*] and Adivasis, Muslims, Sikhs, Christians and weaker sections. [*Interruptions*]

It is not an accident that the Prime Minister does not feel uncomfortable to survive and be sustained in power by those who were full of hate for Mahatma Gandhi. [*Interruptions*]

Mr. Speaker, as you have rightly pointed out, all kinds of remarks were permitted in the previous days during this debate, and nobody then considered that they were irrelevant. We had listened to them very carefully.

However, I must congratulate those members and leaders of the ruling Party whose eyes were opened by the Aligarh riots and who had the courage to tell the truth and identify the danger. High personages have warned the Prime

Minister that the Government might not last for the Government's failure to hear the danger signals and to find answers to the crying problems of our people.

This Government has created conditions of civil war in Bihar and unprecedented organized communal violence in Aligarh, Lucknow, Kanpur, Amroha, Varanasi and in so many other places.

If Harijans are burnt alive, if innocent Muslims, men women and children, fall victim to the daggers of assassins and if all accepted national policies which kept this country together for the last 30 years after independence are being systematically reversed, the Prime Minister has reasons to forget his life-long association with my illustrious father, Jawaharlal Nehru.

By the toil and sweat of agricultural labour and the sustained effort of our farmers, we have been liberated from dependence on foreign aid, but neither minimum wages nor remunerative prices for produce are being ensured. Industrial workers had contributed to increased production in our factors especially in the public sector, but now the Government's attitude towards, and policies for them are threatening their fundamental rights and the existence of their organisations. [*Interruptions*]

I charge the present government of weakening the foundations laid by Gandhiji and built upon by my father, of surrendering the sovereign right of India to use nuclear technology for our vital interests, of diluting the policy of non-alignment, of weakening the public sector, of denigrating our indigenous science and technology and of inviting multinationals, surreptitiously though in a big way, to control the commanding heights of our economy.

I accuse the present government of tarnishing our image at home and of lowering India's prestige in the world.

The failures of this Government are leading to its isolation from people everywhere. The ineptitude of this government has destroyed the cohesiveness of the administration and created a situation of uncertainty and insecurity. Cynicism is growing. If this situation is not reversed it will provide a fertile soil for the growth of fascism.

I say all this not in anger but in deep sorrow, yet say it I must in the interests of our country and our people who are the ultimate sovereign.

It is my firm conviction that the fight between the forces of fascism and socialism in India and in the world is now reaching a decisive stage and if I may quote the Prime Minister of Zambia, "the dying horse kicks harder". Only at our peril can we afford to lose sight of these trends.

Mr. Speaker, Sir, and distinguished members of this august House, I should like to submit with the utmost sincerity that I would cheerfully sacrifice even my life [*Interruptions*] let alone the membership of this House, if by so doing I could promote the cause of our country. As a British poet has written: "All else must be sacrificed to this great cause. I fear no hardships. I have counted the cost." The Janata Party knows and the Prime Minister knows—indeed every man, women and child in India know that if the drama of a kind of impeachment of a former Prime Minister is enacted, its sole purpose is not to sole any national problem but to silence a voice which they find inconvenient.

If the government believes that by sending me to prison or banishing me from this House, the voice of protest against their wrong policies will be silenced, they are woefully mistaken. Their erroneous policies have created problem of such dimensions that no longer can the bogey of Indira Gandhi keep the government in power or their party united. We must find principled answers to the problems confronting our country. This government has landed this country into a deep crisis which it is in no position to resolve.

I am not guilty of the crimes of which I am being charged by this government. Nor do I believe that this government is concerned about such crimes. How can it be? Never in the 30 years of Independence has there been such shameless corruption, such blatant misuse of power [*Interruptions*] the forced retirement of some of the best amongst our civil servants, the deliberate and persistent harassment not only of political workers but of the defenceless average citizen. No, these are not what the Janata Party considers crimes. But they dare not publicly admit to what they do consider my real guilt and the guilt of my party.

My father said "We are sentenced to hard labour." And so we are. But that hard labour is a privilege for it means the service of the people. And it brought with it not the reward of riches but of something much more valuable and much more rare—the trust and affection of the people.

What have been the crimes of my party and myself in the eyes of the Janata Party?

(1) That we were able to weave the strands of our diversity into a strong national fabric, by respecting all religions, by giving full play to the personalities of the different regions, by enriching all our languages and by encouraging local pride and initiative. This was secular nationalism.

(2) That we strengthened the economy, harming none yet making every attempt to redress the imbalance of centuries by special help to the weaker and neglected sections, the minorities, the smaller men in any group. This was democratic socialism.

(3) That we held our head high in international affairs. Not imitating, not boasting, not cringing. Just being ourselves—Indians, belonging to a very special civilisation. Self-reliant, self confident. This was non-alignment.

The pages of history are strewn with the names of innocent people who have been hounded to death or otherwise victimized for their convictions. Some of the greatest men and women have been subjected to persecution. Many, many have gone before me, but I did have the honour of personally knowing a few.

I am a small person but I have stood for certain values and objectives. Every insult hurled at me will rebound. Every punishment inflicted on me will be a source of strength to me.

My voice will not be hushed for it is not a lone voice. It speaks not for myself, frail woman, and unimportant person. It speaks not for a so called 'total revolution' involving smugglers, dacoits and other such, but for the deep and significant changes in society which alone can be the basis of true democracy and a fuller freedom which alone can ensure justice, and help to create a better man.

The atmosphere in this House has been reminiscent of the scene in Alice in Wonderland, when all the cards rise up in the air and shout, "Off with her head"! My head is yours. My box has been packed these several months; we had only to put in the winter things.

I have stated some of the points in my case. There are others equally relevant and telling. I am now in the hands of the Hon'ble members.

'Uphold Secular Values', Rajiv Gandhi's inaugural speech at the national symposium on 'India's Struggle against Communalism' New Delhi, October 8, 1986

While we have given the highest priority in our development to the war on poverty, we cannot afford to ignore all the other aspects that go with the development of the country. Development cannot mean merely economic development. It must include social, cultural, political and human development. Unless we are able to develop in all these spheres also, we will find it very difficult to fight this battle against communalism. Secularism is the bedrock of our nationhood, secularism as defined not in the English dictionaries, where it is defined as 'non-religious' or 'anti-religious', but secularism the way Panditji defined it as Sarva Dharma Samabhava which allows every religion to flourish in our country. Every community, every caste, every linguistic group must be allowed freedom to flourish, prosper and develop, yet they must be woven into one India, to a unified India. India is not just a mere geographic expression or a political entity. India dates back to thousands of years; the boundaries have changed, the politics have changed but still India has remained India. It is the thinking, it is the thought, it is an inner spirituality that makes India.

No matter who conquered us, no matter if we were enslaved, that concept and that idea was not threatened and did not die and that is our strength today—the idea that all people from all faiths, all castes, all languages, all cultures are equal and must get equal opportunity; the concept that there is always something more that we can learn from outside to assimilate and to absorb, to enrich our own culture with what comes to us from outside. It is these ideas which have given us strength from the times that the Aryans swept into India and came into contact with the highly developed Dravidian civilisation. Perhaps that synthesis brought about the beginning of India as we would like to define it today. Conquerors have been attracted to India throughout history by its rivers, by its fertile plains, by deltas, by the knowledge and wisdom that prevailed in India. But with every conqueror we gained something. In battle, in war, you might win some, and you might lose some, but ultimately the concept of India, the idea of India was so powerful that no matter who won the battle or who lost the battle, it was India that gained and became stronger—culturally stronger, economically stronger. It is this idea, this concept of mingling the old with the new, which has given us a fusion, new inputs, new development in our civilisation while keeping alive our own culture, our heritage, what we have always valued, whether we go back to Alexander and the Bactrians which synthesised into the Gandhara culture, the Suryavamsha and the Chandravamsha clans which then brought us the Rajputs. Our Christian community in Malabar is much older than the Catholics of the West. Whether it is the Arabs, the Mongols, the Turks, the Persians who brought us the Bhakti movement and the Sufi Ulema, it has always been a history of infusion of the new into the old, never rejecting one culture or one civilization completely, like it happened in many other areas of the world. It is this that gives us our strength today.

And it is this that is challenged by the concept of fundamentalism and communalism which is totally contrary to everything that India is and has always stood for. If we are to preserve this concept of India then we must be able to fight these divisive forces, these parochial forces that threaten us today. Being an Indian cannot be merely holding and Indian passport; it must be being a true Indian in the spirit in which India has been through the centuries, recognising what India is and rejoicing in the diversity and strength of India. Unless we are able to bring this into the hearts of our people and the minds of our people, India will remain threatened by these divisive forces.

Throughout history our civilisation has developed by cross- fertilization and acceptance of different cultures. It has weakened whenever we have enclosed ourselves or we have cut ourselves off, shut ourselves off, from other cultures and other civilisations. When we talk of communalism or fundamentalism, we are cuttting ourselves off and shutting ourselves off from other cultures, and other civilisations, and we are reducing our strength, we •are weakening ourselves. To make India strong we must cut across these barriers, remove these narrow walls. Unity of India will only come about with deep respect for all faiths and beliefs and this deep respect characterises most Indians. How many countries can we think of where people from one religion visit the religious places of other religions? Perhaps India is one of the few countries where as an ex-pression of faith people from one religion will visit temples, mosques, gurudwaras, churches of other religions; Sikhs go to temples, Hindus go to gurudwaras; Sikhs, Hindus, Muslims, everyone go to mosques. The fact is that in India faith is so deeply ingrained that we find religion in every religious place, we do not have to be confined to our own narrow parameters and these narrow parameters are becoming narrower as religion reduces itself more and more to ritual and the religious aspect of it gets lost and the ritual aspect becomes more and more prominent. We have to pull back from this drift and bring India back to the acceptance of a much deeper faith, a dharma if we can define it in that sense.

The fight against communalism and fundamentalism cannot be fought by the police and the law and order machinery. That can only be a very short term, temporary measure. And we must see how we can face this challenge. Yes, certain amount of police action is necessary, the law and order machinery must be seen to function when law and order is threatened, but we should try and restrict this action against those people who are motivated in a certain different way. Perhaps, motivated from beyond the confines of our boundaries and they must be challenged and they must be faced squarely and that is the job of the police machinery. But the greater task and the much harder task is once more to bring about a feeling, a mood, an atmosphere in the country that does not allow communalism and fundamentalism to develop.

We have taken a step with the new education policy because we feel that the beginning must be in the school, a beginning perhaps must also be in the home and we must bring about an atmosphere where the correct values—correct perhaps is a difficult word—but the right values are imbibed in our younger generation. We have talked so much of secularism. At every chance we get, we would like to say that we are secular but this is the time for us to think about what we mean by secularism and how this secularism is to be propagated. Like I said in the beginning is it negative secularism which avoids mentioning any religion, touching any religion? Is our secularism to be limited to an attempt to separate politics from religion? Is it to go further to try and build that inner spirituality that is a part of being Indian? Is it to go beyond to build a faith? These are the questions that we must answer for ourselves and develop a system which goes in the right direction. Gandhiji and Panditji started this in this direction and we do not have to go very far; we only have to reach out to their writings and their speeches to find out that new direction again—a direction that will transcend religious differences, yet build on the values that we have inherited from all the religions that have flourished in our country. It is time that we discuss this, talk about this amongst ourselves, openly, perhaps in the newspapers, in the journals and debate it and come to conclusions which will give us a direction that can be put into the education policy, that can be given to society—a direction that is acceptable to our people by and large, a direction that will strengthen India and perhaps, most of all, will result in much faster economic growth which seems to be such a mania with us today. But without human development it is very difficult to have economic development. It is only a short-term development, economic development, that is possible if we ignore the human aspect.

It is only with such a thrust that we will be able to challenge the fanatics and extremists, the terrorists who exchange weapons for arguments, who exchange violence for ideology. If the communal virus in Punjab specially is to be tackled, it can only be done if we tackle it on a broader front and not just on the limited front of countering the terrorists, the known hardcore terrorists. Yes, we must do that, we are doing that; the Punjab Government has been successful, Shri Ribeiro (Police Chief) has been successful, but the more successful they are, the more desperate the terrorists will become, the more desperate they are, the more action we will see, like we have seen, in the recent weeks, but we must be prepared to face those challenges. The direction that we have given for countering terrorism must not be changed on both fronts, on the human front, on the social front as well as on the police front. We must tackle it on both fronts and confront it. By tackling terrorism on two fronts in this manner, we are not showing a weakness, we are showing in fact much more strength and if we persist, which we will do, normalcy will be restored in Punjab.

We have to build a country that Gandhiji and Panditji dreamed of, that Indiraji set out to build, where there is communal harmony, where we live as brothers and sisters, where we can hold our heads high—a country which makes us proud to be a member of the comity of nations. Secularism cannot be indifference to religion, like I said, it must be a positive direction as Gandhiji and Panditji had shown us. We must get back to redeveloping that direction in today's situation, in today's reality and then take it to every corner of our country.

Finally, it gives me a great pleasure to inaugurate this seminar. It is an important seminar and I see a lot of distinguished people present here today. I look forward' to reading about some of your views; there is a little time, perhaps I can hear some of your views as well, and to look towards you to help us bring back the values that we all hold so dear, that we feel are slipping out from our civilisation. It is a subject which requires the topmost national importance and many of you here have devoted a lifetime in studying this subject. I look forward to your contributions.

'Focus on Panchayati Raj', Rajiv Gandhi's speech (in Hindi) while inaugurating the Panchayati Raj Sammelan of Northern states, New Delhi, January 27, 1989

I am happy to attend this Sammelan. First, I wish to thank the Ministry for choosing such an appropriate day for this Sammelan, which falls between our 40th Republic Day and the anniversary of the martyrdom of Gandhjji. When *we* adopted our Constitution on the first Republic Day, we promised to give power to the people. Gandhiji fought against the British, the imperialist forces, for achieving this object. I am particularly happy that we have got an opportunity to discuss this seriously during the next two days. I have a complaint which I wanted to make in the end, but I am making at the outset. Bhajan Lalji has invited eight thousand people to come to Delhi but he has fixed only two days and one night for discussions. I am told that the entire time will be utilised if only two per cent of the invites speak for five minutes each. I feel that in such a short duration we cannot discuss these matters well. I hope Bhajan Lalji will extend the Sammelan by another two days, to enable at least double the number of speakers to express their views. I hope he will do so and will also extend the arrangements in the camp.

After Independence, we had promised in the Constitution, to strengthen the third level of our democracy. The first and the second levels which are governed from Delhi and the State capitals have been. Strengthened following several elections, and no one can weaken them. The third level, however, is weak, and it affects the first two levels also, because, people at the top level have become paper tigers and the structure has become hollow. This has to be set right by strengthening the Panchayati Raj institutions. To strengthen our democracy in Delhi and in the State capitals, it is essential to strengthen the democratic institutions at the Panchayat level. To gear up the development process, it is necessary to strengthen the Panchayati Raj institutions at district, block and village levels.

In the last one-and-a-half year we have done many things in this context. We began by organising discussions with the District Magistrates and Collectors. We talked to the Secretaries and the Chief Secretaries. There were discussions in our Party and in the Ministries. We have come to you after doing our home work. I hope we will help you and fulfil the promises we had made. Promises were made during the freedom struggle and in our Constitution but no one effectively implemented them. The people at the top level were busy strengthening their own positions in politics as well as in administration and completely neglected the federal institutions. Whenever elections to the Panchayats were held, they remained nominal. And for the last 10-20 years, mostly nominated members are running these institutions (Panchayats). This cannot strengthen the base level. The devolution of power to the grassroots level as promised could not be effected and whatever was done was generally in an arbitrary manner. In some States where devolution of power had been implemented a member was nominated to the local bodies by the administration or a Minister was placed there. What actually happened? The decision-making authority remained either with the State Government or with the administration, and it could not filter down to the base level.

In addition, sufficient resources were not made available for the upliftment of the rural population, and the meagre amount provided was not spent according to the needs of the rural people. In our development planning and implementation, the participation of the Panchayati Raj institutions was lacking. What was the net result? The result was that the power—which Gandhiji and Panditji wanted to be given to the people and for which our Constitution also provided—did not actually reach them. It meant that the plans and the schemes made, could not in reality cater to your needs. The development programmes which were worked out from Delhi and the State capitals could neither improve your conditions nor remove your difficulties. The result was that even after the completion of those schemes; their full benefit could not reach you.

Whatever economic development was achieved could not be effective because there was a vast gap between the preparation of the schemes and their implementation. The result was that even for the solution of trifling issues, the people looked to the Government. I can quote the example of my own constituency which I have known minutely as to how people come to me even with small problems. There must be some lacuna somewhere that MPs, MLAs and even Chief Ministers come to me with trifling matters: Those issues which can be tackled at the village level should be dealt with there. If the Central Government is involved in such issues, what requires to be done can neither done well nor in time. You know, there are many procedural requirements in the implementation of a project which involves many people, and these only create problems. When we attempt rural development from Delhi, we are unable to detect all the loopholes which only you can plug, being on the spot. The result is that you come with complaints that development schemes are not being properly implemented.

We must ensure that our people are not totally dependent on the Central Government or the State Governments for all types of development works. They should themselves have a feeling of participation in development programmes and the process of social change. This will require that the gap between the administration and the people be bridged. We have to see that people, whether they are in politics or in Government, should not rush to Delhi or State capitals for the redressal of every grievance. If development work can be planned at the district, block or village level it should be taken up there itself. If this is not done, schemes will be delayed and so will their implementation.

We wanted to remove social injustice and atrocities on the weaker sections but this task has not yet been completed. Even today atrocities are perpetrated on weaker sections, on Scheduled Castes and Scheduled Tribes and on women. We want to involve people in nation building. We want everyone in the country to take initiative in such work. This, however, has not been fully accomplished and the result is that a system of power-brokers has emerged in our country, whether it is politics or the development process. For any work that is to be done, people have to please some power-broker. We have to break this system and to do this; we have to devolve maximum power to Panchayati Raj institutions. This was the desire of Gandhiji and Panditji. But that spirit got lost on the way. We will, however, try to give you strength on the lines Gandhiji and Panditji wanted.

It is essential to give power to the common people. We have to pay special attention to the weaker sections, the Scheduled Castes, the Scheduled Tribes and women. We have also to take special care of linguistic and other minorities and protect them. We have also to keep a watch so that devolution of power to grassroots is not usurped by the rich and those who derive power from the caste structure. The Panchayati Raj system should ensure social justice to the poor, to the weaker sections. I would like to have your suggestions on these issues.

I want you to speak openly on these issues during the four days of the *Sammelan*. But you should remember that whatever system of devolution of power is evolved, it must ensure protection of the weak. The elections should be held in time and the weaker sections should freely participate in the elections. If need be, some sort of reservation could be evolved. You have to think how to fill the reserved seats or posts. Should these be filled by election or by nomination? Should we follow the procedure adopted in some countries where the candidate defeated with the minimum margin is also declared elected? Or should we adopt some other method? Every system has its own strong points.

There are various systems—each with its own weakness and strength. You have to consider these systems from different angles.You have to pay special attention to the weaker Sections and tell me how they can be helped. Another method can be what was, at one time, in vogue for elections to the Lok Sabha, the system of multi-member constituencies. Yet another method could also be one of setting up social justice committees and special committees in areas inhabited by Harijans, Adivasis, minorities and other weaker sections.

You have to discuss seriously and evolve some kind of a relationship between Panchayati Raj institutions and the State Governments. You have to discuss it minutely because any mistake can stop the development process. You have to ponder over the relationship of Collectors and District Magistrates with Zila Parishads and their Chairmen. Again, you have to think which institutions would function under the Zila Parishad, under the block and at village level.

You must discuss how development schemes can he implemented most effectively. You should not be engaged in creating small kingdoms because these will only further weaken us. The relationship of municipal areas with Zila Parishads is an important factor, whether they should maintain equal status with Zila Parishads. or work within them or under them. Each system has its own strength and weakness. If a district government is formed, it will strengthen the Zila Parishad. Small towns within such a set-up will become focal points of development. On the other hand if Zila Parishads are kept outside the district administration it will focus greater attention on the development of rural areas. Both the systems are relevant in their own way. You have to find out a way so that a balance can be maintained. Today it is not sufficient only to plan for the development of rural areas. Educated youth are looking for a different type of employment and better facilities for which they migrate to small towns and cities. You must evolve a framework that draws upon the strengths of the alternative systems. You must evolve a system which accelerates the work of removing poverty. You must discuss what role can be played at the district, block and village levels in the planning process.

I have asked the Planning Commission to formulate plans from the district level for the Eighth Plan. They have assured that a beginning will be made. Constraints of time may not permit us to make a beginning on the scale we had envisaged but we will find a way out. I hope that by the second or third year of the Eighth Plan, this work will get off the ground well and that there will be co-ordination between the State Planning bodies and the Planning Commission.

Then, there is the major problem of resources. You must ensure proper utilization of resources. I feel that if we keep on giving resources we are doing today, that will not lead to proper development. You will keep on asking for funds and nobody will see whether work is being carried out properly or not. For the most part you do not keep in view your actual requirements when funds are made available from very far away and programmes are also made at some distant place. You have your eye on what is surplus with the Government and what you can get from it. The other point is that these funds are not linked with raising resources. That is why you must find out whether at the district and lower levels some resources can be raised. Whether you can be given some powers to raise revenue and in what way could these be given.

You will also have to discuss how power will be devolved. When the Panchayati Raj system was initiated, the responsibility of giving power to local bodies was with the States. Often power given by one hand was taken away by the other. This should not happen again. How should the power be given to you? Straight from the Centre or from the States to the local bodies? No one should be able to take this power away from you. Should the

Constitution be amended and in what manner and to what extent? What is the minimum amendment required and what is the maximum that should be done? At the very minimum, timely elections to panchayats must be ensured and these bodies should not be dissolved without valid reasons. If for some reason they are dissolved, there should be a provision for their re-election as is the case for our Lok Sabha or State Assemblies. This is the minimum requirement. There can also be much more. You must reflect which is the best middle path and how we can reach it. We do not want to give you Panchayati Raj institutions as they were. We want to renew and strengthen the institutions that we give you, so that elections are held in time and real power is in your hands. We have also to learn from the past 25 years of experience, what we could achieve and what we could not, where the weakness lies and how it can be remedied. Responsibilities should be well defined and resources should be properly allocated to you. Above all we must ensure that weaker sections are protected and that they are not weakened by this system but in fact gain strength from it.

I hope this new system will cater to the actual needs of the people. It must ensure that past mistakes are not repeated. I hope that democracy will reach the grassroots. To achieve this object, we have to break the hold of power-brokers and give real power to the districts, blocks and villages—to the people who, live there.

Even a four-day period for such discussions is not sufficient and therefore, a questionnaire has been given to you. I hope you will study the questionnaire seriously, complete it and return it to us. I assure you that we will go through the questionnaires filled up by you, thoroughly and try to incorporate your suggestions.

I hope that I shall be with you again on the fourth day and for a longer period. I have kept two and a half hours apart to be with you. I have spoken a lot today, but on that day I will speak less and listen more to you. And I hope that you will speak openly without any reservation.

I see that only a few women are present here. I hope Bhajan Lalji will see to it that women delegates get full opportunity for expressing their views. In the end, I welcome you to Delhi, and I hope that the arrangement made for your stay here is comfortable, inspite of the chilly weather. If there are any shortcomings, do please let us know and we will try our best to remove these.

I saw you sitting in two blocks yesterday in the Republic Day function. I am sure you must have enjoyed the parade.

It is appropriate that you visited the Samadhi of Gandhiji before beginning your deliberations. You have before you very significant work—work linked with the thoughts and ideals of Gandhiji and an integral part of our freedom struggle, which in a way was left out and must be completed now. I give you my good wishes for the success of your discussions. When I meet you on the fourth day of the Sammelan, I hope to get from you good and solid answers to the questions which I have posed before you.

'Youth and National Development', Rajiv Gandhi's speech while presenting the National Youth Awards 1986-87, New Delhi, January 18, 1988

THE NATIONAL YOUTH Week commenced on 12 January with the celebration of' Swami Vivekananda's birthday. Swami Vivekananda attained his spiritual prime when he himself was very young. His example is an inspiration to our generation and to your generation of Indian youth.

Swami Vivekananda's creative interpretation of our ancient traditions kindled in our people a new pride in themselves, a new pride in our heritage. Our youth responded to his exhortation to rise above the petty confines of caste, creed, and religion. Jawaharlal Nehru said of Vivekananda: "He was no politician in the ordinary sense of the word and yet he was, I think, one of the great founders of the modern movement of India. Directly or indirectly he has powerfully influenced the India of today."

Swami Vivekananda brought in a new kind of spirituality, combining inner spiritual wisdom with the rational scientific temper. While the Christian world was struggling to reconcile the literal interpretation of the Old and the New Testaments with Darwin's Theory of Evolution, Swami Vivekananda demonstrated the inherent compatibility in our traditions between spiritual insights and scientific perceptions.

We are one of the world's oldest civilizations and one of the youngest nations. Our country's demographic profile has undergone a major revolution. Now, there is a preponderance of youth. This is a decisive factor in determining our nation's destiny. It is, therefore, incumbent upon us to look very hard at the problems of the youth. At the same time, it is incumbent upon the youth to look at the problems of the nation. Youth must prepare themselves for the responsibilities which lie ahead. With this in view, we have strengthened the range of programmes addressed specially to the youth.

Perhaps, the foremost is the New Education Policy. The fundamental aim is to orient the young mind to face the challenges of the twenty-first century; the challenges at both the moral and material levels. At the material level, it must include the acquisition of aptitudes and skills to deal with the new technologies which incessantly impinge upon our everyday lives. At the moral level, we must make youth and the coming generations the masters of technology and scientific development so that humanity doesn't become slave to technology and science but is able to direct it for the benefit and development of the human beings of our world. Technology is only a tool. How it is used depends on the training given to the minds and hands that are to use it.

I would not go into the details of the long list of programmes. The Minister for Human Resource Development has covered most of them in his speech. What is important is that we must have a good interaction between youth and the development of our society. If this interaction is to be really useful, it is not good enough for the youth merely to participate in these programmes. They must also go out on their own to seek opportunities for service, opportunities in our *mohallas,* in our *bastis,* in our villages, where you can help in changing our society, in strengthening our society, in bringing it out of its old-fashionedness in some places, at the same time preserving all that is best in what we have inherited. In a sense, your task must be to take the initiative, not look merely to the Government or other organisations to bring about the changes that are required in our society. You must do what Gandhiji had called Constructive Work—going amongst the people with adult education, with sanitation. You must make people help themselves. The education of girls is particularly important because that is one of our bigger problems today and it is not a problem that we from Government alone can easily solve. It will be solved quickly and easily only *if* society is willing to tackle it.

There are myriads of other such tasks that can be done and must be done today. The litmus test of our efforts lies not in the mobilisation of youth in large numbers for social service, but in the motivation of youth so that they mobilise themselves and come into the mainstream of our development process. Initiative is the key word and this is what we must develop amongst all our people.

We need to augment greatly our basic data and information about the youth in the country, especially in the light of the growing importance of youth in our population profile. It is essential that we take up these tasks with the utmost urgency. Our data bases today are woefully inadequate. To fill this lacuna, we have taken in hand various research and documentation projects. This is a fruitful area of study, specially for youth. You can contribute both by looking at the problems of the youth and by raising the level of thinking, from merely demanding on a short-term, day-to-day basis, to going into problems much more deeply, studying them and drawing our attention to the solutions that you find. We hope that these opportunities will create many able scholars who will distinguish themselves in these fields.

Lastly, I wish to congratulate all those who have received awards today in recognition of the work that they have done. The purpose is not only to recognise their excellence and their contribution, but equally to serve as an incentive to others to achieve what today's winners have achieved.

I shall leave you with a message from Swami Vivekananda: "Devote yourselves heart and soul to one principal duty, the duty of raising the masses of India, awakening them and uniting them."

Meeting of All India Congress Committee Opening Remarks by the Congress President, Sonia Gandhi, New Delhi, April 6, 1998

Distinguished Members of the Congress Working Committee, Fellow-Members of the AICC,

May I extend to each one of you a very warm welcome to this session of the All India Congress Committee. You have elected me President of this great organization. I am aware of the awesome responsibility you have placed upon me. It is with deep humility that I accept this privilege. I pledge myself to serving the Party with sincerity and dedication.

Men and women of very high eminence have held this office. For a century and more they have defined the destiny of this great nation. It is they who brought us our freedom. It is they who have built modern India. They have moulded the Congress into the prime instrument and expression of our national consciousness. It is through the Congress that the nation has rediscovered its sense of purpose. It is through the Congress that we as a people have forged our unity. It is the Congress that has developed the dynamics of people's action.

From the very inception the Congress has stood for a free, democratic, just and secular India. I pay homage to Mahatma Gandhi, who ensured that the 20th century would be for India—and the world—the century of national liberation.

I pay tribute to his team of noble disciples who brought us to freedom—Motilal Nehru, Chittaranjan Das, Sardar Patel, Rajaji, Maulana Azad, Jawaharlal Nehru, Rajendra Prasad, Sarojini Naidu, Subhas Chandra Bose. I pay tribute also to the Congress Prime Ministers of Independent India, who between them gave our country for and a half decades of democratic governance, raising prosperity and stable governments. I pay special tribute to Indiraji and Rajivji who have become martyrs in the service of our country. I salute all my other distinguished predecessors and pray that I shall prove worthy of them.

I have come to this office at a critical point in the history of Party. Our numbers in Parliament have dwindled. Our support base among the electorate has been seriously eroded. Some segments of the voters—including our tribals, dalits and minorities—have drifted from us. We are in danger of losing our central place in the polity of our country as the natural party of governance. At the centenary session of the Congress back in 1985 Rajiv Gandhi had pointed out certain weakness in the working of the Congress Party.

He asked; "What has become of our great organization? Instead of a party that fired the imagination of the masses throughout the length and breadth of India, we have shrunk, losing touch with the masses." It was by firing the imagination of our people that Gandhiji won us our freedom. It was by firing the imagination of the people that Panditji and indiraji built an India of which the nation was proud. And it was through what he called "a politics of service to the poor" that my husband sought to ignite the imagination of the people.

In his centenary speech, he etched the outlines of the programme he had in mind: "The power to shape their own lives must lie with the people .... Vibrant village panchayats must discuss, deliberate and decide the choices to be made." unquote He called this the "challenge to the Congress cadres". "It is up to us, the workers of this great organization," he said: "to spread in every village and every hamlet of India, to mobilize the people, to guide them, to stand by their side when they are denied their due..." To this rejuvenate the Congress, Rajiv Gandhi emphasized two key issues. One, the role of ideology, policies and programmes in the everyday life of the Party. He said: "The ideology of the Congress has acquired the status of an heirloom, to be polished and brought out on special occasions. It must be a living force to animate the Congress workers in their day-to-day activity. Our ideology of nationalism, secularism, democracy and socialism is the only relevant ideology for our great country." And the instrument for carrying the Congress policies to the people had, of course, to be the humble Congress worker. But the genuine Congress worker remains unheeded and unrecognised. He is not only the last to be heard but also the least heard. I see it as my primary task as Congress President to restore to the Congress the vision of the Congress centenary—Power to the People through the panchayats; and Power to the Congress worker through democracy within the Party.

I am no saviour, as some of you might want to believe. We must be realistic in our expectations. The revival of our Party is going to be a long drawn process, involving sincere hardwork, from each and everyone of us. But I do have an abiding faith in the path shown to us by our leaders in the past. It is the only path that will lead us to our goal. And I believe we can attain it if we act together and hold together. In practical terms, our task is to give the people of India an organization that stands for them, that fights for their rights and is anchored to the principles on which our nationhood is founded. We must shun what is expedient and stand by what is right. That is what Gandhiji taught us. This simple truth wrested for our Independence from the mightiest military power then known to history.

This simple truth is what Panditji practised—and made India a role model for other emerging national, a voice heard with respect around the world.

Our is the oldest, most venerated Party in the country. It is the only Party with adherents in, literally, every village, every mohalla, every basti. Ours is still, notwithstanding recent reverses, the most representative Party in the country, the only political mirror which reflects all the glorious diversity of this vast and wonderful land. It is, therefore, a national imperative, not merely a partisan requirement, that we store the Congress to its former primacy. It is the only Party whose fundamental adherence to secularism has never been diluted.

Gandhiji said all great political parties needed faithful agents to implement their policies and programmes. We have in our ranks lakhs of dedicated, efficient, talented men and women. They combine the energy of youth with the wisdom of age. We are the one Party that excludes none and includes all—both genders, all ages, every caste, every creed, every class, every region. For our workers to fulfil the role of faithful agents of the Party, they cannot be mere playthings of the leadership. Our leadership must in fact emerge from the grassroots. It must reflect the aspirations of the grassroots. It must be sensitive to the demands of the grassroots.

My priority will be to reinforce the role of the ordinary worker in the organization of the Party. I appeal to all office holders from panchayat and block level upwards to be mindful of the grievances of grassroot workers and ensure that they are heard with courtesy and understanding. This alone will give us an organizational structure representative of the Party, responsible to the Party, and therefore, responsive to the Party. It is our immediate task to reverse these trends. To my mind, this can be achieved only through a radical programme of introspection and reflection. We need nothing less than the complete revitalization of the Congress, a return to the time when the Congress was the instinctive first choice of the electorate. I have set in motion a process by which appropriate committees have been appointed and asked to visit the States where we have done badly.

The findings and conclusions of these committees will be carefully studied, analyzed and acted upon by the Working Committee. In the next few months there will be Vidhan Sabha elections in several States. It is imperative that our Party starts preparing for them from now. But cutting across States are some broader issues that deserve our immediate attention and require concrete and corrective action. Our Party has to renew itself by attracting the best and the brightest of the young to join and contribute to its growth. Youth needs encouragement; youth needs opportunity; youth needs training.

Youth is idealistic. It is wary of the unsavoury. It is inspired by the moral high ground. We will spot promising young talent; we will nurture it; we will promote it. We will identify with the aspirations of the new generation and make them feel that, establishment though we are for over a century, we are conscious of their concerns and responsive to their quest for answers. Ours will be a Party which gives real responsibility to the youth. Ours must also be the Party which gives real responsibility to women. Tokenism will not do and is, indeed, offensive. Women must not find themselves shelved and marginalised into just their frontal organization.

It is my purpose to bring them to the Party's mainstream. At the grassroots, reservations for women in the panchayats have opened vast opportunities for their political empowerment and active participation in governance. We must however give much higher priority than we have done to identifying and readying women candidates for election to the panchayats and nagarpalikas at all levels. In the State Assemblies and Parliament, we will be unflinching and resolutely committed to reservations for women in our legislatures. We must so comport ourselves that the women of India identify with the Congress as their Party of preference. We have not made sufficient efforts to engage community leaders in serious dialogue or win them over to our way of thinking.

All our political energies seem to be concentrated on elections. In between lethargy overtake us. We must resist this. Indiscipline and indifferent performance should have no place in our Party. We must be in constant touch with our constituents. For Party workers, this means living and moving among the people. Four our parliamentary and legislative representatives, it means spending a significant part of every month travelling to every corner of their respective constituencies. And our emphasis should not only be on elections but on pressing social, economic and political issues of the day. Through this we will be able to fulfil or broader social and political agenda. Thus will we restore our links with the society and communities we serve. The AICC, the PCCs, the DCCs, the Block Committees and the primary units all need streamlining and toning up.

I intend to apply my mind to administrative restructuring so that our Party becomes an effective instrument for mobilizing the people and translating our policies and programmes into action. I plan to travel extensively to see for myself how this is unfolding on the ground. To be systematic in our approach, I propose to appoint a Monitoring Committee which will supervise programme implementation and report directly to me. It will charge immediate goals and ensure that we keep track of our progress. Immediately after this session of the AICC, I will address myself to the working of our frontal organizations which need effective and purposeful leadership and orient their role to what the people of our country need.

The NSUI, the Youth Congress, the Seva Dal and the Mahila Congress must become active agents for the betterment of society. They can no longer remain, as they have tended to be, the closed preserves of special self-perpetuating groups. They ought to welcome all those who are interested in the welfare and improvement of the lives of our people, especially the poor and disadvantaged. They should not be mere stepping stones to a political career; rather, they should be instruments for the propagation of our policies and programmes. These bodies should be examples of sustained and dynamic action. They should be in the forefront of campaigns on such social issues as female infanticide, child marriage, dowry deaths, atrocities on women, the exploitation of the underprivileged, caste and communal violence, and discrimination in any form. They must be in the vanguard of the promotion of literacy, the legal rights of women, gender equality and family planning. This is a vast agenda and it will constructively absorb the energies of our active workers. We have slipped perilously in the esteem of the educated, the urban and the young voter. It was our party which lowered the voting age to 18 from 21; yet, as the average Indian voter gets younger and more educated, it is our Party which has suffered reverses. To this large and influential segment of the electorate, some of their disenchantment with us arises from our Party being seen as soft on corruption and criminalization. The impression has gained ground among them that we want to cling to power or achieve it at any cost.

We need to build bridges with the intelligentsia, with young professionals, with educated voters, with universities and institutions of higher learning and research where opinion makers are reared. We must revive the culture of informed discussion in the Congress Party. We will chart changes and new courses as the situation requires by holding Narora-type camps. We cannot represent the diversity of India and shy away from frank discussion. At such camps we should aim to strive for consensus if not unanimity. At these camps the participants should also reflect on the more uplifting and enduring aspects of our political activity. We must raise fundamental questions which should be of relevance to the party in the next century. We will also strengthen our Parliamentary wing and the legislature parties. They need analytical expertise and sound intellectual support.

To this end, I am constituting committees which will meet regularly and provide inputs to our parliamentarians for use in debates in both Houses. These committees will also track the performance of the government in vital areas, and help formulate bills that the Congress will table. They will also interact with scholars, intellectuals, business groups, NGOs and others.

To eliminate certain misgivings, we need to put in place a transparent and accountable system of party financing. The people of our country are no longer willing to forgive trespass in this area. We need reform at a wider, national level involving all political parties. But while we will need a broader consensus, we must be prepared to put our own house in order. In my judgement it is essential to ensure a clean, transparent and accountable system of financing. It is an acknowledged fact that donations are made to all political parties, including the Congress party. We cannot single-handedly change this system. But to make a beginning, we should change our election oriented emphasis towards raising financial resources on a sustained, on-going basis.

I would like to commend the Kerala Pradesh Congress Committee in this regard and use its funds raising drive from the public as an example for others to follow. I also appeal to the elected representatives at the district, pradesh and national levels to give a portion of their income for party work. There is no reason why at the end of the year we cannot have a balance sheet that acknowledges the source and utilization of such funds. In this context I would like to draw your attention to the decision taken by the Congress Working Committee in November '96 and September '97 where all office holders of the Party are expected to submit annually a statement of their assets and liabilities to their respective PCCs, and AICC as the case may be.

Another area of people's dissatisfaction is related to the manner in which some of us conduct ourselves both in and out of legislative bodies. There has been a marked deterioration in this regard. Our democracy has no room for rowdyism and disruption. We must honour the traditions of our Parliament and gain the confidence of the people by setting high standards of moral and political behaviour. Having said that I must stress that our members will be expected to severely and relentlessly oppose any attempt at diluting policies and programmes central to the well-being of our people. For this our members must be at all times fully prepared with facts and data to effectively expose the Government.

I now draw your attention to a subject which has aroused some controversy. This relates to the programmes of liberalization and globalisation. We have been told that we have compromised with our basic economic ideology. It was at a time of grave economic reforms. It was a path charted out by my husband and carried forward by Shri PV Narasimha Rao. Rajiv Gandhi had set the economy on the road to rapid growth and transformation while keeping at the forefront the need to protect the poor and disadvantaged from any ill-effects of social change. First of all, we need to build a strong resurgent economy which can grow annually at 7-8 per cent. We need this order of growth to create new job opportunities for our expanding labour force and to increase the resource base of our economy so as to devote more resources for poverty alleviation Programmes.

Economic reforms—liberalization and measured opening out to the rest of the world are essential for this purpose. At the same time, we need well designed strategies to empower the poor to benefit more effectively from processes of development. To ensure its sustainability, the reform ought to be seen as making a substantial difference in the daily lives of ordinary citizens, Particularly those who live in destitution and deprivation. I am aware of the doubts and fears about liberalization and globalisation. It is our duty to dispel them. It is our task to reassure the people in this regard. We must make sure that the government in office does not betray their interests in any way. We must insist on a much greater emphasis on basic social services, such as, education, health, implementation of land reforms and improvement of credit delivery systems for the poor.

While it is true to say that in the nineties economics, finance and trade occupy centre space, it must at the same time be remembered that the economy exists to serve the people and to meet their basic needs. We cannot lose sight of wider ethical issues and concerns such as equity and the environment. Gandhiji emphasised this time and again. Nehru's concept of mixed economy has stood the test of time even though the nature of the mix must vary with the changing needs of the time. However, State intervention can be effective only if politics recaptures the high moral ground and its role as a purposeful instrument of social change.

For generations past, it has been the policy of the Congress Party to work for international peace and harmony, for justice and equality among people and nations. This approach was charted by Jawaharlal Nehru, and evolved by Indira Gandhi and Rajiv Gandhi. Congress party policies gave the world Non-alignment, opposition to nuclear weapons and a voice to hundreds of millions the world over fighting for their liberation. We cannot allow such a great legacy to be squandered.

Our foreign Policy framework created by Jawaharlal Nehru , nurtured and strengthened by Indira Gandhi and Rajiv Gandhi has stood the test of time It is a tribute to his foresight and wisdom that a broad consensus on foreign policy issues has existed for the past 50 years with some satisfaction. But there is great change and movement around us. we have to learn from the experience of the past and apply it to the emerging future. Nothing remains still, nothing remains unchanging. That goes for us too. The Congress Party will adapt to the needs of the future.

Yet, even as we do so, we must never forget why we are here, why we are assembled and why we exist as a Party. And that is to serve the people of our great country and t fulfil their dreams. We will be able to do this only as a united, rejuvenated and invigorated Congress Party.

As Rajiv Gandhi said:

"As we build today so will be the tomorrow. Together we will build for an India of the 21st century. Together we will transform. What needs transformation? Together we will face challenges and obstacles to progress. Together we will create an India that is strong, wise and great—a flame of peace and tolerance."

Let us dedicate ourselves to this task.

Thank you!

Jai Hind.

Concluding Remarks of Congress President, Sonia Gandhi, at Vichar Manthan Shivir, Pachmarhi (September 4-6, 1998) on September 6, 1998

Friends,

We have had a most pleasant, stimulating and refreshing three days at Pachmarhi. On your behalf I thank Digvijay Singhji and his team for making our stay here so comfortable. I also wish to thank Nawal Kishore Sharmaji and his colleagues in the Coordination Committee for having organised this Shivir in such a fine manner. Hundreds of Congress workers have toiled day and night to make our Shivir a success. My thanks to them as will to the residents of Pachmarhi who had helped us as guests for four days, I can only say—expect us to come back.

I wish we could have stayed longer not just for the Chintan and the Manthan but certainly to enjoy Pachmarhi as it should be enjoyed.

You have all heard from the Chairman of the five groups. You have also read the reports of the five groups.

The reports show that the discussions have been free and frank.

The reports show that there has been debate, there has been introspection, there has been refraction and there has been a tremendous sense of participation.

This augurs will but let me hasten to add that Pachmarhi is just the beginning.

We should endeavour to make such Shivirs an annual feature at the National and State level, not to routinise them but to give ourselves the opportunity of pausing once in a while and of reviewing where we are and where we are headed.

We will ensure that future Shivirs will bring in more young men and women.

Friends, the Congress represents like no other political party does, the diversity and plurality of India.

That is why we should not even aim for unanimity on all issues. Differences are inevitable and indeed even desirable.

But I believe that a consensus has been reached on a large number of political, economic, agricultural, foreign policy and organisational issues at this Shivir. I congratulate the Chairman of the five groups for having crafted such a consensus which has all the elements of durability in it. There is really no fundamental differences amongst us. There are differing viewpoints, there are differing perspectives. But there is really no basic conflict. The Shivir has conclusively established this.

In the last three days, I sensed an atmosphere and ambience of team spirit. This is most encouraging and needs to be sustained. I cannot stress enough the absolute essentiality of unity and discipline in the Party at all levels, including among top leaders. If we are united, nothing can stop us and we will meet any threat, overcome any obstacle and win any battle.

I am sure we will rise to the occasion. I am sure we will work cohesively transcending narrow personal interest and keeping the larger good of the Congress and the country in mind.

I do not want to repeat the ideas and the issues we have been discussing in details these past few days.

However, allow me to recall some of the main tasks that form part of our agenda for rebuilding the Congress.

We will take up the ideological crusade against communalism of all kinds and from whatever source it emanates.

We will work tirelessly to recapture our political and social base in the vital states of Uttar Pradesh and Bihar. West Bengal and Tamil Nadu will also receive special attention.

We will give adequate representation to a whole new generation of Dalits, Adivasis, Backward classes and minorities in our Party organisation at all levels particularly women.

We will revitalise the Party organisation at the national, state, district, block and village level and inject into it dynamism that is sustained in the service of the people.

We will restore the ethical and moral foundations of the Congress, the foundations that made the Congress India's foremost political institution.

We will make our election machinery more effective and at the same time work to make polities an instrument of social change and transformation once again.

We will strengthen the institutions of parliamentary democracy.

We will move to once again become the party that people from all walks of life identify with and support in a sustained manner and the party that reflects the hopes and aspirations of all sections of our society.

A number of recommendations have been made in this Shivir to help us respond meaningfully to these challenges.

The Working Committee has already considered these suggestions which have been incorporated in the final statement.

In addition, some of the recommendations will require a review of our Party Constitution, a task which I am confident will be completed very soon.

I also want to say that while we make every effort to come back to power both at the Centre and in various states. We can also enrich the political, economic and social life of the country even by being in the Opposition.

There are many tasks we can and will take on apart from the most fundamental task of exposing the government in power.

We will launch Abhiyans, Jathas, campaigns and movements on basic socio-economic issues. We must mobilise and organise the poor and the disadvantaged in order to empower them. We will take up pressing national causes like population, literacy, Panchayati Raj, land reforms, social justice and gender equality. We will strengthen our traditional bonds with the working classes both in the organised and particularly in the unorganised sector. We will continue to fight for our Kisans and Khet Mazdoors.

The fact that we had a separate group here on agriculture reflects the primacy we give to the welfare and well-being of our farmers and cultivators.

Above all, we will harness the idealism and energy of our younger generation in nation-building activities. We will ensure that the transition to a new generation of leadership at all levels is made.

Friends, there has been much talk about the Congress's attitude towards a coalition government.

The fact that we are going through a coalitional phase at national level polities reflects in many ways the decline of the Congress.

This is a passing phase and we will come back again with full force and on our own steam.

But in the interim coalitions may well be needed. I have already stated in my opening remarks that we will not shirk from our Constitutional obligations as and when they arise. But we will do so without compromising on our basic philosophy and on our priorities as articulated by the five groups here at Pachmarhi.

In the last few months, I get the feeling that the country, fed up with over two years of non-governance, is waiting to give us another chance. I get the feeling that more and more people who moved away from us are once again coming around to the point of view that only the Congress has the experience, the expertise, the energy and the enthusiasm to provide an effective government that will revive the stagnant economy, arrest the price rise, get new investments flowing once again and improve our standing in the world.

We should, however, not be complacent. But we must recognize that the tide seems to be turning. We must consolidate and take full advantage of this changing situation. We must prove ourselves worthy of the confidence and the trust that the people are increasingly reposing in us.

Friends, we depart from this beautiful and picturesque place with fond memories. The woods and the hills of the Satpura have given us a new vigour. We go back conscious of the many challenges that await us. We go back strengthened in our resolve and unwavering in our commitment to meet and respond to these challenges. We go back with a renewed sense of purpose, with a renewed sense of hope and with a renewed sense of determination. I do not want to minimise the obstacles in our path, the pitfalls in our journey. But we go back in the knowledge that each and every one of us will strive relentlessly and inspire others to do so as well and move firmly ahead on the path we have chosen, the path to a new Congress and to a new India.

JAI HIND!

Presidential Address at 81st AICC Plenary Session Bangalore, March 18, 2001

I welcome all of you to the first plenary session of the All India Congress Committee in the 21st century. My fellow Congress workers, I express to you my profound gratitude for giving me such an overwhelming mandate.

We are meeting in this great State of Karnataka that has had such a glorious history, and that has produced some of the greatest sons and daughters of our country. On this occasion, I salute the memories of all our freedom fighters and martyrs. Karnataka is the repository of much that is of the best in our culture and civilisation. This land has a special place in Congress history, having hosted the only session 77 years ago over which the Father of our Nation presided. The recent history of our Party—the stray thoughts of Indiraji in the Lalbagh Glass House 32 years ago that electrified and transformed India is also part of the lore of this vibrant city.

I am deeply conscious of the confidence and trust you have placed in me. I stand before you against the backdrop of an awesome heritage. It is a heritage that gave India independence, a heritage that has shaped a modern nation from an ancient civilisation. It is our great Party that made the 20th century in India a Congress century. It is our pledge that the 21st century too shall be a Congress century.

Through the first half of the 20th century, it was the relentless struggle and immense sacrifices of our Party which wrested Independence through non-violence from what was then the mightiest empire known to world history. And through the second half of the century, it was again the Congress, which shaped the modern nationhood of free India. The Mahatma took us from colonial bondage to national liberation. His greatest disciple, Jawaharlal Nehru, then translated independence for the nation into freedom for our people.

In how many countries has a Constitution drawn half a century ago endured? In how many has democracy come before development? In how many has the military restrained itself from political involvement? Where but in India did affirmative action begin to give equal opportunity to the most oppressed sections of society? Which other country has our wonderful diversity? Where else does secularism flourish in such a profusion of plurality?

Politics, as Gandhiji kept reminding us, is about morality and ethics. Through half a century of freedom, we have been guided by the talisman Gandhiji gave us—the worship of Dardiranarayana: we have placed the poorest of the poor at the centre of our concerns. Their good has been the measure of our achievement. The welfare of the deprived has been our over-riding priority at all times.

It has not been smooth sailing. Within months of freedom, we lost the guiding hand of the Father of the Nation, assassinated by the enemies of secularism. Through the seventeen years of his stewardship of independent India, Jawaharlal Nehru was challenged by the forces of disruption within and the forces of subversion without. The communalists within were vanquished. And those who, from the outside, sought to make India a client state soon learned that India's foreign policy is the external expression of its internal sovereignty.

In his brief term of office, Lal Bahadur Shastri faced the threat of famine at home and Pakistani aggression across our borders. His response was Jai Jawan, Jai Kisan. Over the next two decades, Indiraji grew into the greatest woman leader in contemporary history, focusing the mind of the country on its first and primary duty Garibi Hatao. She launched the Green Revolution and sparked the White Revolution. She was instrumental in liberating Bangladesh. Then came Rajivji, the youthful symbol of India's hopes and aspirations, the translator of Gandhiji's Poorna Swaraj into Gram Swaraj, the architect of India in the 21st century, the man who ushered India into the age of information technology. You all know how today's champions of IT criticized him when he inverted his vision of information technology amidst criticism by today's champions of IT. Right through the eighties, under Indiraji and Rajivji, spectacular growth was registered in every sector of economic activity, specially agriculture, industry and science and technology. For the youth of the nation, it was a time of great expectations. Rajivji had set before the new generation the goal of India occupying its historic and rightful place in world civilization. We were moving towards that objective but sadly that dream could not be realized because of Rajivji's martyrdom. Finally, the last Congress government led by Shri PV Narasimha Rao in the 1990s has rescued India from its gravest economic and political crisis into which a mere 18 months of non-Congress governance had plunged the nation.

Unlike other all coalition Governments the Congress has given stability to our polity and progress to our economy. Economic policy under non-Congress governments at the Centre is proving an accelerating disaster.

We are meeting here at a time when the economy is experiencing a deceleration of growth and is in the grip of an investment famine. Employment growth has come to a virtual standstill. All that the BJP-led coalition can do is to mount an ideological assault and destroy the edifice of the public sector built up with the savings of lakhs and lakhs of our people. A public sector that has given India industrial muscle, that has developed backward regions and that has given numerous jobs to men and women belonging to the weaker sections of society.

We are meeting here at a time when farmers all over the country are facing acute distress. Prices of most agricultural products and commodities have collapsed. Instead of owning up to its responsibilities and focusing on the demands of our kisans, of our khet mazdoor everywhere, the Central Government is content to make the WTO the alibi for its own incompetence and for its inability to deal with the flood of imports. Right through the eighties and till the mid-nineties, agricultural exports boomed bringing prosperity to our farmers. But in the last few years, in the absence of stable policies, exports of farm products have stagnated.

We are meeting here, when for the first time since the Bengal Famine of 1943, we are facing the tragic paradox of full godowns but empty stomachs. The BJP-led coalition government has doubled the prices of foodgrains for the poor. This has led to a decline in their purchase from ration shops. Foodgrain stocks have mounted to almost 50 million tonnes, on the other hand in the face of poverty and malnutrition, there has been no effort to launch a massive food-for work programme that would not only provide employment in the most vulnerable regions of the country but also help build community and social assets. This is what we would have done as a matter of the highest priority if we were in power.

We are meeting here when pernicious efforts are being made to tinker with our Constitution by the BJP-led coalition. Our Constitution is a magnificent document put together by some of our most brilliant minds. Our Constitution is our most valuable legacy, a charter for a quiet and peaceful revolution. It has laid the foundations for and strengthened the roots of representative democracy in our country.

We are meeting here at a time when dangerous attempts are relentlessly made by the RSS-BJP combine to saffronise the country's public institutions, to undermine its secular educational system. Our politics is being made blatantly partisan. Efforts are afoot to impose an artificial homogeneity on a vastly heterogeneous social fabric. Those who claim to speak on behalf of Indian culture are, in fact, destroying the very essence of that culture. Those who claim to champion Indian values are, in fact, subverting the very foundation of those values. Even on Ayodhya, the BJP has not genuinely distanced itself from the publicly declared agenda of the RSS-VHP and so-called Dharma Sansad combine. These very people are now threatening to take the law into their own hands while the BJP leadership look the other way. The Prime Minister's own statements have given rise to serious apprehensions about his real beliefs and intentions.

We are meeting here at a time when the central government continues to vacillate over that profound symbol of Indian secularism—Jammu and Kashmir. My heart goes out to the families of those who have fallen victims to terrorist violence. I have seen for myself their continued sufferings. These killings have not stopped. Inspite of three extensions, the ceasefire initiative has failed to produce the desired results. Different elements of the Government are at odds with each other over whom to deal with, how to deal with them and in what direction the dialogue must move. The ceasefire initiative is not an end in itself. I have said so before and I will say it again—we are more than prepared to support initiatives, back policies, that brings peace to Jammu and Kashmir and restores tranquillity to the lives of our brothers and sisters in that beautiful region. But, where I ask, is that policy? Some elements of the Sangh Parivar have floated the idea of trifurcating the state. There must be balanced regional development within Jammu & Kashmir, but let me categorically say with all the firmness at my command that the Congress will never, I repeat never, accept the partition of Jammu and Kashmir.

We are meeting at a time when the foreign policy of the country is in disarray. The end of the Cold War vindicated non-alignment, which has been the great contribution of the Congress to international affairs. But instead of building on it, the BJP-led coalition has abandoned this major pillar of Indian foreign policy and diplomacy. We are meeting here today when a fifty-year national consensus has been broken by the BJP. India has become a nuclear weapons state. But all of us are in the dark about the government's nuclear doctrine. This doctrine is absolutely essential if we are to ensure that nuclear weapons are never used either by design or accident. The Central government has had with it for 18 months, a draft nuclear policy prepared by its National Security Advisory Board. We do not know the fate of this policy. We believe India must assume a leadership role in all international efforts to eliminate weapons of mass destruction.

Friends we are meeting here under the shadow of the shameful exposure of the BJP-led government's insatiable appetite for gratification even at the cost of our defence forces, of our nation's security. The recent exposure has torn the mask of self-righteousness from the ugly face of corruption and venality. What had long been whispered in the corridors of power has now being telecast to the world. For a fistful of riches, the men and women who rule in the name of high principle have sold the honour of the seats they occupy. There can be no forgiveness. There can be no mercy. The BJP-led coalition Government has lost the moral right to govern. Let the message go forth from Bangalore that we will fight every battle, wage every war, make every sacrifice to ensure that the country is liberated from the shackles of this corrupt, shameful and communal Government. I have met with all PCC Chiefs and CLP leaders last night with a single-point agenda: namely, a plan of action to expose the corrupt and venal BJP and its allies. This plan of action is being released tomorrow in New Delhi. Let the states, districts, cities, towns and villages of India reverberate the cry of the Congress that the BJP-led coalition at the centre has betrayed the nation.

We meet here not just to draw the nation's attention to the misdeeds of the BJP-led coalition government in New Delhi. We meet here today also to remind the nation Why Congress? Why should the Congress be the first choice, the only choice for today's youth, for all Indians worried about the present and concerned about the future.

The Congress mirrors India in all its diversity. It represents, like no other party does, the plurality of India. It is the only pan-Indian party that draws its support and sustenance from each and every section of our society, that appeals to and derives its encouragement from all Indians, irrespective of caste, community, religion, language or region. Other parties use our diversity to divide us. We are the only party that uses our diversity to keep us united, the only party that recognises that without social harmony, nothing else is possible. A fractured India cannot prosper. A divided India cannot progress.

Other parties bring politics into development. We bring development into politics. Ours is the politics of vikaas. This is derived from our basic philosophy of socio economic justice, social harmony and mutual tolerance. Other parties discover the virtues of a moratorium on contentious issues when they come to power but when they are out of power, they forget this virtue. On the other hand, in or out of power, we remain faithful to our policies and programmes. Today, the performance of the Congress-ruled states stands out when contrasted to what is happening in states not administered by us.

Only the Congress can ensure a strong Centre, strong states and strong local bodies in villages, towns and cities. If we do not watch out, regionalisation of our polity could lead to parochialism and a weakening of the national will. This is so very essential for maintaining the political unity of India. The challenge is to maintain a fine sense of balance among the Centre, the states and local bodies. We need to strengthen administrative and fiscal capacities at each of the three levels. Each level must draw support from and feed into the others. It is only the Congress that can work this balance and keep our polity functioning in an integrated and inter-dependent manner.

Above all, while we devolve greater economic, political and financial powers to states, and while panchayats and nagarpalikas emerge as the first tier of our democracy, the central government must retain an overall sense of purpose and direction. India is one and many at the same time. That has to be preserved and nurtured. It is only the Congress that can understand and work this balance because of its history, its basic character and long years of administrative experience.

It is only the Congress Party whose very core is secular. We need no certificate for this. For us secularism is an article of faith. We are a Party whose leaders have become martyrs at the altar of secularism. Secularism, for us, is freedom of religion, not freedom from religion. For us, secularism is not religion *versus* religion. It is about rescuing Indian culture from the merchants of hate and the peddlers of poison. It is about recalling the immortal message bequeathed to us millennia ago, "Truth is One, the Paths are Many". Pandit Jawaharlal Nehru reminded us that the edifice of India is one on which layer upon layer of thought and reverie has been inscribed and yet no succeeding layer has completely hidden or erased what had been written previously. And it was Maulana Abul Kalam Azad who, as Congress President said at Ramgarh in 1940, I quote "It was India's historic destiny that its soil should become the destination of many different caravans, of races, cultures and religions. Even before the breaking of the dawn of history, they started their trek into India and the process has continued since. This vast and hospitable land welcomed them all and took them to her bosom" unquote. I firmly believe in this sacred legacy.

Since we last met at Calcutta, we have amended our Party Constitution to guarantee adequate representation for and participation of the weaker sections of our society in the Party organisation at all levels. The Congress is by every Indian, for every Indian and of every Indian. But at the same time, we have a special responsibility for bringing women, dalits, adivasis, minorities and backward classes into the social, economic and political mainstream. I reiterate what I first said on April 6, 1998 when I took over as Congress President—that the weaker sections demand parity, not charity. And that is what we have set out to do. And this is what we will continue to do.

Elections are the very lifeline of a political party. They are the very lifeline of any democracy. It is, therefore but natural, that we gear ourselves for elections whether they be for panchayats, nagarpalikas, Vidhan Sabhas or the Lok Sabha. But surely there is more to politics than electoral ups and downs. But surely we must look at politics through a larger perspective than that of elections alone. Politics is about social transformation. Politics is about providing an arena for debate on issues vital to the future of our society and crucial to the welfare and well-being of our people. Politics, as Gandhiji kept reminding us, must have a fundamental moral and ethical foundation. How many of us actually stop and ponder about this wider meaning of politics, about its larger social vision? That is what I want all of us to do even as we strengthen ourselves electorally. Once we give politics a new meaning, I am sure it will begin to attract the best and the brightest to its fold, it will begin to attract sections of our society who have alienated themselves from the political process.

I now want to say something about an issue that has a great bearing on our image and on our performance, on how we perceive ourselves and how others perceive us. I can no longer keep silent on this issue and this has to do with Party unity and discipline. It is true that there are differing viewpoints and perspectives among ourselves. We must allow differences to be aired and discussed openly and democratically. But, Unity is the need of the hour. We must learn to subjugate personal agendas for the greater good of the causes we espouse and champion—that of social harmony, of political stability and of economic growth. There is nothing impossible for us if we remain united if we function cohesively and with a spirit of collective endeavour.

The concept of service or seva is central to our organizational philosophy. It is a pleasant coincidence that the founder of the Seva Dal, Dr. N.S. Hardikar, was a noble son of Karnataka. It was his vision that gave our Party organization a special dimension. Every time I see Seva Dal volunteers, both men and women, saluting the tricolour, I hear them singing the Vande Mataram and other patriotic songs, or see them standing in the sun, helping and directing enthusiastic crowds at our Party programmes, or working tirelessly to help people in natural calamities as in Orissa and Gujarat, my heart swells with pride. There is much we owe this army in white. The example of Seva Dal must be emulated by all of us. Our Party Constitution enjoins every active member to participate in and contribute to social welfare causes. And when we look around us, there are many causes crying out for our attention. Let us show to the world that the Congress workers are passionate in their commitment to the party and compassionate in their service to society. The Indian Youth Congress and the NSUI, cradles of our future leadership must turn their vitality and energy to sewa and shramdan, even as they articulate issues of day-to-day concern to the younger generation.

Rajivji changed the face of rural India by providing reservations for women in panchayats. The Mahila Congress must link up with these elected representatives so that empowerment and development programmes can be reached to every home, particularly those in poverty and deprivation.

You are all aware of the political tasks that await us. We need to rebuild the Congress in states like Uttar Pradesh, Bihar, Tamil Nadu and West Bengal. We face elections in five states in the next sixty days. All of us must throw ourselves unitedly into winning these elections. I know that the people of Kerala and Assam are tired of five years of CPM and AGP misrule respectively and are ready to give us a fresh mandate. But there is no room for complacency. In Tamil Nadu and Pondicherry our alliance seems certain of victory. In West Bengal, we have taken a principled position, a position that will stand us in good stead in the future. We must continue to identify ourselves with the aspirations of the people in these states.

We need to give the party organisation at all levels a new sense of vitality. Where we are in power, we have to fulfill the expectations of the people and where we are not in power we have to play the role of a responsible and watchful opposition, mindful of people's interests. And there are many issues relating to the Party organisation itself that will need to be addressed. During my interaction with a large number of workers across the country, a number of views and suggestions come to me. I shall share with you some of them. Some party workers feel that we need to abolish the distinction between active and primary members and have only one kind of membership. Others think that we must move away from the district and adopt the parliamentary or assembly constituency as the basic unit. I intend to call another Pachmarhi-type Chintan Shivir sometime in the next six months so that all of us, particularly the next generation of Congress leaders, can have an opportunity for a meaningful debate and discussion. Besides the Party's internal organisational matters, there is one issue that should concern all political parties. This relates to how parties are financed. We have talked enough about this but have made little headway. I believe that we in the Congress should take the lead to put in place a more transparent and honest system of financing political activities.

During the Freedom struggle, the Congress was more than a political movement for Independence. It was a catalyst for fundamental social change and reform. We must return to that role. In and out of power, the Congress Party must take up larger societal issues, issues like literacy, population growth, environment, public health and AIDS, atrocities on women and children and implementation of social legislation. These and other such issues can no longer be seen only in the context of government programmes. They demand our full-fledged attention as political activists and mobilisers.

Let me also share with you another very deep concern of mine. As I travel and go around the country, I become painfully conscious of the vast deprivation and poverty that still stalks our country. But do our lifestyles reflect that reality? Is it not true that we, those who belong to the privileged sections of society, "talk poor and live rich". How many of us practice austerity and simplicity in our lifestyles, shunning ostentation and vulgar display of wealth. Insensitivity in our public conduct leads to callousness as a way of life. This is both socially disruptive and immoral. Gandhiji had said "my life is my message". We should aspire to make his message the model for our own lives.

Today we are not in power at the Centre, but we have nine CMs. It is a matter of great satisfaction that Congress State governments are today recognised as being the trendsetters in economic and social policy, in promoting economic growth, in giving good governance. Their performance stands out in stark contrast with the track record of non-Congress state governments. On your behalf, I would like to congratulate all our Chief Ministers. But much more awaits us. Much more needs to be done to meet the expectations that people have of us. I have directed the CMs to pay personal emphasis on the issue of administrative reforms to ensure a responsive and accountable administration, to ensure that the voice of citizens in their day-to-day interface with the government agencies and institutions is heard and their concerns addressed. The harassment of all citizens, particularly of those whose voices are never heard must end. The Congress Chief Ministers must pay special attention to integrate environmental concerns with developmental necessities. We have made great progress. But this has extracted a heavy ecological price. We must not make the next generation pay this price.

The renaissance of the Congress is a national need. The country requires a revitalised Congress. Today, we rededicate ourselves to the historic task of building a new Congress, a Congress proud of its past, a Congress mindful of the present and confident of its future, a Congress which will give new hope to India, particularly to its poor, under-privileged and the oppressed.

Jai Hind!

Congress President's Opening Speech at Conference of Congress Chief Ministers at Guwahati April 12, 2002

This is the third meeting of Congress Chief Ministers. A warm welcome to all of you.

Last time we met on June 16th 2001, we welcomed the new Chief Ministers of Assam and Kerala. Today, we welcome the new Chief Ministers of Manipur, Punjab and Uttaranchal. The significance of this has not been lost on the nation that while the BJP-led government rules or misrules in Delhi, the Congress has 14 Chief Ministers of its own. We cannot, however, afford to rest on our laurels. Congress governments must continue to stand out as ever-expanding silver linings in the dark clouds created by the BJP.

We have met twice before in Delhi. By holding this meeting in Guwahati, I want to emphasise the importance we place on this region and on the development of the seven sisters.

The agenda for this interaction is with you. We will have presentations by Chief Ministers on some of their special programmes and innovative schemes that have wider replicability.

This meeting is, to exchange experiences and learn from each other. We are here not for self-congratulation but for critical appraisal and to identify what more we need to do, to fulfill our commitments to the people, especially to the weaker sections of society—the Dalits, the Adivasis, the Backward Classes, the religious Minorities and—how I can forget—Women. We have also circulated the detailed record of discussions at our previous two meetings and it is my sincere hope that the Chief Ministers would have followed-up on them. The purpose of such conclaves, let us remind ourselves, is to provide specific guidelines for action.

We are meeting against the background of one of the darkest periods in our post-independence history. The images I have seen, the stories of utter despair and desolation that I have heard during my recent visit to Gujarat will not leave me for a long time to come. How can it be said that these atrocities were perpetrated by people of one religion or the other? The perpetrators of these atrocities have violated all tenets of all religions.

The fact that Gujarat continues to burn is a most damaging assault on our secular polity. The CWC met recently and was unequivocal in demanding the resignation of the Chief Minister who has singularly failed in discharging his Constitutional obligations and responsibilities. It is clear that the Central Government condones a situation where Indians are targeted on the basis of their faith. The Central Government sees nothing wrong in a Chief Minister whose law and order administration, is so infected by the politics of communalism, that it victimises officials who took a courageous stand against communal violence.

We in the Congress Party must take an unambiguous, unequivocal stand. We must reiterate our conviction that Indian civilisation is a celebration of diversities. We must emphasise our commitment to the fact that all those who live in this country are equally and I underscore—equally—entitled to the protection of law, irrespective of the community they belong to. What has happened in Gujarat starting from Godhra has shaken this image of ours as a land in which people of different faiths live harmoniously with each other. Who else but those deriving inspiration from the killers of the Mahatma, could have defiled the sanctity of the Sabarmati Ashram?

Secularism is India's destiny. An India that is not secular will simply not survive, let alone progress. This is the time for each and every one of us to reaffirm our faith in secularism. The debate on secularism is the on-going battle between an overwhelming number of Indians, steeped, in their own religions yet tolerant and respectful of other faiths, and a handful of Indians, self-appointed guardians of their own faiths, fanatically convinced of their own righteousness. The overwhelming number of Indians want to live in peace and goodwill. A handful of Indians seek to disturb that peace by their bigotry and narrow-mindedness. The overwhelming number of Indians want to move forward, to look ahead. A handful of Indians want us to be prisoners, of a past invented and interpreted by them.

This is the real battleground for secularism. It is to rescue/protect India's great religions from the zealots of obscurantism, from the merchants of fundamentalism, from the purveyors of hate and poison. It is this vision of secularism that the Congress has always stood for and practiced. It is this vision of secularism that is in danger. The Congress alone represents the overwhelming number of Indians of all faiths who want to live and work in an atmosphere of peace and amity, in an environment of mutual accommodation and acceptance.

Let me make it absolutely clear: any individual or any organization preaching or practising the politics of hate and threatening the very existence of our secular fabric must be dealt with without fear or favour according to law. My directive to you from this Guwahati conference, is that there must not be any compromise, under any circumstances on this under a Congress Government.

Now on to the main agenda itself.

I find that there are a very large number of schemes and programmes that go under the category of "centrally-sponsored" or "central sector" schemes. The numbers and sums involved are huge. For example this year, in rural development alone, quite apart from rural infrastructure, central allocations are close to Rs. 12,000 crore. But the funds actually disbursed by the Centre are far less than funds budgeted. I am told that sometimes the utilization by some States is less than the amount disbursed. Such a situation is not acceptable. Such a situation is unacceptable. It goes without saying that Congress governments must make full use of these funds on time. The Central Government has to continue to play a principal role in the financing of rural development and social sector schemes. And such schemes must draw on the experiences of various States.

In addition to the large number of central schemes, there are also numerous others launched by the States themselves. It is time we begin to pay serious attention to their effective convergence. I do get the impression that resources are being spread out thinly. At the block level, many people have told me that there are over 200 schemes to be managed and monitored. We must concentrate on fewer schemes that are sharply targeted at the most vulnerable of our society.

Even if integration were to take some time, could we focus on a few key strategic interventions that will make a dramatic difference to the lives of the people immediately? I have corresponded with most of you on issues like cooperatives, tenancy laws, marketing of agricultural produce, decentralization and Panchayats, primary education and environmental conservation. I am happy that progress has been made in some of these areas. Butt there are many other equally crucial interventions. Small and marginal farmers will have their lives transformed, if we are able to reduce the cost of credit and other inputs and ensure their timely and adequate availability. The accelerated creation of rural jobs, particularly through self-employment and schemes of micro-finance, will bring new prosperity to our villages. Social housing, water supply and sanitation are other examples.

As a nation, both at the Centre and in States, we have to increase investments in crucial areas like agriculture, education, health and nutrition. Inadequate public investments in physical and social infrastructure are costing the country heavily. But while we increase outlays, we should also focus on outcomes. This is where concurrent evaluation and social audit become particularly important. It is unfortunate that we still measure achievement in terms of how much money is spent and not by what physical output or service is delivered. We must improve the quality of government expenditure, just as we enhance its quantity. The close involvement of the beneficiaries themselves as well as of NGOs and social action groups as partners, will go a long way in improving the impact of public spending.

Quality of government expenditure is of paramount importance all over the country but even more so in the North-East. This is a resource-rich region that requires vastly greater investment in basic infrastructure. The region also faces a variety of problems on account of its location. These have to be tackled sensitively, yet effectively. The nation has to find the resources needed to accelerate the development of the North-East. At the same time, the expenditures must benefit the people and create community assets. The alienation of the youth and persisting militancy and insurgency are matters of grave national concern that must be addressed by all political parties.

Congress-governed States must take the lead in issues of national concern that have emerged in recent years. For instance, four of the most seriously AIDS-affected states happen to be Manipur, Nagaland, Maharashtra and Karnataka. Similarly, two of the States with the worst sex ratios are Punjab and Delhi which, paradoxically, also happen to be among the most prosperous States. Some of our states have sharp disparities within them; Karnataka and Maharashtra, for example, have a number of Districts with very poor human development indicators. The evil of child marriage still continues to stalk large parts of many States. Social legislation must be enforced strictly along with education and awareness-building. This is an area where the Party must play an active role. Meanwhile, other traditional concerns also remain. Foremost among them to me personally is malnutrition. How can we tolerate that over half our children are born underweight, that millions go hungry every day, inspite of overflowing godowns.

I can hardly over-emphasise the centrality of good, effective governance and the need for a new administrative culture. Good governance has many dimensions. Ensuring that legislated minimum wages are paid is good governance. Assuring the welfare of the unorganized sector, in which over 90 per cent of our work force is employed, is good governance. Vigorous implementation of legislation that was passed during Rajivji's tenure as Prime Minister to curb atrocities on the weaker sections of society, is good governance. In recent months, we have been made painfully aware of a simple truth that, at its most fundamental level, ensuring law and order, maintaining social peace and harmony, is good governance.

Some of our States have passed Freedom of Information Acts. Has that made the entire administration more open, more accountable and more responsive? Has this helped in placing power in the hands of the people? Some of our states have set up "Administrative Reforms Commissions". What has happened to their recommendations? Is the professional, autonomous and even-handed functioning of the police being ensured? How can we make the police and administration more sensitive to the concerns of all people and particularly of the poor and the minorities? Rajivji believed that empowering local governments was the first step to good governance. To what extent is this belief being borne out in practice? To what extent are Congress governments implementing the 73rd and 74th Constitution Amendments both in letter and spirit? I am particular that our States start training programmes on a massive scale for all elected representatives to local bodies. We must also aggressively combat the deep-rooted cancer of corruption. If a Chairman of a Public Service Commission stands indicted as has happened in one state, how can ordinary citizens have any confidence in the administration?

I do recognize that States have to take hard and tough decisions to restore their fiscal system to health. It is unfortunately true that the structure of public expenditures today bears no relation to pressing socio-economic priorities. We cannot fulfil our commitments to the weaker sections of society if the state of public finances remains as fragile as it is today. This is a great political challenge. How do we take the people into confidence and sustain their support? How do we ensure that the gains are not monopolized by a few while the pains are borne by the many? We remain firmly committed to a welfare state but such a state must have a strong and growing investment capacity. Bankruptcy of the type that stares each and every state in the face is anti-poor. Revenue mobilization, expenditure priorities and discipline and greater investment in the social sectors must go hand-in-hand. Congress governments must reinforce their commitment to responsible and fiscally sustainable economic management. Another important area is power. I urge the Chief Ministers to give their personal attention to reforms in the power sector so that all section of society get reliable and adequate power at affordable rates very quickly.

Austerity begins at home. If we want society to make sacrifices today for a better tomorrow, we must ourselves take the lead and set an example for others to follow. In a country like ours, the kind of ostentatious display of wealth we see is unacceptable. So also is the tendency to arrogantly display the trappings of authority and power. I must honestly admit that there is a lot of this in our system. I would go to the extent of suggesting that we collectively boycott such exhibitions. We must practice what we preach. I am proud that some of our Chief Ministers are role models for simplicity and sincerity. Our entire party must learn from them. The people of India, I am convinced, will participate in any painful fiscal adjustment that is demanded of them if they are convinced that those who govern are honest and are rooted in political morality.

I had mentioned right at the outset that one of the main purposes of this meeting is to provide a renewed impetus to programmes for the weaker sections of society. This is not an electoral compulsion but a moral imperative. The Congress draws its strength from, appeals to and has a place for all people of India. We want all people to improve their quality of life and better their standard of living. Even so, we must pay special attention to the cause of the Dalits, Adivasis, Backward Classes, religious Minorities and Women. In this connection I would urge all of you to pay close attention to the recent Bhopal Declaration which is a 21st century charter for the emancipation of Dalits and Adivasis. Of special significance are the recommendations concerning land redistribution, irrigation, education and economic advancement. On religious minorities, you are all aware of

Indiraji's comprehensive 15-point programme launched in 1983. Rajivji set up an elaborate monitoring mechanism. Two years ago, I myself announced a comprehensive intensified 7-point programme. These must engage your personal attention on a sustained basis.

Let me now turn to a couple of party-related issues in Congress-governed states.

Whenever I travel I am met with complaints from party workers that in the states where we are in power, it is the bureaucracy that is dominant and that there is very little interaction between the Party and the Government. We have to bear in mind that we are, first and foremost, a political party. Unless the party machinery and organization at all levels, feels and gets a sense of close participation, we will not be able to effectively communicate and project whatever we are doing. How should we be projecting our achievements, not in the spirit of boasting about them, but to keep people informed and make them aware of our work? This is where political leadership and mobilization is required and where constant communication and outreach becomes essential. We hear repeated mention of the so called anti-incumbency factor. I personally feel that the cause of anti-incumbency is actually indifferent governance, non-performance. I am confident that credible achievement and responsive political management will neutralize this factor.

Our states have to work and do business with the Centre. Yet, at the same time, in many instances where the BJP-led Government's policies go against our beliefs, we must oppose the Central government. I find that the imperative of such a nuanced approach in a Parliamentary democracy is not fully understood and appreciated. Hence, I personally have to hear criticism as to why is the Congress opposing something in Delhi when its own Chief Ministers are supporting it. Much of this criticism is unjustified and deliberate. Even so, the policies of the Sate Government must be in harmony with the basic principles of the Party's policies.

Friends, a fractured India cannot prosper. A divided India cannot move forward. An India whose secular foundations and moorings are sought to be deliberately destroyed cannot hold its head high, either domestically or internationally. The people of India know this. The nation's eyes are on us. Expectations are very high. The people of India are once again recognising that the Congress is the natural party of governance. A historic responsibility has devolved upon all of us but more directly on all of you—the Chief Ministers—a responsibility to practice a new politics, a politics in which economic growth and social development have absolute primacy, a politics in which the welfare and well-being of the weaker sections of society have overriding priority, a politics that unites, not divides, a politics that takes the entire country forward with dignity and pride. That has always been the Congress commitment. To this commitment we re-dedicate ourselves this afternoon, on the banks of the mighty Brahmaputra.

PM's Intervention in the Lok Sabha on the Right to Information Bill debate May 11, 2005

THE PRIME MINISTER (DR. MANMOHAN SINGH): Mr. Speaker Sir, I am very grateful to you for granting me permission to intervene on a very important and critical Bill, which is before this august House.

Sir, all modern societies or complex societies, they require strong and purposeful Government to steer them. In our own country, Government expenditure, both at the Central level and at the level of State and local bodies, accounts for nearly 33 per cent of our gross National Product. At the same time, the social and economic imperatives require our Government to intervene extensively in economic and social affairs. Therefore, the efficiency and effectiveness of Governmental processes are critical variables, which will determine how our Government function and to what extent it is able to discharge the responsibilities entrusted to us by the electorate.

Now, it is, therefore, of utmost importance that when Governments account for such a large proportion of total national expenditure, when Governments interfere extensively with the way ordinary citizens of the country go by doing their business, these powers should be exercised with utmost caution and utmost concern for public welfare in the widest sense of the term.

Civilized Governments everywhere have been searching for ways and means to deal with problems of corruption, problems of ineffectiveness of Governments at various levels. We have the judiciary; we have the representative institutions of parliamentary system of Government to check both corruption and to ensure that monies that are voted for truly subserve the public purpose. But, it has been found that it is not enough that Governments should go to the people once in five years.

It is necessary to find other means of empowering out citizens to feel that processes of governance truly serve the public purpose. The right to information is a quest for that sort of mechanism, which will empower our citizens with information, which enables them to judge for themselves whether or not Governments are functioning in accordance with what can be considered as *public interest* in the widest possible sense of the term. It goes without saying that all information can be misused also. Therefore, much will depend upon how information seekers approach their tasks. I do recognize the dangers that are inherent in such a situation because in our society information is power. But one way of ensuring that this power is as widely distributed as possible is to ensure that access to information is not a monopoly of the few.

The Bill lays down architecture for accessing information which is simple, easy, time-bound and, in my view, inexpensive. It has stringent penalties for failing to provide information or affecting information flow in any way. In fact, it imposes obligation on agencies to disclose information, *suo moto,* thus reducing the cost.

We all know that in development there are linkages. We all know that the benefit meant for the poorer sections of the people do not reach them. We all know that the public funds meant for serving the causes of the poor and the downtrodden are, in fact, eaten up by more influential sets of people. The Right to Information will, I hope, give our public-spirited people another instrument through which they will be able to prevent this patent misuse of public fund or public patronage. I, therefore, feel that this Bill is a historic Bill. What it seeks to do is to strengthen the foundations of our democracy. It seeks to promote the cause of a transparent humane administration. It seeks to make our administration more accountable than ever before.

Therefore, I feel, with the passage of this Bill, we see the dawn of a new era in governance processes, an era of performance of efficiency, an era which will ensure that benefits of growth flow to all sections of society, an era which will eliminate the scourge of corruption, an era which will bring the common man's concerns to the heart of all the process of governance, an era which will truly fulfill the hopes of the founding fathers of our Republic.

Great responsibility will rest on the shoulders of those who seek information, and also those who will administer this Act. I do hope that we have, in this country, men and women who know how to draw a right balance. We need a strong and purposeful Government. We need Government processes, which rise to the challenges of our time, which would enable us to ensure that this country moves forward to realize its chosen destiny. At the same time, I am also convinced that the future of this country is to strengthen the foundations of democracy. And, this Bill is an important step forward in promoting a culture of transparency, a culture of accountability, and to ensure that Governments do work to promote the public good in the widest possible sense of the term. That was the ambition of the founding fathers of our republic.

In keeping with the commitment made by the Congress Party the right to Information Act is a historic legislation passed on 15th June 2005. Earlier, there was a weak Freedom of Information Act. Now, in keeping with our belief that information is an entitlement, we have a strong Right to Information Act whose theme is greater disclosures. It will bring about transparency and accountability in public administration at all levels in significant measure. Citizens in villages, towns and cities have been empowered to demand and actually get information on policies, programmes and projects that affect their day-to-day lives. The enforcement of this Act is one of the most important means by which another equally historic legislation passed by Parliament last month The National Rural Employment Guarantee Act will be subject to continuous social audit and be under constant public scrutiny for effective implementation. As an example, muster rolls and the list of public works would, for the first time, be publicly available. Social action groups, NGOs and civil society organizations can use the provisions of the Right to Information Act on behalf of the poor and weaker sections of society so as to make sure that the various rural development and social welfare schemes deliver benefits to the people as intended.

Speech of Congress President Sonia Gandhi at the Congress Parliamentary Party, General Body Meeting, March 4, 2010

Welcome back after Holi. You may recall that I could not address the CPP General Body in December last year since the Parliament session ended abruptly because of the Opposition's disruptive attitude.

Let me begin by congratulating the Prime Minister on a very successful visit to Saudi Arabia. The warmth of his welcome and the positive outcome only add to our country's prestige. This was the first visit by a Prime Minister since Indiraji in 1982.

Close to nine months have elapsed since the people of India clearly reaffirmed their faith in the Congress Party and gave us the opportunity to serve them for a second term. These months have by no means been easy. We have faced many political and economic challenges. While some of them like the drought and the global economic crises have tested us, we have come through and remain firm to our dedication and resolve.

Addressing the issue of food prices continues to be our foremost priority. We have responded to this pressing concern with all the resources at our command. Despite the fact that this was a crisis born of circumstances outside our control, the Government has put in place proactive policies to mitigate the hardships of the people. We had a day-long discussion on this subject last week in both Houses. Both the Finance and the Agriculture Ministers spoke in great detail on all that has already been done and on the steps that will be taken to reduce the rate of inflation of food items. The Prime Minister has also met with chief ministers and has sought to remind them of their own and responsibilities. They must ensure that the PDS functions properly, and that wherever necessary de-hoarding operations are carried out effectively. The food price inflation detracts from the UPA's outstanding accomplishment in sustaining high economic growth that is so essential for generating resources for social welfare programmes and inclusive long-term prosperity.

Left-wing extremism continues to be another major challenge. Our government is committed to addressing it both from the developmental and the law and order perspectives in partnership with the states affected. Both have to go hand-in-hand. I am happy that our Finance Minister has provided adequate funds, for an integrated action plan to combat this problem.

Speaking of the Budget that was presented just a few days back, Pranabji has already briefed you yesterday about its salient features and on the various new initiatives that have been launched. I am sure this input will help you in countering the Opposition's propaganda. We have many essential social obligations and to meet them it is necessary to raise resources. I congratulate the Finance Minister for a fine and delicate balancing act which has been widely welcomed.

The social security fund for workers in the unorganised sector has finally taken shape and will soon become operational. The expenditure emphasis on agriculture, rural development, infrastructure and social empowerment stands out boldly in the Budget. It is for all of us now to play our part in ensuring that the benefits of these programmes as well of those launched during UPA-I reach the intended beneficiaries.

Friends, over the last five years, we have built a structure of legal entitlements for the *aam aadmi*—starting with the Right to Information and the Right to Work in UPA-I, and followed by the Right to Education in the first few months of UPA-II. We are now ready for the next step of placing the draft Food Security Bill for discussion in the public domain. This was perhaps the most important pledge in our Manifesto last year.

Other than the Right to Food Security, I personally attach the highest importance to the Women's Reservation Bill. So many years have passed since Rajivji first unveiled his vision of empowering us women. It is a matter of pride that even though it has taken so long, it is our Government that has cleared the legislation in Cabinet. This year is on 8th March is the centenary of International Women's Day. What a gift to the women of India if on this important day this historic legislation is introduced and passed!

We have taken steps to improve coordination between the party and Government, to keep our MPs better informed on issues likely to be raised by the Opposition, and enhance the quality of our parliamentary interventions. From time to time, ministers will brief all of you on important programmes and schemes in their charge. The Rural Development Minister has already done so. I urge all of you, especially my younger and first-term colleagues, to take full advantage of these opportunities.

Criticism, differences and debate are an integral part or a democracy. But the manner in which the Opposition sought to disrupt the presentation of the Budget last week is not in keeping with the democratic norms and traditions that we cherish. The disruptive approach of the Opposition was evident to the entire nation. If they look back, they will recall the constructive cooperation extended to the NDA in the six year's when we were sitting on their benches in the Opposition.

In almost all my addresses to you I have felt compelled to refer to another issue, that of attendance. Regular attendance is part of our basic duty' and responsibility.

Even to sit and listen to Parliamentary proceedings is an education in itself. The time has come to take poor attendance on the part of members seriously.

I cannot end without making a reference to the terror attacks in Pune and in Kabul in which a number of our countrymen were killed. On your behalf, I express our collective sorrow and anguish at these incidents. There are forces operating from both outside our country and from inside who are determined to destroy the bonds of social harmony that unite our people, and to thwart our economic progress. Our resolve to fight these forces remains firm, uncompromising and undiminished.

Annexure IV

Brief Life Sketches of Congress Presidents

(1) Womesh Chandra Bonnerjee (Bombay, 1885; Allahabad, 1892)

Born 1844, Started the *Bengalee* newspaper. Got the Jeejeebhai Scholarship in 1864 and went to England. Was called to the bar, 1887. Advocate, Calcutta High Court, 1868. Soon attained highest place in the profession. Made Standing Counsel of Government. Thrice declined seat on the bench. Fellow of the Calcutta University, 1880. Chosen by the University to Bengal Legislative Council. President, First Session of Indian National Congress, Bombay 1885. Attended successive sessions and took part in the discussion of various resolutions such as appointment of a Parliamentary Committee, 1888. Member of the Congress delegation to England, 1890. Left India in 1902 and settled in England. Considerable practice at the Privy Council, unequalled services to the British Committee of the Indian National Congress. Died in 1906.

(2) Dadabhai Naoroji (Calcutta, 1886; Lahore, 1893; and Calcutta, 1906)

Born 1825. Lecturer in Elphinstone School, 1845. Founder of several public institutions. Started *Rast Goftar,* a Gujarati weekly, 1851. Went to England as representative of Cama & Co., 1855. Became their partner later. Founded the East India Association 1867. Professor of Gujarati in the University College, London. Returned to India, 1869. Gave evidence before Fawcett Commission, 1873. Appointed Dewan of Baroda, 1874. Nominated to Bombay Legislative Council, 1885. Contested unsuccessfully Holborn seat for Parliament, 1886. Lord Salisbury calls him "back man". President, Indian National Congress, Calcutta, 1886. Lahore, 1892 and Calcutta, 1906. Elected to Parliament from Central Finsbury, 1892. Defeated in Parliamentary election of 1889 and 1905. Published his great book, "Poverty and Un-British Rule in India." Died in 1917.

(3) Badruddin Tyabji (Madras, 1887)

Born 1844. Educated in London. Was called to the bar, April 1867. Established lucrative practice. Secretary to the Anjuman-i-Islam 1880 and later its President. President, Bombay Presidency Association. Nominated to the Bombay Legislative Council. President, Indian National Congress, Madras, 1887. Appointed Judge of the Bombay High Court, 1895. Presided over the Mahomedan Educational Conference, Bombay, 1903 and pleaded for women's education and abolition of purda. Was associated with Aligarh College. Died August 11, 1909.

(4) George Yule (Allahabad, 1888)

A prominent merchant of Calcutta. He was elected to preside over the Indian National Congress held at Allahabad in 1888. Sheik Raza Hussain Khan in supporting his election produced a fatwa from the spiritual leader of the Sunni Community at Lucknow. From that time he took great interest in the Congress movement and when in 1890 at Calcutta, the Government returned the invitation to the Congress session, he fulminated against the "Dogberry clothed in little brief authority." Yule was of considerable help in strengthening the British Committee of the Indian National Congress. Died 1892.

(5) Sir William Wedderburn (Bombay, 1889; Allahabad, 1910)

Born 1836, Member of ICS. Cooperated with Hume in his efforts to channelise Indian political discontent. President, Indian National Congress, Bombay 1889 and Allahabad 1910. Connected with the British Committee of the Indian National Congress. Tried to bring about a rapprochement between the Congress and the Muslims. Toured throughout the country. Successive sessions of the Congress passed resolutions appreciating his meritorious services to the Congress cause. Wrote a number of books and did considerable propaganda for India. Died 1918.

(6) Sir Pherozeshah Mehta (Calcutta, 1890)

Born 1845. Went to England in 1864 and called to the bar. Entered the Municipal Corporation of Bombay and served it long and brilliantly. Founder

President of the Bombay Presidency Association. Associated with the Congress from its very inception. Member, Bombay Legislative Council, 1886. President, Indian National Congress, Calcutta, 1890. Elected to the Imperial Legislative Council, 1893. Chairman, Reception Committee of the Congress, Bombay, 1904. Knighted, 1902. Took keen interest in the rights of Indians overseas. Visited England for Congress propaganda. Vice-Chancellor of the Bombay University. In 1911, started the Central Bank of India. Founded the *Bombay Chronicle* in 1913. Died 1915.

(7) P. Ananda Charlu (Nagpur, 1891)

Born 1843. Lawyer in 1869. Was a delegate to the first Congress held in Bombay in 1885. Since then, till his death he was an ardent Congressman. The India Council was the main target of his attack at successive Congress sessions. He described it as "the oligarchy of fossilized Indian administrators who were superannuated for service in India." President, Indian National Congress, Nagpur, 1891. Member of the Imperial Legislative Council 1895-1903. Put up a plucky fight for freedom of speech. "He was a shining light of the South Indian political firmament for nearly two decades and though he never had a following or a school of thought behind him, he was a notable personality with a rugged eloquence, all his own." Died 1908.

(8) Alfred Webb (Madras, 1894)

Irish member of the House of Commons, whose co-operation for the Indian movement was enlisted by Dadabhai Naoroji and W.C. Bonnerjee. Was a stalwart fighter of the Irish freedom movement. Was an active member of the British Committee. Died 1908.

(9) Surendranath Banerjea (Poona, 1895; Ahmedabad, 1902)

Born 1848. Entered the Indian Civil Service, 1871. Dismissed after 3 years. Professor of English and later founder of the Ripon College, which he managed for many years. Prominent member of Indian Association. First political leader to make extensive all-India tours. Went to England in 1880 on Congress deputation. Member of the Bengal Legislative Council 1893-1901. Editor, *Bengalee*, President, Indian National Congress at Poona, 1895 and Ahmedabad, 1902. Great orator. Took leading part in opposing the

Bengal partition but disapproved of the Boycott movement. Sided with the Moderates in the Congress split at Surat in 1907. Member, Imperial Legislative Council. Left Congress after 1919 and joined Liberal Federation. Supported Montagu-Chelmsford Reforms and became Minister for Local Self-Government in 1919-1921. Framed and passed Calcutta Municipal Act in 1923. Defeated by a Swarajist in the elections of 1923. Author of his memories, "A Nation in Making". Died 1925.

(10) Rahimatullah M. Sayani (Calcutta, 1896)

Born 1846. Fought against heavy odds to obtain higher education and passed MA, LLB. Appointed Justice of the Peace and the Fellow of the Bombay University and later, Member of the Syndicate. Elected to the Bombay Corporation, 1876, and as its President in 1888. Secretary of Anjuman-i-Islam. Appointed member of the Bombay Legislative Council, 1888. President, Provincial Conference, Ahmedabad, 1893. President, Indian National Congress, Calcutta, 1896. Elected to the Imperial Legislative Council, 1896. Took notable part in budget speeches. Died 1902.

(11) C. Sankaran Nair (Amraoti, 1897)

Born 1897. Advocate and Journalist. Conducted *Madras Review* and associated with *Madras Law Journal.* Secretary, Devastanam Committee. Fellow of Madras University, 1889. Nominated to Madras Legislative Council 1890. President, Indian National Congress, Amraoti, 1897, Judge of the Madras High Court, 1908. Presided over the National Social Conference, 1908. Appointed Education Member in Viceroy's Executive Council 1915. Resigned from his post as protest against Punjab atrocities. Opposed non-cooperation and wrote "Gandhi and Anarchy". Sir Michael O'Dwyer field libel suit. Justice McCardie awarded damages, and heavy costs against Nair. President of All Parties Conference, 1921. Member of the Council of State since 1920. Cooperated with the Simon Commission. Died 1934.

(12) Ananda Mohan Bose (Madras, 1898)

Born 1846. Professor of Mathematics. Later, proceeded to England. President, Cambridge Union. Returned to India in 1874 as Barrister. Successful practitioner and owner of Tea Estate in Assam. Fellow of Calcutta

University, 1877. Nominated to Bengal Legislative Council, 1886. But elected by his University, 1895. Ardent Brahmo. President of New Sadharana Samaj. Went to Germany, 1897. Did valuable work in England. President, Indian National Congress, Madras, 1898. Participated in Bengal Partition agitation from sickbed. Died 1906.

(13) Romesh Chunder Dutt (Lucknow, 1899)

Born 1848. Entered Indian Civil Service, 1869. Appointed District Officer, 1883. Regional Commissioner, 1894. Resigned from I.C.S., 1897. Published "Peasantry of Bengal", "History of Literature of Bengal", translation of Rigveda, "History of Civilization in Ancient India", and other books. Lived in England from 1897-1904. Lecturer in Indian History at the University College, London. President, Indian National Congress, Lucknow, 1899. Returned to India, 1904. Was Dewan of Baroda State. Member of the Royal Commission on Decentralization 1907. Was a Moderate. First Indian economist to study and write on Indian agrarian problems. His works are classics on the subject. Died 1909.

(14) N.G. Chandavarkar (Lahore, 1900)

Born 1855. Editor, *Hindu Prakash* from 1878-1889. Enrolled as lawyer, 1881. Practised successfully. Went on Congress deputation to England in 1886. Fellow of Bombay University and Justice of Peace. Ardent Brahmo and mainstay of Prarthana Samaj. President, Madras Hindu Social Reform Association anniversary and Provincial Conference, Karachi, 1896. Elected in Bombay Legislative Council by University, 1887. Re-elected in 1899. President, Indian National Congress, Lahore, 1900. Judge of the Bombay High Court 1901. Chief Justice, 1909. Knighted in 1910. Dewan of Indore, 1914. Vice-Chancellor, Bombay University. Co-operated with the Montagu-Chelmsford Reforms and became first President of Bombay Legislative Council. Keen social reformer and Moderate. Died 1923.

(15) Dinshaw Eduljee Wacha (Calcutta, 1901)

Born 1844. President, Bombay Corporation for 30 years. Member, Millowners Association for 45 years. Member, Improvement Trust from 1898-1919. Associated with the Congress from the beginning. Joint General

Secretary of Congress from 1886-1913. President, Indian National Congress, 1901. Secretary, Bombay Presidency Association from 1895-1915. President, Bombay Presidency Association from 1915-1918. Member, Bombay Legislative Council from 1915-1916, and of Imperial Legislative Council from 1916-1920. Governor of the Imperial Bank of India, 1920. Left the Congress after 1919. President, Western India Liberal Association from 1919-1927. President, Bombay Provincial Liberal conference, 1922. Member of the Council of State, 1920. Died 1936.

(16) Lal Mohan Ghosh (Madras, 1903)

Born 1849. Barrister at Calcutta. Went as delegate of Indian Association to England in 1879. Participated in Ilbert Bill controversy. Most eloquent and powerful orator. Twice contested seat in English Parliament as a Liberal but failed. Returned to India in 1884 and resumed practice. Member, Indian Legislative Council, 1892. President, Indian National Congress, 1903. Later retired from politics and took to literature. Died 1909.

(17) Sir Henry Cotton (Bombay, 1904)

Born 1845. Educated in England. Entered I.C.S. in 1867. Was District Magistrate at Midnapore for 11 years. Held other responsible posts and was Chief Secretary. Home Member to the Government of Bengal. Retired form I.C.S. as Chief Commissioner of Assam. Published his "New India" in 1885. His Indian sympathies and differences of opinion with Lord Curzon stood in the way of his becoming a Governor. President, Indian National Congress, Bombay, 1904. Elected to the House of Commons, 1905. Died 1915.

(18) Gopal Krishna Gokhale (Benares, 1905)

Born 1866. Joined Deccan Education Society in 1884 as Professor of English in Fergusson College. Came under the influence of M.G. Ranade. Secretary, Sarvajanik Sabha. Attended Congress in 1890. Went to England 1896, to give evidence before the Welby Commission. Elected to Bombay Legislative Council, 1899. Imperial Legislative Council, 1902. President, Indian National Congress, 1905. Went to Africa and met Gandhiji and took interest in South African Indian question. Endeared himself to all. Known for simplicity of character, intellectual powers and long and selfless service to the country.

Founder and President of Servants of People Society. Leading expoonened of Moderate school. Died 1915.

(19) Rash Behari Ghosh (Surat, 1907; Madras, 1908)

Born 1845. Top lawyer in Calcutta High Court. Member, Bengal Legislative Council, 1889. Member of the Imperial Legislative Council in 1891 and 1893. President of the Faculty of Law, Calcutta University from 1893-1895. Chairman of the Reception Committee of the Calcutta Session of Congress in 1906. President, Indian National Congress, Surat, 1907 and Madras 1908. Member of the Congress delegation to England 1917. Presided over the joint session of Indian Congress Committee and the Council of the Muslims League at Calcutta, 1917. Protested against the internment of Mrs. Besant. Gave away large donations to Calcutta University. Died 1921.

(20) Madan Mohan Malaviya (Lahore, 1909; Delhi, 1918)

Born 1864. Took to journalism and edited *Indian Union* from 1825-1899. Practised Law from 1892. Member, Provincial Legislative Council 1902-1912. President, U.P. Medical Conference, 1908. President, Indian National Congress, Lahore 1909 and Delhi 1918. Member, Imperial Legislative Council from 1912-1918. Resigned as a protest against the Rowlatt Act. Member, Industrial Commission from 1916-1918 and wrote Minority Report. Founder, Benares Hindu University and its Vice-Chancellor from 1919-1939. Member, Central Legislative Assembly from 1924-1930. Resigned as a protest against Imperial Preference policy. Imprisoned twice during the Civil Disobedience Movement from 1930-1932. Delegate to the second Round Table Conference, 1931. President of the two banned sessions of the Congress in 1932 and 1933. President, Hindu Mahasabha 1923, 1936. Resigned from Congress Parliamentary Board, 1934 on the question of communal award and formed Nationalist Party. Retired from active politics due to old age. Died 1946.

(21) Bishan Narayan Dar (Calcutta, 1911)

Born 1864. Set up practice as barrister in 1887. Participated effectively in the Madras Congress of 1887 and 1894. Member, Calcutta Municipal Corporation. President, U.P. Conference at Lucknow in 1908. President,

Indian National Congress, Calcutta, 1911. Member of Bengal Legislative Council, 1914. Chairman of the Reception Committee of the Congress at Lucknow, 1916. Noted writer and public man of U.P. Died 1916.

(22) R.N. Mudholkar (Bankipore, 1912)

Born 1857. Fellow of Elphinston College in 1877. Set up law practice in C.P. Established Berar Trading Co. Ltd. Started *Vaidarbha* newspaper. Established Berar Sarvajanik Sabha in 1888. Was its Secretary till 1898. Joined Indian Congress in 1898. Congress delegate to England, 1890. Secretary, Reception Committee of the Congress session at Amraoti 1897. Organized branch of the Indian Famine Charitable Relief Fund 1897. President, C.P. and Berar Provincial Conference at Raipur, 1897. Sided with Moderates after Surat split. President, Indian National Congress, 1912. Died 1921.

(23) Nawab Syed Mohammad Bahadur (Karachi, 1913)

Born 1869. Came from a famous family of Jagirdars, Khan Bahadur Nawab, 1897. Member of Madras Legislative Council from 1900-1902. Later, member of Imperial Council. First joined Congress, 1894. Chairman, Reception Committee Madras Session, 1903. Member of standing Committee of the Congress, 1906. President, Indian National Congress, 1913. Joint Secretary 1915, 1916 of the Congress. Died 1916.

(24) Bhupendranath Base (Madras, 1914)

Born 1869. Started practice as a lawyer, 1884. Captained the volunteer corps Calcutta Congress, 1886. Chairman of the Reception Committee of the Congress at Calcutta in 1911. Took leading part in the Unity-partition agitation but was moderate by temperament. Was a member of the Bengal and Central Legislative Councils. President, Indian National Congress 1914. Vice-Chancellor of the Calcutta University for 2 years. Member of the Council of the Secretary of State for India. Joined the Liberal Federation. Died 1924.

(25) Satyendra Prasanna Sinha (Bombay, 1915)

Born 1864, Ran away to England in 1881 and with the help of a scholarship prosecuted his studies. Was called to the Bar in 1886. Returned to India and set up practice at Calcutta. Spoke at the Calcutta Congress. Advocate General of Bengal, 1908. First Indian to be made Law Member of the Viceroy's Executive Council, 1909. President, Indian National Congress, Bombay, 1915. Represented at the Imperial Conference, 1917. Represented India at the War Conference, 1917 and again 1918. Was made Under Secretary of State. Raised to the peerage as Lord Sinha of Raipur. Piloted the Government of India Bill through the House of Lords. Member of the Judicial Committee of the Privy Council. First Indian to be appointed Governor. Governor of Bihar and Orissa 1921. Resigned after one year. Died 5th March 1928.

(26) Ambica Charan Mazumdar (Lucknow, 1916)

Born 1851. Graduated in 1873 form the Presidency College, Calcutta and later became an MA. Qualified as a lawyer and set up practice in 1879. Was associated with the Congress almost from its very inception and spoke at several sessions of the Congress. Great orator. Participated in the Anti-partition agitation. Represented Bengal at the War Conference. Member of the Legislature for two terms. President, Indian National Congress. Lucknow, 1916. Wrote "Indian National Evolution". Died in 1922.

(27) Annie Besant (Calcutta, 1917)

Born in London 1847. Married, December 1867. A son and daughter. Legally separated from husband in 1873. Came under the influence of Charles Bradlaugh and was appointed Vice-President of National Secular Society and Sub-Editor, *National Reformer* 1877. Knowlton Pamphlet prosecution. Formed the Malthusian League. Came in contact with Madame Blavatsky 1882. Leaned towards socialism and conducted the Socialistic paper *Our corner*, 1813. Edited *Link,* 1888. Joined the Theosophical Society, 1889. Attended Labour Congress, Paris, 1889. Visited Chicago Parliament of Religions in 1893. Came to India November, 1893. Started School at Benares in 1892, which developed into the Hindu University Central College, 1904. President of the Theosophical Society June 1907. Inaugurated Home Rule agitation. Started *Commonweal* a weekly and *New India* a daily. Prohibited entry into Bombay and C.P. Interned at Ootacamund in June 1917. President, Indian National Congress, Calcutta, 1917. Supported the Montagu-Chelmsford Reforms and opposed Gandhiji's non-cooperation. Supported independence resolution at Madras Congress, 1927. Powerful speaker, writer, organizer and social worker. Made India her home and was a great force in Indian regeneration. Died 1933.

(28) Syed Hasan Imam (Bombay, 1918)

Born 1871. Went to England in 1889 and was Secretary of the Indian Society. There, worked for Dadabhai Naoroji's election. Called to the Bar and returned to India in 1892. Excellent practice in Patna and Calcutta. Judge of the Calcutta High Court in 1911. Resigned and reverted to Patna Bar in 1913. Gave equal donations to Benares and Aligarh Universities. President, Behari Student's Conference, Gaya 1909. President, Behari Provincial Conference, 1917. Trustee of the Aligarh College in 1911. President, Indian National Congress Special Session Bombay, 1918. Supported Gandhiji's Satyagraha movement against the Rowlatt Bills. Led the Home Rule League Deputation in England. Joined the Indian Muslim delegation in London to present the case of the Turks. Sympathized strongly with the Khilafat and Congress movement and participated in the Civil Disobedience Movement with his family from 1930-1932. Evidence before Lee Commission in 1924 memorable. Staunch nationalist throughout his life. Brother of Sir Ali Imam. Died 1933.

(29) Motilal Nehru (Amritsar, 1919; Calcutta, 1928)

Born 1861. Brilliant lawyer. Attended a few early sessions of the Congress. President, U.P. Provincial Conference, 1918. Services in the Punjab. Came under the influence of Gandhiji. President, Indian National Congress, Amritsar, 1919 and Calcutta 1928. Gave up his extensive practice as leading non-cooperator. Organized boycott of Prince of Wales. Arrested and sentenced to six months, 1921. Joined C.R. Das and founded Swaraj Party, 1922. Elected to the Central Assembly, 1923. Leader of the opposition. Gandhi-Das-Nehru Pact, 1924. Leader of Swaraj Party after death of Das, 1925. Re-elected to Central Assembly in General Election, 1926. Trip to Europe, 1927. President of Committee to draft constitution for India, 1928. Organized the boycott of the Simon Commission. Acting President of the Congress, April 1930. Leader Salt Styagraha. Arrested and sentenced to six months in June. Gifted of Anand Bhavan to Congress. Released in September. Died February 1931.

(30) Lala Lajpat Rai (Calcutta, 1920)

Born 1865. Joined the legal profession and established extensive practice at Lahore. Early in life came under the influence of Dayanand Saraswati and for years engaged in Arya Samaj activities. Helped in founding D.A.V. College and other institutions. Visited England in 1895 as a delegate of the Congress. Chief extremist leader with Lokmanya and Bipin Chandra Pal. Arrested in 1907 and deported to Mandalay but was released after six months. Thereafter, became foremost leader of the Punjab. Went to America during the war but had to stay there till 1919 as his passport was withheld. Published *Young India*, banned in India and England. President, Special session of the Congress at Calcutta in August, 1920. President, Indian Trade Union Congress. In 1921 and 1922 underwent two terms of imprisonment. Elected to the Central Legislative Assembly in 1923 as a Swarajist but later formed the Nationalist Party and successfully contested the 1926 election. Author of many books. Moved the resolution on boycott of the Simon Commission in the Assembly. Led the boycott demonstration at Lahore on the 30 October 1926. Assaulted by police, he said, "Every blow aimed at me is a nail struck in the coffin of British Imperialism in India." The injuries hastened his death. A trust of his properties for Servant of People Society formed, Library and Hospital. Died 1928.

(31) C. Vijayaraghavachariar (Nagpur, 1920)

Born 1852. Associated with the Congress from its very inception. Member of the Committee to draw up the Congress constitution 1887. Member of the Madras Legislative Council from 1885-1901. Member of the Indian Congress Committee, 1899-1900. President, Madras Provincial conference, Calicut, 1900. Collection work for "India" 1901-02. Actively participated in Benares Congress, 1905. Spoke in Calcutta Congress. Stood aloof from Congress since Surat split in sympathy with the Extremists. Member, Imperial Legislative Council from 1913-1916. Reappeared in the Congress after Lucknow session of 1916. Took active part in the special session held at Bombay in 1918 and in the session at Amritsar 1919. President, Indian National Congress, Nagpur, 1920. Did not agree with non-cooperation. Later, supported the Hindu Mahasabha and presided over one session. A staunch nationalist to the end of his life. Died 1943.

(32) Hakim Ajmal Khan (Ahmedabad, 1921)

Born 1865. Belonged to a family of reputed Hakims. Muslim scholar and divine. Took to medicine and became the leading Unani Physician in Delhi. Went on an extensive pilgrimage in the Middle East, 1904. Visited Europe in in 1911. Visited the leading Hospitals of England and the Continent. Wrote several treatises on medicine. Member of the Muslim League and later Vice-President, Chairman of the Reception Committee, Indian National Congress, Delhi, 1918. Came under the influence of Gandhiji. A prominent non-co-operator and Khilafatist. C.R. Das, President-elect of Ahmedabad Congress being in Jail, Ajmal Khan was unanimously elected in his place. President, Civil Disobedience Committee, 1922. Participated in the Unity Conference, 1924. Foremost exponent of Hindu-Muslim unity. Member of the Working Committee of the Congress till death. Trip to Europe for reasons of health 1925. Died 1924.

(33) Chittaranjan Das (Gaya, 1922)

Born 1870. Educated in Calcutta and England. Enrolled as a barrister, 1903. Appeared in many sensational cases (1907-1911) like the Manicktolla Bomb Case, Decca Conspiracy Case and the Munitions Board Case. Member of the Congress Punjab Enquiry Committee. Advocated obstruction at the Amritsar Congress, 1919. Opposed non-cooperation at the Calcutta special session but accepted it at Nagpur in 1920. Suspended his immense practice. Organised the boycott of the Prince of Wales. Elected President of the Ahmedabad Congress, 1921, but arrested 15 days before the session. Sentenced to six months' imprisonment. In 1922, presided over the Congress at Gaya and founded the Swaraj Party. In 1923 the Swarajists entered the Councils but Das refused to form a ministry in Bengal. Presided over the All-Indian Trade Union Congress at Lahore. In 1924 captured the Calcutta Corporation and became the first Mayor. Gandhi-Das-Nehru Pact, Satyagraha at Tarakeswar. Presided again over the All India Trade Union Congress. Made over his entire property to a trust for the service of the country. Died at Darjeeling, 1925.

(34) Maulana Abul Kalam Azad (Delhi, 1923; Ramgarh, 1940)

Born at Mecca in 1888 and passed childhood in Arabia. Educated at the Al Azhar University, Cairo. After coming to India, settled in Calcutta. Started

Urdu weekly *Al-Hilal*. Suppressed by the Government. Started *Al-Balagh*. Arrested and interned along with the Ali brothers. After release, joined the Congress under the leadership of Gandhiji. Leading Khilafatist and pre-eminent non-cooperator. Imprisoned alongwith Deshbandhu Das 1921-1922. President, Special Session of the Indian National Congress at Delhi, 1923 and Ramgarh session 1940. Continued as President upto 1946. Suffered imprisonment several times in connection with the Salt Satyagraha and the Civil Disobedience Movement, 1932. Acting Congress President, 1930. Member of the Working Committee for over two decades. Leading Muslim divine, scholar, powerful writer and orator. Arrested on the 9 August 1942 and detained in the Ahmednagar Fort. Minister for Education in Interim Government and Indian Dominion, 1947. He was free India's Education Minister till his death on 22 February 1958.

(35) Maulana Mohammad Ali (Cocanada, 1923)

Born 1878. Educated at Aligarh and Oxford. On return from England, was for sometime in the service of the Nawab of Rampur and also of the Baroda State. In 1907 took to journalism and established and edited the *Comrade,* an English Weekly published first at Calcutta and later at Delhi. Pamphlet "Come into Macedonia and help us" forfeited, 1914. Interned on the outbreak of the war, October 1914. Released in 1919 and attended Amritsar Congress. Became leader of the Khilafat movement and ardent follower of Gandhiji. Led a Khilafat deputation to England, 1920. Member, Working Committee of the Congress. President, All India Khilafat Conference, Karachi, 1921. Declared unlawful for Muslims to serve in the army. Arrested at Waltair in September 1921 and sentenced at Karachi to 2 years. President, Indian National Congress, Cocanada, 1923. Associated with the Unity Conference, 1924. Opposed the Nehru Report on the independence issue and communal settlement. Drifted away form the Congress. Delegate to the first Round Table Conference. Died in England, 1931.

(36) M.K. Gandhi (Belgaum, 1924)

Born 1869. Barrister at Bombay and later South Africa. Led an Indian Ambulance Corps during Boer War and Zulu Revolt. Satyagraha in South Africa and the Gandhi-Sinus agreement. Kaira Satyagraha and the

Champaran Agitation. Became undisputed leader of Congress after 1920. Inaugurated and led the Khilafat and Non-cooperation movements from 1920-1922. Arrested and sentenced to 6 years imprisonment, 1922. Released February 4, 1924. President, Indian National Congress Belgaum, 1924. Devoted the next 6 years to constructive programme. Inaugurated the Salt Satyagraha, April 1930. Imprisoned January, 1932. Fast unto death against Communal Award. Award modified. Released in 1933. Formed Harijan Sevak Sangh. Retired from Congress, 1934 but remains undisputed leader and adviser of the Congress. Worked for Bihar Earthquake Relief, Rajkot imbroglio and fast, 1939. Inaugurated individual Civil Disobedience, 1940. Formulated Quit India move, 1942. Arrested and detained, August 9, 1942. Twenty-one days fast in February, 1943. Life partner Kastuba died in detention, February 1944. Released in May 1944. Toured Noakhali and Bihar for riot relief. Opposed to partition scheme but advised country agree to Mountbatten Plan. Stemmed communal riots in Calcutta and later at Delhi. Assassinated by a fanatic at Birla House, Delhi, January 30, 1948.

(37) Sarojini Naidu (Cawnpore, 1925)

Born 1897. Educated at Hyderabad and Cambridge. Published three volumes in poetry in English which have been translated into many languages. Fellow of the Royal Society of Literature in 1914. Herself a Bengali Brahmin, she married a Madrasi non-Brahmin. Joined the Indian National Congress, 1915. Went to England in 1920 and did propaganda. Returned Kaiser-i-Hind medal to Government. Member, Working Committee of the Congress. Visited East Africa and Kenya. Work appreciated by Congress. President, Indian National Congress, Cawnpore, 1925. Toured and lectured America in 1928. Participated in the Salt Satyagraha and was jailed. Delegate to the Second Round Table Conference, 1931. Acting President of the Congress, 1932. Jailed again. Connected with the Women's movement. Offered Satyagraha in the individual Civil Disobedience Movement. Was arrested again on the August 9, 1942 and detained with Gandhiji at Aga Khan Palace. Nursed Gandhiji during famous fast in 1943. Released soon thereafter on grounds of health. Chairman, Asian Relations Conference, Delhi 1947 and member Constituent Assembly, Governor, U.P. in 1947. Died 1948.

(38) S. Srinivasa Iyengar (Gauhati, 1926)

Born 1874. Prominent lawyer and soon became the leader of the Bar. Member of the Madras Senate, 1912-1916. President of the Madras Social Reform Association, 1916-1920. Advocate-General, 1916-1920. Returned his C.I.F. and resigned his membership of the Council in 1921. President, Tamil Nadu Provincial Congress Committee. Elected to the Central Assembly. Elected president of the Indian National Congress, Gauhati, 1926. Elected Deputy Leader of the Opposition in the Central Assembly. Member of the Working Committee of the congress for a number of years. Took leading part in the demonstrations against the Simon Commission. Started the Independence of India League and fought the Nehru Report on the question of Independence. Withdrew from public life in 1930. Died 1941.

(39) Dr. M.A. Ansari (Madras, 1927)

Born 1880. Educated at Allahabad and Deccan. Joined the Edinburgh University in 1901. House Surgeon, Charing Cross Hospital. Resident Medical Officer, Lock Hospital and Clinical Assistant St. Peter's Hospital, London. Returns after 10 years stay in Europe. Organised the All India Medical Mission to Turkey in 1912-1913. Took leading part in the Home Rule Agitation, 1917-1918. Elected President All India Muslim League, 1920. Active leader of the Khilafat and Non-cooperation movement. President, Khilafat Conference, Gaya, 1922. President, Indian National Congress, Madras, 1927. Participated in the Salt Satyagraha and the Civil Disobedience Movement and was imprisoned. Founder President, Congress Parliamentary Party, 1933. Largely responsible for Congress accepting the parliamentary programme. Retired from active politics due to bad health in April 1935. Died 1936.

(40) Jawaharlal Nehru (Lahore, 1929; Lucknow, 1935; faizpur, 1937; New Delhi, 1951; Hyderabad, 1953; Kalyani, 1954)

Born 1889. Educated in England. Called to the Bar. Secretary, Home Rule League, 1918. Member, A.I.C.C. since 1918. Leading non-cooperator, jailed in 1921 and 1922. General Secretary of the Congress, 1923. President, Allahabad Municipality, 1924. Visited Europe and Russia in 1926. Attended Congress of Oppressed Nationalities, 1927, Brussels. Moved Independence resolution at

Madras Congress. General Secretary of the Congress, 1927. President, All India Trade Union Congress, Jharia, 1928. Independence of India League. President, Indian National Congress, Lahore 1929; Lucknow 1935 and Faizpur, 1937. Arrested, April 1930. Released in October and again arrested. Gandhi-Irwin Truce, leads agrarian movement in U.P. Arrested December, 1931. Released August, 1933. Arrested February, 1934. Released September 1935 and left for Germany where Kamla Nehru was ailing. Kamla died shortly after. Whirlwind tour for Congress election success, 1936. Resigned from working committee 1937. Great Anti-Fascist, helped Spanish Republicans. Visited China. President, National Planning Committee. Sentenced to 4 years R.I. November 1940. Released December, 1941.

Represented Congress in talks with Cripps. Arrested August 9, 1942, detained at Ahmednagar Fort. Released in 1946. President All India States Conference. Head of the Interim Government 1947. First Prime Minister of Independent India. Architect of India's Foreign Policy. Advocated the Five Principles of peaceful co-existence—Panchsheel. Also formulated policy of non-alignment and along with Tito and Nasser launched the first Non-Aligned Conference in Belgrade in 1961. Initiated the planning process and laid basis for socialistic pattern of society based on democratic principles. World statesman, powerful writer. Died on May 27, 1964

(41) Sardar Vallabbhai Patel (Karachi, 1934)

Born 1875. Passed the pleader's test and started practicing at Godhra. Later went to England and was called to the Bar. Shifted his practice to Ahmedabad. Flourishing lawyer. Entered public life in 1916 as an associate of Gandhiji. Came into prominence as a national leader, first at Kaira Satyagraha and later Nagpur Flag Satyagraha. President, Ahmedabad Municipality in 1927-28. Led the Bardoli no-tax campaign. Participated in Salt Satyagraha and went to jail in 1930. President, Indian National Congress, Karachi, 1931. Arrested alongwith Gandhiji in January, 1932 and imprisoned without trial under Regulation III of 1818 till July 1934. Chairman, Congress Parliamentary Sub-Committee 1935-1939. Was arrested and detained a number of times. He was free india's Deputy Prime Minister and Minister of Home Affairs from August 15, 1947 till his death in December 1950. His greatest achievement was the integration of the Indian States.

(42) Dr. Rajendra Prasad (Bombay, 1934)

Born 1884. Brilliant academic career. Professor, University Law College, 1914-1916. Later became the leader of the Bar at Patna. Member, Senate of Patna University since foundation. Collaborated with Gandhiji in Champaran Agrarian Struggle, 1917. Gave up his extensive practice in 1920. Registrar, Bihar Vidyapith. Chairman of the Reception Committee of the Gaya Congress, 1922. President Bihar Provincial Congress Committee for a number of years. Participated in the Salt Satyagraha and the Civil Disobedience movement 1930-1932 and was jailed several times. Member of the Working Committee of the Congress all through. Organised the Bihar earthquake relief. President, Indian National Congress, 1934. Prominent Right Winger. Member, Congress Parliamentary Sub-Committee. Acting President of the Congress 1939, after the resignation of Subhas Bose. Offered Satyagraha in the Individual Civil Disobedience campaign. Arrested in August and detained at Patna and Hazaribagh throughout. Member Interim Government. President, Constituent Assembly of India. Minister for Food and Agriculture of Indian Dominion Government. President of Indian Republic 1950-62. Great Scholar and author of "India Divided". Died 28 February 1963.

(43) Subhas Chandra Bose (Haripura, 1938; Tripuri, 1939)

Born 1987. Entered the Indian Civil Service but resigned to join the non-co-operation movement in 1921. Arrested along with Deshbandhu Das 1921-1922. Manger, *Forward,* 1922-1924. Member, Calcutta Corporation and Bengal Legislative Council, 1924. Chief Executive Officer, Calcutta Corporation 1924. Arrested under Regulation III in 1924, released in 1927. Took prominent part in the Simon Commission Boycott. G.O.C. of Volunteers at Calcutta Congress 1928. Mayor of Calcutta, 1930. President, Bengal Provincial Congress Committee for many years. Participated in the Salt Satyagraha and was jailed. In 1932 interned as State prisoner, but released and asked to go to Europe for medical treatment. President, Indian National Congress, Haripura 1938. Re-elected President, Tripura Session 1939, but resigned due to differences with the Congress High Command. Inaugurated the Forward Bloc. Was elected member of the Central Assembly while in prison, 1940. Was subsequently released due to ill-health. Disappeared from the Calcutta residence on 26 January, 1941. Escaped to Germany and later to the eastern front. Set up provisional Indian Government and the I.N.A. Died in an air crash in 1945.

(44) J.B. Kripalani (Meerut, 1946)

Devoted his early life as educationist. Professor in Muzaffarpur College in Bihar. Associated with Gandhiji in Champaran Satyagraha. Greatly influenced the youth in favour of national service in Bihar. Later joined Benares Hindu University in 1919. Was in-charge of Gujarat Vidyapith 1922-1927. Organised and ran the Meerut Gandhi Ashram centre of constructive work. Service in Bihar Earthquake. General Secretary of the Congress 1934-1946. Married Sucheta in 1934.

Author of books on Gandhian ideology. Last imprisonment in 1942 August movement. President of the Congress in 1946.Resigned Congress Presidentship in November 1947 on important issues of policy of the Congress Government.

(45) B. Pattabhi Sitaramayya (Jaipur, 1948)

Born 1880. Studied in Madras and started Medical practice at Masulipatnam. Inspired by the Swadeshi upsurge he entered public life in 1906 and distinguished himself in politics in Andhra. Renounced his lucrative practice in 1916 and became a full-time worker of the Congress. In 1919 he started an English journal, *Janmabhumi* which served as the organ of the Congress. His fearless writings often led to the Government framing seditious charges against him. President of Andhra Provincial Congress Committee in 1938, the President of the Indian National Congress in 1948. Governor of Madhya Pradesh in 1952.

Pattabhi was imprisoned several times. Besides political activities, devoted his energies to the constructive programmes and founded several institutions. As the historian of the Congress, was a forceful proponent of Gandhism.

(46) Purushottam Das Tandon (Nasik, 1950)

Born 1882. Started his career as an advocate of the Allahabad High Court. He took active part in the Rowlatt Bills. He joined the non-cooperation movement, leaving his profession, he organised in 1921, the *kisans* in U.P. on a provincial basis, in 1923 he was elected President of the U.P. Congress Committee. Was prominent among the leaders of the Civil Disobedience movement in U.P. and was responsible for the non-rent campaign among the *kisans* in the province. In 1937, when the Congress formed the Ministry in U.P., was elected Speaker of the U.P. Legislative Assembly. Was placed in detention during the 1941 and 1942 Movements. He was speaker of U.P. Assembly from 1946-50. In 1950, was elected President of the Congress. A great patron of Hindi. Died in 1962.

(47) U.N. Dhebar (Avadi in Madras, 1955; Amritsar, 1956; Indore, 1957; Gauhati, 1958; Nagpur, 1959)

Born 1906. Rajkot. His father Shri Naval Shankar was a god-fearing and truthful man. "Nothing must be done except what is right," was his motto. Dhebar accepted these principles and practiced them all through his life. At the age of nine he lost his mother. Deaths of his two younger sisters, one brother and two paternal uncles also occurred in his early life. There was a big family under the charge of his father with a very poor income.

All the events in the family and the poverty which Dhebar saw at an early age and also the moral courage of his father made a deep impression on the mind of young Dhebar. This provided the basis for his philosophy of life. He matriculated from the Saurashtra High School, Rajkot in 1922. During his four and half years stay in a solicitor's office as a dispatch clerk he privately studied for law and passed, with distinction in Hindu Law, the Bombay High Court Pleaders examination in 1928. He started independent practice in the courts of Western India States Agency at the age of 24 and soon established himself as a sound civil lawyer. He visited the rural areas around Rajkot and witnessed the widespread misery in the village due to the impossible burden of taxation. In 1936, he gave up his legal practice and shifted to a village near Rajkot to live among villagers and work for their emancipation.

At that time, Gandhiji came to Rajkot. Dhebar called on Gandhiji and discussed his programme of constructive work. The Mahatma gave his blessings. Dhebar adopted Gandhiji's twin principles of truth and non-violence for guidance in his life. He worked day and night for relief, economic betterment, fight, against social evils and injustice, political and social organisation and above all Gandhian constructive programmes in the Saurashtra area intensively.

(48) N. Sanjiva Reddy (Bangalore, 1960; Bhavnagar, 1961; Patna, 1962)

Born 1913. Joined the Congress in the 1920s. Became the Secretary of the Andhra Provincial Congress Committee in 1938 and held that office during the next eight eventful years.

Was arrested in 1940 and was in jail till 1942. His freedom was, however, shortlived for he was re-arrested when returning from Bombay after attending the AICC Session which passed the "Quit India" resolution. He was detained first in Vellore Jail and later in Amraoti Jail from which he was released alongwith other leaders in 1945.

Was Minister for Prohibition, Housing and Forests in the Kumaraswami Raja Ministry in Madras, 1949 to 1951.

The State of Andhra came into existence in 1953 and he was Leader of the Congress Party in the Legislature. Mid-term elections to the Andhra State took place in the summer of 1955. Sanjiva Reddy was responsible for the strategy of a united front in the elections which resulted in the success of the Congress beyond its expectations.

He soon became Chief Minister of Andhra Pradesh when in a straight contest, he defeated the then Chief Minister Mr. Gopala Reddy. He became the President of the AICC in 1960. The 66th and 67th Sessions were also chaired by him. Sanjiva Reddy was President of India between 1977 and 1982 (January).

(49) K. Kamaraj (Bhubaneshwar, 1964; Durgapur, 1965; Jaipur, 1966)

Kumaraswami Kamaraj born in Virudhunagar in 1903, belonged to a Nadar family. He had little scope for receiving education and became full involved in politics from his boyhood. Joined the Non-Cooperation movement at the age of 18 and joined the Salt Satyagraha movement at Vedaranyam. From 1940 to 1954 was President of the Tamilnadu Congress Committee. Was in the Working Committee of the AICC from 1947 till the Congress spilt in 1969. Was elected to the Madras Legislative Assembly in 1937 and again in 1946.

Became Chairman of the Virudhunagar Municipal Council in 1941. In 1946 was elected to the Constituent Assembly of India and in 1952 to the Parliament of independent India. In 1954, became the Chief Minister of Madras. In 1965, became the President of Indian National Congress and presided over its annual session at Durgapur. Died in 1976.

(50) S. Nijalingappa (Hyderabad, 1968; Faridabad, 1969)

Born Bellary District in 1902. Passed lower secondary examination at Devanagere. Passed S.S.L.C. from Jagaduru of Murugi Mutt, and continued studies at the Collegiate High School, Bangalore and the Central College and graduated in 1924. Set up law practice at Chitaldrug in 1926. Was debarred from legal practice in 1940. Was imprisoned in 1939, 1942-1947. President Mysore Congress Committee 1945-46, of Karnataka Pradesh Congress Committee 1954, of Mysore Pradesh Congress Committee 1960-62; Member Constituent Assembly 1946-50. Member Parliament 1952-1956; Member Mysore Constituent Assembly 1948-1950; Chief Minister 1956-58; Chairman, Indian Oil Corporation Ltd. 1962; Chief Minister 1962-68; President Indian National Congress 1968 and 1969.

(51) Babu Jagjivan Ram (Bombay, 1969)

Born 1908. Educated at Patna University, B.H.U. and Calcutta University, Married Indrani Devi 1935. Social and political worker. During the 1930s secretly circulated pamplets about the Congress Movement. Offered individual Satyagraha and was arrested in Patna. Imprisoned in 1940 for one year. Detained under "Quit India" Movement in August, 1942. Released in October 1943 on medical grounds. He was Union Minister for Labour, 1946-52. Minister for Communication, 1952-56; Transport 1956-57; Railways 1957-62; Transport and Communications 1962-63; Labour & Employment 1966-67; Food, Agriculture, Community Development 1967-70; Defence 1970-74; Agriculture & Irrigation 1974-77; again Defence 1977-79. Was also Deputy Prime Minister of India from January 1979 to July 1979.

(52) Dr. Shankar Dayal Sharma (Calcutta, 1972)

Born 1918. Educated at St. John's College, Agra, Allahabad University, Lucknow University, Fitzwilliam House, Cambridge University, Harvard Law

School, London University, Lincoln's Inn. Married Smt. Vimla Sharma 1950. He was General Secretary, Indian National Congress 1968-72. President, Bhopal District Congress Committee 1951-52 and M.P. Pradesh Congress Committee 1967-68, was Member, Planning Commission's Team on Community Projects and Chairman, Working Group on Industries and Training of the Committee of Review of Rehabilitation work in West Bengal. He was also the Editor of the *Lucknow Law Journal*. Member Bhopal State Legislative Assembly 1952-56. Member Madhya Pradesh State Legislature 1956-71. Cabinet Minister in M.P. Government 1956-67. Was Chairman, Committee on delegated Legislation of M.P. State Assembly till March, 1971. President Indian National Congress 1972-74. Member All India Congress Committee for 28 years. Union Minister for Communication, October 10, 1974 to March 24, 1977. Governor of Punjab from November 1985. Vice President of India 1987 to 1992. President of India from July, 1992 to July 1997.

(53) D.K. Barooah (Kamagatamaru Nagar, Chandigarh, 1975)

Born 1914. He was educated at Nowgong Government High School and at Banaras Hindu University. He was imprisoned in 1930, 1941 and 1942. He was Secretary of the Assam Pradesh Congress Working Committee 1953-54. He was deputed to supervise elections in PEPSU, Andhra and Delhi. He had been Member of the Constituent Assembly, 1949-51 and was a Member of the Lok Sabha 1952-57. (He was also Deputy Chief Whip of Congress Party in Parliament during this period.) He was Minister of Education and Co-operation in the Assam Government for some time and later became Minister of Petroleum and Chemicals, Government of India in 1973. He was unanimously elected President of Indian National Congress at the 75th Plenary Session of the Indian National Congress held at Kamagatamaru Nagar (Chandigarh) in 1975. Elected to the Rajya Sabha in 1973 and again in 1974.

(54) Indira Gandhi (New Delhi, 1978; Calcutta, 1983)

Born at Allahabad on November 19, 1917. Indira Gandhi was influenced in her childhood by Mahatma Gandhi, Motilal Nehru, Jawaharlal Nehru and other great leaders of the Indian freedom movement. From the early years, she was active in the national liberation struggle. During the 1930 movement, she formed the "Vanar Sena" a children's brigade to help freedom fighters.

In the late twenties, she had her schooling in Europe, where her mother Kamla Nehru spent some time for medical treatment and later in Pune and Bombay. In 1935, she enrolled in Rabindranath Tagore's Visva Bharati, but had to leave after a few months to accompany her ailing mother to Europe.

She became a member of the Indian National Congress in 1938. Soon after her return to India in March, 26, 1942, she married Feroz Gandhi, who was himself a valiant freedom fighter. She attended the session of the All India Congress Committee in August 1942 which adopted the famous "Quit India" resolution. Soon thereafter, she was arrested and imprisoned until her release in May 1943.

Her public activity entered a new phase with India's independence in 1947. She took over the responsibility of running the Prime Ministers' House. The Congress, which had been her political home ever since her childhood, soon drew her into leading political roles, first as member of the Congress Working Committee in 1955 and later as member of the Central Parliamentary Board in 1958. In 1959, she was elected President of the Indian National Congress. She oriented Congress thinking and action towards basic issues confronting Indian society and enthused the younger generation in the task of nation-building.

When Jawaharlal Nehru died in May 1964, Indira Gandhi was persuaded by Lal Bahadur Shastri to join his Cabinet as Minister of Information and Broadcasting.

On January, 19, 1966, after the death of Lal Bahadur Shastri, she was elected leader of the Congress Parliamentary Party and sworn in as Prime Minister on January 24, 1966. She led the nation in that capacity until March 1977, and again from 1980 to October 31, 1984, when she, like the father of the Nation, fell to an assassin's bullets.

(55) Rajiv Gandhi (Bombay, 1985)

At 41, Mr. Rajiv Gandhi was the youngest Prime Minister of India, perhaps one of the youngest elected heads of Government in the world. His mother, Indira Gandhi, was eight years older when she first became Prime Minister in

1966. His illustrious grandfather, Jawaharlal Nehru, was 58 when he started long innings of 17 years as free India's first Prime Minister.

Besides being the harbinger of a generational change in the country, Mr. Gandhi received the biggest mandate in the nation's history. In the elections to the Lok Sabha, which he ordered as soon as the mourning for his slain mother was over, his party, the Congress, got a much higher proportion of the popular vote than in the preceding seven general elections and captured a record 401 seats out of 508.

Such an impressive start as the leader of 700 millions Indians would have been remarkable under any circumstance. What makes it even more so, indeed unique, is that Mr. Gandhi was a late and reluctant entrant into politics even thought he belongs to an intensely political family that has served India for our generations both during the freedom struggle and afterwards.

He was born on August 20, 1944, in Bombay. He was just three when India became independent and his grandfather became Prime Minister. His parents moved to New Delhi from Lucknow. His father, Feroz Gandhi, became an M.P. He earned a reputation as a fearless and hard working Parliamentarian.

Rajiv Gandhi spent his early childhood with his grandfather in the Teen Murti House, where Indira Gandhi served as the Prime Minister's hostess. He briefly went to school at Welham Prep in Dehra Dun but soon moved to the residential Doon School in the Himalayan foothills. There be made many lifelong friendships and was also joined by his younger brother, Sanjay.

After leaving school, Mr. Gandhi went to Trinity College, Cambridge, but shifted to the Imperial College, London, soon enough. He did a course in mechanical engineering. He really was not interested in "mugging for his exams", as he was to say later.

By this time it was clear that politics did not interest him as a career. According to his classmates, his bookshelves were lined with volumes on science and engineering, not works on philosophy, politics or history. Music, however, has had a pride of place in his interests. He liked western and Hindustani classical music as well as modern music. Other interests included photography and amateur radio.

His greatest passion, however, was always flying. No wonder then that on returning home from England, he quickly passed the entrance examination to the Delhi Flying Club, went on to obtain a commercial pilot's licence and soon became a pilot in Indian Airlines, the domestic national carrier. Meanwhile, at Cambridge, he had met Sonia Maino, an attractive Italian who was studying English there.

The two were married in New Delhi in 1968. They stayed in Smt. Indira Gandhi's residence in New Delhi with their two children, son Rahul and daughter Priyanka. Theirs was a very private life despite the surrounding din and bustle of political activity.

But Sanjay's death in an air crash in 1980 changed all that. Pressures on Mr. Gandhi to enter politics to help his mother, then besieged by many internal and external challenges, grew. He resisted these pressures at first but later bowed to their logic. He won the by election to Parliament, caused by his brother's death, from Amethi in U.P. The Constituency returned to him by a whopping margin that too has become a national record.

For no one could have ascended to power—becoming both Prime Minister and Congress President—in more tragic and tormenting circumstances than Mr. Gandhi did in the wake of Indira Gandhi's brutal assassination on 31 October 1984. But he wore the awesome burden of personal grief and national responsibility with remarkable poise, dignity and restraint.

Congress lost the 1989 elections and Mr. Gandhi became the leader of the opposition. The National Front collapsed in early 1991 and elections were announced for May, 1991. He died in a tragic bomb blast on 21st May, 1991 at Sriperumbudur in Tamil Nadu.

A modern-minded, decisive but undemonstrative man, Mr. Gandhi was at home in the world of high technology. And, as he had repeatedly said, one of his main objectives, besides preserving India's unity, was to propel it into the twenty-first century.

(56) P.V. Narasimha Rao (Tirupati, 1992)

Shri Pamulaparti Venkata Narasimha Rao was sworn in as the Ninth Prime Minister of India on June 21, 1991. He was born on June 28, 1921 in Vangara, Karimnagar district of Andhra Pradesh. He had his education at Osmania

University, Hyderabad, Bombay University and Nagpur University, and had a Bachelor degree in Science and Law.

Shri Rao entered into public life as a student, at the impressionable age of 15-16, like many others during the freedom struggle. Starting from the "Vande Matram" movement launched by students of the Osmania University, Hyderabad against the discriminatory attitude of the then Nizam's Government, Shri Rao became a part of the agitation launched by the Hyderabad State Congress under the leadership of Swami Ramananda Tirtha. He, however, continued his studies with short breaks and obtained his Law degree from Nagpur University. After a short spell of practice in Hyderabad High Court, he was drawn into the Lawyer's agitation and later became a full-fledged Congress worker. He rose quickly in the Congress ranks and eventually became the General Secretary of the All India Congress Committee.

He was a member of the Andhra Pradesh Legislative Assembly for 20 years (1957-1977) and a Minister in the Andhra Pradesh Government from 1962 to 1971. He served as the Chief Minister of the State during 1971 and 1973. He was the General Secretary of the All India Congress Committee from 1974 and 1976. He was elected to the Parliament in March 1977. In the 1980 General Elections, he was re-elected from Hanamkonda (Andhra Pradesh); and in December 1984 and November 1989 he returned to Lok Sabha from Remtek constituency in Maharashtra.

He was Minister, External Affairs (January 1980 to July 1984); Home Affairs (July 1984 to December 1984); Defence (December 1984 to September 1985); Human Resource Development (September 1985 to June 1988); Health & Family Welfare (additional portfolio) (July 1986 to February 1988); and External Affairs (June 1988 to December 1989).

(57) Sitaram Kesri (1997-98, Calcutta)

Shri Sitaram Kesri was born in Bihar (Danapur) near Patna in 1919. He was a member of the Indian National Congress and was the President of Congress from 1996 to 1998.

Elected to the Lok Sabha from Katihar Lok Sabha Constituency (fourth) when he won on a Janata Party ticket and was given a last moment call by then Bihar Janata Party President S.N. Sinha; he represented Bihar in the

Rajya Sabha several times: July 1971 to April 1974, April 1974 to April 1980, July 1980 to July 1986, April 1988 to April 1994, April 1994 to April 2000. He was Union Minister during the reigns of Indira Gandhi, Rajiv Gandhi and P.V. Narasimha Rao as Prime Minister of India.

In 1967, he was elected to the Lok Sabha from the Kathiyar constituency. After that he became a member of the Rajya Sabha for longer than he had been in the Lok Sabha.

One high-point in his career was when Kesri was appointed AICC treasurer by Mrs. Indira Gandhi following her return to power in 1980. Kesri retained the post for nearly two decades.

Kesri played an important role in national politics much before becoming the treasurer of the Congress party. Immediately after the 1971 elections, which he lost, he was accommodated in the Rajya Sabha and soon Indira Gandhi entrusted him with the task of easing out leaders from U.P. Kesri died in 2000.

(58) Sonia Gandhi

Born 9 December 1946. President of the Indian National Congress. Studied at the School of Languages, Cambridge. Presently, Chairperson of the United Progressive Alliance in the Lok Sabha and the leader of the Congress Parliamentary Party. Joined the Congress Party as a primary member in the Calcutta Plenary Session in 1997 and became party leader in 1998. Holds the record of having served as Congress President for 10 years consecutively.

Mrs Sonia Gandhi contested the 1999 Lok Sabha elections from Bellary, Karnataka and Amethi, Uttar Pradesh. In Bellary, she defeated the veteran BJP leader, Sushma Swaraj. In 2004 and 2009, she was re-elected to the Lok Sabha from Rae Bareli in Uttar Pradesh.

She was elected the Leader of the Opposition of the 13th Lok Sabha in 1999. As Leader of Opposition, she called a no-confidence motion against the NDA government led by Vajpayee in 2003. In the 2004 general elections, Mrs. Gandhi launched a nationwide campaign, criss-crossing the country on the *Aam Aadmi* (ordinary man) slogan in contrast to the 'India Shining' slogan of the BJP-led National Democratic Alliance (NDA) alliance. She countered the BJP asking "Who is India Shining for?" In the election, she won by a large margin in the Rae Bareilly constituency in Uttar Pradesh. Following the unexpected defeat of the NDA, she was widely expected to be the next Prime Minister of India. On 16 May, she was unanimously chosen to lead a 15-party coalition government with the support of the left, which was subsequently named the United Progressive Alliance (UPA).

Re-elected from Rae Bareilly in May 2006 by a huge margin of over 400,000 votes. As chairperson of the National Advisory Committee and the UPA chairperson, she played an important role in making the National Rural Employment Guarantee Act and the Right to Information Act into law. Under her leadership, India returned the Congress-led-UPA to a near majority in the 2009 general elections with Manmohan Singh as the Prime Minister. The Congress itself won 206 Lok Sabha seats, which was the highest total by any party since 1991.

Annexure V

Members of the Interim Government of India

In August 1946, Congress decided to join the Interim Government in response to the call of the British Government to facilitate the process of transfer of power. The Interim Government, which assumed office on 2nd September, 1946, consisted of the following persons:

1.	Lord Wavell (Governor General)	President
2.	Pandit Jawaharlal Nehru	Vice-President and Member in-charge of External Affairs and Commonwealth Relations Departments.
3.	Sardar Vallabbhai Patel	Home, Information and Broadcasting.
4.	Dr. Rajendra Prasad	Food and Agriculture
5.	Mr. M. Asaf Ali	Railways and Communications (Post and Air)
6.	Mr. C. Rajagopalachari	Industries and Supplies
7.	Mr. Sarat Chandra Bose	Works, Mines & Power
8.	Dr. John Mathai	Finance
9.	Sardar Baldev Singh	Defence
10.	Sir Shafat Ahmed Khan	Education and Arts, Health
11.	Mr. Jagjivan Ram	Labour
12.	Syed Ali Zaheer	Law
13.	Mr. Cooverji Hormusji Bhabha	Commerce

After some time the Muslim League decided to join the Interim Government. Some members appointed earlier resigned to make room for the Muslim League nominees. They were: (1) Sarat Chandra Bose, (2) C. Rajagopalachari (3) M. Asaf Ali, and (4) Sir Shafat Ahmad Khan and (5) Syed Ali Zaheer. The following five nominees of the Muslim League joined the Interim Government, Incharge of the Ministries noted against their names.

1.	Liaquat Ali Khan	Finance
2.	I.I. Chundrigar	Commerce
3.	Abdur Rab Nishtar	Posts and Air
4.	Ghazanfar Ali Khan	Health
5.	Jogendra Nath Mandal	Law

Annexure VI

The Central Cabinet
(As on August 15, 1947)

1.	Pandit Jawaharlal Nehru	Prime Minister, External Affairs, Commonwealth Relations and Scientific Research
2.	Sardar Vallabbhai Patel	Deputy Prime Minister, Home, Information & Broadcasting & States
3.	Maulana Abul Kalam Azad	Education
4.	Dr. B.R. Ambedkar	Law
5.	Shri Rafi Ahmad Kidwai	Communication
6.	Dr. John Mathai	Railways & Transport
7.	Shri C. H. Bhabha	Commerce
8.	Sardar Baldev Singh	Defence
9.	Smt. Raj Kumari Amrit Kaur	Health
10.	Shri R.K. Shanmukham Chetty	Finance
11.	Mr. Jagjivan Ram	Labour
12.	Dr. Rajendra Prasad	Food & Agriculture
13.	Dr. Shyama Prasad Mukherjee	Industry and Supplies
14.	Shri N. V. Gadgil	Works, Mines and Power

Annexure VII

Provincial Chief Ministers (Premiers)
(As on August 15, 1947)

1.	Assam	Shri Gopinath Bordoloi
2.	Bihar	Dr. Shri Krishna Sinha
3.	Orissa	Dr. Hare Krushna Mehtab
4.	West Benal	Dr. Prafulla Chandra Ghosh
5.	United Province & Oudh	Shri Govind Ballabh Pant
6.	East Punjab	Dr. Gopichand Bhargava
7.	Central Province	Pt. Ravishankar Shukla
8.	Madras Presidency	Shri T. Prakasam
9.	Bombay Presidency	Shri B.G. Kher